A Penny Saved

R.S. Yeoman and His Remarkable Red Book

A Personal Recollection and Biography
by
Kenneth E. Bressett

Whitman Publishing, LLC
PUBLISHING SINCE 1934

Dedication

If Dick Yeoman were with us today, I know how pleased and proud he would be to celebrate the 75th anniversary of his amazing *Guide Book of United States Coins*. I am also sure that his first consideration would be to thank the thousands of individuals who contributed to making it such a success throughout the years. Without their help, no single effort could have achieved the degree of accuracy and usefulness that have come together to make this book a universally recognized standard reference for coin collectors.

If it were possible, Yeoman would want to personally thank everyone who ever made a suggestion, pointed out an error, added a piece of new information, or otherwise contributed throughout the years to refine the content of the *Red Book*. Unfortunately, the list is too long, and memory too unreliable, for me or anyone to attempt such an accounting. Be assured that your contributions have all been appreciated and recognized for their impact on the betterment of the hobby. To that end, this tribute publication is dedicated to each of you, with thanks and gratitude.

Ken Bressett
Colorado Springs, Colorado

A Penny Saved:
R.S. Yeoman and His Remarkable Red Book

Whitman Publishing, LLC
Publishing since 1934
Whitman.com

1974 Chandalar Drive • Suite D • Pelham, AL 35124
ISBN: 0794849016
Printed in the United States

Correspondence concerning this book may be directed to Whitman Publishing, Attn: A Penny Saved, at the address above.

Whitman®

Contents

Foreword

by Jeff Garrett

A Penny Saved is a comprehensive and personal retrospective of A *Guide Book of United States Coins* and the people behind its creation and evolution. There is no better person to write this volume celebrating the historic diamond anniversary of the *Red Book* than Ken Bressett, editor emeritus of our hobby's essential reference.

My first trip to the American Numismatic Association Summer Seminar was in 1974, and Ken was my instructor that week. In those days he was employed full-time at Whitman Publishing and had been the editor of the *Red Book* for years. I had decided to take his class on U.S. colonial coinage. It was a subject that I knew very little about, and Ken did a great job explaining this somewhat complicated area of the market.

I could not have known that more than 40 years later, I would step into his role as the next senior editor of the *Red Book*.

Many people make no attempt to collect colonial coins because they do not understand them. This is a mistake—U.S. colonial coinage is fascinating and represents an excellent value. Very few coins offer such an incredible combination of rarity, historical significance, and affordability. There are many mega-rarities in the colonial series, but there are dozens of issues that can be purchased for a few hundred dollars.

As was the case over 40 years ago, Ken Bressett is still one of the best instructors in this compelling

◄ **Jeff Garrett and Ken Bressett at the American Numismatic Association World's Fair of Money banquet, Chicago, August 2015.**

▲ Jeff Garrett, Ken Bressett, Dennis Tucker, and Dave Bowers review *Red Book* pages in an Editorial Summit at Whitman Publishing headquarters in Atlanta, May 2011.

area of the market. His work for the *Red Book* will live on, even though he has retired as senior editor. Indeed, the *Red Book* continues to serve as a wonderful guide for anyone getting started with colonial coinage—or any other series.

Over the decades, Ken, Dave Bowers, I, and the *Red Book* team have continuously improved the editorial content of the book. We have expanded the *Red Book*, the *Blue Book*, and *Mega Red* considerably. Most people who buy the *Red Book* do not appreciate the incredible amount of information this reference contains. The section on early U.S. coinage is probably the most valuable part.

In recent years, several pages have been added to the colonial section discussing "Foreign Coins in the Colonies." Many hobbyists do not realize that foreign coins were legal tender in the U.S. until 1857, and continued to circulate in the remote interior even after that. Evidence of their ready use as money is easily seen in the large quantities of these coins found in shipwrecks.

The *Red Book* coverage of U.S. colonial coinage starts with the Sommer Islands (Bermuda) coinage. The Bermuda Islands were named for Juan de Bermúdez, who is believed to have stopped there in 1515. He left behind a few hogs, and 100 years later the island was overrun with the animals. Thus, the first coins struck for the English colonies in the New World, issued in about 1616, feature a hog as the main device and became known as Hogge Money, or "Hoggies." It's stories like these that make coin collecting such a fascinating pursuit.

The historical information about U.S. coinage is important. But the *Red Book* is also one of the finest price guides ever published. What makes it special are the 100-plus contributors who help with pricing each year. Every effort is made to enlist top experts in each series of United States coinage. No single person could duplicate the combined knowledge of this esteemed group.

The rare-coin market is ever changing, and my job is to reflect those changes in the most important annual numismatic reference. The 2022-dated edition of the *Red Book*, issued in 2021, is the 75th, and the entire team conducted a page-by-page review to offer the latest in numismatic scholarship. We also reviewed the grades priced, which reflect current market conditions and collector interests.

My goal as senior editor of the *Red Book* is to make it an indispensable resource for beginners and advanced collectors alike. The *Guide Book of United States Coins* is probably the only numismatic publication that every collector and dealer keeps within arm's reach at all times.

The future of numismatics is bright, and many people have discovered coin collecting in recent years. For most of them, the *Red Book* is one of their first purchases. It is critically important that we provide these newcomers with the information they need to enjoy this great pursuit. I look forward to helping the *Red Book* evolve with the hobby in the coming decades.

Jeff Garrett
Senior Editor, *A Guide Book of United States Coins*

▲ Walter Ostromecki Jr. and Ken Bressett at the Numismatic Literary Guild awards banquet, Los Angeles, August 2009. Ken holds an "Extraordinary Merit" plaque for *The Fantastic 1804 Dollar, Tribute Edition*.

▲ Ken Bressett examining an ancient coin with David M. Sundman, Chicago, August 2015.

HONORING KENNETH BRESSETT
Ken Bressett
EDITOR EMERITUS
"Mr. Red Book"
HONORING KENNETH BRESSETT
Ken dedicated the Whitman Guide to Coin Collecting to his wife, Bert, "the very real love of my life. . . . Without her patience, help, and understanding I might not have undertaken this work."

Publisher's Preface

Whitman Publishing

For more than 50 years, Kenneth Bressett skillfully shepherded the *Guide Book of United States Coins*—the hobby's beloved "Red Book"—as its coordinating and senior editor. For generations of coin collectors he has been the face of the *Red Book*, much as R.S. Yeoman was to earlier hobbyists.

I never met Ken's predecessor in person. Yeoman was winding down in the mid-1980s, when my own life as an active young collector was just gearing up. But working as Ken's publisher and frequent collaborator for the past 16-plus years, I've come to know R.S. Yeoman quite well. I've learned from Ken the "Yeoman way" of thinking about and managing the *Red Book* and the *Blue Book*, and now *Mega Red*. His philosophy and approach have become second nature to me. Notice when I say "his philosophy and approach," I don't specify whose—because Yeoman's and Bressett's are one and the same. Not only did Ken learn his mentor's style, but he has thoughtfully and steadfastly emulated it since the 1960s. That's a remarkable demonstration of one professional's respect for another.

Meanwhile, a defining part of Ken's personality is constant humility in spite of his own brilliance and productive hard work. "If it takes a village to raise a child," he's told me, "then equally it takes a large, dedicated group of individuals to produce a formidable publication like the *Red Book*." He quickly gives credit to the generations of coin collectors and dealers whose contributions have made

◀ At the March 2018 Whitman Coin and Collectibles Expo in Baltimore, 100 limited-edition commemorative lapel pins were given away to lucky collectors.

▲ *Red Book* Research Editor Dave Bowers and Editor Emeritus Ken Bressett (both seated) are two founding members of the Rittenhouse Society. Here they are surrounded by members of the Society who attended the American Numismatic Association World's Fair of Money, Anaheim, 2016. Left to right: P. Scott Rubin, George Frederick Kolbe, Joel J. Orosz, David Fanning, Wayne Homren, Denis Loring, Mark Borckardt, Jeff Garrett, Bill Bugert, Barbara Gregory, Ron Guth, John Dannreuther, Tom DeLorey, John Kraljevich, David W. Lange, Len Augsburger, Neil Shafer, Doug Mudd, David T. Alexander, Dennis Tucker, and guest Deb Wurtz.

the book a success. And of course he credits the vision and energy of Yeoman and others who founded the *Blue Book* and *Red Book*, as well as all the typesetters, assistant editors, graphic designers, factory workers, distributors, retailers, and others who have done their part. Ken's modesty and courteous generosity only add to the kudos he himself so richly deserves.

Please forgive me for straying from the purpose of a book's preface. (I'm an antiquarian. Antiquarians are, by default, sentimental, and this is a sentimental book.) Traditionally a preface is used to describe the process of how a book came to be, and why it was undertaken in the first place. Its intent is not to praise the author—that's partly what the foreword is for. And it's not to introduce the subject matter—that's for the prologue or introduction. So let me preface *A Penny Saved* and tell you how and why the book came about.

First, the "why": Surely every book that's seen 75 editions and sold in the tens of millions has a story to tell, and deserves to have it told. As Ken has said, "It would be impossible to appreciate the story of the *Red Book*'s birth and development without a broad knowledge of its author himself; the publisher and printing facility that produced it; and the throng of talented individuals who contributed to its creation and continued success." He further observes, "Sad as it is, most of the participants involved in producing the early editions are no longer with us, and even the best of memories tend to fade with time." Ken wanted to bring together as much

information as possible before it was lost to future generations. He took up the challenge of reconstructing the *Red Book*'s historical background based on his personal knowledge and close working association with Whitman Publishing over many decades.

Whitman has been in business for more than a hundred years. Racine was its home for decades. Then, from the 1980s to early 2000s, the company and its ownership and management moved a few times—from Wisconsin to New York and down South, with points in between. Unfortunately, some of the physical moves resulted in a gradual loss of material culture—historical records, old letters, corporate items like plaques and awards, and similar artifacts.

"The task at first seemed nearly impossible," Ken said, "until recent investigation uncovered a treasure trove of factual material related to every phase of *Red Book* production." This allowed us to present much previously unknown (or unpublished) background of when, why, and how the *Red Book* came about. The trove included R.S. Yeoman's personal papers, documents, files, correspondence, and artifacts related to his long and successful life and career.

▲ Part of Ken Bressett's legacy as a supporter of numismatic research and writing: in 2010 Whitman Publishing and the ANA jointly established the annual Kenneth E. Bressett Young Numismatist Literary Award, for researchers aged 18 to 22. (Here, Ken is pictured with Whitman publisher Dennis Tucker and 2010 award winner Will Robbins.)

▲ At the March 2018 Whitman Baltimore Coin and Collectibles Expo, *Red Book* fans assembled for a giveaway of the hardcover 72nd edition, which featured a gold-foil portrait of Editor Emeritus Kenneth Bressett on the back.

Equally exciting was the almost simultaneous discovery of much of the original Western Archives, described by Ken as "documentation, data, background stories, and materials from Western Publishing Company files, including perhaps every numismatic book ever published by the firm, and curiosities that no one ever dared to think still existed."

Ken proposed a manuscript to Whitman in the summer of 2019. I'll never forget meeting with him about it at the American Numismatic Association World's Fair of Money that August, in Chicago. The idea of celebrating R.S. Yeoman's life, sharing coins from Yeoman's own collection, publishing his handwritten notes, telling the *Red Book* story and of the old days at Western and Whitman—it was a dream manuscript pitch!

Much of the detailed architecture of chapter 1, the story of Western Printing & Lithographing and the birth of Whitman Publishing, is built on the foundation of Frank J. Colletti's *Guide Book of the Official Red Book of United States Coins*. (That book, volume 14 in Whitman's Bowers Series, is highly recommended for its fascinating edition-by-edition study of Yeoman's famous scarlet tome.) To that foundation Ken added material and information from the Western Archives and other resources. In several places the assistance of David W. Lange, preeminent scholar of the history of coin albums and folders, was crucial. Robert Kelley, museum specialist and photography

◄ Ken Bressett, unable to attend the March 2018 Baltimore Expo in person because of the winter weather, nevertheless was a constant presence! Senior Editor Jeff Garrett autographed *Red Books* next to a poster with his portrait.

director for the American Numismatic Association, beautifully photographed many of the medals, framed portraits, books, and other vintage artifacts. Stack's Bowers Galleries opened its auction archives for images of coins, tokens, paper money, and medals, common and rare. Lawrence Block, Lincoln Higgie, Ed Metzger, and Neil Shafer shared personal memories of their work at Whitman Publishing. Ken was aided in the enormous task of studying, sorting, organizing, and presenting the story by Barbara J. Gregory, recently retired longtime editor of the ANA's popular magazine, *The Numismatist*. Other individuals and companies helped in many ways, as noted in the credits and acknowledgments.

Of course, the brightest mint luster on *A Penny Saved* is Ken Bressett's personal involvement as author. He can recount the true stories, expose the myths and legends, and confirm the hidden facts because he was eyewitness to most of the *Red Book*'s history. On top of that, his own remarkable life is presented as a warmly personal autobiography, found in chapter 6.

So that's the "why" and "how" of *A Penny Saved*. This book itself now becomes part of the *Red Book* story. If you're a collector of United States coins, you're already part of the story, as well. And after you read *A Penny Saved* and learn the history of Western Printing, Whitman Publishing, R.S. Yeoman, and Ken Bressett, you'll be able to share this remarkable story of our hobby with the next generation of collectors.

Dennis Tucker
Publisher, Whitman Publishing

◄ Ken Bressett and Barbara Gregory reviewing archival materials in 2020.

THE HANDBOOK OF UNITED STATES COINS

GUIDE BOOK OF UNITED STATES COINS

A CATALOG OF MODERN WORLD COINS

PUBLISHED BY WHITMAN PUBLISHING COMPANY, RACINE, WISCONSIN • R. S. YEOMAN, EDITOR

August 13, 1959

Mr. Kenneth E. Bressett
28 Woodbury Street
Keene, New Hampshire

Dear Ken:

Thanks for your letter of August 9 and the report on your expenses.

I am hoping for a check to reimburse you to be included with this letter.

It's too bad you were delayed in your trip home, but it probably was the fastest route possible. Only 10 minutes and you had to wait an entire night to make up for it.

Make the best deal you can with your long-distance movers. We will pay the bill in any case. Have them send the bill directly to Whitman Publishing Company, attention Pete Foerster. The reason for that is, I will probably be on the West Coast at the time you arrive. I've already made arrangements for the bill to be accepted and paid.

I'm sure we will be ready for you whenever you can arrive. If you should find it necessary to delay a few days, we can always start your employment whenever it occurs. It really isn't important to be here on the exact first day of September.

I have given Mr. George Kurten your Social Security number, so that is taken care of.

During the past week, I have been checking the Canadian Coin Book and am making a start on Dr. Judd's Pattern Book.

I'll be glad for anything you can give me concerning the Lawrence Bros. of Anamosa.

Say hello to Bertha and give our best to your children!

Very truly yours,

Dick

R. S. Yeoman

RSY:rc

Prologue

This is the story of Richard S. Yeo, better known to most coins collectors as R.S. Yeoman, and his extraordinary *Red Book*, as seen through the eyes of several generations of readers who were instrumental in making the book an essential part of their involvement in numismatics, the hobby of coin collecting. It is a memorial dedicated to the thousands of contributors who adopted the book as an extension of their own connection with coins and helped in numerous ways to make it inclusive, relevant, detailed, accurate, and as timely as possible for the past three-quarters of a century.

The year 2021 marks the 75th anniversary of annual editions of *A Guide Book of United States Coins*, a book that has become a universal favorite among coin collectors for longer than any similar reference. In fact, it surpasses the longevity record for almost any other kind of chronicle. Although *Webster's Dictionary* and *The Old Farmer's Almanac* hold the nation's records for being updated and published every year, the *Guide Book* is definitely a formidable challenger. And, as the dictionary does with Mr. Webster, the *Red Book* continues to carry the name of its creator.

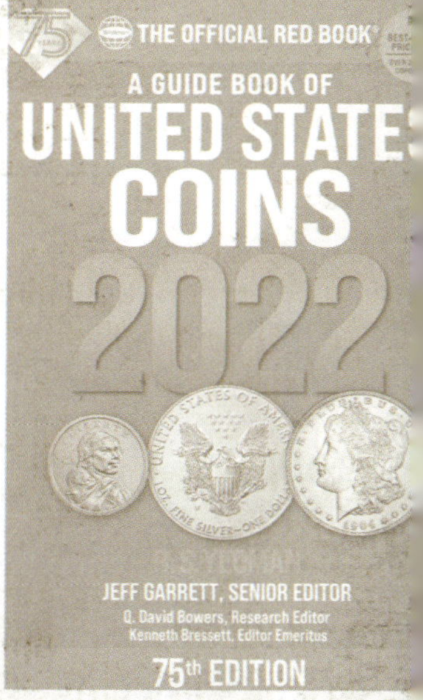

Along with its contemporary publication *How to Win Friends and Influence People* by Dale Carnegie (one of the most inspirational books in my life), the *Red Book* continually holds its place as a leader in the field of popular nonfiction publications. *How to Win Friends* is a self-help book that was first published in 1936. Since then, more than 15 million copies have been sold worldwide, making it one of the best-selling nonfiction books of all time. In

2012 it was number 19 on *Time* magazine's list of the 100 most influential books. A recent Library of Congress survey ranked Dale Carnegie's volume as the seventh most influential book in American history. Its annual sales exceed 100,000 copies.

By comparison, the annual *Red Book*'s circulation and popularity far surpass any of those statistics. Although *Red Book* sales numbers usually are not publicized, it has been reliably calculated that more than 25 million copies have been sold since the book was first released in 1946. And it has been estimated that three or more people tend to see or use each copy. Equally impressive is the *Red Book*'s core support of faithful followers who, on average, purchase a new edition every year or two. A rough calculation indicates that one-third of American adults have at some point seen or used a copy of the book.

The reasons for the *Red Book*'s longevity and popularity are its detailed information about the technical aspects of each coin, as well as its accurate and unbiased assessments of retail values. When it first appeared in 1946, it was one of the few such price guides not produced as a sales catalog by a dealer. It was then and still is widely appreciated as an independent reporting on the annual state of the market and a record of price movements.

In addition to this essential price guide, Yeoman produced a number of other related numismatic books covering both wholesale and retail coin values, world coins, and other popular subjects, as well as a wide array of coin-collecting boards, albums, holders, and whatever else he felt would benefit collectors in pursuing their hobby.

In the early days of publication, *A Guide Book of United States Coins* was subjected to the wartime shortages of paper and other curtailments. Fortunately, red Kivar®—a latex-saturated, simulated leather material—was

▲ *Red Book* Senior Editor Kenneth Bressett and son Philip at the ANA World's Fair of Money, August 2010, Boston.

▲ A banner from the March 2018 Whitman Baltimore Coin and Collectibles Expo.

▲ Ken Bressett (left) with Leroy "Pete" Foerster and R.S. Yeoman at work on the *Red Book* in 1959.

▲ Q. David Bowers: "More than any other single factor, the *Red Book* is a missionary for getting people interested in collecting coins. No other effort comes even close."

▲ Ken Bressett autographing a *Red Book* and talking coins with Young Numismatist Cole Hendrickson, at the ANA World's Fair of Money, August 2016, Anaheim.

▲ The editors of the 75th-edition *Red Book*: Research Editor Q. David Bowers, Senior Editor Jeff Garrett, and Editor Emeritus Kenneth Bressett (ANA World's Fair of Money, August 2018, Philadelphia).

readily available for making the case (cover) of the books. In time the books took on the color as a nickname, and today the term *Red Book* and what it stands for are commonly known to every serious coin collector.

I was intimately involved with all aspects of the book almost since its inception. I had the privilege of working with R.S. Yeoman for more than 10 years and knowing him for more than 30, until his untimely death in 1988. Our first meeting, some 65 years ago in 1956, is discussed in this book. I was not alone in my association with the author. He had a talent for seeking and finding skilled help that would be beneficial to making his book as complete as possible.

"A penny saved is a penny got."—Benjamin Franklin, 1758

Follow along now as I present insights, anecdotes, history, and the story of how the *Red Book* came to be what it is today, and what might be expected for it in the future. A good deal of this material is Yeoman's personal commentary that has never before been published. Much has been gleaned from what is known as the Western Archives, a collection of notes, articles, clippings, and photos that were preserved by Yeoman himself or as part of the original Western Printing reference library and records collection.

The story begins with a look at the printing industry and the company that made all this possible through its interest in producing low-priced, family-oriented products to entertain and amuse a nation during the hard times of a major depression and war.

Kenneth Bressett
Editor Emeritus, *A Guide Book of United States Coins*

THE GOLDEN HOME AND HIGH SCHOOL
ENCYCLOPEDIA
VOLUME 2
LINCOLN
PLASTIC COATED
JOKER

Chapter 1

Western Printing & Lithographing Company

STARTING AN EMPIRE

Western Printing Company in Racine, Wisconsin, began as West Side Printing Company. By 1907 the small print shop was sinking into debt and it probably would have vanished into oblivion if not for the enterprise shown by its part-time bookkeeper, Edward H. Wadewitz. The son of German immigrants, Wadewitz had moved to Racine at age 17, leaving only to attend Pott's Shorthand College in Pennsylvania. By 1907, when he was 29, he had held a number of jobs, at one time working at his cousins' trunk factory. Now, seeing the opportunity to go into business for himself, he bought the foundering print shop with a combination of back-pay owed to him by the company's owner and funds loaned by his brother Albert. He was joined by another brother, William; printer Catherine Bongarts Rutledge; and Roy A. Spencer, who worked for the Racine *Journal* as a printer, and who would later became mayor of Racine. Together they reversed the fortunes of the

West Side Printing Company and quickly earned a reputation for reliability and fair dealing among Racine's rising manufacturing companies.

By 1910 the company was prospering enough to justify investment in a new lithographic offset press, which was reflected in the business's new name, Western Printing and Lithographing Company. The growing firm relocated to the grand six-story Shoop Building, named for a famous patent-medicine entrepreneur who was one of Western's clients. Among Western's other customers was a Chicago publishing company, Hamming-Whitman, that specialized in children's books. This business relationship soon turned into a liability, however: after printing an order of thousands of books for Hamming-Whitman, Western discovered that the publisher was verging on bankruptcy and unable to pay for the job.

▲ Edward H. Wadewitz, seen here in 1910, was born in 1878. Wadewitz was a first-generation German American who grew up in rural northern Wisconsin and moved to Racine in 1895, aged 17, to make a life for himself. He started out as a woodworker in his cousin's trunk factory. There he greatly improved efficiency by developing an assembly-line setup. Applying his business mind to accounting classes at a YMCA night-school, he saved enough money to go to Pennsylvania, where he graduated from Pott's Shorthand College, a small business school. Then he returned to Racine and began work as a bookkeeper. Wadewitz was the savior of the struggling West Side Printing Company, which he eventually bought after the owner couldn't pay him for his bookkeeping. Under the leadership of E.H., as he was known, the firm would grow into Western Printing and Lithographing.

▲ Roy A. Spencer, a printer with experience in the newspaper world, partnered with Edward and Albert Wadewitz and helped transform the West Side print shop into one of Wisconsin's biggest businesses. In *Golden Legacy*, historian Leonard S. Marcus describes Albert: "After enjoying a stint in the U.S. Navy and finding that he did not like the printing business, Al . . . chose early on to sell his one-third share of the business to the other partners and return to sea as a member of the Merchant Marines."

Spencer took the role of president with E.H. Wadewitz as treasurer, secretary, and general manager. The *1916 Racine County Wisconsin History* described the former printer's devil: "In politics Mr. Spencer maintains the attitude of a non-partisan, voting according to the dictates of his judgment and the exigencies of the case." In the late 1930s he would serve as mayor of Racine.

◄ The original basement operations of West Side Printing Company in 1907. From left to right: Roy A. Spencer; Catherine Bongarts Rutledge; Edward H. Wadewitz; William R. Wadewitz; and William Bell (who worked for the company only a short time).

◄ West Side Printing circa 1909, by which time it had moved to the first floor and basement of 548 State Street in Racine. In the center is Ernie Boernke. The woman in the back is Johanna Erickson Wiechers. William R. Wadewitz, brother of founder Edward Wadewitz, is seated on the railing, foreground. Historian Leonard S. Marcus describes him: "Bill—or W.R.—who was fourteen years younger than E.H., remained with Western for the rest of his working life, succeeding E.H. as president in 1952 when E.H. was elevated to the position of chairman of the board."

Western took ownership of the stock and Edward Wadewitz, inexperienced as he was in sales, set about trying to sell the books to recoup his company's losses. His unexpected success in finding buyers led him to decide to acquire the bankrupt company in 1916.

A partner and vice president of the bankrupt publishing firm bore the name of Whitman, and Wadewitz suggested that this name be adopted for the new publishing venture. Whitman Publishing Company was therefore organized as a subsidiary and the first meeting of stockholders (five in number) was held on February 26, 1916, at which time there was made "a motion that the purchase be made from Western of all stock, plates, and accounts receivable, giving Western Printing and Lithographing Company, in consideration thereof, a note for the sum of $20,000, secured by a chattel mortgage." The company was relocated to Racine and staffed with two salesmen.

Wadewitz, serving as secretary-treasurer of the new subsidiary, estimated that sales for the year 1916 would reach at least $60,000. "Total sales for this year up to, and including March 6, amount to $3,500," he said, "and this is at a time when both the salesmen are spending most of their time at the factory getting ready for their trips." In setting up the venture, an entirely new concept of publishing was introduced whereby, for the very first time, the company produced its own line of products that were mass produced and sold to the five-and-ten-cent stores throughout the country. It was an eminently successful and mutually beneficial philosophy of selling that prevailed for a period of over 50 years.

▲ There was a fourth Wadewitz brother, the eldest, Otto, who "joined the company a few years after Bill and worked for Western for many years while also becoming a local figure of note" (Marcus). Historian Steve Wheeler, writing in the publication *RYC Roots* in 2016, described the eldest Wadewitz brother: "Otto's machinist skills were needed to operate and maintain the stationary steam engines that powered the fast-growing printing plant. He was one of the few people able to operate the large engines that powered the printing machines with belts and drive shafts." Otto Wadewitz was an influential benefactor of the Racine Yacht Club and served five terms as its Commodore, from 1933 to 1937, helping it weather the Great Depression. He is pictured here in a late-1930s portrait and in a bronze bust (by artist Paul Ring) currently in the Racine Yacht Club library.

The Shoop Building in 1910 became the home of the freshly expanded and renamed Western Printing & Lithographing Co. The building was named for Dr. Clarendon I. Shoop, one of the last of America's old-time patent-medicine purveyors. His six-story Racine landmark would be placed on the National Register of Historic Places in 1978.

▶ Western's impressive headquarters was featured prominently on its company letterhead.

NEW CHALLENGES AND OPPORTUNITIES

The many other iterations of the Whitman organization are somewhat confusing. In the beginning, the Whitman name was merely used as a brand designation for several products created by the parent company known as Western Publishing, or more properly as Western Printing and Lithographing Company. The main office was based in Racine, Wisconsin, for many years and became famous as a producer of children's books, jigsaw puzzles, playing cards, and games. It was also a commercial manufacturing printer for many large firms. In its heyday Western Publishing was renowned as the producer of *Little Golden Books, Big Little Books*, and other family-related entertainment products, including an extensive line of numismatic books, coin boards, albums, and related fare.

▼ Western's new "Main Plant"—its headquarters, as of 1928—was built specifically for the needs of a modern graphic-arts firm. Its completely climate- and humidity-controlled printing facilities were among the first such in the world.

◀ The front entry of the old Western headquarters building, in a more recent view.

In 1925 the company took on the challenge of manufacturing playing cards, which demanded particularly high precision in color alignment and die cutting; by acquiring the specialized equipment and expertise this product required, Western soon positioned itself as an industry leader. By 1928 the company had a staff of 300, necessitating a move to new quarters: the "Main Plant" on Mound Avenue, a cutting-edge facility (complete with air conditioning) that was designed and built to meet Western's needs. The company established a smaller plant in Chicago that same year to handle printing jobs for that area more conveniently.

During the Great Depression, between 1929 and 1933, Western acquired exclusive rights to all the Walt Disney–licensed characters and established an eastern printing plant in Poughkeepsie, New York. From 1938 to 1962 Dell Publishing and Western produced comic books featuring Western's characters. In 1938 a joint effort between Western and Simon & Schuster was undertaken.

The Great Depression, rather than handicapping Western, actually served to increase demand for its products. Inexpensive pastimes like jigsaw puzzles and board games became more popular than ever among families who could no longer afford more costly forms of entertainment, and Western was operating around the clock to meet demand. Its specialized die-cutting equipment could also be put to use on a new paper-based product that would have an unimaginable impact on the company's fortunes—and the face of American coin collecting.

▲ *Walt Disney's Bambi*, published by Western in 1941.

RICHARD S. YEO ENTERS THE SCENE

It was during this period that the young, talented Richard Yeo was added to the staff as part of the marketing team in 1932. Dick had previously worked for the Milprint Company in Milwaukee, where he was involved with the distribution of greeting cards. His initial position with Whitman concentrated on sales, sales promotion, and advertising. In 1934 a fortuitous event changed Dick's life and added a new dimension to Whitman's products. A Wisconsin engineer and coin collector named Joseph Kent Post had recently begun making cardboard holders for minor-denomination coins. Before Post's innovation, collectors had few options for housing their coins: cabinets and special albums were expensive, and storing coins in envelopes, the thrifty alternative, kept them hidden from view. At only 25¢ each, Post's coin boards provided an affordable and attractive way to store a collection.

Post and his family initially made the boards themselves, later arranging with two separate companies to do the printing and hole-punching. Western Printing could carry out both steps, however, and it made sense for Post to transfer the manufacture of the boards to this company—and later the marketing as well. In Yeo's account of the event, Whitman eventually assumed the rights to Post's product when he was unable to pay the company's bills. Post dropped out of the picture at that point, and his invention became the beginning of a numismatic upheaval.

Yeo was assigned to market the company's new product, and he quickly realized that it was poised for success. The boards were considered a

▼ Western's factory and office complex in 1947.

◄ Edward H. Wadewitz at the age of 70. The Wisconsin entrepreneur was in his mid-50s when young Richard Yeo was hired to work for Whitman. Wadewitz passed away in 1955, having seen Whitman Publishing grow into an influential part of his business.

challenge—almost a game—that demanded no great investment of money or time; anyone could go through their pocket change and extract a penny or nickel here and there without feeling a financial pinch, and the satisfaction of filling a board was not limited by age or educational level. Whitman employees were even taking the boards home to fill. The extraordinary popularity of the new boards had an enormous impact on coin collecting, creating massive numbers of new collectors, boosting the values of collectible twentieth-century minor coins, and changing the face of the numismatic community.

Yeo himself would later point out, "Up until this time, numismatics had been almost exclusively the pursuit of intellectuals[:] . . . researchers, historians, museum curators and the like." The coin board transformed all this. Now the hobby saw an influx of young, working-class collectors, and their collecting zeal focused on modern coins, not antique rarities. Many of the new collectors held jobs in which they handled small change often during the course of their work: waiters, cashiers, streetcar conductors—and paperboys like the young Richard Yeo. Coin collecting was no longer reserved for the elite; it was everyone's hobby.

In 1940 Whitman launched its coin folders, offshoots of the original coin board, which offered greater storage capacity, protection, and convenience. As developer and promoter of the folders, Yeo saw that the line was expanded to include many additional denominations and both American and foreign coins. Although coin folders had been introduced in 1939 by the Daniel Stamp Company (Dansco), Whitman was the first company to effectively market and publicize them. As a result, numismatist David W. Lange (a specialist on the subject) has noted, "The Whitman folders quickly became the industry standard for decades afterward."

Yeo's involvement with marketing the boards and folders steered his professional life firmly in the direction of numismatics. In his own words, "I somewhat timidly broke into the national numismatic scene by attending such events as the 1940 ANA convention in Detroit and meetings of the Chicago Coin Club, and I represented Whitman at the 1940 Hobby Show in Chicago. When we came along with the coin boards, things started to really come alive. The show provided their first formal public appearance."

Because he was there only to display the boards, not to sell them, would-be buyers were referred across the aisle to an enterprising young coin dealer, Ben Dreiske. The future founder of Rare Coin Company of America (Rarcoa), Dreiske would go on to be of great help in producing the original *Red Book*. This was just one of many important friendships Yeo formed in the numismatic community around that time. Events like these did far more than introduce the neophyte numismatist to new connections in the hobby—they also gave Dick the inspiration for writing the *Handbook of United States Coins* (the "Blue Book") as a means of adding to the educational aspects of collecting coins as a pastime. After the *Blue Book* would come the *Red Book*. Each would add its own unique energy to another revolution in coin collecting.

▲ Whitman coin boards (and, later, folders) gave everyday Americans an easy way to collect coins from their pocket change.

▶ A "Lincoln Penny Collector" board, copyrighted 1934 by J.K. Post and manufactured by Whitman Publishing.

Lincoln
PENNY COLLECTOR
The idea is to collect a complete set of pennies in the best available condition.
The numbers under the dates on the card indicate the approximate millions coined each year at each mint.
"S" below the date on the penny indicates San Francisco mint—"D", Denver—No mint mark, Philadelphia.
Victor D. Brenner designed the penny. His initials appear at the bottom edge of the tail of first issue 1909 only.
There are some pennies dated 1922 without mint mark in circulation though Phila. claims to have made none.
Clean your specimens with a soft eraser or a little vinegar before placing them in the board.
WHITMAN PUBLISHING CO., RACINE, WISCONSIN
Made in U. S. A.

The Standard Catalogue of United States Coins
INTRODUCTION.
SILVER COINS OF THE EARLIEST PERIOD.
New Hub Coin Book of American and Foreign Coins
30th EDITION
Published by
AUCTION SALE
THE SECOND PART
RARE COINS
The Numismatic Scrapbook Magazine
15c
June 194
In This Issue
Isle of Man Internment Camp Money
Portraits of Lafayette On Bank Notes
The Greeks Had A Word For It
The Story Behind The Token
Coins of Barcelona
AN ELABORATE
PRICE ONE DOL

Chapter 2

Before the Red Book

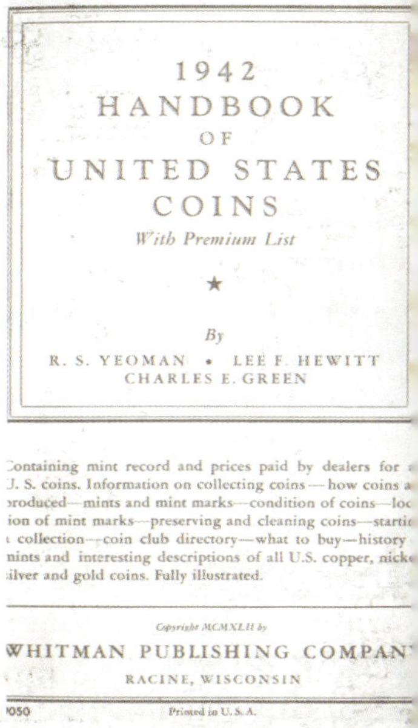

1942
HANDBOOK
OF
UNITED STATES
COINS
With Premium List

★

By
R. S. YEOMAN • LEE F. HEWITT
CHARLES E. GREEN

Containing mint record and prices paid by dealers for all U. S. coins. Information on collecting coins—how coins are produced—mints and mint marks—condition of coins—location of mint marks—preserving and cleaning coins—starting a collection—coin club directory—what to buy—history of mints and interesting descriptions of all U.S. copper, nickel, silver and gold coins. Fully illustrated.

Copyright MCMXLII by
WHITMAN PUBLISHING COMPANY
RACINE, WISCONSIN

Printed in U.S.A.

EARLY REFERENCES

The *Red Book*, of course, was not the first or only price guide for collectors in the past. And it was not born like Venus, arriving on shore in the form of a fully grown woman. When coin collecting caught on in America in the mid-nineteenth century, available information for pricing coins was very limited. Most collectors seeking coin values had to make do with what they could derive by studying auction catalogs or dealers' price lists. Although auction records could provide a fair representation of cost, price lists were influenced more by dealers' desire to make money than by any inclination to provide a fair market value. In 1859 a collector had little more to rely on than the very untrustworthy reference work by Montroville W. Dickeson, with the expansive title *American Numismatical Manual of the Currency or Money of the Aborigines, and Colonial, State and United States Coins*.

The information void was somewhat alleviated a few years later by John Walter Scott when he

founded J.W. Scott & Company, which would become one of the largest stamp-and-coin businesses in the world. He would ultimately, in fact, found two businesses under his own name. As early as 1871, Scott published a price catalog for American coins, and in 1875 he founded the *Coin Collector's Journal*, a magazine that continued publication through 1888. (It would be revived nearly half a century later by an even more important figure in numismatics, Wayte Raymond.) A shorter-lived publication, his *American Journal of Philately and Coin Advertiser*, lasted only from 1879 to 1886. Perhaps Scott's greatest contribution to the development of the coin-pricing reference was his 1906 *Standard Coin Catalogue No. 1: The Silver Coins of the World, to Which Is Added U.S. National and Territorial Gold*. It was reprinted in 1916 as a companion to his 1913 *Standard Coin Catalogue No.2, Coins of the World, Copper, Nickel, Lead and Brass*, which included values for U.S. minor coins. By R.S. Yeoman's reckoning, the collecting community then had to face a hiatus of nearly 20 years before an equally useful resource came on the scene: Wayte Raymond's *Standard Catalogue*.

In 1884 Scott sold his original business, which had become known as the Scott Stamp & Coin Company, but financial reverses led him to launch another stamp company five years later under the J.W. Scott moniker. After successfully defending a lawsuit brought by the purchasers of the first Scott company, he settled into a thriving career as a stamp dealer. In 1906, the same year that his influential *Standard Coin Catalogue* first appeared, Scott joined what was then known as the American Numismatic and Archaeological Society. (The next year it would revert to its original name, by which it is still known today: the American Numismatic Society, or ANS.) When Scott died in 1919, however, he was most famous for his contributions to the field of stamp collecting.

In the late nineteenth century Boston coin dealer William von Bergen released the first of two influential references on contemporary coin pricing. *The Rare Coins of America, England, Ireland, Scotland, France, Germany, and Spain*, which was first published around 1885 and would go through numerous editions, is a fascinating look at the coin market of this time. It sold for $1 in hardcover and was, according to von Bergen's note, "bound in cloth and gold, gilt edge." Von Bergen's focus was clearly commercial, as can be seen in his "Terms to Agents and Collectors":

> In order to meet the constantly increasing demand for rare coins, a few intelligent and respectable persons (ladies or gentlemen) can have profitable employment in collecting them, and by following the instruction given here can make at least $7 per day, and some day an agent might make $100 or $1000 if he is lucky enough to

> come across a lot of rare coins of which the owner does not know the value. . . . [But] a collector ought not to depend upon buying coins to make his pay, but upon selling the Coin Books.

As a reference to coin values, *Rare Coins* is far from objective: the prices given are what von Bergen was willing to pay for the coins listed, and his own collecting preferences served as the arbiter of value. To read this book is to take a fascinating trip through time and into the mind of this collector. Von Bergen describes Civil War tokens, for example, this way: "Issued by different parties during the late war of the Rebellion. There are about 500 different patterns. None are very valuable, and average not over 5 cents apiece. I have no use for them and do not buy them at present."

▲ The cover of the fifth edition of William von Bergen's *Rare Coins* book, measuring a convenient 4 by 6-3/8 inches.

Other listings also reveal interesting idiosyncrasies. For the silver three-cent piece, von Bergen makes it clear that "positively uncirculated ones or proof only [are] wanted. 1851 to 1863 I do not want." Regarding two-cent pieces, he states, "only those coined in 1872 and 1873 are wanted, and they must be strictly proofs or uncirculated." Under the heading "One-Cent Piece, Nickel" he asserts that "I only buy those coined in 1856, for which I pay—proofs, \$5.00; uncirculated, \$2.00. Positively no other dates wanted." Although these strict limitations on date may startle today's collectors, von Bergen deserves a place in numismatic history for popularizing various scarce dates. It should also be remembered that at the time this book was published, some dates that are now much sought after were fairly common; even the 1877 Indian Head cent was readily available in pocket change.

Notice also that there is no mention in von Bergen's text of the various mintmarks. Not until the 1893 publication of A.G. Heaton's *Treatise on the Coinage of the United States Branch Mints* would collecting by date *and* mintmark become popular. Now popularly known simply as *Mint Marks*, the treatise pointed out that coins issued by branch mints were often far scarcer, and thus more valuable, than those struck at the Philadelphia mint. Heaton's book would launch a new development in the collecting of coins—one that was unknown even four years earlier. (Augustus Goodyear Heaton, an artist as well as numismatist, would go on to be the third president of the American Numismatic Association.) Von Bergen followed up *Rare Coins* with *The Rare Coin Encyclopedia (Universal Coin Dealers Directory)*, which also went through numerous editions; the last was published in 1907.

Not to be outdone by the increasing number of pricing references, Farran Zerbe, the president of the American Numismatic Association from

THE

Rare Coins of America,

ENGLAND, IRELAND, SCOTLAND, FRANCE,

GERMANY, AND SPAIN.

THIS BOOK CONTAINS

A Complete List of and Prices paid for Rare American Gold, Silver, Nickel, Brass, Tin and Copper Coins, Fractional Currency, Colonial, Continental and Confederate Paper Money; a List of all Counterfeit U. S. Treasury and National Bank Notes and Canadian Bank Notes, and How to Detect Them; the Market Value of all Nations' Coins and Bank Notes in U. S. Money; a List of and Prices paid for Rare English, Irish, Scotch, French, German and Spanish Coins.

ILLUSTRATED WITH ABOUT 150 CUTS,

SHOWING OBVERSE AND REVERSE OF EACH GROUP OF RARE COINS, MADE FROM COINS COSTING OVER $6,000.

SEND ALL COINS TO

NUMISMATIC BANK, BOSTON, MASS.

FIFTH EDITION.

NOTE.—It is impossible to establish a fixed price good for any length of time for Rare Coins, inasmuch as the supply and demand is constantly changing, and this of course effects the prices paid. I give on page 107 the most important changes which have taken place up to January 1st, 1891.

▲ Farran Zerbe's aluminum "business card," shown at actual size.

◀ Workers weighing scrap silver for coinage at the Philadelphia Mint, 1888. At the time, coin collectors paid little attention to mintmarks and collected mainly by date. That would change with the publication of Augustus G. Heaton's *Treatise on the Coinage of the United States Branch Mints*.

1908 to 1910, designed and issued a novel variation to suit his interest in the coin business. His aluminum "business card," or token, measures 50 millimeters in diameter and contains prices he was willing to pay for all valuable United States coins.

THE COLORFUL B. MAX MEHL

One of the most famous, influential, and downright colorful figures in twentieth-century numismatics, Benjamin Max Mehl (pronounced "Mail"), was born in Lithuania in 1884 and settled in Fort Worth, Texas. At just 11 years old he began a home coin business, and he was not yet 20 when he joined the American Numismatic Association and placed his first ad, which appeared in the December 1903 issue of *The Numismatist*. A few months later in 1904, he issued his first publication: *Catalogue of Fine Selections of Choice United States Gold, Silver, and Copper Coins, Private and Territorial Gold, United States Fractional Currency*. By 1916 Mehl's Star Rare Coin Company had prospered to the extent that he was able to pay $25,000 for the construction of his own office building, which he later depicted on the cover of his catalogs.

Mehl's numismatic venture was incredibly successful. It is estimated that at one time more than half the mail received at the Fort Worth post

▶ B. Max Mehl as a young coin dealer and in later life.

▲ The *Star Coin Book*, 31st edition (circa 1937), shows off the impressive B. Max Mehl Building.

office was addressed to him. By the mid-1920s he was spending $50,000 annually on advertising—a small fortune by the standards of the day. Mehl was also the first coin dealer to use the new medium of radio to reach the public. In what was probably his most famous advertising venture, during the Great Depression he spent millions of dollars on ads that offered a then-substantial $50 for a 1913 Liberty Head nickel. Mehl must have known that his offer was hollow—only five pieces were known to exist, and these were already held by a collector. However, his campaign prompted countless people to search for the elusive treasure, eager for the distraction from everyday life and hopeful for sudden riches. Succeeding generations continued to search for these coins (none of which ever came into Mehl's possession). The expensive promotion was a huge success for the brilliant marketer, creating countless new coin collectors—and therefore customers. Throughout his career, the man Q. David Bowers has called "the numismatic equivalent of P.T. Barnum" did more to popularize the hobby of coin collecting than anyone before him. Not until the advent of R.S. Yeoman would one man be so influential in popularizing coin collecting among the general public.

The work Mehl is best remembered for, today generally referred to as the *Star Rare Coin Encyclopedia*, was published in different forms and under different names. In format it was clearly influenced by von Bergen's *Rare Coin Encyclopedia*, and recent research also shows some overlapping of content between Mehl's and von Bergen's coin-pricing books. It is still unclear whether Mehl purchased the rights to von Bergen's work, chose to imitate his predecessor, or worked in concert with him. The first incarnation of Mehl's best-selling reference, *The Star Coin Book: An Encyclopedia of Rare American and Foreign Coins*, cost 50¢ and was issued through the Mehl-owned Numismatic Bank of Texas. Most editions of this book were 112 pages long, with much of that length devoted to American coins. Yet, of the 44 pages of photographs in the catalog, 27 illustrated ancient coins, for which no values were noted. The practice of including pictures of ancient coins would continue throughout Mehl's publication of *The Star Coin Book*.

Like his predecessor von Bergen, Mehl did not usually reference mintmarks. In most instances, he simply listed the year of production and the price he was willing to pay. He would include the mintmark information

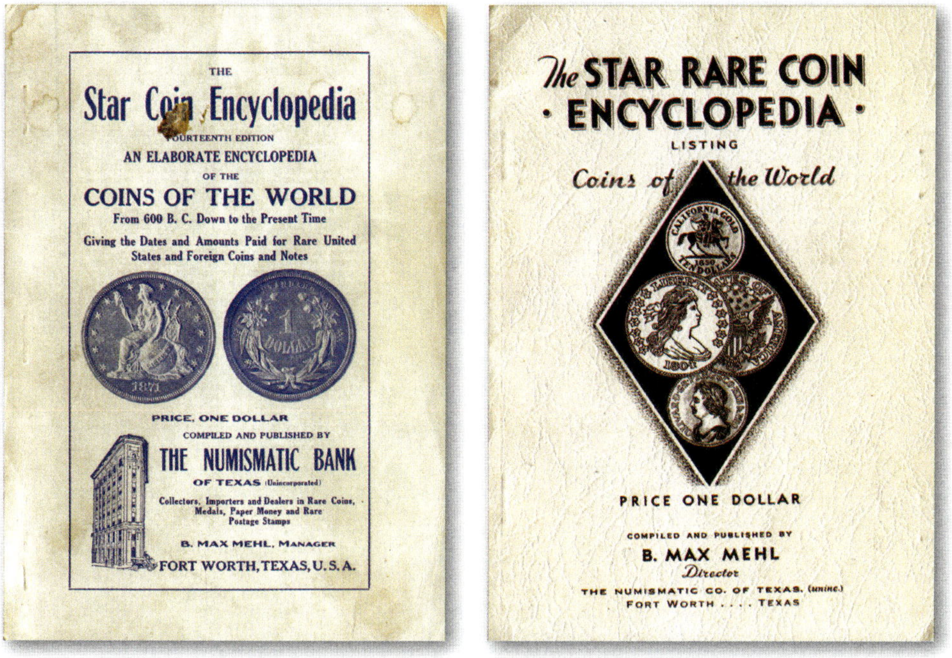

◄ Two Mehl catalogs from 1916 and 1944.

if it applied to a specific coin he wanted, but collecting by mintmarks had not yet become common practice. Eventually, *The Star Coin Book* gave place to a longer reference, *The Star Coin Encyclopedia: An Elaborate Encyclopedia of the Coins of the World*. At 208 pages, it included illustrations and values of many foreign coins, as well as a number of essays. Although it carried a price tag of $1, for many readers it was well worth the cost. Regarding mintmarks, in the 14th edition's section on dimes, for example, the mints of origin were listed for only four dates. Among these was the 1894-S Barber dime, valued at between $50 and $100. In the quarter-dollar section, which contained listings through 1893, mintmarks were included for only two dates. A brief section of the book entitled "Mint Marks That Command a Premium" supplemented (and occasionally repeated) the standard type listings with specific values for particular dates and mintmarks, but at the equivalent of about two text pages, this list could hardly be called exhaustive.

Another idiosyncrasy of the *Encyclopedia* listings was its organization. Even by the time the 51st edition was released in 1944, some coins were listed as a group rather than by individual date. In the section on Barber dimes, for example, appears a listing for 1892 to 1905-O issues as a single entity, with values of between 20¢ and $1. Mehl's books and promotional ventures have landed him a place in numismatic history as one of the premier architects of twentieth-century coin collecting. By telling the public that they could start collecting simply by glancing through their loose change, Mehl introduced the idea that numismatics was a pastime for everyone, not just the elite. He was instrumental in popularizing coin collecting and brought unprecedented numbers of people into the hobby.

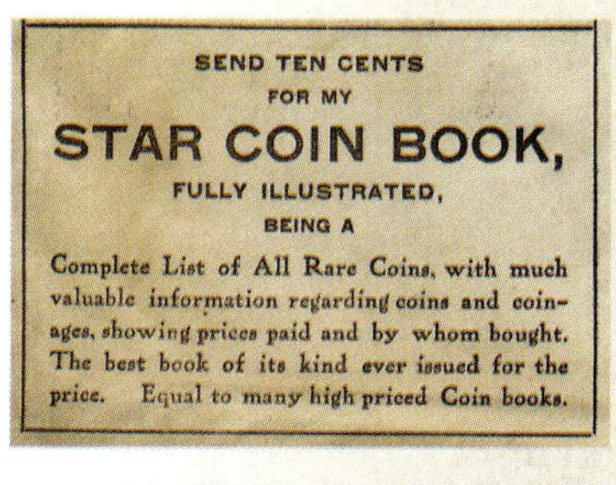
SEND TEN CENTS
FOR MY
STAR COIN BOOK,
FULLY ILLUSTRATED,
BEING A
Complete List of All Rare Coins, with much valuable information regarding coins and coinages, showing prices paid and by whom bought. The best book of its kind ever issued for the price. Equal to many high priced Coin books.

▲ Mehl advertised extensively—from full ads down to text boxes on his company envelopes (as seen here).

▲ Mehl issued this promotional token (actual size, about the diameter of a half dollar) to advertise his books and coin sales.

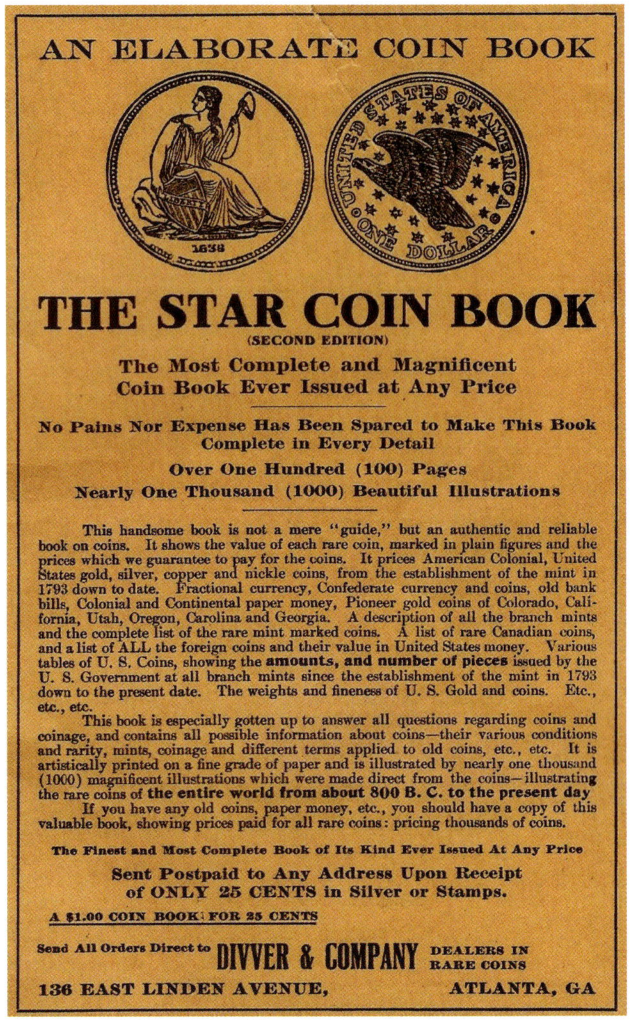

AN ELABORATE COIN BOOK

THE STAR COIN BOOK

(SECOND EDITION)

The Most Complete and Magnificent Coin Book Ever Issued at Any Price

No Pains Nor Expense Has Been Spared to Make This Book Complete in Every Detail

Over One Hundred (100) Pages

Nearly One Thousand (1000) Beautiful Illustrations

This handsome book is not a mere "guide," but an authentic and reliable book on coins. It shows the value of each rare coin, marked in plain figures and the prices which we guarantee to pay for the coins. It prices American Colonial, United States gold, silver, copper and nickle coins, from the establishment of the mint in 1793 down to date. Fractional currency, Confederate currency and coins, old bank bills, Colonial and Continental paper money, Pioneer gold coins of Colorado, California, Utah, Oregon, Carolina and Georgia. A description of all the branch mints and the complete list of the rare mint marked coins. A list of rare Canadian coins, and a list of ALL the foreign coins and their value in United States money. Various tables of U. S. Coins, showing the **amounts, and number of pieces** issued by the U. S. Government at all branch mints since the establishment of the mint in 1793 down to the present date. The weights and fineness of U. S. Gold and coins. Etc., etc., etc.

This book is especially gotten up to answer all questions regarding coins and coinage, and contains all possible information about coins—their various conditions and rarity, mints, coinage and different terms applied to old coins, etc., etc. It is artistically printed on a fine grade of paper and is illustrated by nearly one thousand (1000) magnificent illustrations which were made direct from the coins—illustrating the rare coins of **the entire world from about 800 B. C. to the present day**

If you have any old coins, paper money, etc., you should have a copy of this valuable book, showing prices paid for all rare coins: pricing thousands of coins.

The Finest and Most Complete Book of Its Kind Ever Issued At Any Price

Sent Postpaid to Any Address Upon Receipt of ONLY 25 CENTS in Silver or Stamps.

A $1.00 COIN BOOK FOR 25 CENTS

Send All Orders Direct to DIVVER & COMPANY DEALERS IN RARE COINS

136 EAST LINDEN AVENUE, ATLANTA, GA

► The inside-back cover of the March 1909 *Numismatist* promoted Mehl's book, for sale by an Atlanta-based distributor, Divver & Company.

OTHER EARLY REFERENCE BOOKS

A lesser-known pioneer reference that attempted to organize the rather chaotic listings of United States coins was Ben Green's *Numismatists' Reference and Check Book, Being a List of Coins Issued by the U.S. Mint and Branches With Principal Varieties, Private Issues of Gold, Paper Fractional Currency, and Encased Postage Stamps, With Provisions For Checking and Recording The Pieces In A Collection*. Published in 1902, it was a valiant effort, with a title nearly as long as its 112 pages, and undoubtedly a useful tool for early collectors. It bears no relationship to the somewhat similar *Mint Record and Type-Table, United States Coins* issued by Charles E. Green (no relation to Ben Green) in 1936, mentioned here in connection with Yeoman's *Handbook*.

Yet another influential price reference of that era was the 1934 *New Rare Coin Book* published by New York City dealer Thomas L. Elder, a 100-page catalog listing prices paid for valuable coins of America as well as just about everything else from ancient to modern times. It carried this stern warning: "Prosecution will promptly follow all infringements on this work."

WAYTE RAYMOND'S INFLUENCE

New York coin dealer Wayte Raymond is not as widely known today as some of his numismatic brethren, but he brought distinction—and many new collectors—to the hobby by creating high-quality coin-pricing guides. After Raymond's death in 1956, John J. Ford Jr. wrote an obituary that provides most of the information available today on this private man. The first such tribute ever to win the American Numismatic Association's Heath Literary Award, it tells us that Raymond, who was born in Connecticut in 1886, started his numismatic career as a vest-pocket dealer. In 1912 a $500 loan from his parents enabled him to leave his position as a bank teller and become a full-time coin dealer. A quiet, unassuming man who avoided the spotlight craved by so many other dealers, Raymond was well regarded by his contemporaries for the thorough research and desire for accuracy that he brought to his publications. He also designed and sold the popular National Coin Albums. Today he is acknowledged by numismatic scholars like David T. Alexander as being the twentieth century's "godfather of quality numismatic publishing," producing reference works that did not make their author rich but greatly stimulated numismatic interest and activity. As Q. David Bowers observes in his essay "Inside the *Red Book*," "any survey of pivotal figures in American numismatics during the [twentieth] century must have Raymond near the top of the list."

▲ Coin dealer, numismatic writer, and publisher Wayte Raymond.

Raymond's most famous reference work debuted in 1934, the same year that he went to work for the Scott Stamp & Coin Company. Originally this book was titled *Standard Catalogue of United States Coins and Tokens*; later, tokens would be dropped from both title and contents. The *Standard Catalogue* soon became the leading numismatic reference of its day. David T. Alexander calls it "the first truly objective pricing guide covering the broad field of U.S. coinage," and, as an annual publication (at least initially), it was also the first coin-pricing guide to be regularly updated. The early editions are notable in part for their invaluable information relating to U.S. tokens. In the first edition, the section on Hard Times tokens spanned a then-unusual ten pages and included illustrations. Raymond's listings included both hand-drawn illustrations and photographs of early merchants' tokens, and a section on Civil War tokens and cards. By listing these tokens, Raymond greatly furthered the hobby of collecting them.

▼ An advertisement from the February 1911 issue of *The Numismatist*.

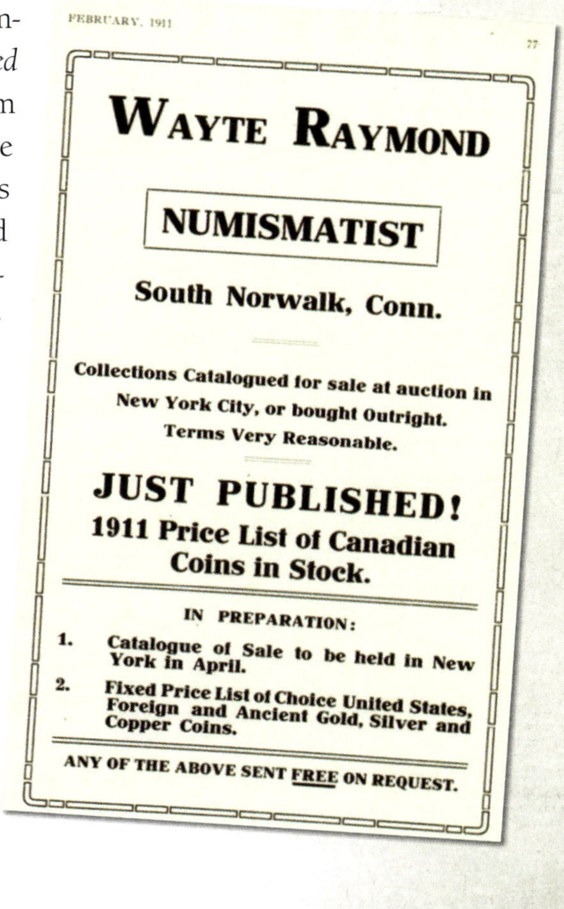

Yet, at the same time, the catalog was awkwardly organized in certain ways. The minor coinage (that struck without silver or gold, such as cent and nickel coins) is clearly listed by date and mintmark within each coin's type. Inexplicably, however,

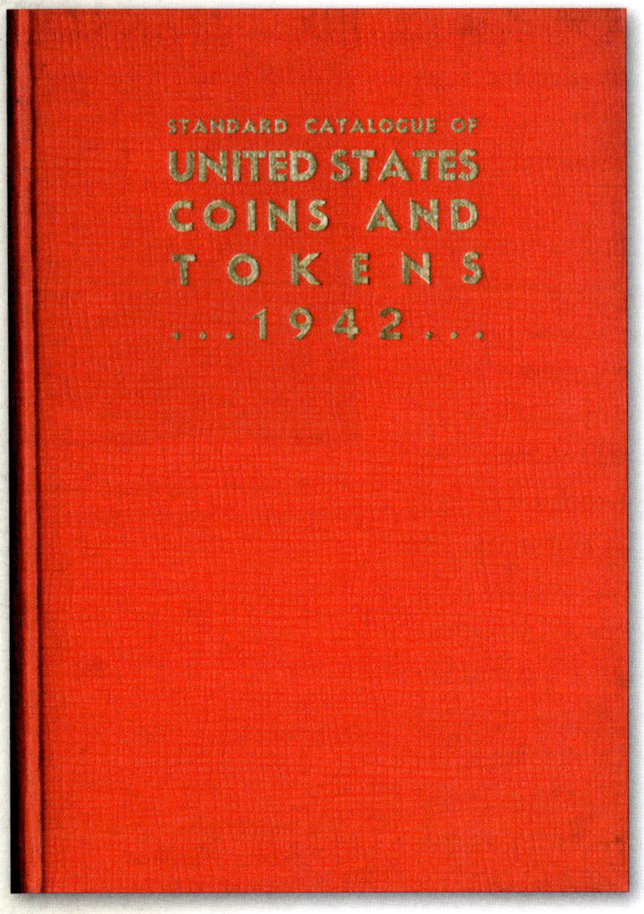

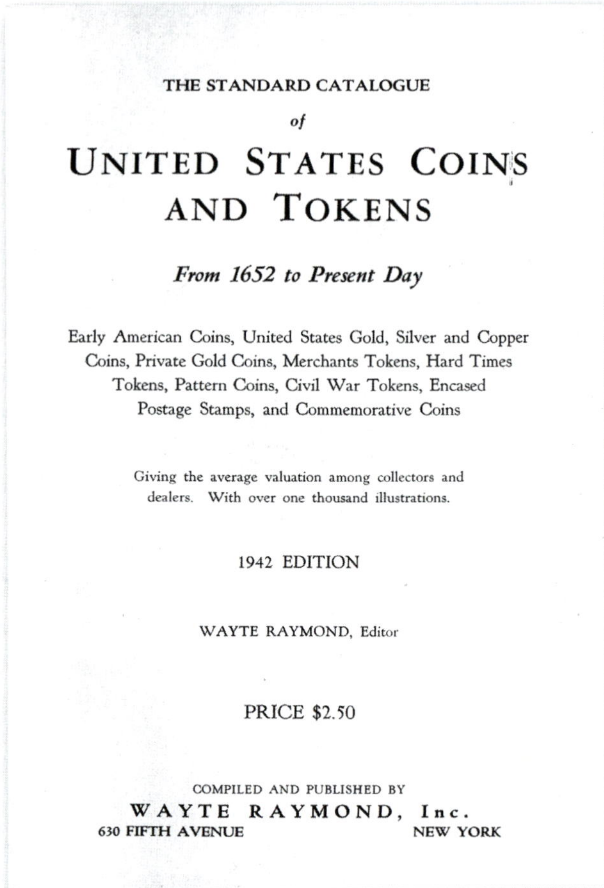

THE STANDARD CATALOGUE

of

UNITED STATES COINS
AND TOKENS

From 1652 to Present Day

Early American Coins, United States Gold, Silver and Copper Coins, Private Gold Coins, Merchants Tokens, Hard Times Tokens, Pattern Coins, Civil War Tokens, Encased Postage Stamps, and Commemorative Coins

Giving the average valuation among collectors and dealers. With over one thousand illustrations.

1942 EDITION

WAYTE RAYMOND, Editor

PRICE $2.50

COMPILED AND PUBLISHED BY
WAYTE RAYMOND, Inc.
630 FIFTH AVENUE NEW YORK

▲ **The 1942 edition of Wayte Raymond's *Standard Catalogue of United States Coins and Tokens*.**

a different method was used in the silver and gold coinage sections. These coins, rather than being arranged by series, were listed by the mint at which they were produced. This unwieldy system required users to search by mint—and to be aware of which mint produced which dates.

The *Standard Catalogue of United States Coins and Tokens* continued to be released annually through 1942. Each edition after the first was dated a year ahead of its publication date, a convention that would also be used in Yeoman's *Guide Book*. In 1943 Raymond published a supplement that contained values for minor, silver, and commemorative coinage. This 16-page pamphlet was priced at 25¢—rather expensive if you consider that the full clothbound 1942 edition was $2.50 and the 1940 edition was then available for a discounted price of $1. When the book reappeared in 1944, its name had been shortened to *Standard Catalogue of United States Coins*, and the 60 pages devoted to tokens had been removed. The remaining listings were completely reworked so that all dates and mints were listed within their appropriate headings, rather than being organized by mint.

Although the *Standard Catalogue* would no longer appear on a regular annual basis, Raymond continued publishing his popular reference even after a potential competitor emerged in 1946, in the form of Yeoman's *Guide Book of United States Coins*. Interestingly, while the 14th (1950)

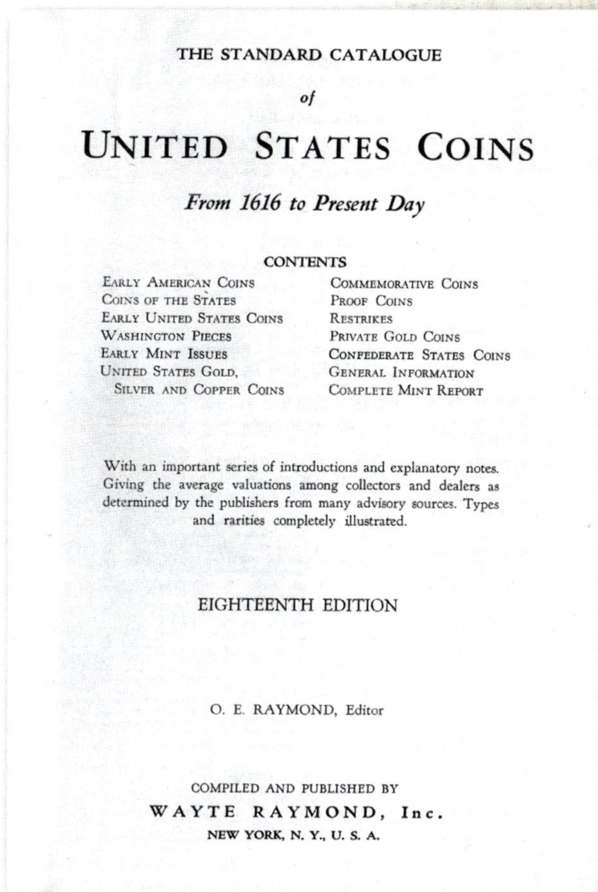
THE STANDARD CATALOGUE

of

UNITED STATES COINS

From 1616 to Present Day

CONTENTS

Early American Coins	Commemorative Coins
Coins of the States	Proof Coins
Early United States Coins	Restrikes
Washington Pieces	Private Gold Coins
Early Mint Issues	Confederate States Coins
United States Gold, Silver and Copper Coins	General Information
	Complete Mint Report

With an important series of introductions and explanatory notes. Giving the average valuations among collectors and dealers as determined by the publishers from many advisory sources. Types and rarities completely illustrated.

EIGHTEENTH EDITION

O. E. RAYMOND, Editor

COMPILED AND PUBLISHED BY
WAYTE RAYMOND, Inc.
NEW YORK, N. Y., U. S. A.

▲ The 18th edition of the *Standard Catalogue* (1957).

edition of the *Standard Catalogue* listed 32 contributors, the 15th (1951) edition listed only the editor, Wayte Raymond. When the 16th edition was published in 1953, however, John J. Ford Jr. was credited as associate editor and Walter Breen as researcher. Raymond had taken the innovative approach of sending Breen to the National Archives in Washington, D.C., to investigate original historical documents relating to U.S. coinage. The research Breen carried out at Raymond's behest broke new ground in numismatic scholarship and further helped to establish the *Standard Catalogue* as a landmark reference.

In 1953 the catalog's title was changed to include "The," and the volume was released as *The Standard Catalogue of United States Coins*. Most likely, this was an attempt by Raymond to establish his publication as *the* definitive reference on U.S. coins. But the 1953 *Standard Catalogue* ended up being the second-to-last edition issued. The final one was released in 1957, after Raymond's death; his widow, Olga (credited as O.E. Raymond), served as editor of this edition. For the first time, mintages were given in an easy-to-read format—at least, those from 1936 to 1956. Mintage quantities for earlier years, on the other hand, were still presented as they had been previously, in the back of the book and copied in tabular style from the report of the director of the Mint, which was difficult to comprehend.

Wayte Raymond's achievements in the field did not end with the *Standard Catalogue*. During its publication, he revived J.W. Scott's *Coin Collector's Journal*, and under his direction it enjoyed a successful run from 1934 to 1954. Raymond also produced numerous other books, such as *The Standard Paper Money Catalogue* in 1940 and *Coins of the World: 20th Century Issues*. This popular title saw five editions, the last of which appeared in 1955, and a counterpart publication, *Coins of the World: 19th Century Issues*. Published in 1947, this book too was later succeeded by another edition. In honor of Raymond's contributions to numismatic literature, the ANA created the Wayte and Olga Raymond Memorial Award for literature. It is awarded to authors of articles in *The Numismatist*, the ANA journal, that display "original and comprehensive research in U.S. numismatics."

LEE HEWITT'S *NUMISMATIC SCRAPBOOK MAGAZINE*

At around the same time that Wayte Raymond was revolutionizing his coin-pricing guide, Chicago printer and coin collector Lee Hewitt launched his own highly influential publication. Hewitt was reportedly inspired by the flood of commemorative coins emerging at the time, and in January 1935 he began production of the *Numismatic Scrapbook Magazine* at the Chicago printing shop he owned with his brother, Clifford. Published monthly, the *Scrapbook* became a respected and popular periodical, praised by R.S. Yeoman in particular for being "no-nonsense, non-technical," and "down-to-earth." Q. David Bowers recalls that in the 1950s it was "the be-all and end-all in monthly coin market spirit and information." Hewitt continued as editor until 1968, when he sold the magazine to Amos Press, which published the title until 1976. As popular as it was, however, Hewitt's magazine did not regularly provide comprehensive coin pricing information—leaving a need that he filled in the 1950s by printing a basic wholesale buying list called *United States Rare Coin Value Guide* that could be imprinted with a dealer's name and sold by them for 50¢.

◀ The January 1940 issue of Lee F. Hewitt's *Numismatic Scrapbook Magazine*. R.S. Yeoman felt that "coin collecting . . . came alive in the modern sense" when the magazine was launched in 1935. Hewitt was also influential in the start of the Central States Numismatic Society in 1939.

THE ADVENT OF THE *BLUE BOOK*

To support and increase sales of Western's emerging line of coin boards, Dick Yeo (not yet known by his pseudonym of R.S.

Yeoman) foresaw the need for an unbiased and factual source of information about current values of coins, as well as the historical background that made them desirable collector's items. Building collectors' confidence in the hobby would increase the market base and add to sales and profits. A new, inclusive book on the subject was now the objective for the neophyte numismatist, who set about in an orderly manner to explore the field and quickly learn where and how to obtain reliable information to meet his needs. Close at hand were the Racine Numismatic Society, the Chicago Coin Club, and the Milwaukee Numismatic Society, as well as numerous seasoned local collectors and dealers. Yeo did not rely solely on the published works of the past, because he quickly learned that they were often biased and unreliable.

Among his earliest and most trusted teachers were stalwarts like Charles Green, Lee Hewitt, and M. Vernon Sheldon of Chicago, as well as Dan Brown and Hubert Polzer of Milwaukee. The most influential of these was Green, who in 1936 published *Mint Record and Type-Table, United States Coins by C. E. Green*, a popular book that was essentially a checklist of all U.S. coins with mintage figures and side comments on many of the issues, but with no indication of individual values.

While not a price guide, the style, scope, and information in this book were a well-suited model arrangement that greatly influenced the construction of what was to become the *Blue Book*. Hubert Polzer, a long-time Milwaukee dealer, not only assisted Yeo with his expertise but subsequently gave up his assistant, son-in-law Pete Forrester, who was hired to work at Western as sales manager for coin products.

With the assistance of his core group and many others, Yeo researched, organized, and printed the first edition of the *Handbook of United States Coins* in 1942. World War II caused the book to skip a couple of editions in those early years. It quickly became a staple of the hobby, providing average dealer buying prices for U.S. coins. Before long, the popular guide was known among collectors by the color of its cover, as the *Blue Book*. It made R.S. Yeoman—as Dick Yeo's authorship was styled—a numismatic household name.

▲ A 1910 medal of the Chicago Numismatic Society, precursor of the Chicago Coin Club. Many of the coin dealers who assisted on the first *Blue Book* hailed from the Windy City.

R.S. YEOMAN, LEE F. HEWITT, AND CHARLES E. GREEN

The covers of each edition of the *Handbook* from the first in 1942 through the 13th, dated 1956, indicate the co-authors are R.S. Yeoman, Lee F. Hewitt, and Charles E. Green. Hewitt's fame was especially widespread because of his publication, which was named *Numismatic Scrapbook* in 1934; *The Numismatic Scrapbook* in 1935; and later *The Numismatic Scrapbook Magazine*. Green, while one of the leading numismatic authorities of

▲ Two versions of the 1936 Green *Type-Table* cover were printed. One shows the copyright holder to be H.W. Gumaer, a little-known collector and book dealer from Cortland, New York.

the time, was more generally known as a professional coin dealer. The three names continued to be used on the cover until they were dropped from the 1957 edition and the designation was changed to "By R.S. Yeoman." That credit continued to be used until the 36th edition in 1979, when "Edited by Kenneth Bressett" was included on the title page. Beginning with the 57th edition, in 2000, and thereafter I was credited on the cover as editor, until my retirement as editor emeritus in 2018. At that time Jeff Garrett became senior editor, only the third person to fill that role for the *Blue Book*.

Charles Elmore Green (1894–1955) was a Chicago coin dealer and author who in 1936 wrote the *Mint Record and Type-Table, United States Coins* and was a contributor to the *Handbook* until 1955. He closed his retail store in 1955 but continued to do business by mail out of Skokie, Illinois, until his death. His wife, Ruth, managed the business under the name R. Green until 1959. Both were active members of the Chicago Coin Club and close friends of Yeoman's. Charles had been injured in the first World War and suffered from complications thereafter, with occasional hospital confinement and restricted activities.

Lee F. Hewitt (1911–1987) was the founder and publisher of *Numismatic Scrapbook Magazine*, issued monthly from 1935 to 1968. He was a contributor to *Coin World* and author or co-author of several publications, as well as being one of the three major influences and assistants to Yeoman in constructing the original *Handbook*. Lee and his younger brother Clifford were partners in the Hewitt Brothers printing company in Chicago, where the *Scrapbook* was published. A dynamic contributor to the success of their magazine was their associate editor, Arlie R. Slabaugh, who served as editor, writer, and linotype compositor in the production of the magazine, often writing fill-in articles on the spot while setting type. Although Slabaugh was not part of the original 1942 work on the *Handbook*, he did later write two editions of *United States Commemorative Coinage* that were published by Whitman in 1962 and 1975, and he was a contributor to the *Whitman Numismatic Journal*.

▲ Lee F. Hewitt.

◄ Yeoman's *Handbook of United States Coins* bore a striking resemblance to Green's *Mint Record and Type Table*, from the rounded corners on the cover to the overall presentation and content.

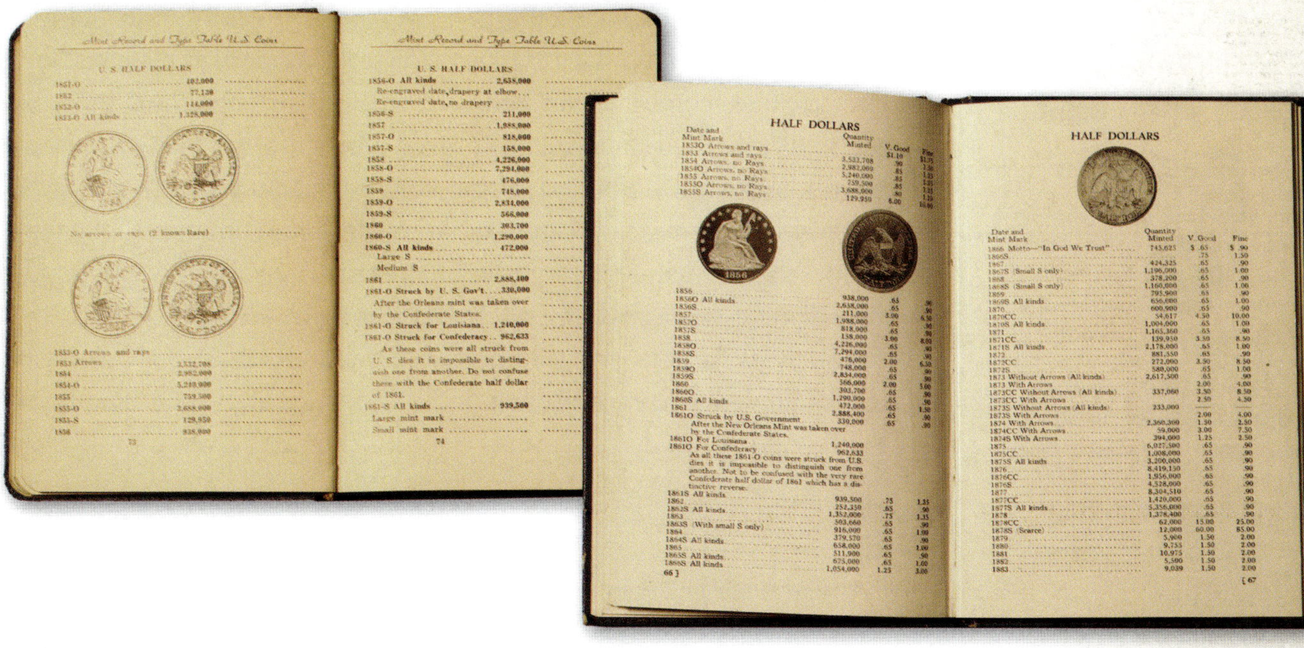

1942
HANDBOOK
OF
UNITED STATES
COINS
With Premium List

★

By
R. S. YEOMAN • LEE F. HEWITT
CHARLES E. GREEN

Containing mint record and prices paid by dealers for all U. S. coins. Information on collecting coins—how coins are produced—mints and mint marks—condition of coins—location of mint marks—preserving and cleaning coins—starting a collection—coin club directory—what to buy—history of mints and interesting descriptions of all U.S. copper, nickel, silver and gold coins. Fully illustrated.

Copyright MCMXLII by
WHITMAN PUBLISHING COMPANY
RACINE, WISCONSIN

9050 Printed in U.S.A.

▲ The title page of the first *Blue Book.*

In addition to the principal editors, contributors, and multitude of special helpers, all of whom deserve thanks for making the *Handbook* one of the most revered and useful numismatic references, a question might still be asked as to exactly who did the original research and writing. Yeoman certainly provided the concept and undoubtedly gathered the necessary material, and he must be given credit as the originator. Yet after careful consideration it seems unavoidable to conclude that it must have been Charles Green who provided the inspiration and much of the factual material in the very first edition of the *Handbook*. Beyond the size, shape, color, and layout of Green's *Mint Record and Type-Table, United States Coins*, there is undeniable proof that much of the wording and listings are identical. Using the trio of names as co-editors was not only due credit but also a mark of the scrupulousness of Yeoman, who always strove to show his appreciation for everyone who helped with his quest to improve and promote the coin-collecting hobby.

Before the end of 1942, changes were already being planned to correct, update, and enhance the listings in the first edition of the *Handbook*. The Western Archives holds Green's personal copy of the *Type-Table* book showing his notations for future additions and changes, which were later implemented in the *Handbook*. Further, in the second edition the extensive "Coin Club Directory" was eliminated to provide space for expansion and additional pictures. A new feature was added explaining the regulations about hoarding gold coins and the lapses in coinage of some silver dollars. A list of current Whitman coin-folder titles was added to the last page. Most noticeably, the rounded-corners feature for the cover and pages was eliminated.

DISTINGUISHING MARKS

1864 BRONZE INDIAN HEAD CENT WITH "L" ON RIBBON

A magnifying glass is necessary to see this detail. Only a very fine or uncirculated specimen will show this small initial. If the coin is turned slightly (so Indian faces observer) the highlighted details of the "L" will appear to better advantage. The "L" is the initial of the engraver, Longacre.

Small Motto — Large Motto

TWO CENTS OF 1864

Details explain the differences in these two well-known varieties. Observe the D in God, it is narrow on the large motto. The stem to the leaf shows plainly on the small motto variety. There is no stem on the large motto coin.

LINCOLN CENTS SHOWING LOCATION OF INITIALS V D B

(At top) 1909 Initials appear on reverse. (At right) Initials appear beneath shoulder, 1918 and later.

1918-S QUARTER 8 OVER 7

A variety of this kind is rarely found in coinage of the twentieth century.

[13

▲ The *Blue Book* gave hobbyists a 12-page primer on coin collecting. For R.S. Yeoman and his team, accurately cataloging every U.S. issue was a major challenge. Mintage figures were not readily available. Even the records of the United States Mint could be confusing and, in places, unreliable.

The *Handbook of United States Coins* was popular with coin collectors from the start, and its ongoing enhancements and updates made it more so. Yeoman would later write about how it began to satisfy the "long-felt need among American collectors" for "a low-priced standard reference book of United States coins and kindred issues." Even so, something more was needed: "While the *Handbook* has proved a boon to the many thousands of coin board enthusiasts and casual coin collectors who are concerned principally with elementary information, or with premium prices," he wrote in 1946, "there remains a vast group of intermediate collectors who require a guide book containing more advanced features."

That new, more extensive volume would debut as the *Guide Book of United States Coins*—a reference that would be forever known as the "Red Book."

▶ This advertisement for the first edition of the *Handbook of United States Coins* appeared in the January 1942 issue of *The Numismatist.*

Know WHAT YOUR COINS ARE WORTH—HOW AND WHAT TO COLLECT

HANDBOOK OF UNITED STATES COINS

With Premium List

- **AUTHORITATIVE**
- **UP-TO-DATE**
- **FULLY ILLUSTRATED**

Whitman's 1942 Handbook of United States Coins is coat-pocket size 5 x 7½ inches, cloth bound with gold stamped board cover. This beautiful 128-page volume is written in simple everyday language. It is indispensible to the beginner and advanced coin collector alike.

Features Never Before Found in Books Costing Less Than One Dollar Are Included in This Handbook

Here are a few feature sections that make this the outstanding coin book of a generation:

Illustrations showing location of mint marks on all denominations • Mint records • How coins are produced •Determining condition of coins • Preserving and cleaning coins • History of mints • Halftone illustrations of all commemorative and regular type coins • Premium list giving prices paid by dealers, etc.

Price 50¢ in Stores • 65¢ Postpaid from WHITMAN PUBLISHING CO., Racine, Wis.

SEND FOR *Free* . . .
WHITMAN HOBBY CATALOG

Twelve illustrated pages listing 25 different coin folders, also match book collectors, stamp albums, nature guides, etc.

WHITMAN PUBLISHING CO.
Dept. HK
RACINE, WISCONSIN

Dealers: Write for quantity prices.

HANDBOOK OF
UNITED STATES
COINS
With Premium List
A GUIDE BOOK
of
A GUIDE BOOK of
UNITED STATES
COINS
1947
BY R. S. YEOMAN

Chapter 3

The Red Book Story

GENESIS

The early success of the *Blue Book* gave impetus for a second, more detailed reference that would show the average prices coin dealers were charging for their wares. Richard Yeo—or R.S. Yeoman, as collectors knew him—was by then well aware of the task at hand, as well as the competition to be faced. He was a quick learner and problem solver, but the ongoing World War II was an obstacle that caused many delays, changes, and contingency plans. In retrospect, while the numismatic world went nearly dormant, Yeoman was given the opportunity to hone his skills, develop a publishing strategy, and perfect a quality product that would be ready for collectors as soon as things returned to normal. And he did exactly that through his foresight, ingenuity, and collaboration with friends and specialists who provided additional expertise, help, and guidance.

▲ The war effort in the 1940s was a nationwide call to action. Americans were encouraged to reduce consumption, reuse and recycle household goods, grow our own food, and ration consumables for the war effort. Part of that rationing, for book publishers like Whitman, included paper.

In Yeoman's words, "The *Guide Book* was in the planning stage when Adolf Hitler went berserk, and we put the project in cold storage for the duration." The wartime paper shortage brought new publishing restrictions, so that starting in 1943 paper supplies were allotted to publishers according to their previous year's paper use. In practice, this meant that although a successful volume like the *Blue Book* could, and did try to, continue its annual publication, going forward with the planned companion volume would have eaten into the paper allotment for other, established books that Whitman published. As a consequence, the *Red Book* would not debut until 1946. Yeoman would later observe that the postponement "was not all bad, for it gave me time to meet some key people and discuss details and features with them." Among these key people were coin dealers Aubrey Bebee, Bill Clark, Stuart Mosher, and Hubert Polzer, who assisted Yeoman in the intensive research that he carried out during the enforced delay.

A Guide Book of United States Coins was published in November 1946, with a cover date of 1947. The system of postdating each edition has confused later generations of readers, but at the time it was not unusual; Wayte Raymond's *Standard Catalogue* also carried a cover date one year ahead of its publication date, which might even have influenced the decision to date the *Guide Book* this way. The distinctive color of the cover, which would later give the book its enduring nickname, was Yeoman's choice because it was a "good, bright, attention-getting color." In fact, the early editions are closer to maroon than red, and not until the 10th edition would the now-standard red shade appear. The term *Red Book* first appeared as a subtitle on the cover in 1963 for the 16th edition.

The *Guide Book* contained much more material than its predecessor, with the most prominent content being, of course, the retail values in the listings. To assemble those values, Yeoman drew on a distinguished panel of contributors in the trade. Because the *Red Book* was created to provide *unbiased* values for coins, all of the values were averaged from multiple contributors' input—no small feat, particularly as the panel of contributors grew in number. The list of contributors in the first edition reads like a who's who of numismatists of the day:

A.E. (Aubrey) Bebee
Malcolm O.E. Chell-Frost
William L. Clark
Damon G. Douglas
Charles E. Green
Ted R. Hammer
A. (Abe) Kosoff
Abner Kreisberg
Edmund E. Lamb
Stuart Mosher
Hubert L. Polzer
Lewis M. Reagan
Max M. Schwartz
Farran Zerbe

RATIONING MEANS A FAIR SHARE FOR ALL OF US

Office of Price Administration
Washington, D. C.

☆ U. S. GOVERNMENT PRINTING OFFICE : 1943—O-523856

Starting with the first edition, which named the 14 contributors, Yeoman surrounded himself with many of the era's most knowledgeable and distinguished numismatists. In 1971, he described them this way:

> Contributors to the *Guide Book* were then and still are volunteers who come to us with price projections annually, and with full knowledge that their data will be merged with that of their fellow experts and averaged for listing in the catalog. This dedicated group represents every geographical region, age group, and degree of knowledge and experience. They are truly a cross-section of our American numismatic community. Since taking the editorial helm in 1965, Kenneth Bressett has carried on the tradition of bringing the finest numismatic minds to the creation of the *Red Book*.

The innovative new *Guide Book* was warmly greeted, and its popularity illustrated by the fact that the initial printing of 9,000 copies quickly sold out, and just a few months later (in February 1947) another 9,000 copies were printed. Yeoman noted that he and his staff took the opportunity to go back to press with a second print run to make "a few corrections and

▶ The *Guide Book of United States Coins*—"not to be confused with any other coin book," extols this advertisement from the December 1946 issue of *The Numismatist*.

Waiting for the War to End

During World War II, Western had a contract with the U.S. Army Map Service to produce maps for soldiers in the field, and it also manufactured books and playing cards, which were sent overseas. In 1945 Western also produced an inexpensive Bible that was extremely popular both in the United States and abroad. Despite the wartime shortages and demand for necessary paper products, the company was poised to embark on something entirely new.

New Aid for Collectors

WHITMAN'S *GUIDE* BOOK OF U. S. COINS

IT'S BIG! 256 pages of information

IT'S HELPFUL! Illustrations and data for every collector

Handsomely bound in cloth, with gold-stamped cover. Size 5⅛ x 7¾ inches. Contains 256 pages of data and illustrations. Only $1.50.

● One of the best ways to increase the pleasure to be derived from your coin collection is to know the interesting history of the various U. S. issues. Whitman . . . publishers of the Handbook of U. S. Coins, now in its 5th Edition . . . has just published the new, *Guide Book* of U. S. Coins, not to be confused with any other coin book. A new, different kind of Catalog and Standard Price List—1616 to Date—it includes such valuable information as • Brief History of American Coinage (Fully Illustrated) • Early American Coins and Tokens • Early Mint Issues; Regular Mint Issues • Private, State and Territorial Gold • Silver and Gold Commemorative Issues; etc. Get your copy today!

See Your Coin Dealer or Write to the

WHITMAN PUBLISHING COMPANY

DEPT. HT • RACINE, WISCONSIN

▲ This set of 1946 cents was likely given out by Whitman Publishing to celebrate the first edition of the new *Guide Book of United States Coins.*

revisions." The most widely known change is the footnote on page 135 clarifying the 1903-O silver dollar statement, which has since become the identifying distinction between the first and second printings. (See the appendix for more differences between the two printings.)

It is no surprise that Yeoman would seize the opportunity to make every possible improvement in the new book. When the *Guide Book* first appeared, it faced potential competition from Wayte Raymond's *Standard Catalogue of United States Coins*. Raymond's numismatic reference was in its 11th edition by 1946 and was well established as the reference serious numismatists turned to first, while Yeoman was still not a well-known figure in the field of coin collecting. Whitman's ability to mass-produce books was one competitive advantage, as it could price the *Red Book* at less than the *Standard Catalogue*. Within a few years, the fledgling publication took the older book's place as the number-one reference for collectors of U.S. coins.

Yeoman's rapid success was partially due to his canny marketing strategy. The *Standard Catalogue* was mainly available through coin dealers, and unless a collector lived in one of the larger cities, it could be obtained only by mail. Whitman, on the other hand, placed its products in a wider variety of less-specialized retailers, such as hobby shops, general bookstores, and even department stores. At $1.50, the *Red Book* was also significantly cheaper than the $3.50 *Standard Catalogue*. Yeoman reasoned that coin collecting was a sufficiently popular topic that an annual price guide would have wide appeal for the general public. At the same time, he believed the *Standard Catalogue* would continue merrily on its way as a specialized (and high-priced) book for advanced collectors. The two were not viewed as competing publications. As a reference that was both more readily available and more affordable than its closest competition, Yeoman's new book further boosted the growing popularity of coin collecting, a trend that had started with Whitman's popularization of the coin board. Yeoman would later reflect, "It is my belief that the *Red Book* was needed as a bridge between the coin board or commemorative coin collectors, and the professional dealers, the ANA, and even the Treasury department."

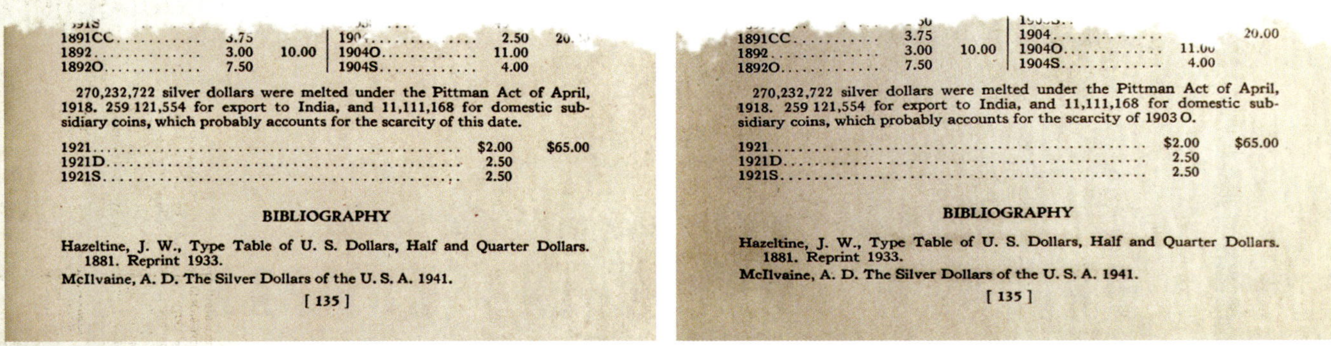
1891CC.......... 3.75 | 190...... 2.50
1892.......... 3.00 10.00 | 1904O.......... 11.00
1892O.......... 7.50 | 1904S.......... 4.00

270,232,722 silver dollars were melted under the Pittman Act of April, 1918. 259 121,554 for export to India, and 11,111,168 for domestic subsidiary coins, which probably accounts for the scarcity of this date.

1921.......... $2.00 $65.00
1921D.......... 2.50
1921S.......... 2.50

BIBLIOGRAPHY

Hazeltine, J. W., Type Table of U. S. Dollars, Half and Quarter Dollars. 1881. Reprint 1933.
McIlvaine, A. D. The Silver Dollars of the U. S. A. 1941.

[135]

1891CC.......... 3.75 | 1904.......... 20.00
1892.......... 3.00 10.00 | 1904O.......... 11.00
1892O.......... 7.50 | 1904S.......... 4.00

270,232,722 silver dollars were melted under the Pittman Act of April, 1918. 259 121,554 for export to India, and 11,111,168 for domestic subsidiary coins, which probably accounts for the scarcity of 1903 O.

1921.......... $2.00 $65.00
1921D.......... 2.50
1921S.......... 2.50

BIBLIOGRAPHY

Hazeltine, J. W., Type Table of U. S. Dollars, Half and Quarter Dollars. 1881. Reprint 1933.
McIlvaine, A. D. The Silver Dollars of the U. S. A. 1941.

[135]

▲ Page 135 of the first edition of the *Red Book* (first and second printings).

"Look at What He Has Accomplished!"

by Lincoln W. Higgie III

In October 1938, Richard S. Yeo approached my father, Lincoln W. Higgie Sr., with questions concerning numismatics and coin collecting in general. Yeo had come to Racine from his native Milwaukee to work for Whitman Publishing Company and was given the "penny boards" section of the children's games department to develop and expand.

My father was a founder of the Racine Numismatic Society, and he invited Yeo to accompany him and my mother to a coin convention being held in Des Moines, Iowa. A few weeks after that convention I was born. In later years, with so very many coin conventions behind all of us, there were numerous stories about the destiny of those people driving off to Iowa together in the autumn of 1938.

My parents' birthdays were August 24 and 25, just about a week after Yeoman's. Every year they exchanged birthday cards and letters. In his last birthday letter to my parents in 1987, Yeoman fondly recalled that trip to Iowa and their friendship during the years that followed.

How excited my father was when the first *Guide Book of United States Coins* appeared! Yeoman had brought copies to the Racine Numismatic Society meeting, and the results were electrifying. Over the years, how many times Daddy would be reading that book and say, "I still can't believe that this man came to ask me about numismatics and coin collecting. Look at what he has accomplished!"

Yeoman remained faithful to the Racine Numismatic Society and to the many friendships he made there. He encouraged young people like me and the sons of other members to attend meetings, picnics, banquets, and other

▶ Advertisements in *The Numismatist* for early editions of the *Red Book*.

▲ Dick Yeoman was a co-founder of the Numismatists of Wisconsin.

club events. Usually he had a "story coin" to show us. It could have been a widow's mite, piece of eight, or his wonderful 1848 CAL. quarter eagle, whose story he would relate. Thus, he would lead us to higher levels of intellectual study and collecting pleasure well beyond the completion of a penny board. His tastefully mounted exhibitions of story coins at major coin club functions were fascinating to collectors and non-collectors alike.

Although Yeoman himself never collected any coins in a Whitman coin album, he realized there was a large audience for that product. He edited and produced a wide variety of coin albums for collectors. He would bring the latest album to a coin club meeting and suddenly some of the "wise eyes" collectors would rush out to get the key dates for whatever new series was going to be collected in this way. Clever pressmen and typesetters in the plant liked being able to "get in early" on a series of coins as well. Yeoman enjoyed creating a collecting frenzy every so often, and it would perk up the sales of Whitman albums or books.

Growing up as I did with collectors as family members and Yeoman as a mentor, I was hopelessly hooked on numismatics. My brain filled up with coins and their stories from Croesus to the Franklin half dollars. Ties of friendship were nurtured with other collectors, dealers, and experts, which proved to be among the most rewarding of our lifetimes.

High school and university studies in Wisconsin and Germany were always enhanced by the added historical and art-historical knowledge I had gained through numismatics. After my graduation from the University of Wisconsin, Yeoman asked me to work for him as an editor and writer. My dreams had come true! Happily, I have a gift for writing, and with Yeoman's coaching I learned a great deal more. By the end of 1961 I had written and edited several books, and it was time for me to return to Europe. Yeoman helped me to get a position as foreign correspondent for *Numismatic News* with our good friend Chet Krause, and off I went.

As I visited numerous royal and national coin collections in Europe and the Near East as a newspaper man, I was always well received because I was a protégé of R.S.

Yeoman. The finest European numismatic scholars openly admired Yeoman as a pioneer with a gift for organizing and presenting not only American but also world coins in such a lucid fashion. They saw that he was the best working example for future generations to follow in promoting our hobby.

By virtue of his intelligence and interest in numismatics, he taught millions of people an appreciation of history, art history, and economics via numismatics. No assemblage of professors could claim to have educated so many people in this way.

Yeoman understood that the history of every nation is reflected by its money. Price guides had been printed before he came along, but he understood how to explain in very precise language the story of the coins. He told you where the coins fit into the picture puzzle of the nation's history, to the delight of the scholar and common man alike. He also told you what to pay for a coin and got you looking for a rare date or mintmark in your change. He had created the basic formula for the success of a coin book in modern times.

However, as important as it is to appreciate Yeoman as an author who was a pioneer in his literary style, we must also admire his talents as a businessman and manufacturer. He had to learn about the printing trade and the functions of the typesetter, pressman, binder, and shipper. He had to know how much and what kind of paper, ink, bindery materials, and glue to order, and when to schedule new press runs. Then he would go to coin conventions to find reliable people to wholesale and retail his books and coin supplies. These people often profited greatly from Yeoman's favors. Likewise, they frequently had good suggestions from which Yeoman would prosper.

Yeoman learned to do a lot of jobs, and he had to do them all right. As his success grew and the responsibilities multiplied, he needed full-time professionals to shoulder various responsibilities. For him, it was a lucky day when he found Ken Bressett.

My collection of Yeoman books continues to be a source of happiness. Like revisiting an old friend, I'll read them over again from time to time. The memories come back, and I can see Yeoman at his desk, deep in thought with one of his workbooks, polishing a sentence to define and immortalize a coin for his readers. I also see us with a typesetter who has pulled the individual lead letters out of a type case, has put them on his "stick," and is assembling a page of cold lead type. These typesetters were all prima donnas, but Yeoman and Bressett knew how to flatter them to get a nice job. Some typesetters were coin club members and would later point with pride to various pages of the *Red Book* which they had set with Yeoman's approval. A lot of people in Racine, Wisconsin, also took pride in their part of the success story of Yeoman and his wonderful books.

THE BOOKS WE TREASURE

I remember clearly the time, when I was in fourth grade, when our teacher, Sister Teresa, taught the class the proper way to open and care for a new book. Looking back, I suspect it was mostly to be sure that classroom books were carefully preserved for use by future students, but it was also a good drill for learning to appreciate books beyond their value as sources of knowledge and entertainment. I watched with close attention as Sister Teresa, an obvious bibliophile, took a book and carefully opened it to allow the pages to fan out without breaking the tight binding. Then she took a whiff of that new-book odor of fresh ink that we all know so well . . . and something that I still do today. She then checked for any imperfections, to carefully smooth out any tiny bends or folds. Last was a stern warning against writing or marking anything in the book or abusing it in any way. Surely there was a place in Dante's Inferno for anyone ever doing that.

While I still adhere to this training, I freely admit to abusing some of my books by using a duplicate copy as a working reference tool. Those are crammed full of side notes, additional information, clippings with occasional comments, and other references. Often they are my quickest and handiest way to locate important information when needed.

This early interest in books, combined with my background in the printing industry and love of numismatics, were surely the impetus for what turned out to be my lifelong career.

One does not have to be a confirmed bibliophile to appreciate fine books, and I maintain that all books have their place in the learning process on any given subject. Each should be studied and evaluated for its individual merits. A knowledge of what reference books exist, where to find them, how to use them, and how to locate wanted information is the measure of their usefulness.

▲ The only vintage *Red Book* advertisement known to be printed in red (from the program of the 1949 Central States Numismatic Society convention). It promotes the 3rd edition.

CAN YOU TELL A GOOD BOOK BY ITS COVER?

Despite the old adage, a lot can be learned by the look of a book's cover. Generally, a high-quality book will have an attractive, well-made cover, although not necessarily one with hand-tooled leather and all the trimmings. Commercial-quality books today are expected to be attractive and hardbound, with a headband, neatly squared edges, and a title on the spine, all featuring a prominent and well-respected author. Sadly, some very important numismatic books today are lacking in a quality look because of hasty preparation or a failed attempt at self-publishing. The quality of authorship, which is of highest importance to any book, cannot be ascertained by any cover, no matter how attractive or unpleasant it may be, and if desired, any book can be improved by having it re-bound to one's own satisfaction. (Some of the most respected and heavily used public library

books have been re-bound with simple blank covers to extend their lifetime on the shelf.) This is something occasionally seen with used *Red Books* and can be a source of confusion with the rare experimental production books discussed in chapter 6. So, you really "can't tell a book by its cover," or by its price. It is the content that really matters, and the numismatic world has been blessed by a plethora of fine publications over the years, and especially so in the past couple of decades. I hope you appreciate them all, and the prodigious effort that goes into producing them. Here are some things about the making of a worthwhile book that most people have forgotten or have never thought about.

CONSTRUCTING A SUCCESSFUL PUBLICATION

It takes scores of people with various talents to make a comprehensive book out of an author's creative dream, plus an equal number of specialists to print, package, promote, and bring the finished product to market. It usually begins with careful strategic planning and coordination between the author, editors, marketing experts, and a full production team including type setters and layout experts, as well as the printing, binding, and inspecting crews. There are scant records remaining to tell about the multitude of behind-the-scenes workers who contributed their talents to make the *Handbook* and *Guide Book* the classic books they came to be. Yeoman knew them all, and I had the good fortune to get to meet most of them in my time, but over the years way too many have become but fading memories and nameless faces.

▲ Typesetter Wil Winters, 1962: one of the many workers behind the success of the *Red Book*.

16TH EDITION GUIDE BOOK SHOWS MAJOR REVISIONS

R. S. Yeoman, author and editor of the GUIDE BOOK, inspects a press sheet during the current printing of the 16th edition.

The new 16th edition of A GUIDE BOOK OF U. S. COINS by R. S. Yeoman is now on the press and running on schedule so that it will be ready for shipment to all jobbers and will reach them by July 2. Collectors all over the country will be looking forward to this new edition with great anticipation because of the many special features that are being offered in this revised edition. The shipping of these books will be carried out on an exacting schedule so that dealers throughout the country will be able to receive their books on nearly the same day and be able to take care of the many collectors who want to be the "first" to get a look at this new book.

This year's Red Book has been enriched with numerous improvements. Some of these include more condition columns, mint totals adjacent to the date, grading guides for each coin type, alphabetical arrangement of commemoratives, new pictures, latest coin discoveries and accurate coin valuations. One of the questions that many collectors will be asking concerns the latest numismatic discovery, the 1938 D over S Buffalo nickel. Because of the importance of this coin, it will be listed in the new book.

The reorganization of the GUIDE BOOK extends far beyond the printed copy that you will be selling. Unseen changes include a new method of selecting price contributions. Approximately 40 qualified dealers and collectors throughout the country are used for sources for price information. Starting this year approximately 20 per cent of these sources will be changed each year in a program to allow new people to participate in supplying information. This will give a much broader base to the prices and assure an accurate average of prices used throughout the country. All of the information submitted by the panel of price contributors has been averaged together in our office and the final tabulation gives the prices used in the book.

The method of printing the GUIDE BOOK has also been changed. This year we have switched from letterpress to offset lithography. Two giant high-speed presses are used to print the books. 64 pages are printed on a single sheet and the sheets are then transferred to the second press where the other side of the sheet is printed with another 64 pages. This gives a total of 128 pages on each enormous sheet of paper and thus only two sheets of paper are used for an entire 256-page book. This faster method of printing was necessary to produce enough books to be able to supply all jobbers with their initial requirements of the GUIDE BOOK. After this first surge of business is over, additional

quantities of the book will be printed to take care of the entire year's needs.

This year brilliantly printed window streamers are being packed in every case for initial shipments. These window streamers announce the fact that you have Red Books available and indicate some of the major revisions in this edition.

As dealers, you will realize the importance of passing along the good word about the revised GUIDE BOOK. Our recent survey indicated that many collectors purchase this book only every two or three years. We feel that this is the year that nearly every collector will want to have the new revised edition. Do not be caught short and miss out on sales because of lack of sufficient merchandise.

Members of the Coin Division inspect the Pack-O-Matic shipping facilities which speed the packing process.

▲ The June–July 1962 issue of the *Whitman Coin Supply Merchandiser* gave a detailed overview of revisions in the 16th edition of the *Red Book*. In the photograph at lower-right, R.S. Yeoman and Kenneth Bressett inspect Whitman's new "Pack-O-Matic" system.

Charles Green and Lee Hewitt have already been recognized in chapter 2 for their considerable influence on the style of the *Blue Book*, for which their names appeared on the cover alongside Yeoman for the first 13 editions. Hewitt and Yeoman became close friends through their frequent meetings at the Chicago Coin Club. Green undoubtedly added his numismatic expertise to the pricing information, as did several other collectors and dealers with whom Dick became acquainted in his whirlwind quest to learn all he could about the subject while preparing to enter the competitive field of publishing pricing information.

Fortunately, through the existence of a first-edition copy of the *Red Book* that was preserved by Yeoman, we know the name of the Western employee who set the type and made the initial layouts for both the *Blue Book* and *Red Book*. Yeoman's handwritten inscription in that book, which has been preserved in the Western Archives, says the compositor was John Larsen.

▲ 1960: R.S. Yeoman, assistant editor Kenneth Bressett, and production manager Pete Foerster examine a *Red Book* press sheet, with pressman Al Rivers keeping an eye on production.

Although I never met Mr. Larsen, I will always hold him in high regard for his insight and skill in arranging the book in an orderly and easily usable format, unlike others of that time. Most of his innovations continue to be used today as standards for organizing date, mint, and pricing, without a thought about who first devised the system or what it took to set the type, one letter or number at a time, as compositors had to do in those bygone days.

Since the early 2000s, the star compositor of the modern-day Whitman Publishing, Matt Heller, has done an equally outstanding job of organizing the complex spacing of text, pricing, grades, and pictures into an attractive and easily readable arrangement. His task is equally daunting, though considerably faster because of modern typesetting software, equipment, and other facilities. Today one of the major challenges to organizing each edition of the Whitman books is the problem of how to accommodate all of the new Mint issues, pictures, and pricing columns each year.

In every edition are new issues of circulating coins, commemorative coins, bullion pieces, Proof and Mint sets, popular or recently discovered die varieties, or other new special information. This content must somehow be added to an already nearly full book without taking up too much page space or leaving something out. It is the job of a compositor to make this happen without any noticeable changes. In the initial strategic planning for any book, the first thing to be considered is the number of pages that will be needed. The number has to be divisible by 16 because of the way paper is folded into "signatures" and made ready for binding. This means that regardless of how the book needs to be expanded, the compositor cannot simply add one or two pages. When needed, it usually takes a full signature of 16 or 32 pages to accommodate even a couple of new pages.

One innovation that Yeoman used was what he called the "accordion effect," which involved adding special stories, pictures, or features that could be used when needed, or removed or replaced until it became necessary to add another signature. The system is still in use today and works well at a time when so many new Mint products are being made each year.

Still, the question looms frequently as to what to do when the traditional *Red Book* becomes unwieldy. One solution seems to be that it could be split into two volumes, perhaps covering different collecting interests or one volume with classic listings and another covering modern issues.

▲ 1965: Yeoman explains *Red Book* printing processes to two guests on a tour of Whitman's facilities, with Pete Foerster (now director of sales) observing.

Foerster joined the Whitman coin supply division in 1956, and was handling marketing operations when I came on board full-time in 1959. Before joining Whitman he ran his own coin shop in Milwaukee for ten years. He would leave the company in 1969 and return to coin dealing.

Yeoman and I used to discuss this often. His concern was always that it would be nearly impossible to coordinate the number of books printed for each volume, because the demand would likely be different for each.

The original strategic planners of the early editions of the *Red Book* consisted of Yeoman, Green, and Hewitt, who had also done the same work for the *Blue Book*. Soon, other experienced helpers were added to the "inner circle" of specialists who were responsible for the growth and continued improvement of the text. A professional staff of editors, artists, technicians, and printers has always been an indispensable part of the team that produces the books that proudly bear the Whitman name. In addition to Dick and myself, the people who have been among the most influential team leaders over the years are Glenn Smedley, Ed Metzger, Dave Bowers, Dennis Tucker, and Jeff Garrett.

Very few books of any kind have continued to remain in print for more than a dozen editions. To do so for 75 years is an admirable record. The *Red Book* owes its success to all of the people who have added their help and support to this achievement. One of the highest compliments for the

▶ 1971: A *Red Book* milestone—the printing of the 10 millionth copy. Assembled to witness the event are (left to right): Kenneth Bressett, Neil Shafer, R.S. Yeoman, Ed Metzger, and Holland Wallace.

book that I remember is the time that Mint Director Eva Adams was asked about a certain mintage figure, and she replied: "I'm not sure about that; just look it up in the *Red Book*. That's what I do."

Without the assistance of Ed Metzger, there would have been no easy connection between those who composed the Whitman books and the production staff who manufactured them. It was a team operation from conception to point of purchase. The following are some of Ed's recollections of the time he worked at Western as production coordinator and in many other capacities:

> It's hard to believe that the *Red Book* is in its 75th year. I think it was in its 12th or 13th edition when I was hired to work at Western for Dick Yeoman. As I recall, my first assignment when I joined the department was to enter the dealer prices by hand on the annual *Red Book* coin valuation analysis sheets—a different color for each dealer. It was a time-consuming, and tedious job. It would be several years before we were able to do it by keying the prices directly into a computer that even gave average totals. Thank God for technology! Today these tasks can be done almost instantly for a much larger participation.
>
> Other things I remember regarding the *Red Book* were discovering the missing page from the 16th edition, and the commotion that caused. And, I won't forget the fun we had with the first edition of the *Official A.N.A. Grading Standards* book, when the staff and I managed to produce a press-sheet without the names of the co-authors (Bressett and Kosoff) on the title page. The look on Ken's face when it was given to him for a final press check, and his reaction, went down in the annals of Whitman history. Everyone in the office was in on the joke, and to this day we still will not let on how it was done.
>
> One other memory was when both Whitman Coin Products and I were presented an ANA Presidential Award in 1995 for the work done to further the hobby of coin collecting and the contributions made by the department to that end. I don't think Whitman Coin Products would have been as successful as it is if we didn't have the group of people we had. We were one big happy family, and I was proud to be part of it.

▲ Ed Metzger.

A Lifelong Obsession

by Doug Winter

I can't remember exactly when I received my first *Red Book*, but I'm certain that it was obtained as a result of nagging my Mom, who controlled the family purse strings at that time. I do know that I was about seven or eight when I got my first copy (which I still have) and that I read it every night until I had mintage figures memorized for most coins.

I would have to regard the *Red Book* as one of the great contributions to twentieth-century American numismatics, right up there with coin folders and coin albums. Think of the millions of copies of the *Red Book* that have been sold and think of how many prominent dealers and collectors began their lifelong obsession with American coins as a result of this incredible book. I should know, because I'm one of them.

◄ Hobbyists with R.S. Yeoman at the 1968 Racine Numismatic Society coin show, held in Kenosha, Wisconsin. From left to right: Leroy Jakubowski, Bill Spencer, Roy Miller, and Yeoman. Spencer first met the author of the *Red Book* in 1951, at the age of 13, and he later became a coin dealer. "Yeoman was always helpful to the young numismatists," he recalled.

The Original and the Second "Mr. Red Book"

by Joel J. Orosz

Two Whitman book series, the *Handbook of United States Coins* and *A Guide Book of United States Coins*, both truly numismatic institutions, were the inspiration and dedication of *two* men, who first established, then refined these series for decades. One, Richard Yeo, was the founder, consummate salesman, and ambassador; the other, Kenneth Bressett, was the scholar and developer. The story of their joint achievement, annually renewed, is worthy of note and remembrance.

Richard Yeo was a son of the Badger State, blessed with a flair for design and a knack for making friends. Whitman Publishing of Racine, Wisconsin, hired Yeo in 1932 and soon put him to work selling coin boards, and later, the celebrated blue coin folders beloved by generations of young collectors. Although new to numismatics initially, he wasn't afraid to ask specialists for guidance.

As R.S. Yeoman, Yeo continued as editor of the *Red Book* for nearly a quarter century, making it into the most trusted guide for retail prices and earning him the title "Mr. Red Book." Throughout the 1960s he appeared frequently as a brand ambassador for his many publications at coin shows, conventions, and clubs, where he autographed books and charmed collectors with his modest demeanor and engaging personality. By the time of his retirement in 1970, he had proven his pen name truly apt, for his "yeoman's service" benefitted not only Whitman Publishing, but all of numismatics.

Of all of Yeoman's many achievements, perhaps the greatest was mentoring his successor. Ken Bressett of Keene, New Hampshire, became a numismatist while in his teens. He had printer's ink in his veins, as one of his early jobs was as a "printer's devil" in the twilight years of the hot-lead printing process. In the mid-1950s Yeoman was attending a coin show and Bressett discussed with him some questionable items in the *Guide Book*. Instead of taking offense, Yeoman recognized his talent and later engaged him as a freelance editor. Whitman hired Bressett in 1959, with his responsibilities encompassing the *Blue Book* and *Red Book* series. By 1962 he was made assistant editor and later managing editor in 1965, giving Yeoman more opportunities to be a roving ambassador. Bressett's tenure as editor lasted an astonishing 53 years; even after his formal retirement in 2018, he has continued with special projects for

Whitman. It was natural, therefore, that following Yeoman's death in 1988, Bressett inherited the title of "Mr. Red Book."

Bressett's stewardship was lengthy, and also quietly revolutionary. He enhanced not just two book series but an extraordinarily successful and truly beloved numismatic institution. A glance at the 1966- and 2019-dated editions of both the *Red Book* and the *Blue Book* shows how vastly he (often with some behind-the-scenes help from his son, Philip) improved these iconic products. They employ similar organizational schemes, but everything from the typeface to the factual content was enriched. Page counts nearly doubled, incorporating new coin issues, and novel research expunged old errors and added important fresh findings. Timely special features were added. Ken Bressett achieved the highly improbable: he supervised production of two successful books and for five decades simultaneously preserved and reinvented them—a seamless fusion of tradition and transformation.

Two men, two enduring book series, three-quarters of a century; one shared sobriquet. Only the oldest coin collectors of 2021 can remember numismatics without the *Blue Book* or the *Red Book*, all thanks to the extraordinary exertions of not one "Mr. Red Book" but two.

The 2007 Limited Edition of the *Red Book* featured a dual portrait of R.S. Yeoman and Ken Bressett by numismatist Charles Daughtrey.

THE *RED BOOK* COMES OF AGE

The emergence of the *Red Book*, and its increasing popularity, began to cause a decrease in the yearly publishing schedule of Wayte Raymond's *Standard Catalogue* and put it at a disadvantage next to the *Red Book*, which quickly established a reliable annual publication schedule (the sole exception being its hiatus in the year 1950). After Raymond's death in 1956, his wife, Olga, was listed as editor in the 18th and last edition of this catalog, with John J. Ford Jr. and Walter Breen given credit for consultation and research. Within a decade, the *Standard Catalogue* had ceased publication, in effect ceding the field to the *Red Book*.

Yeoman had improved upon the format of Raymond's reference in several ways. He eliminated the dust jacket and reduced the size from 6-1/4 by 9 inches to 5-1/4 by 7-3/4 inches, resulting in a more "pocket friendly" book. The addition of type-coin descriptions, including design details and many designers' names, made the book easier to use than its competitor. The *Red Book* offered not only values and variety listings but also valuable background on type coins. For the collector who wished to learn more about specific coin types, Yeoman included bibliographies for many sections. The *Red Book* also provided the collector with a short introduction

▼ The first edition of the *Red Book* listed early quarter dollars in three grades: Good, Fine, and Uncirculated. Mintages for all regular U.S. coin issues were given in 18 pages of charts in the back of the book.

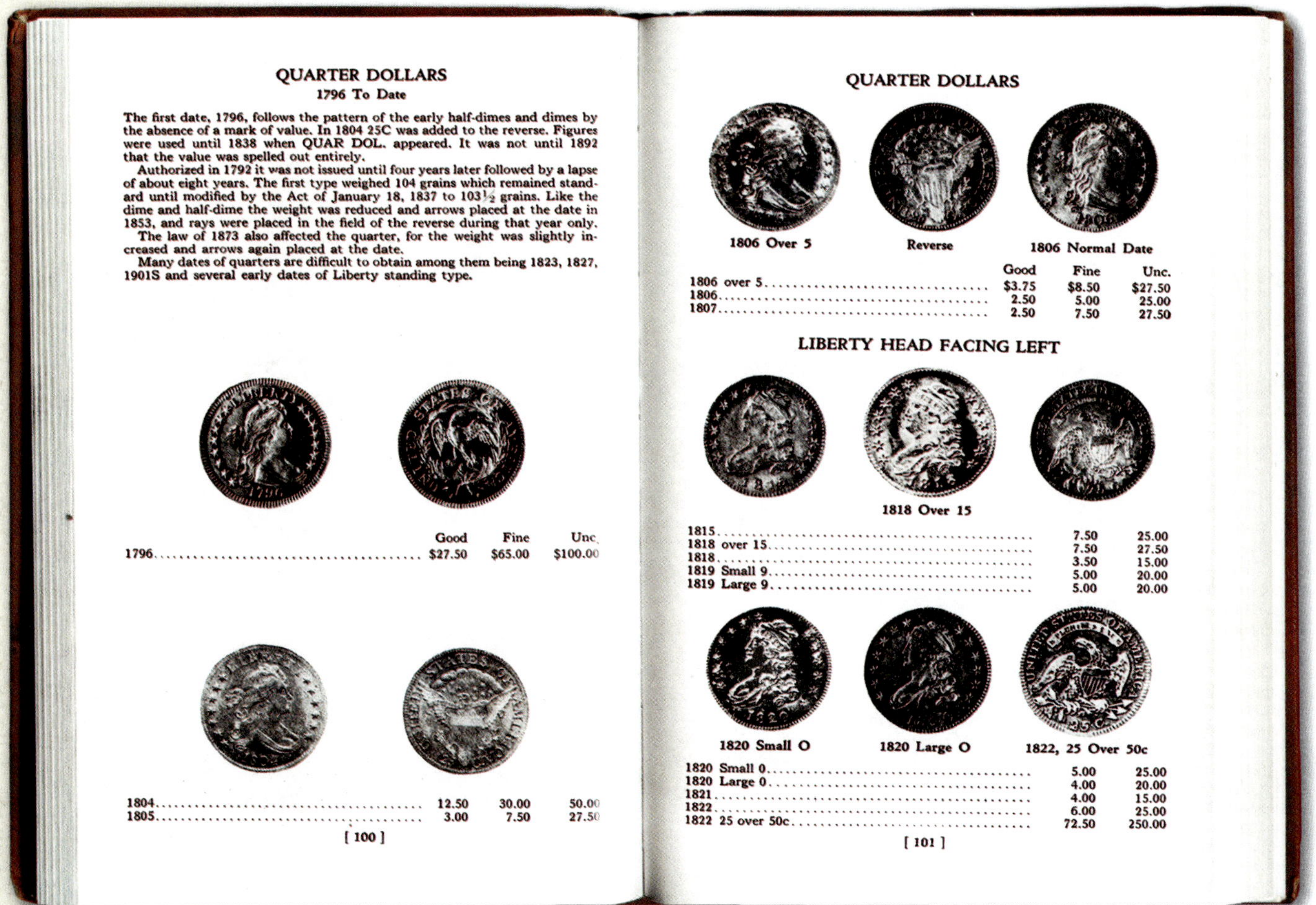

QUARTER DOLLARS
1796 To Date

The first date, 1796, follows the pattern of the early half-dimes and dimes by the absence of a mark of value. In 1804 25C was added to the reverse. Figures were used until 1838 when QUAR DOL. appeared. It was not until 1892 that the value was spelled out entirely.

Authorized in 1792 it was not issued until four years later followed by a lapse of about eight years. The first type weighed 104 grains which remained standard until modified by the Act of January 18, 1837 to 103½ grains. Like the dime and half-dime the weight was reduced and arrows placed at the date in 1853, and rays were placed in the field of the reverse during that year only.

The law of 1873 also affected the quarter, for the weight was slightly increased and arrows again placed at the date.

Many dates of quarters are difficult to obtain among them being 1823, 1827, 1901S and several early dates of Liberty standing type.

	Good	Fine	Unc.
1796	$27.50	$65.00	$100.00
1804	12.50	30.00	50.00
1805	3.00	7.50	27.50

[100]

QUARTER DOLLARS

1806 Over 5 — Reverse — 1806 Normal Date

	Good	Fine	Unc.
1806 over 5	$3.75	$8.50	$27.50
1806	2.50	5.00	25.00
1807	2.50	7.50	27.50

LIBERTY HEAD FACING LEFT

1818 Over 15

	Good	Fine	Unc.
1815		7.50	25.00
1818 over 15		7.50	27.50
1818		3.50	15.00
1819 Small 9		5.00	20.00
1819 Large 9		5.00	20.00

1820 Small O — 1820 Large O — 1822, 25 Over 50c

	Good	Fine	Unc.
1820 Small 0		5.00	25.00
1820 Large 0		4.00	20.00
1821		4.00	15.00
1822		6.00	25.00
1822 25 over 50c		72.50	250.00

[101]

to and history of each coin. In addition, Yeoman introduced an innovative section, "Quantities of Coins Struck." Before he listed them in the *Blue Book*, mintage quantities had not been available without referring to sometimes unreliable Mint records. The convenient mintage amounts shown in the *Red Book* made it a major improvement over most other retail coin-pricing books.

The Rest Is History

by Q. David Bowers

Here I am in 2021, the research editor for *A Guide Book of United States Coins*. In retrospect, 69 years ago I would hardly have been able to believe it. How lucky I am!

In 1952 someone told me that Robert L. Rusbar, tax collector for my town of Forty Fort, Pennsylvania, had a very nice collection of rocks and minerals, so I made it a point to give him a call. I was greeted cordially, taken into the basement office of his home, and shown box after box of colorful garnets, sulfur clusters, quartz crystals, and the like.

▲ Q. David Bowers in a 2010 portrait medal honoring his importance to the American Numismatic Society.

After a session with rocks and minerals, Bob asked me if I collected coins, to which I replied in the negative. He took from a safe a Whitman album of Lincoln cents, pointed to one of the first openings, and told me he had paid $10 for that particular coin. He carefully explained that it was a Lincoln cent made in the first year of issue, 1909, with the initials of the designer, Victor David Brenner, V.D.B., on the reverse—but that alone did not make it valuable. With only these features, it would be worth just a few cents. However, beneath the date was a tiny "S" signifying it had been made in San Francisco. This letter or mintmark, hardly visible, jumped the value from a few cents up to the $10 he had paid during a visit to the rare-coin concession at Gimbel's department store in New York City.

I felt absolutely certain that as soon as I left his office and looked through some pocket change, I would find *several* 1909-S V.D.B. cents—after all, a copy of the *Guide Book* that he showed me revealed that 484,000 had been minted.

Continued on next page.

Certainly, in the town of Forty Fort alone there must be hundreds just waiting for me!

Bob Rusbar gave me a couple of blue Whitman coin folders and a few mint-marked Lincoln cents to get me started. Soon, my two Lincoln cent folders were nearly full—with no 1909-S V.D.B., 1914-D, or 1931-S—but with most everything else.

I bought the latest edition of the *Guide Book* (1952). The coin bug bit me and wouldn't let go. Almost before I learned to pronounce *numismatist* I was beginning to be one. From finding Lincoln cents in circulation I went to other series, including Mercury dimes and Standing Liberty quarters, both of which were common. Barber dimes were seen occasionally and Barber quarters even more often. Barber halves—nearly always worn to the point of virtual smoothness, About Good and Good—were available with some frequency, perhaps one out of every 200 or 300 half dollars examined. Although I never tried, I imagine that in 1952 and 1953 it would have been easy enough to have put together a set of half dollars 1892 to date from circulation. I never did find a Liberty Seated silver coin for face value.

Meanwhile, I sought to gain more knowledge. I re-read the introductory material in the *Guide Book* and all the headings for the later listings and committed most details to memory. (Somehow, I was endowed with the ability to memorize trivia and obscure information.) Not one to do things halfway, I decided to take the bull by the horns and write to the Philadelphia, Denver, and San Francisco mints to see how many older coins they could supply, and order Proofs from each. Back came mimeographed form letters from each institution informing me that Proofs were made only at Philadelphia, and that no back-dated coins were available, and giving me other basic information.

My numismatic interests continued to expand, but my budget remained fixed. My father made the wise suggestion that if I wanted to collect a lot of coins, I should investigate other ways to earn money. Mowing lawns wouldn't do it. And I had yet to find a 1909-S V.D.B. cent. I began buying coins wholesale at Wilkes-Barre (Pennsylvania) Coin Club meetings and elsewhere and selling them retail. The rest, as they say, is history.

Many things have changed in the world and in numismatics, but the *Guide Book* remains as ubiquitous and as useful in the hobby as it has always been. Just as it was for me nearly 70 years ago, I envision future generations of numismatists relying on the *Guide Book* to be their one-volume source for most basic information about American numismatics, history, mintages, and values. How delightful the excursion has been!

One drawback to both the *Red Book* and the *Standard Catalogue* was the lack of information on grading coins. Both books listed the values of coins in various grades, but neither reference explained specifically how the grades were determined. At the time, no commonly accepted grading guides were available, and collectors had to depend on local dealers for their knowledge and grading skills. Standardization of the meaning of grades for different coin types would have to wait for Martin R. Brown and John W. Dunn's *Guide to the Grading of United States Coins*, issued more than a decade later, whose grading system would be incorporated into future *Red Book* editions. Despite this drawback, the *Red Book* was well received. *The Numismatist*'s review of December 1946 spoke enthusiastically of the "general excellence of the book" and also another important selling point: "a high-class job of printing and binding at a remarkably modest cost." The press run for the second edition, published later in 1947, was substantially increased; 22,000 were originally printed, but 3,000 went unsold and were destroyed.

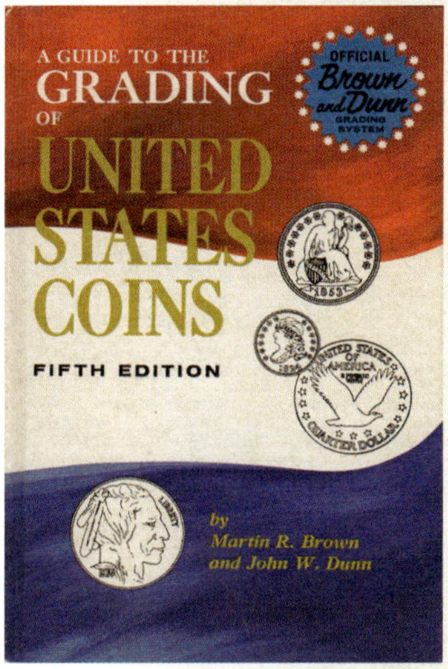

▲ Brown and Dunn debuted their guide to coin grading in 1958. The book proved popular, and Whitman Publishing soon acquired rights to it.

In the 1950s the *Red Book* established itself firmly as the go-to book for thousands of collectors. Few other reference books for coin collectors were available at that time, and the periodicals of the era did not pose serious competition. *The Numismatist*, the ANA's official journal, was held to be "more of an erudite journal and record of club meetings," in the words of Q. David Bowers. The popular *Numismatic Scrapbook Magazine*, as has been discussed previously, did not offer the range of coin-pricing data provided by the *Red Book*. Not surprisingly in these circumstances, the print run of each successive *Red Book* edition increased. (The possible exception to this trend is the fifth edition, which is difficult to locate today and has been said to have had a reduced print run because of paper shortages caused by the Korean War.) By 1959 more than 100,000 copies were being printed each year.

Bowers recalls, "You had to be there to appreciate the impact the *Guide Book* had at the time. Each year in the mid-1950s, dealers, collectors, and anyone else even remotely interested in coins would await the new edition and then eagerly peruse it to find out what his or her coins were worth. . . . Regardless of what you wanted to know, Yeoman's *Red Book* was the be-all and end-all for such information. It was, without question, *the* source."

The 1960s saw a coin-collecting boom in America unlike any before or since, and the *Red Book*'s fortunes went hand in hand with the trend. By the middle of the decade, the *Red Book* was a best seller, ranking fifth among modern nonfiction titles—right after *Betty Crocker's Picture Cook Book* and just before Dale Carnegie's *How to Win Friends and Influence People*. The *Blue Book*, no slouch itself, ranked number 12 on the same list.

Western Growth in Other Fields

In the early 1950s Western purchased Guild Press, Inc., a publisher of Catholic books, religious greeting cards, and gift wrap. In 1955 it built a new specialty printing plant in Hannibal, Missouri. Western achieved sales of $63 million in 1957, the year of its 50th anniversary. In the same year the company acquired Kable Printing Company, a large rotogravure magazine printer. All were fortunate expansion moves that created more capacity for printing and distributing the ever-growing line of coin-supply merchandise. America's interest in hobbies and leisure-time pursuits was rising.

With partners Dell and Simon & Schuster, the company sponsored the Story Book Shop on Main Street, U.S.A., in Disneyland, which opened on July 17, 1955, and closed on April 1, 1995. In addition, it was one of the initial investors in the park by virtue of being a part-owner of Disneyland, Inc.

Western and Pocket Books, Inc., formed Golden Press, Inc., at the end of 1958, following their joint purchase of all *Golden Book* properties from Simon & Schuster. The arrangement called for Western to continue to create and manufacture *Golden Books*, which Pocket Books would promote, sell, and distribute. By 1959 over 150 *Little Golden Book* titles had sold at least a million copies, and more than 400 of the 1,000-plus *Golden Book* titles were in print in 13 languages.

In 1960 the name Western Publishing Company was adopted and common stock was issued, a large percentage of which was immediately purchased by management and employees. Late in 1961 Golden Press successfully published its 20-volume *Golden Home and High School Encyclopedia*, with total sales of nearly $39 million. Western then had the distinction of being the largest creator and publisher of children's books; the largest producer/distributor of children's games made from paper or paper products; and the largest creator/producer of comic books.

Because of its prominence, Western was frequently asked to consider new products. One such request came in

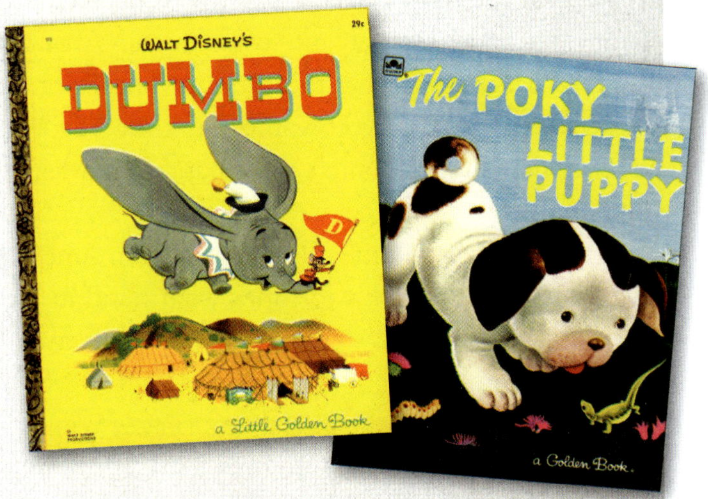

► *Golden Books* and various Disney properties were all part of the larger Whitman Publishing family.

▲ Hugh M. Knight, president of the Chicago Coin Club, created a "Coin Store" game, which he convinced Whitman to produce and market. Very few were sold.

1962 from an acquaintance of Yeoman's. The proposal was a family game called "Coin Store," devised by Hugh M. Knight, president of the Chicago Coin Club. Since it was intended to be manufactured by Western Printing and Lithographing Company, Knight proposed that it should be added to the Whitman coin-supply line as a special feature item.

I remember the incident quite well. Dick and I were members of the Chicago Coin Club along with Hugh Knight, and he kept imploring us to produce the board game that he had devised. After repeated coaxing, we directed him to the game department. It wasn't much of a novelty and was not unlike many other board games of that era. It was also complex, with many pieces, coin terms, and moving parts. Western agreed to produce it like any other commercial printing job and assist in distribution. Knight was required to pay for the printing and other expenses. Unfortunately, very few were ever sold, and eventually the leftover stock was either destroyed or liquidated as distressed merchandise.

Western Printing and Lithographing, the largest unit of Western Publishing Company, accounted for about 40 percent of sales. Artists & Writers Press, Inc., one of 14 active subsidiaries, created books for publishers and commercial customers, including *Golden Books*, Betty Crocker cookbooks, the "Arts of Mankind" series for Golden Press, and the four-volume *Harper Encyclopedia of Science* for Harper & Row. Capitol Publishing, purchased in 1961, originated and produced educational materials and games for children, as well as toys and novelty products. The Kable Printing division produced over 125,000 monthly magazines, other periodicals, and catalogs. The Watkins-Strathmore Company, acquired in 1957, made children's books and games, including Magic Slate. Meanwhile, Whitman published nearly every type of juvenile and adolescent books, numismatic books, coin cards, a wide variety of games, playing cards, crayons, and gift wrap. Western also had a Canadian subsidiary (established in 1959) and a French company (introduced in 1960).

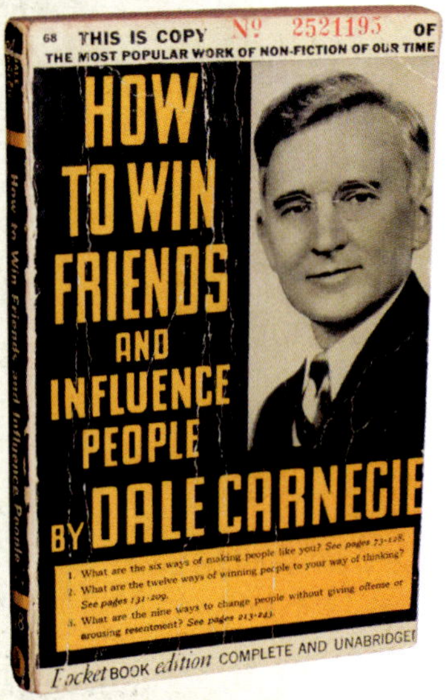

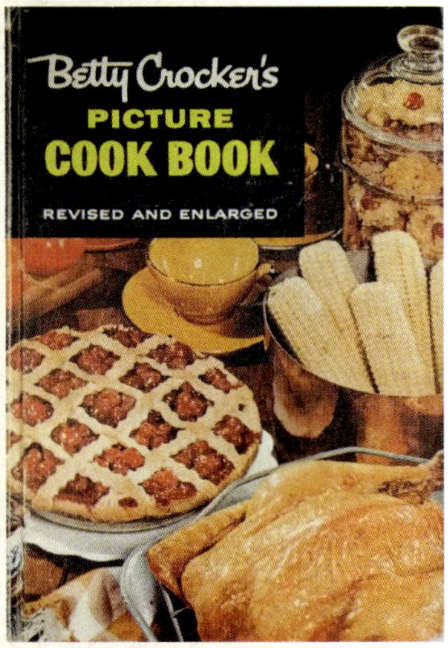

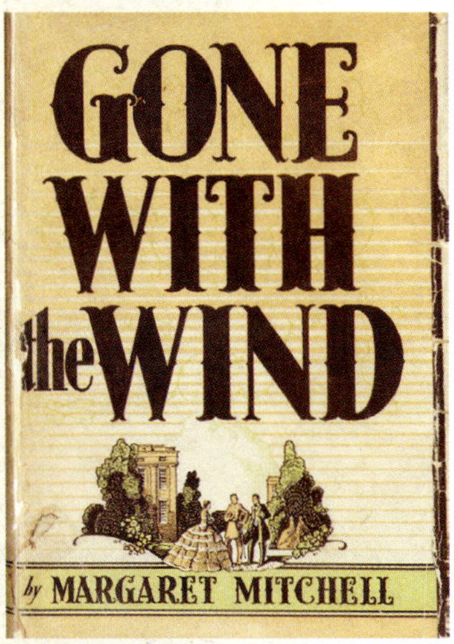

▲ The *Red Book* has been in good company among the best-selling nonfiction titles in American publishing—and has even given popular fiction a run for its money.

Perhaps even more impressive, the *Red Book* was ranked ninth in the top ten all-time best sellers, tabulated through 1965—just behind Margaret Mitchell's *Gone with the Wind*!

It was also at this time that the *Red Book* set a record for copies printed and sold: the 18th (1965) edition went into multiple printings to satisfy the high demand, and the final count came to a staggering 1.2 million copies. Although the exact print runs and sales figures of the following years are confidential, this remains the high-water mark of *Red Book* sales. The triumph of the *Red Book* was all the more notable because serious competition had begun to emerge. Before 1960 periodicals like *The Numismatist* and Lee Hewitt's *Numismatic Scrapbook* posed little competition because they did not regularly include comprehensive coin pricing. *Numismatic News* was founded in 1952 by Chester "Chet" Krause, who would become a good friend of Yeoman's, but it would be a number of years before this modest weekly newsletter developed into a major publication. The emergence in 1960 of *Coin World*, the first successful weekly numismatic newspaper, presented more of a challenge. In 1963 the *Coin Dealer Newsletter*, popularly known as the "Greysheet," appeared.

The 1960s also saw some reconfiguring behind the scenes. In 1959 I joined the *Red Book* staff, and in 1963 I began inheriting editorial duties from Yeoman, whose position was shifting more toward managerial responsibilities as the staff expanded. Just two years later, the company was restructured. A line of stamp-collecting books and supplies was added, and Whitman Publishing became the Whitman Hobby Division of Western Publishing. During this decade the *Red Book* was also supplemented, for a short time, by the *Whitman Numismatic Journal* (subtitled "A Monthly Magazine Devoted to All Phases of Numismatics"). This monthly publication, whose staff included Yeoman as editor-in-chief and myself as managing editor, was published from January 1964 to December 1968. According to a 1968 advertisement, the *Journal* "will keep your copy of the *Guide Book of United States Coins* always up-to-date."

Retailers who stocked Whitman coin products also received a newsletter that kept them informed of the latest news about the *Red Book*, the *Blue Book*, and other Whitman coin titles. This newsletter was published as the *Whitman Coin Supply Merchandiser* from 1960 to 1966, then resumed in 1969 as the *Stamp and Coin Supply Merchandiser*, reflecting the company's acquisition of the stamp division during the interim. However, by 1971 the stamp line had been cancelled, and the newsletter was discontinued. The next year it was revived as the *Coin Supply Merchandiser*, and it ran under that name through the end of 1974. In its various incarnations, the *Merchandiser* held a wealth of inside information on the evolution of the *Red Book*.

◄ Neil Shafer worked at Whitman Publishing from 1962 to 1981. "The *Red Book* was always the product of primary importance," he recalls. "My participation in the preparation of the book was somewhat limited, as my particular fields of activity centered more on world numismatics. Yet each year around April, when the next edition was in earnest preparation, I was called upon to work alongside Dick Yeo and Ken Bressett in entering values and doing anything else there was to be done editorially in order to get the book ready for publication." Here, Shafer is seen with Yeoman in 1969, examining world coins and paper money. "My work on the *Red Book* remained pretty much the same through Dick Yeo's retirement in 1969 and Ken Bressett's 1980 departure," Shafer says. "At that time, and for only a single year, I became the coordinating editor. Ken then resumed the position and maintained it admirably for many more years."

Meanwhile, of course, Yeoman did not merely sit back and admire the success of his two popular series. Expanding into other areas of collecting, he continued to bring important reference books to the market. He scored another hit with *A Catalog of Modern World Coins* (1957), which listed thousands of coins from the period of 1850 to 1955. It was later joined by a second publication, *Current Coins of the World*, which began at the point where *A Catalog of Modern World Coins* concluded. Working together, the Whitman staff produced more than 300 hobby-related titles and products.

Yeoman was rightfully proud of his creations and always willing to speak about them at club meetings and coin shows and in interviews. As memory aids, and to keep his stories straight, he often used crib notes with pertinent dates, information, anecdotes, and an occasional joke or two to keep the presentation interesting. On one such occasion, someone in the audience asked a detailed question, to which Yeoman replied: "The reason I wrote that book was so I could look that up whenever I needed the information." Included in the sidebars here are some of his handwritten prompts, which are preserved in the Western Archives. These may have been used as part of a club talk or perhaps in a training session for some of the sales staff, most of whom were initially unfamiliar with the hobby and its components or the customers they were serving.

How the *Red Book* is Put Together

by R.S. Yeoman

[These handwritten notes likely outlined a presentation for a coin convention or club meeting (circa 1965).]

- Originally a step up from the *Handbook* [*Blue Book*].
- Meant as a "guide" reflection of the coin market.
- Selection of panel:

  Size of dealer

  Type of dealer—store, mail order

  Geographical location
- Coordinator—was Glenn Smedley, Frank Miller, now Ken Bressett
- Special current record kept for auctions—Walter Breen

48 active panelists

10 specialists

Mechanics of price revisions

- Send out interleaved books of last edition to all selected panelists.
- Master sheets prepared—describe colors assigned to every panelist
- Averaging

Meeting in a secret place

- About 50 hours. Two sessions—Division of book and method of printing and binding. 1st and 4th part of book first. Early American, half cents, commemoratives, private gold and miscellaneous.
- Middle two sections are main task.
- New grading columns added each time, increases, [plus a] policy on mint errors.

Policy on mint errors

Must be die error, such as a "1942 over 41" dime. Proven by popularity; many available, visible to the naked eye. Not concerned with coins resulting from mistreated dies (gouges), malfunction of coinage machinery (off-center, etc.), or imperfect quality of blanks, laminations, etc.

Miss Adams and the upside-down *Red Book*. [This humorous incident is described on page 157.]

Fort Madison Meeting

by R.S. Yeoman

[These rough notes were made by Yeoman, probably for a sales meeting about the Red Book scheduling process (October 15, 1966).]

1934—Coin boards

1940—Coin folders

1941—Handbook of United States Coins

1942—Paper shortage, war contracts, *Red Book* preparation

1946—Publish *Red Book* (dated 1947); 20th this year

Program for Revising Catalog

January 2—Mail material and instructions to panelists

February 20—deadline

Special master sheets—every date and mintmark

Type of contributors—geographic and method

Prominent and small

Assignment of colors and symbols

—for quick check

—for detecting extremes, high or low

—easy to spot any manipulation

Averaging

March 15-20—meeting at secret place. At least one professional outsider—1,000 mi. Purpose of outsider is to explain any pattern and minute change. Be advisor.

April 1-6—Final copy to composing room. Proofreading to May 1.

May—Printing and binding.

June 10—Finished books prepared as finished. All orders go "first," starting June 20-25. Farthest first.

July 1—On board with all dealers.

Blue Book has same pattern.

October delivery this year—next week.

Next year, 25th edition.

INTEREST IN THE *RED BOOK* SPREADS

By the start of the 1970s, *Red Books* were becoming collectible themselves. The 1971 *Red Book* introduced a new feature, "Old *Red Books* Never Die," which demonstrated the usefulness of the fund of historical price data furnished by a collection of old *Red Books*. The chapter observed that *Red Books* were already becoming collectibles and offered some observations on what made them attractive and interesting to collect. One of the most important aspects of preserving old editions of these books was that they served as a record of coin values throughout the years that could be used to establish market and pricing trends, as well as evidence of what collectors might have paid for their coins (if they had no other records for tax purposes).

Following Yeoman's retirement in 1970, he continued a detached working relationship with the company that continued well beyond his move to Green Valley, Arizona, in 1978. Always concerned for the welfare of the operation and the staff employees, he carried on through correspondence and phone calls with me, editorial assistant Jenny Martin Tomaszek, and others to stay informed and offer assistance during the transition. Times were changing in the late 1970s and early 1980s, and disruptions were being felt throughout the entire corporation because of a merger with Mattel. One of the numismatic repercussions of the corporate shake-up was the coin-supply department's move from Western's main building on Mound Avenue to the less luxurious "Creative Center." Some of the staff were assigned to different positions as replacements for those who resisted the changes and resigned. Richard Giese, the marketing manager, was transferred to a different department and replaced by Richard Thompsen, leaving me to find a replacement for him. Unforeseen at the time was the possibility that I was destined to join the exodus—and that's precisely what happened, in 1979. Among the stalwarts who remained to operate the business were Dick Thompsen and Ed Metzger, both of whom eventually became the department managers and ran the business, while I and my team of special helpers acted as satellite numismatic consultants and pricing coordinators for the various publications.

▼ By the 1960s, "autograph parties" and other book-signing events were part of the *Red Book* experience. Fans lined up to get R.S. Yeoman's signature every chance they could (as seen here in 1969).

Space was at a premium in the Creative Center, and although the coin department had its own section and offices, there was scant room for the reference library, viewing tables for the large-size press sheets, or storage of the components of current and past editions of the many books and products that were needed for reference and archival purposes. Throughout the years, samples of all books had been preserved in the company reference library, and now they had to be condensed or destroyed. Included were several boxes of early *Red Book*s, which I believe accounts for a number of them that seem to have appeared on the market at about that time. Unfortunately, many others were destroyed.

No one can describe the early years of the legendary *Red Book* better than the author himself. Fortunately, he did exactly that in 1983 and published it as a special editorial feature in the 37th (1984) edition of the *Guide Book*. In this reflective account, titled "The *Red Book* Story," Yeoman describes how the book came to be, its early growth in popularity, and many of its trials and successes. At the end, he stated that a second and concluding article would be published in a later edition. Unfortunately, he was never able to complete the mission. Yeoman's original manuscript is reproduced here:

The *Red Book* Story—Part 1

by *R.S. Yeoman*

I was pleasantly surprised, at a recent numismatic convention, to be shown a very special first edition (1947) copy of *A Guide Book of United States Coins*. An elated bourse dealer had purchased it at an auction a short time before. The inscription on the flyleaf made it unique. It read "Copy Number One." Beneath that line I had dedicated and autographed the book to the late Stuart Mosher, then-editor of *The Numismatist*. He had been a particularly supportive friend, who was constantly available for timely advice and encouragement when the catalog was little more than a dream. He was one of several experts who came forward with guidance and counsel when the pieces were being put together. As a matter of fact, from the very beginning and throughout the years, the numismatic fraternity has given continuous timely support in editorial, statistical and valuation updating whenever requested.

The Stuart Mosher copy is, perhaps, the most noteworthy, but is only one of a surprising number of early editions that have surfaced recently. There are increasing signs that more and more collectors are assembling sets of back editions and, understandably, the elusive first edition is the ultimate target of those avid searchers.

I have been asked a number of times what led to the *Guide Book*. Of course, the Whitman marketing group did not confer one day to say "Let's get into the numismatic market." Actually, several fortuitous factors came together

Continued on next page.

during the Great Depression period of the 1930s, a time when thousands of unemployed people were looking for ways to occupy their idle time. Card playing, working crossword puzzles, and assembling picture puzzles were frequent activities to while away the many hours. Our company was turning out playing cards and picture puzzles around the clock in those days, and the die-cutting equipment employed in that production was the door opener for an entry into the then-fledgling numismatic market.

In 1934 our special machinery attracted J.K. Post, a gentleman from Neenah, Wisconsin, with an idea for collecting coins from pocket change using a large cardboard panel with rows of openings that would hold Lincoln Cents. Under each opening, dates and mint marks from 1909 to 1934 were to be printed. He knew that equipment turning out picture puzzles in our factory was just the thing for punching out the holes in his product. He placed an order with us, and we proceeded to manufacture them in sizable quantities.

Later in the year, Post came to us and convinced us that we ought to market the novelty ourselves. He was regularly employed in a position which left little time for distributing the boards. The demand, he said, was beyond his most optimistic expectations. We took his creation into our line and paid him a royalty until 1938, when we made him an offer for the rights and exclusive Whitman ownership, to which he agreed. By 1940 we had redesigned the product from the somewhat cumbersome, large board format to a compact and more secure three panel, hinge-type folder. Since then, this style for most United States coin denominations has been marketed under the Whitman® name. We now had our foot in the numismatic door. The coin board and, in turn, the folder had penetrated the very grass roots of numismatics. Up until this time, numismatics had

▲ Numismatists at the American Numismatic Association's convention of August 24, 1937, examining coins owned by ANA president T. James Clarke (center).

▲ Edness Wilkens, secretary to U.S. Mint director Nellie Tayloe Ross, examining a 1792 half disme and other coins and medals, April 1938.

been almost exclusively the pursuit of intellectuals. The majority of that elite group were researchers, historians, museum curators and the like, generally with an academic approach. Their study of coins and their preservation was, in fact, a virtual science. They were isolated and aloof, and the term "hobby" seldom entered their vocabulary. By contrast, the advanced numismatist of today is highly visible and in greater numbers than ever before. Topnotch numismatists fill the ranks of professional coin dealers, and many have become enthusiastic motivating forces in regional, national and international societies and associations. Most of them freely credit their achievement in the field to the widespread availability of numismatic literature and accessories. It is no surprise that, now and then, one of those experts will confide to me that he started with the "Penny Board."

Yes, the genesis of Whitman accessories, leading to *A Guide Book of United States Coins* (*Red Book*) and other catalogs, was the unlikely coin board. It was one of several compelling influences which started a fad that "left no purse unturned." At the beginning, pocket and purse had supplied nearly all of the coins that filled the empty spaces. Started in homes, the craze spread to neighbors, offices and factories, where buying, selling and swapping went on at a fast pace, keeping the challenge alive and moving.

Perhaps the first and most aggressive influence to alert the public to coin searching was the print media and radio promotions conducted by the famous B. Max Mehl of Fort Worth, Texas. During the early 1930's he relentlessly exploited those will-o'-the wisp coins, the 1804 dollar and 1913 Liberty nickel. Another strong factor in turning the public's eye to coin collecting was the steady flow of new commemorative half dollars emanating from the Mint during the 1930's. Production of proof sets, beginning with the 1936 issues, provided even more collecting momentum. Add to this the down-to-earth *Numismatic Scrapbook Magazine* (founded in 1934 by the enterprising Hewitt brothers), which recognized the growing interest from entry-level enthusiasts when commemorative, proof set and penny collectors needed just such a voice, and the hobby was off and running.

Shortly, the "vest pocket dealer" entered the scene, supplying hard-to-find dates at gradually increasing premium prices. He bought the other fellow's duplicates and eventually expanded to mail order and modest storefront shops. Increasing development spurred the formation of coin clubs in scores of communities during the 1940's. The formative hobby had now been established on a firm foundation. There were professional coin dealers on the scene before the 1930's, but mainly in large cities. To the credit of most of these entrepreneurs, they sensed the future of the upcoming collecting trend and adjusted their sights to the needs of the new breed, the novice collector.

Continued on next page.

In 1940 I somewhat timidly broke into the national numismatic scene and attended a number of numismatic conventions, including the American Numismatic Association Convention in Detroit. Several coin dealers, consulted at those gatherings, came forward with offers of assistance and encouragement to publish a premium (wholesale) catalog. Their rationale for pushing the idea with our particular publishing house was, simply, that established dealers had long sought an unbiased publisher with nationwide distribution, outside the numismatic domain of buying and selling coins. I was made aware that all coin catalogs, then on the market, were published by certain dealers, and other dealers felt uncomfortable dealing in the shadow of a competitor's "price list."

▲ The first ANA convention Dick attended was held in Cincinnati in 1942. Shown here is the official convention medal he received for his participation.

With the timely assistance of a small group of learned professionals, we went to work on the first of our catalogs, the *Handbook of United States Coins* (*Blue Book*). The first edition debuted at the Cincinnati A.N.A. Convention in 1942. Since that modest beginning, it has been revised annually and marketed continuously to become the number-one book on wholesale coin prices in America.

The same concept of unbiased coin valuations led to groundwork for the creation of *A Guide Book of United States Coins* (*Red Book*). This catalog would serve the retail side of the coin market. Like the *Blue Book*, we followed the survey-average technique, with our staff acting as a clearinghouse for a selected panel of contributors. The price evaluations came from experts, mostly dealers, located in various trade areas and types of establishment. The *Red Book* has followed this system of price averaging through the years, and it is our belief that it has had a positive, standardizing influence in all phases of American numismatics. In 1946 the first *Red Book* was ushered into the marketplace bearing a cover date of 1947.

I am frequently asked to disclose how many of the first edition were printed. For the official record, since we have seldom revealed production figures publicly, I am pleased to report that the total quantity distributed was 18,000. There were two press runs which yielded 9,000 books each. The first printing was made during November 1946 and the catalogs were placed on the market immediately. The sell-off was rapid and we were prompted to run a second printing during February 1947. There are some minor differences between the two printings.

We made a few corrections and revisions before going to press with the second printing. To enlighten first edition owners with one significant clue, I direct them to page 135. Near the bottom of page 135, the first printing reads ". . .which probably accounts for the scarcity of this date." This statement was clarified in the second printing to read ". . .which probably accounts for the scarcity of 1903 O."

We proceed to the second edition, which had a total printing of 22,000. Likewise, each succeeding edition, through the eighth, gradually increased but did not exceed 100,000. The largest circulation, before or since, was attained by the 18th (1965) edition, when several printings were necessary to keep up with the quickened demand. That was during the frenzied roll market era. When the final tally came in, we learned that an astonishing 1,200,000 copies had been delivered to the field.

An affordably low price has been the market policy of our company for all its products. The suggested retail price of the *Red Book* has been no exception. We are convinced that its popularity and standing among America's best sellers can be credited largely to that principle. The price per copy, nevertheless, has gradually crept upward with inflation. However, early editions, we find, have an inflation factor all their own.

Back-issue aficionados, who it appears are surfacing in ever-increasing numbers, have created a lively secondary market with unbelievable price tags for certain early editions. Moreover, grading standards apply to the books, much the same as for numismatic specimens.

The 37-year-old *Red Book* story also had its share of embarrassing moments . . . or so we were wont to believe. Though infrequent, there are the occasional production irregularities which go unnoticed by our team of inspectors to enter the marketplace. Our quality-control staff is as efficient as any in the

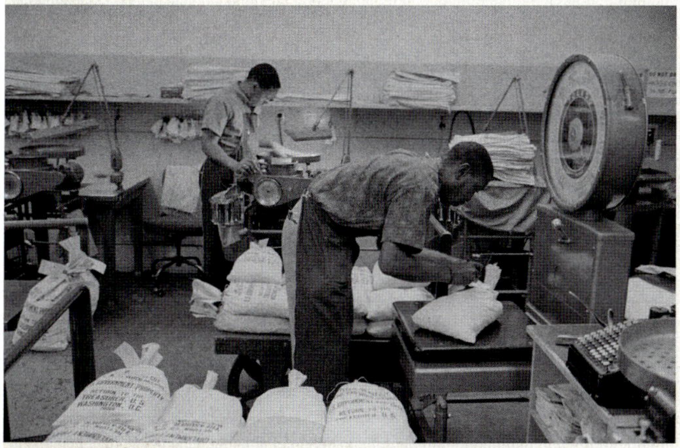

▲ Employees in the Coin Room of the U.S. Treasury Department, June 1964—the year the *Red Book* sold a record-breaking 1.2 million copies.

▲ Western Publishing president Gerald Slade, flanked by Kenneth Bressett and R.S. Yeoman, holds a plaque commemorating the landmark printing of the 10 millionth *Red Book*, 1971.

▲ A 39th-edition *Red Book* with a remarkably misprinted cover and spine.

industry, and they tell me that every attempt is made to inspect each book and sort out all rejects before packing. Nonetheless, they estimate that with every printing, perhaps a few dozen "mistakes" could escape apprehension.

I was a little slow to pick up on the trend, but I became positively aware of the inclination a few years back. The "mint error" syndrome seems to have drifted into the world of publishing as well. Printing and binding discrepancies have taken on a special interest for a growing number of *Red Book* owners. At first, when an occasional convention visitor would come up to me with an obviously imperfect catalog which might have an upside-down or double-stamped cover, laminated pages, missing pages or the like, I would assure the "victim" that Whitman expected to replace the offending volume at no charge. Then I came to realize that each of those enthusiastic folks had no intention of parting with his or her catalog. Rather, they usually asked me to certify in writing adjacent to the manufacturing imperfection snafu, that the mistake was in the nature of a genuine "Mint Error," to be attested to with my signature no less! Yes, there are mistakes in a very few *Red Books* out there in that vast land of numismatics. Somehow, as publishers, we are unique: our errors are not embarrassing; they are sought-after gems!

On several occasions, urgent summons would come from the pressroom to verify typographical errors. Some trips to the press were false alarms. After a few such incidents of press stoppings, however, those eagle-eyed craftsmen came to understand that aberrations such as the 1796 LIHERTY Cent and the 1800 LIKERTY Half Dime were actually historical and got there through someone else's carelessness, committed years before they were born.

Continued on page 68.

▲ An ad from the July 1971 *Numismatist*, honoring the *Red Book*'s volunteers who had 20 or more years on its contributors panel. The service of Bebee, Chell-Frost, Kosoff, and Kreisberg (and, of course, Yeoman) dated back to the first edition.

There are a limited number of *Red Books* which were contrived for special use by the panelists for their price revision work. They are twice the normal thickness, hand-bound in an unprinted red cover (some have the date hot-stamped in gold on spine,) and interleaved with plain, white pages for making notes. Revisions were entered on the blank pages, and when completed the books were returned to us. They were assembled using first, second, fifteenth and all succeeding editions through the twentieth. Not all were used as intended, so there may be a few extant. A unique edition of the *Red Book* is a special copy printed in Braille. Permission was granted to Uncap International, Inc., a California nonprofit organization engaged in promoting hobbies for the disabled. This special version of the catalog was created to accommodate a blind California collector.

A tax accountant once informed me that it was his practice to use his complete set of *Red Books* to appraise collections of deceased numismatists for estate-tax purposes. He explained that, in cases where date of purchase is known but the cost of a coin is not recorded, past editions prove reliable sources for establishing original costs back to the mid-forties. The Internal Revenue Service, at least in his case, accepted this value-source, we were told.

It goes without saying that many collectors, dealers and investment analysts seek out old editions to establish yearly performance data for individual coins in which they are interested. It is wonderful to see the great increase in value, over time, of almost every United States coin. Therefore, to say that the future will see a similar rate of gain over a like period would not be an unrealistic statement to make based on the record. The contributors to both our *Handbook of United States Coins* and *A Guide Book of United States Coins* are a special group.

Over the years, scores of men and women, mostly from the ranks of professional numismatists and from all corners of America, have unselfishly given of their time and talent to work as panelists, supplying us with price evaluations, statistics or historical data.

In the foregoing story, I have named very few people. At every stage of development in the narrative, I could have named a sizeable list of friends and dedicated colleagues whose influence in various ways has made our catalogs successful references for so many.

WHITMAN'S BIGGEST JOBBER

Few people have had a more direct influence on the marketing success of Whitman products than Donald S. Hirschhorn (1927–2020). Yet, he always remained behind the scenes in his usual quiet manner, offering suggestions and help with innovative methods of presenting the hobby to a worldwide audience. In 1965 he displayed his confidence in the coin-hobby market by ordering a full truckload of *Red Books* for his distribution network. Portions of a personal remembrance of his life, business activities, and association with Whitman have been recounted by David W. Lange:

> He was Whitman's biggest jobber (wholesale distributor) throughout the '60s, forming Don Hirschhorn, Ltd., with offices in Wisconsin, Pennsylvania, Massachusetts, Puerto Rico, Canada, and the United Kingdom. He even put out a series of Whitman folders under his name as publisher, that were distributed solely in the UK and the Republic of Ireland. [Together with a special version of Ken Bressett's *Guide Book of English Coins*, with values shown in English pounds.] During the 1970s he broke with Whitman, purchasing the old stamp firm of H.G. Treacher Company and publishing his own line of coin folders under that name or his new Treat brand through 1980.
>
> Donald was born in Brooklyn, New York, on August 30, 1927, to Irving Hirschhorn and Bessie Passoff, both

◀ As reported in *The Westerner*, published for the employees of Western Publishing Co., August 22, 1969: "While all orders for the 1970 *Red Books* were exceptionally large, that of Don Hirschhorn, international distributor of Western coin supplies, was by far the largest—an entire truckload was shipped for first-day sales. Seeing the truck off were (from left) Dick Thompsen and Harold Richow, both of Hirschhorn; and Westerners Jerry Huebner, hobby specialist-wholesale sales; and [R.S. Yeoman], chief editor, Whitman Coin Supply."

> immigrants from Russia. He raised his family in Jericho, Long Island, before moving to Hawley, Pennsylvania, where he and his wife, Sandra, designed and built dream homes there on a lake, and in Boca Raton, Florida.
>
> . . . Donald served as a Technician Fifth Grade in the U.S. Army until 1946. A World War II veteran and member of the Greatest Generation, he was particularly proud of his service while stationed at the Panama Canal Zone, and of his large extended family and reunions to remind younger generations of the contribution family members had made to the United States. His wise and loving counsel to family members will be greatly missed, as will his steadfast, uncomplaining manner and good humor.

COMMENTS, COMPLIMENTS, AND GROWING PAINS

By the 1980s the *Red Book* had become such a firmly established institution that nostalgia was gathering around it. Articles about collecting *Red Books* begin to proliferate: in 1983 Q. David Bowers's "The Guide Book Revisited" appeared in *The Numismatist*; from 1983 through 1986 *Coin World* ran a series of articles by *Red Book* collector and dealer Ed Lesniak, who offered collecting advice and published accounts of newly discovered error copies.

▲ From 1986 to 1997 Whitman issued annual dollar-sized commemorative silver medals for the *Red Book* (as well as companion pieces, each with a different design, for the *Blue Book*). (shown enlarged)

The appeal of the *Red Book* was not merely sentimental, however, as many fans were quick to point out. In 1987 numismatist Colonel Bill Murray wrote an appreciative essay that appeared under the title "'*Red Book*' Still an Informative Guide" in the October 21 issue of *Coin World*. As the title indicates, he stressed the continuing relevance of the venerable guide book and urged the novice coin collector, or "new-mismatist," to explore it:

> If you want to determine the greatest value of the "*Red Book*" for a New-Mismatist, take time to read the words in paragraphs, not just the numbers and column introductions and headings. You'll learn. In fact, I firmly believe that if you know all that is in the "*Red Book*," truly know it, you'll know more about United States coinage than many, not to say most, dealers. . . . Purchase it, and immerse yourself in the material therein. You'll be a better numismatist as a result. Besides, it's fun.

▲ Common reverse for all medals.

Although Murray warned readers that "prices in the coin market change too often and too rapidly for an annual publication to keep pace," he asserted that the price listings in the *Red Book* "still have utility." As proof, he offered the intriguing information that "a small survey conducted a few years ago disclosed that virtually all dealers in United States coins not only owned the '*Red Book*' but purchased one each year. Primarily these dealers use the '*Red Book*' to determine relative values of coins, especially some of the more esoteric varieties not usually listed in the various weekly price guides." It seems that coin dealers, as well as collectors, recognized the usefulness of a library of *Red Books*!

In a similar vein, Q. David Bowers's essay in the November 1987 *Numismatist* discussed the perspective that could be gleaned from examining older editions of the guide. Entitled "The *Red Book*: Great Value for the Money," his discussion provided an insightful look at the history and development of the *Red Book* and mused on some of the changes the famous volume had undergone through the years:

> Though many products deteriorate once they achieve a measure of success, the opposite has happened to the *Red Book*. Over the years it has improved, and this year's edition contains much more information than its predecessor of some 30 years ago. Of course, things were simpler back then—grading was not nearly as complicated—and it can be argued that not as much information was necessary. . . . Back then a coin was either uncirculated or it wasn't; likewise, a proof was a proof—not a Proof-60, Proof-61, etc.

◀ The 1982 *Red Book*, advertised in the July 1981 *Numismatist*, was distinguished by a special 35th-anniversary emblem with R.S. Yeoman's signature.

▶ Q. David Bowers extolled the *Red Book* in a November 1987 *Numismatist* article.

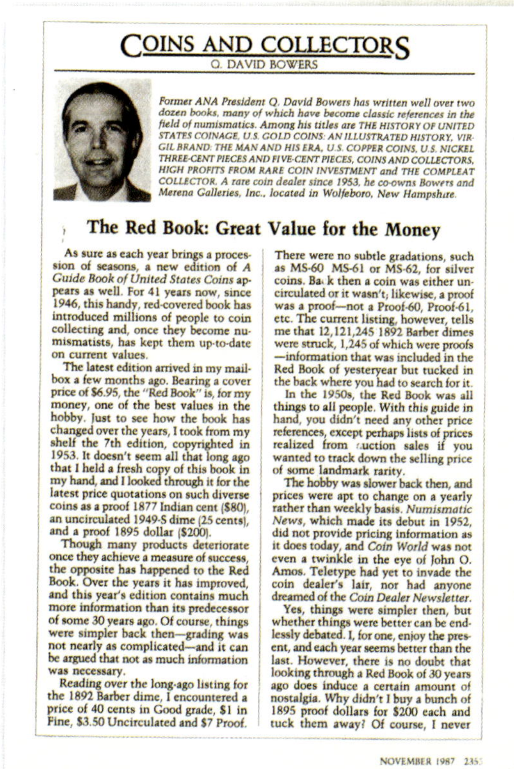

COINS AND COLLECTORS

Q. DAVID BOWERS

Former ANA President Q. David Bowers has written well over two dozen books, many of which have become classic references in the field of numismatics. Among his titles are THE HISTORY OF UNITED STATES COINAGE, U.S. GOLD COINS: AN ILLUSTRATED HISTORY, VIRGIL BRAND: THE MAN AND HIS ERA, U.S. COPPER COINS, U.S. NICKEL THREE-CENT PIECES AND FIVE-CENT PIECES, COINS AND COLLECTORS, HIGH PROFITS FROM RARE COIN INVESTMENT and THE COMPLEAT COLLECTOR. A rare coin dealer since 1953, he co-owns Bowers and Merena Galleries, Inc., located in Wolfeboro, New Hampshire.

The Red Book: Great Value for the Money

As sure as each year brings a procession of seasons, a new edition of *A Guide Book of United States Coins* appears as well. For 41 years now, since 1946, this handy, red-covered book has introduced millions of people to coin collecting and, once they become numismatists, has kept them up-to-date on current values.

The latest edition arrived in my mailbox a few months ago. Bearing a cover price of $6.95, the "Red Book" is, for my money, one of the best values in the hobby. Just to see how the book has changed over the years, I took from my shelf the 7th edition, copyrighted in 1953. It doesn't seem all that long ago that I held a fresh copy of this book in my hand, and I looked through it for the latest price quotations on such diverse coins as a proof 1877 Indian cent ($80), an uncirculated 1949-S dime (25 cents), and a proof 1895 dollar ($200).

Though many products deteriorate once they achieve a measure of success, the opposite has happened to the Red Book. Over the years it has improved, and this year's edition contains much more information than its predecessor of some 30 years ago. Of course, things were simpler back then—grading was not nearly as complicated—and it can be argued that not as much information was necessary.

Reading over the long-ago listing for the 1892 Barber dime, I encountered a price of 40 cents in Good grade, $1 in Fine, $3.50 Uncirculated and $7 Proof. There were no subtle gradations, such as MS-60 MS-61 or MS-62, for silver coins. Back then a coin was either uncirculated or it wasn't; likewise, a proof was a proof—not a Proof-60, Proof-61, etc. The current listing, however, tells me that 12,121,245 1892 Barber dimes were struck, 1,245 of which were proofs—information that was included in the Red Book of yesteryear but tucked in the back where you had to search for it.

In the 1950s, the Red Book was all things to all people. With this guide in hand, you didn't need any other price references, except perhaps lists of prices realized from auction sales if you wanted to track down the selling price of some landmark rarity.

The hobby was slower back then, and prices were apt to change on a yearly rather than weekly basis. *Numismatic News*, which made its debut in 1952, did not provide pricing information as it does today, and *Coin World* was not even a twinkle in the eye of John O. Amos. Teletype had yet to invade the coin dealer's lair, nor had anyone dreamed of the *Coin Dealer Newsletter*.

Yes, things were simpler then, but whether things were better can be endlessly debated. I, for one, enjoy the present, and each year seems better than the last. However, there is no doubt that looking through a Red Book of 30 years ago does induce a certain amount of nostalgia. Why didn't I buy a bunch of 1895 proof dollars for $200 each and tuck them away? Of course, I never

NOVEMBER 1987 235

◀ The September 1988 *Numismatist* featured the *Red Book* as its cover story.

▶ The 1989 edition of the *Red Book* is the end of the collection for those who seek R.S. Yeoman's autographs. He passed away four months after it was released.

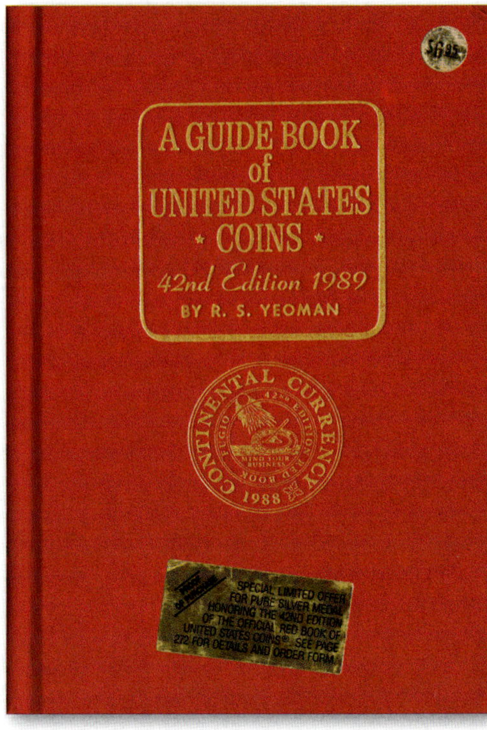

Bowers went on to provide the reader with a sense of how the *Red Book* had fit into the numismatic community during its early years: "In the 1950s, the *Red Book* was all things to all people," he pointed out. "With this guide in hand, you didn't need any other price references, except perhaps lists of prices realized from auction sales if you wanted to track down the selling price of some landmark rarity. The hobby was slower back then."

In 1987 Yeoman was present at the ANA convention as part of the celebration of the *Red Book*'s 40th anniversary. The following year, in 1988, the *Red Book* appeared on the cover of the September issue of *The Numismatist*, in recognition of that issue's main article, "The *Red Book* Story," by Ginger Rapsus. The 42nd-edition *Red Book* even received a two-part review from Bowers, which spanned the December 1988 and January 1989 issues of *The Numismatist*.

Meanwhile, the situation at the book's parent company remained unsettled. In 1982 Western Publishing was bought by Mattel, which made no attempt to restore the coin-collecting line to its former glory. Two years later Western changed hands again, when investor Richard A. Bernstein bought out Mattel's interest in the company. Again, no improvements came about under the new management. The next time the company was put up for sale, in 1992, several years would pass before it found a buyer. Sadly, as this era came to a close, the creator of the *Red Book* was no longer alive to shepherd it as he would have wished to. Richard Yeo died in November 1988 at the age of 84.

◂ The *Red Book* 50th-anniversary medal set illustrated here includes a medal struck over a Peace dollar. Some sets had overstruck Morgan dollars. Each set, numbering 50 in total, contained a one-ounce silver round, an overstruck silver dollar, and a gold-plated round, housed in a red display card stamped in gold with the set's serial number. "Whitman Publishing decided not to publicly distribute these sets," notes researcher Frank J. Colletti, "so they are one of the best-kept secrets of *Red Book* collectibles."

THE ENDURING *RED BOOK*

The 50th anniversary of the *Red Book* in 1996 was a major milestone. A special anniversary cover and a new spiralbound edition marked the occasion, and Q. David Bowers launched a five-part series called "Inside the *Red Book*" in *The Numismatist*. In the same year, Western Publishing was finally sold after four years on the market. The new owner, Richard E. Snyder, changed the company name to Golden Books Family Entertainment—a reflection of his vision for the company, which was to focus on

◂ R.S. Yeoman was featured on a brass medal (mintage 5,000) commemorating the 50th anniversary of the *Red Book*. These were presented in cloth pouches, given away at the 1996 ANA convention in Denver. A hundred pieces were also struck in silver.

▲ To mark the 50th anniversary of the *Red Book*, elongated coins were rolled by the Racine Numismatic Society and distributed at its March 2, 1997, coin show. Approximately 1,000 elongated Lincoln Memorial cents were given away for free to attendees of the show. About 200 five-coin sets were made with Wheat cents, steel cents, Memorial cents, Buffalo nickels, and Jefferson nickels. The sets were sold for $5 apiece.

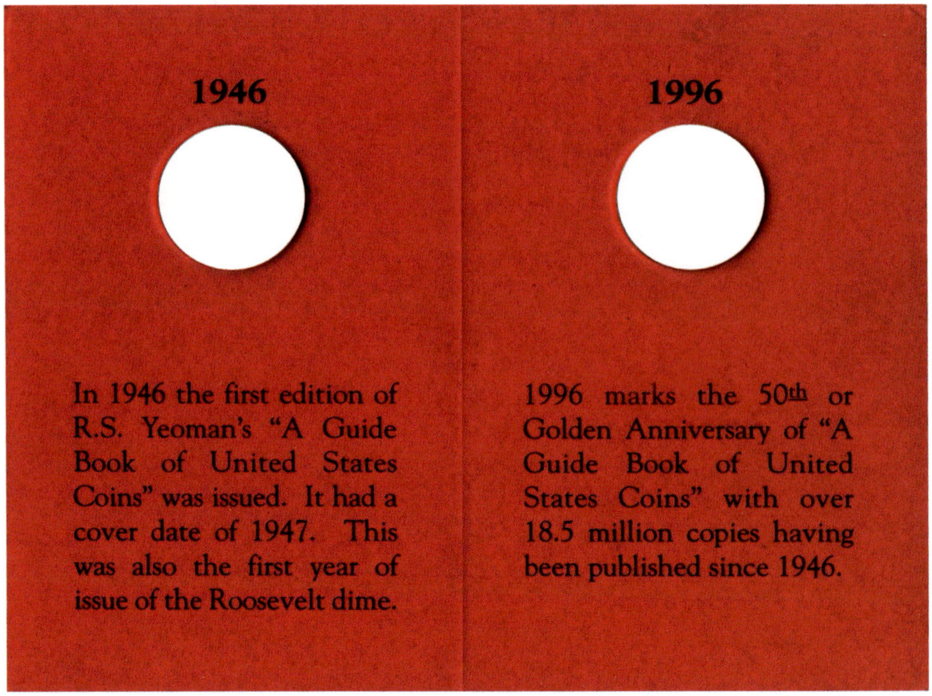

▲ Another commemorative of the *Red Book*'s 50th anniversary: a miniature coin folder (measuring 4-5/8 by 3-1/2 inches) with openings for Roosevelt dimes from 1946 and 1996.

children's publishing. Whitman Publishing was renamed "Whitman Coin Products" and became just a part of Golden's relatively small adult-publication division. Whitman brought steady profits to the division but, as numismatist David Crenshaw observes, "Little was done to reverse the continuing slump in the numismatic line," and the low product inventories allowed other numismatic publishers to take a bigger bite of the market.

Yet another change of hands in 1999 had a more positive outcome: St. Martin's Press of New York City, the new owner, gave the coin division a much-needed boost by overhauling the company's sales strategy and launching products related to the U.S. Mint's 50 State Quarters® Program. This included my feeble attempt to write a booklet, the *Official Whitman Statehood Quarters Collector's Handbook*, even before the coins were actually minted.

The 1990s also saw the emergence of a potentially serious threat to the *Red Book*: the Internet. As the possibilities offered by the new technology grew, more and more numismatists felt obliged to address the question of whether the *Red Book* would be rendered obsolete by online coin-pricing references, which could offer more frequent data updates. In a review, ANA member Susan Headley explained that she prized the book because it was "inexpensive and portable" and pointed out that up-to-the-minute pricing wasn't necessarily a major consideration for the average collector:

> Although the Internet has more up-to-date pricing than the book, this type of information is only useful for high-grade and rare coins. The vast majority of buying and selling is done in collector-grade material, which doesn't change much in value in the short term. Internet price listings are a great source of extra information, but until somebody invents a $15 real-time-pricing coins-based handheld computer, online price lists will not be replacing my *Red Book*!

Likewise, Bowers noted that "the *Red Book* is convenient, portable and offers a very large database of price and mintage information. You don't have to charge its batteries or plug it in, nor does it cost $2,000 or arbitrarily decide to stop working!"

Nevertheless, doubts as to the book's continued relevance would still arise. In a 2002 essay in *COINage*, for example, writer Mike Thorne suggested that the *Red Book* had been eclipsed: "In the early 1950s, determining a coin's value was easy for many dealers: If you were selling, the coin was worth full *Red Book*. . . . Today, the situation is drastically different. The *Red Book* and *Blue Book* still exist, but are pretty limited in their ability to determine a coin's value." At the same time, however, Thorne was enthusiastic about the changes that the *Red Book* had undergone during its long life. Just three years later, reviewing the 2006 edition, he would assert that "the current *Red Book* is much more than just a list of coins and prices" and observe that the presence of competing coin guides had evidently been beneficial to the book.

Further changes were still in store for the *Red Book*. In 2003 St. Martin's Press sold Whitman Coin Products to H.E. Harris & Company, a well-established stamp- and coin-collecting supply firm owned by Anderson Press. Harris and Whitman combined under the name of Whitman Publishing, with the new company's base of operations in Atlanta, Georgia. This alliance of the leading numismatic and philatelic supply firms reinvigorated the Whitman coin-collecting line of books, coin albums, folders, and related items, and supplemented it with an assortment of licensed U.S. Mint products.

► In 2006 Ken Bressett joined R.S. Yeoman on a new medal commemorating 60 years of the *Red Book*. Mintage was limited to 500 in nickel-silver, each in an individually numbered ANACS slab and red slipcase. At a ceremony on the bourse of the ANA World's Fair of Money in Denver that August, Whitman publisher Dennis Tucker presented to Bressett a unique strike in .900 fine gold.

A Teacher's Point of View

by Rod Gillis

As the education director at the American Numismatic Association, I would be hard-pressed to think of anything that helps me more in my day-to-day general activities than *A Guide Book of United States Coins*. I depend on the book because (and I am letting you in on a little secret) I have yet to memorize the mintage number of the 1833 Capped Bust half dime (1,370,000). Of course, the *Red Book* is more than just a listing of facts; it explains, among many other things, how modern Proof coins are struck, the importance of Fugio coppers, and the significance of U.S. patterns.

For me, the most amazing thing about the *Red Book* is its consistency. Yes, the *Red Book* contains more information every year, yet it has always been a steadfast product. There is no such thing as an "off year" for *A Guide Book of United States Coins*. I never had the opportunity to meet R.S. Yeoman, but I am familiar with many of the contributors. I am proud to say that I have worked with Ken Bressett, undoubtedly the driving force behind the *Red Book* for all these years. Ken truly loves to write about numismatics, and he is a real stickler for detail. I believe Ken's mentioned abilities have made the *Red Book* the "go-to" resource for novices and experts alike. His efforts are truly a labor of love.

▲ In 1991 Whitman Publishing issued a special-edition brass-plated aluminum medal with a matte finish, for the 100th anniversary of the American Numismatic Association. The 5,000 medals were given away as premiums at the 1991 ANA show in Chicago.

It occurs to me that *A Guide Book of United States Coins* is much more than just a book; it is an important component of numismatics itself. I cannot tell you the number of times I have been in Ken Bressett's company, either co-teaching a grading class or discussing coins with several young numismatists, and have introduced him to the audience. Suddenly, *Red Books* appear and students ask Ken if he would be kind enough to sign their copy. Ken, being Ken, graciously autographs each book placed in front of him; I never recall him declining. The students have huge smiles on their faces and hold onto their treasures like the rarest coins in their collections. Youngsters and adults walk away feeling that they have arrived. They are now honest-to-goodness coin collectors.

No, *A Guide Book of United States Coins* never outlives its usefulness. Older editions are great to look through, especially if you want to see if you could have afforded a Hawaiian commemorative half dollar in 1969 ($250). In today's world, I do not know what I would do without the latest copy when I field a question on Feuchtwanger tokens. I keep the spiralbound edition on my desk at all times. However, I cannot promise that my most recent copy will not end up looking well used . . . even though it does contain Ken's autograph.

In spite of the competition posed by new technology and other coin-pricing guides, the *Red Book* endured, as did its popularity. Different readers cite different reasons for their loyalty. Q. David Bowers wrote in 1997, "Despite the abundance of timely numismatic references—such as *Coin Dealer Newsletter*, *Coin World* and *Numismatic News*—I rely most on the familiar, red-covered *Guide Book*. It is not that it has more pricing information, but rather because it is so easy to use. It is small enough to tuck into a coat pocket, yet big enough to provide mintage figures, general price indications and a wealth of information."

Numismatist David T. Alexander, in his April 2005 *COINage* article "The '*Red Book*' of U.S. Coins," also cited its ease of use, as well as its familiarity and long history—which carry both the appeal of nostalgia and the sense of stability that may be absent in other areas of coin collecting (and life in general). "In some ways," he concluded, "the public affection that is lavished on the *Red Book* recalls baseball fans' devotion to some of the more lop-eared home teams in places such as Brooklyn or Chicago over the years. Sure, there are things to affectionately criticize, 'but they're our guys, and we're gonna love 'em even if we lambaste 'em!'"

Overall, criticisms were few.

INTO THE FUTURE

The *Guide Book of United States Coins* is constantly changing. From its first publication in 1946 to the current edition, the *Red Book* has been a work in progress. Coin varieties are discovered, new coins are issued, the coin market fluctuates, coin collecting evolves as a hobby—and the *Guide Book* has recorded and responded to it all. Numismatist Joel J. Orosz commented in a letter to me in 2020, "I'm struck by how much you updated the content over the years while staying faithful to the basic framework that Dick Yeoman created."

As coin collecting has changed, the *Red Book* has grown and evolved from a simple listing of two or three different grades of coins to an elaborate catalog that reflects the refinement in grading that later developed. The first edition contained listings for approximately 3,400 different coins, tokens, sets, and other entries. By the 75th edition the *Red Book* had expanded to list nearly 8,000. Now there are as many as nine grades and values for each coin (with more than 32,000 retail valuations in total). The first edition was a compilation of the knowledge of author R.S. Yeoman and 14 contributors. Today Senior Editor Jeff Garrett utilizes the skills and experience of more than 100 contributors, plus myself as editor emeritus, Research Editor Q. David Bowers, and several special consultants. Rather than being a collection of information from a select few, the book now contains the knowledge and research of many contributors, each of whom has broad general knowledge and also works in a specialized niche of the market. Heading this robust team is Whitman Publisher Dennis Tucker, a longtime coin collector himself. His comments tell of his enthusiasm and resolve:

> I'm living a collector's dream: hired as Whitman's publisher in 2004, I actually get to work as a hands-on member of the *Red Book* team. I never guessed that my career in corporate communications and publications would lead me to Whitman Publishing, the maker of the famous scarlet tome. I count among my coworkers Jeff Garrett, Kenneth Bressett, and Q. David Bowers—how much more fortunate can a numismatist be? Ken's *Guide Book of English Coins* was the first world-coin book I ever bought, back when I started to branch into British and European material. And, of course there was many a Bowers title on my numismatic bookshelf. I'm honored to work with the hundreds of pricing contributors and researchers who make the *Red Book* so unique.

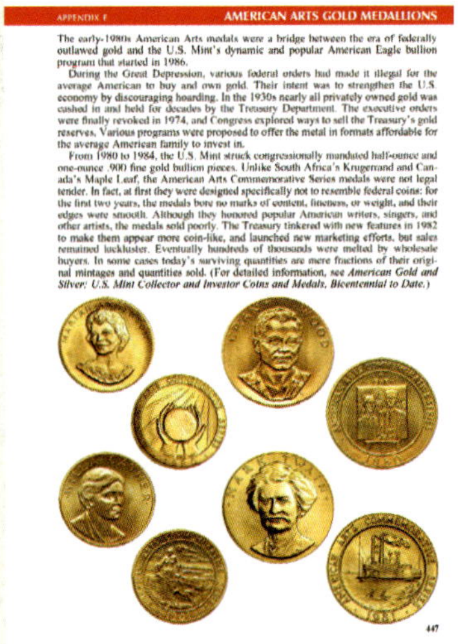

APPENDIX F — AMERICAN ARTS GOLD MEDALLIONS

The early-1980s American Arts medals were a bridge between the era of federally outlawed gold and the U.S. Mint's dynamic and popular American Eagle bullion program that started in 1986.

During the Great Depression, various federal orders had made it illegal for the average American to buy and own gold. Their intent was to strengthen the U.S. economy by discouraging hoarding. In the 1930s nearly all privately owned gold was cashed in and held for decades by the Treasury Department. The executive orders were finally revoked in 1974, and Congress explored ways to sell the Treasury's gold reserves. Various programs were proposed to offer the metal in formats affordable for the average American family to invest in.

From 1980 to 1984, the U.S. Mint struck congressionally mandated half-ounce and one-ounce .900 fine gold bullion pieces. Unlike South Africa's Krugerrand and Canada's Maple Leaf, the American Arts Commemorative Series medals were not legal tender. In fact, at first they were designed specifically not to resemble federal coins: for the first two years, the medals bore no marks of content, fineness, or weight, and their edges were smooth. Although they honored popular American writers, singers, and other artists, the medals sold poorly. The Treasury tinkered with new features in 1982 to make them appear more coin-like, and launched new marketing efforts, but sales remained lackluster. Eventually hundreds of thousands were melted by wholesale buyers. In some cases today's surviving quantities are mere fractions of their original mintages and quantities sold. (For detailed information, see *American Gold and Silver: U.S. Mint Collector and Investor Coins and Medals, Bicentennial to Date.*)

447

APPENDIX E — MODERN U.S. MINT MEDALS

National Wildlife Refuge System Centennial Medals (2003)

In 2003 the U.S. Mint released its first-ever series of silver national medals, to celebrate the 100th anniversary of the National Wildlife Refuge System. Their shared obverse features a standing portrait of President Theodore Roosevelt, who designated Florida's Pelican Island as the nation's first wildlife refuge in 1903.

Sales started with the Bald Eagle variety, available in bronze and .900 fine silver formats. The Salmon, Elk, and Canvasback Duck varieties, in silver only, were released successively every few weeks after that.

The bronze Bald Eagle had no mintage limit, and in fact since then has been reissued in 2008 in the Bald Eagle Coin and Medal Set, and in 2013 in the Theodore Roosevelt Coin and Chronicles Set. The four silver medals all sold out their mintage limits (35,000 for the Bald Eagle and 25,000 for the others).

The silver medals were the first U.S. Mint products made using laser technology to texture their dies. They feature distinctive matte-finish frosted devices on mirror-finish fields. All were struck at the Philadelphia Mint without a mintmark.

	Mintage	Value
2003, National Wildlife Refuge System Centennial, Bald Eagle, bronze	(a)	$5.00
2003, National Wildlife Refuge System Centennial, Bald Eagle, silver	35,000	28.50
2003, National Wildlife Refuge System Centennial, Salmon	25,000	30.00
2003, National Wildlife Refuge System Centennial, Elk	25,000	30.00
2003, National Wildlife Refuge System Centennial, Canvasback Duck	25,000	29.00

a. The Mint established no production limit for the bronze medal. Mintage was ongoing into the early 2010s. At least 22,000 were distributed as part of the Mint's 2008 Bald Eagle Coin and Medal Set, and at least 15,000 in the 2013 Theodore Roosevelt Coin and Chronicles Set.

449

▲ In recent years, when space has allowed, the *Red Book* has included information on American Arts gold medallions, modern United States Mint medals, and other specialized numismatic topics.

◄ The *Red Book*'s editors and publisher rolled out the *Professional Edition* in a presentation at the 2009 Whitman Coin and Collectibles Philadelphia Expo.

PLUS ULTRA: EVOLUTION OF THE *RED BOOK* TO "MEGA RED"

In 2009 Whitman broke new ground by publishing the *Professional Edition Red Book*, an 8-1/2 by 11-inch spiralbound, softcover, expanded version of the traditional *Guide Book of United States Coins*. Numismatists immediately recognized its importance as a supplement to and expansion of the information in the regular edition. Longtime *Red Book* collector Frank J. Colletti, author of the *Guide Book of the Official Red Book of United States Coins*, expressed the feelings of many hobbyists when he wrote to Ken Bressett and Dennis Tucker in December 2009:

> I have been reading the "Professional Edition" *Red Book*. The enhancements over the regular edition make this a truly innovative development in the sixty-year history of the *Red Book*. The new die varieties throughout the book make it a wonderful addition to my library. Thank you for providing us (collectors as well as dealers) with a new invaluable resource.

The *Professional Edition* was published from 2009 to 2014, along with the regular edition.

In 2013 Whitman produced a 352-page "magazine book" format of the *Red Book* called the *Essential Edition*. It was an 8-1/2 by 11-inch perfect-bound, softcover version that continued through five annual editions. The "bookazine" was designed for sale in select markets and featured large-size print and a condensed version of some of the more specialized areas of collecting. Values shown

▼ The first *Professional Edition* of the *Red Book* (2009).

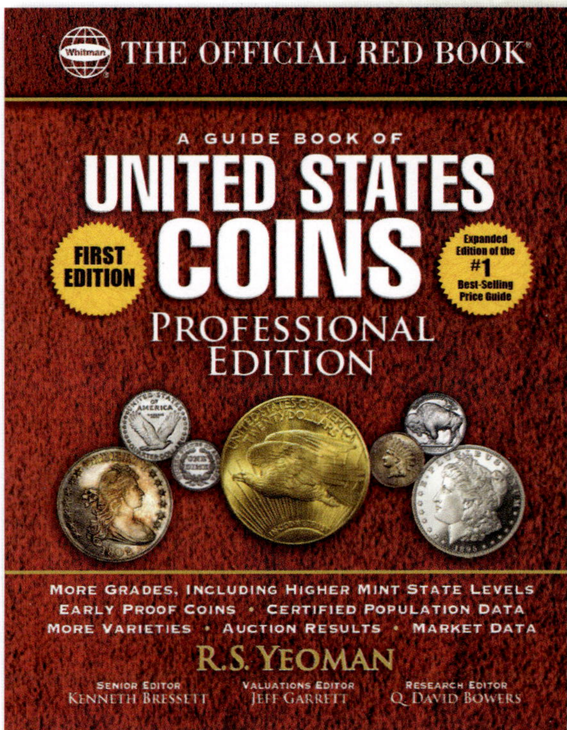

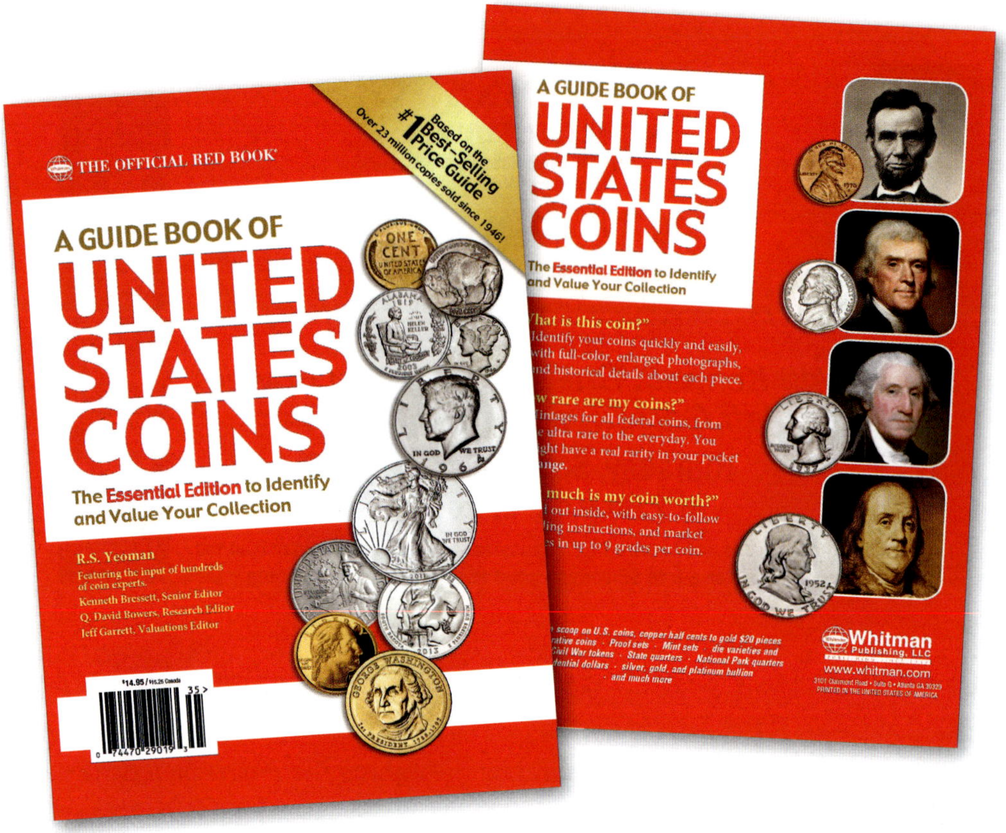

▸ The first *Essential Edition* of the *Red Book* (2013).

for coins were the same as those in the regular *Red Book* of that time. The first edition had a copyright date of 2013 and no date on the cover. The second and subsequent productions of the *Essential Edition* were printed with cover dates one year ahead of publication, like the regular editions.

In a 2014 press release, Dennis Tucker described the *Essential Edition*:

> The *Essential Edition Red Book* focuses mainly on circulating federal U.S. coinage—the cents, nickels, dimes, silver dollars, and other coins most likely to be found in Grandpa's proverbial cigar box or other collections. As with the regular-edition *Red Book*, we promote the *Essential Edition* through mainstream bookstores like Barnes & Noble and Books-A-Million. Beyond that, it's also carried in Sam's Club—the eighth-largest retailer in the United States, serving 47 million members. We're excited to be able to offer this version of the *Red Book* to such a large audience, and to introduce the hobby to a new generation of collectors.

Wayne Homren, editor of *The E-Sylum* (weekly newsletter of the Numismatic Bibliomania Society), opined in the June 22, 2014, edition: "My first thoughts on reading this were, 'I thought the *Red Book* already WAS a mass-market publication,' and 'Boy, they're milking that cow dry.' But improvements over time have greatly enlarged the book, and stripping it back down to the 'essentials' for everyday pocket-change collectors is probably a good idea. I would be much more inclined to buy a copy of this version to give to my neighbors and relatives than I would the regular edition, which has a lot of information, but not of direct interest to them.... I think this is a good step in promoting the hobby to a wider audience." To this, Tucker replied, "Yes, our goal with this edition is to expand the already considerable ambassadorial reach of the *Red Book*, rather than preach to the choir. The *Essential Edition* is a way of putting coin collecting in front of a huge new audience of non-collectors who probably have never even heard of the *Red Book*, but who might be intrigued enough to look up those old Wheat cents and Morgan dollars that Granddad set aside. (And then, with a bit of encouragement, grow into active collectors themselves!)"

Whitman recognized the growing importance of these specialized books and in 2014 began planning for an even bigger new edition. The result of many months of planning was the first *Deluxe Edition* of the *Red Book*, published in 2015. It was described as "a fully illustrated catalog of useful information on colonial and federal coinage, 1616 to date." In reality, it was a virtual encyclopedia of data concerning every aspect of our nation's coinage, including valuations in grades well beyond those listed in the regular editions of the customary *Red Book*. Sometimes facetiously described as the "*Guide Book* on Steroids," it was a gigantic 7 by 10 by 2-1/2–inch tome consisting of 1,504 pages. With the book's immediate popularity, the massive size turned out to be no problem. While it could not be toted around and used like its handier brother, nothing could match it for the plethora of information it contained, and it gained an instant following among serious collectors and dealers. By the second edition, the title was changed to "Mega Red," and it has remained so for the subsequent annual editions. The content has also changed each year to include a more detailed coverage of America's coinage in specific denominations. A Whitman press release described the sixth edition thus:

> The Sixth Deluxe Edition "Mega Red" is the latest expanded version of the hobby's best-selling "*Red Book*" (more than 24 million copies sold since 1946). With pages 30% larger than the regular editions and weighing in at 1,504 pages (more than three times the page count), the new Deluxe Edition MEGA RED includes more historical information, extensive grading instructions with enlarged illustrations, a featured section on half dollars, and valuable essays on collecting and investing in rare coins.
>
> MEGA RED has certified population data, more die varieties, more auction records, and more pricing in more

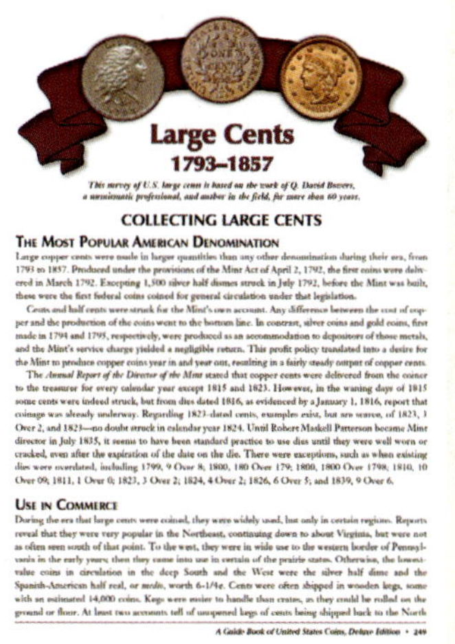
Large Cents
1793–1857
COLLECTING LARGE CENTS
The Most Popular American Denomination
Use in Commerce

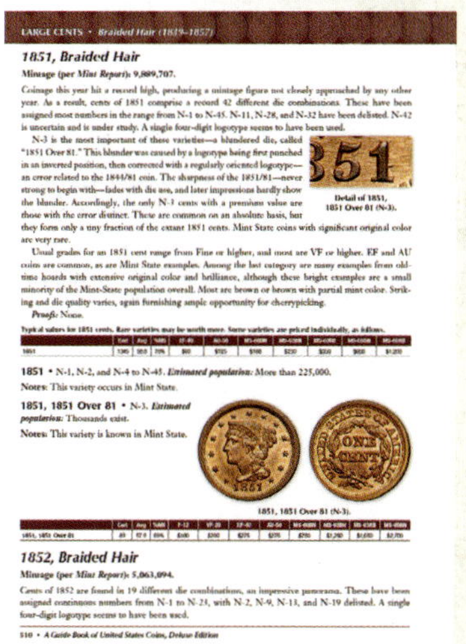
1851, Braided Hair
1852, Braided Hair

▲ The first *Deluxe Edition* of the *Red Book* (later titled *Mega Red*) had an in-depth feature on half cents and large cents. At 364 pages, this special section alone was the size of a normal book.

▲ A "carton poster" (a large point-of-purchase promotional poster, inserted into each carton of Whitman books shipped to retailers) advertising the first *Mega Red*.

grades than the regular *Red Book*. It covers American coinage from colonial times to the modern-day half cents through $20 gold double eagles, plus bullion, commemoratives, proof and Mint sets, significant tokens, errors, and other collectibles. MEGA RED prices more than 8,200 items in up to 13 grades, each with 47,000 individual values, 15,800 auction records, and 6,000 images (thousands of which are updated or new to the sixth edition). Expanded sections and new features in the sixth edition include: an overview price-guide of foreign coins that circulated as cash in the British American colonies; an illustrated history and price guide of So-Called Dollars; insight on counterfeit and spurious coins; advice on collecting and investing in modern gold and silver bullion coins; an illustrated history of half dollars, and more.

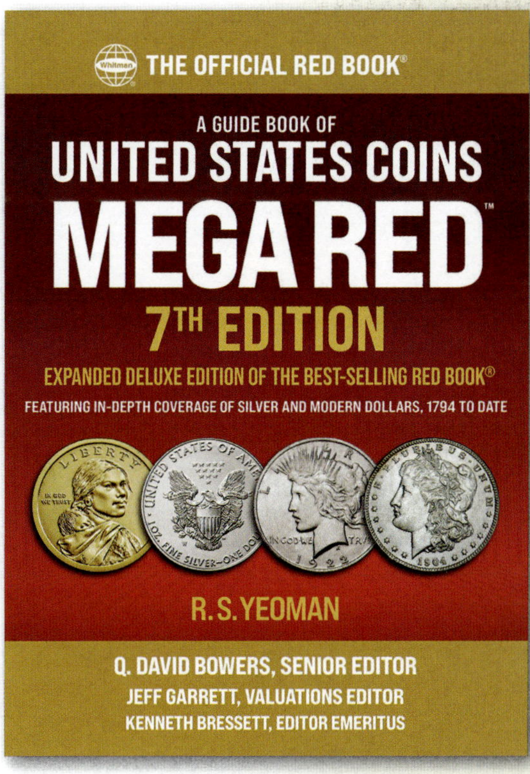

▲ The *Deluxe Edition* of the *Red Book*, now called *Mega Red*, debuted in 2015 and has been issued annually since. The cover style was developed by Matt Jeffirs, an artist and creative director who has worked on many projects within Whitman Publishing and its parent company, Anderson Press.

Mega Red Senior Editor Q. David Bowers recently commented: "It is a good sign that numismatic books are alive and well. More different USA titles have been published in the past 30 years than in the two centuries before it. *Mega Red*, with over 1,500 pages, has become very popular. The Internet is a wonderful source for numismatic and historical information, and I think it inspires people to seek books to add to the experience. While the Internet is a super source for info, it is hard to beat the tactile experience of having a printed book in hand while reading the text and looking at pictures."

Clifford Mishler responded: "I'm very much in Dave's corner here . . . pointedly where the 'Mega Red' is concerned. . . . I've always had a copy or two of the *Red Book* at hand since around 1950/52 . . . but I have and will keep a building set of the Mega Red in my library as long as I am active."

A Penny Saved is a memorial publication dedicated to preserving and remembering R.S. Yeoman's *Red Book* as it has changed and developed over the course of more than six decades. As Thomas Wolfe wrote, "You can't go home again," and neither can we return to the days when a coin was simply either Circulated or Uncirculated. Still, we can look through the window of the past represented by the early editions of the *Red Book* to gain from our predecessors a clearer picture of the hobby, not only as it was but as it may become in the future.

1969-S
547.3 MILLION
1970
1,898.3 MILLION
1970-D
2,891.4 MILLION
1970-S
693.1 MILLION
1971
1,919.5 MILLION
1972-S
380.2 MILLION
1972-D
MY FIRST
FIRST EARNED COIN 1916

Chapter 4

R.S. Yeoman

A BRIEF INTRODUCTION

I had the pleasure of working shoulder to shoulder with Richard S. "Dick" Yeo—known to generations of collectors by his pen name, R.S. Yeoman—for more than a decade, and it was a grand learning experience. We first met and began corresponding sometime around 1954, and in 1959 I became part of Dick's team at Western Printing Company in Racine, Wisconsin. We continued our close association long after he retired in 1970 and moved to Arizona. Throughout that time, I came to know and understand Dick in a way few others did.

A gentle genius, Dick was an amazing man in many ways. His creativity and energy were limitless. Whenever he was faced with a challenge, he always came up with the right solutions. I am sure he could have been a success in any undertaking, but first and foremost he wanted to become a commercial artist. It was only by a twist of fate that, while employed at Western Printing in his chosen field, he was asked to help develop a plan for marketing a novel line of coin boards.

Never one to do anything halfheartedly, Dick fully investigated coin collecting. To his credit, he surveyed some of the leading collectors of the day and quickly formulated a course of action that ultimately led to an extensive and diverse series of books, albums, and related items.

I held Dick in the highest regard as my supervisor, and greatly respected his experience and business acumen. Despite the 24-year age difference between us, we were close friends, and he appreciated my numismatic skills and knowledge. He was always genial and helpful not only to me, but also to his numerous friends, collaborators, and co-workers.

"Coin collecting is a pleasant pastime for idle moments, and a tonic for the mind after a busy day. Even if you decide to discontinue collecting, it is comforting to know that you still have your money. Truly it can be said of this hobby that you can eat your cake and have it too!"—R.S. Yeoman

In 2020 I had the rare opportunity to study Dick's personal files, which are part of the Western Archives. While I was aware of his many accomplishments and challenges, his well-organized folders of letters, newspaper clippings, speeches, and articles provided me a closer look at the workings of his mind and the generosity of his spirit.

As I sifted through his writings, I came across a short piece titled "A Case of Identity." In it, Dick explained that after he and his wife, Marion, retired to Arizona, he tackled the chore of unpacking cartons of books, family souvenirs, clippings, and keepsakes, some going back as far as the 1870s. Few items had dates or descriptions identifying the individuals or events. Frustrated by the process, he resolved to better organize his own photos and clippings. He wrote dates on all newspaper articles, added captions to photographs, and described places and occasions.

"[It is] surprising how our memory fails," he wrote. "Don't assume that in the years to come we WILL recall. . . . After several decades have passed, we all know that 'we shoulda.' And when we pass on, we can't. WHO, WHEN, WHERE, WHAT and even WHY are a must. If a future grandchild comes across any object left behind by you, he has the right to know what he is looking at."

Dick's archival material was indeed well documented, for which I am most grateful. Were it not for his efforts, we would never fully comprehend the man and his indelible numismatic legacy.

I was always impressed by the way he effortlessly performed the three distinct roles in his life. "Dick Yeo" was the devoted family man who enjoyed all the usual activities with his wife and their daughter, Laura Sharon. "Richard Yeo" was the successful businessman. And "R.S. Yeoman" was the consummate hobbyist who made coin collecting a popular pastime for millions of new enthusiasts.

FORMATIVE YEARS

Born in Milwaukee, Wisconsin, on August 15, 1904, Richard Sperry Yeo was the middle son of Frederic and Jennie (Stewart) Yeo. His brother Stewart was born three years before, and William came along three years later; another brother, Frank, had died in 1903.

Dick's paternal grandparents, William and Katie Yeo, lived in Devonshire, England, until 1871, when they immigrated to America and settled in the Midwest. (Interestingly, Dick's surname and pseudonym had historic connections. In medieval Europe, landowners were known as *yeos*, while their captive workers were *serfs*. Freed serfs came to be called *yeomen*.)

Fred, Jennie, and the three boys lived in a middle-class neighborhood. Dick fondly remembered the summers of his boyhood, which he spent with "grandmas and cousins." His Grandparents Stewart lived on the southwest corner of Jefferson and Dundee avenues. The house had "a modern (for that time) cement-block construction . . . built to last," he wrote in a letter to longtime Elgin friends Alwin and Viola Swanson in February 1988. Dick also noted that his family had connections with the Elgin National Watch Company. "Grandpa Yeo was the first employee to be pensioned there, and father sold the daily paper at the factory workers' exit at quitting time."

▲ A copper trade token issued in Exeter, Devonshire, England, in the 1790s.

◀ National Bank Notes of the First Wisconsin National Bank of Milwaukee, 1902. Richard Sperry Yeo was born in "the Brew City" in 1904.

▲ A typical residential street in 1940s Elgin. Many post-war homes were built from kits marketed by Sears & Roebuck.

Elgin, Illinois: A Legacy of Industry

Searching for a fertile settlement site along the stagecoach route between Chicago and Galena, New Yorker James T. Gifford and his brother, Hezekiah, came upon a likely spot in Illinois's Fox River Valley, about 30 miles northwest of Chicago. In April 1835 they founded Elgin, named after a favorite Scottish tune, "The Song of Elgin."

The city showed great promise in the 1850s, and in 1856 the Elgin Academy was founded. The college preparatory school is the oldest co-educational, non-sectarian institution of its kind west of the Allegheny Mountains. Thanks to the water power supplied by the Fox River, Elgin continued to thrive in the 1860s and produced military supplies during the Civil War.

With its ample pastureland and natural springs, Elgin was the perfect environment for raising dairy cattle and became known for its butter, milk, and related products. Gail Borden, who had developed a process for making sweetened condensed milk, established a factory there in 1866.

The thriving community also attracted the attention of the National Watch Company, which was founded in Chicago in 1864. Four Elgin businessmen purchased 35 acres of neglected farmland and donated it to the firm. The company reorganized its operations in 1865 and completed construction of its Elgin factory the following year. In 1874 its name was officially changed to the Elgin National Watch Company. The factory employed generations of Elgin's citizens—including Dick Yeo's grandfather—until its closure in the early 1960s.

Elgin had a population of 5,441 in 1870, a few years before Yeo's father was born there.

► A 1935 plaster model (shown smaller than its 174 mm actual size) of a design for the Elgin Centennial half dollar. The actual coin, with a different view of the Pioneer Memorial statue, was minted in 1936. The coin and the Memorial were both prepared by Trygve Rovelstad—the Memorial itself was not dedicated until many years later, in 2001.

▲ Dick's father, Fred, was born in 1873 and grew up in Elgin, Illinois. Fred's first job was with the street railway. There he manned the car where the trainmen turned in their receipts at the end of their shifts.

◄ The Elgin National Watch Company was founded in 1864 and grew to become one of the largest such manufactories in the world.

Dick attended Riverside High School on Locust Street on Milwaukee's east side, graduating in 1922, three years after the end of World War I. In an interview conducted by Paul Green for the December 16, 1986, issue of *Numismatic News* (part of an extended, eye-opening series), Dick recalled that in 1923, "while making up my mind whether to go to college, I worked for the Wisconsin Anti-Tuberculosis Association. That was a job which gave me a little money to pay for tuition and so on." He entered the University of Wisconsin–Madison (UWM) in the fall of 1923.

▲ In the year Dick Yeo graduated high school, 1922, the United States minted only three denominations of coins for circulation: the Lincoln cent, the Peace dollar, and the Saint-Gaudens double eagle. This $20 gold piece at the time would have been about a week's wages for a newspaper typesetter.

Dick attended college for two years, majoring in industrial arts. He was active in UWM activities, among them the school's literary magazine, where he honed his talents doing "art publicity," and the Arts and Crafts Club, in which he served as president.

According to Dan Brown, a Denver numismatist, coin dealer, and Dick's good friend in later years, "He always had the desire to create and have beautiful things. [Dick's] early ambition was to be an artist. He was art editor of his high school paper. But somehow there was the problem of making a living, and art didn't seem to be the way, so [it] had to wait."

While at the University of Wisconsin, he continued to court Leila Marion Junkerman, his high-school sweetheart, who was two years his senior. When Dick picked her up at her parents' home for dates, he frequently engaged in deep conversations with her father, a Milwaukee dentist, to the extent that Marion wondered who her beau really had come to see. Their romance endured, and Dick and Marion wed in 1925.

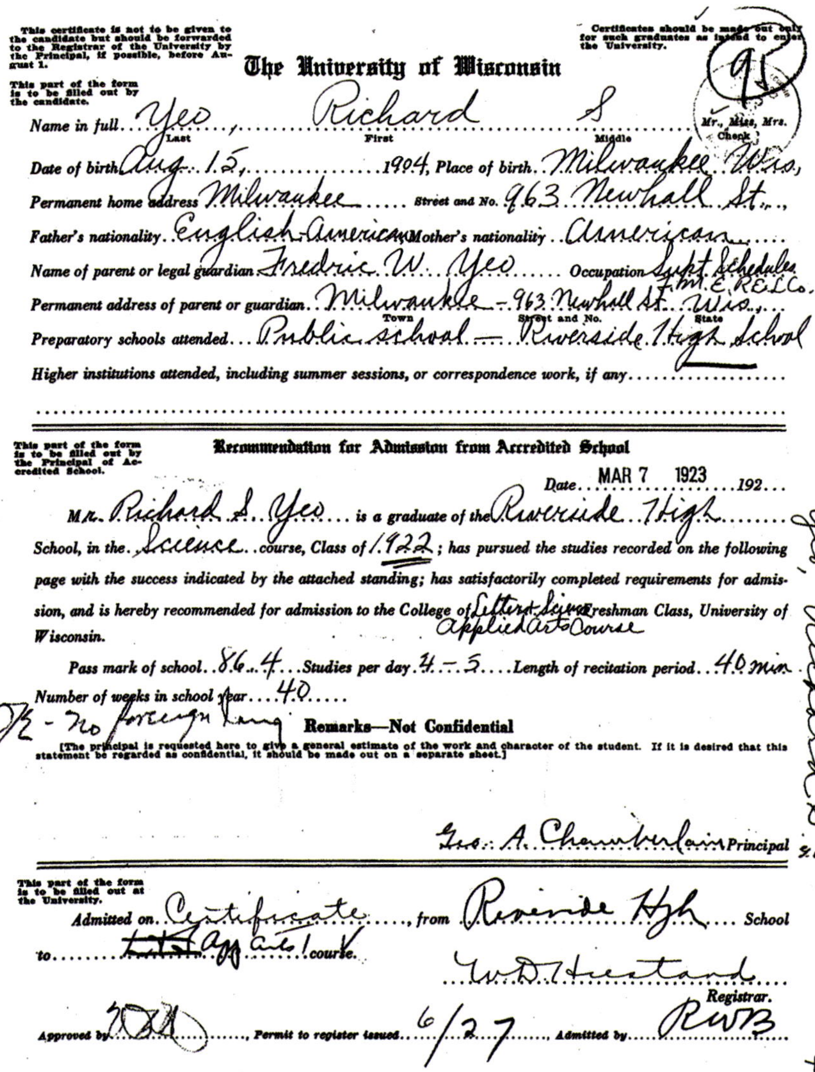

This certificate is not to be given to the candidate but should be forwarded to the Registrar of the University by the Principal, if possible, before August 1.

Certificates should be made out only for such graduates as intend to enter the University.

The University of Wisconsin

This part of the form is to be filled out by the candidate.

Name in full Yeo, (Last) Richard (First) S (Middle) Mr., Miss, Mrs. (Check)

Date of birth Aug. 15, 1904, Place of birth Milwaukee Wis,

Permanent home address Milwaukee Street and No. 963 Newhall St.,

Father's nationality English-American Mother's nationality American

Name of parent or legal guardian Fredric W. Yeo Occupation Supt. Schedules T.M.E.R.&L.Co.

Permanent address of parent or guardian Milwaukee (Town) 963 Newhall St. (Street and No.) Wis. (State)

Preparatory schools attended Public school — Riverside High School

Higher institutions attended, including summer sessions, or correspondence work, if any ...

This part of the form is to be filled out by the Principal of Accredited School.

Recommendation for Admission from Accredited School

Date MAR 7 1923 192...

Mr. Richard S. Yeo is a graduate of the Riverside High School, in the Science course, Class of 1922; has pursued the studies recorded on the following page with the success indicated by the attached standing; has satisfactorily completed requirements for admission, and is hereby recommended for admission to the College of Letters & Science Freshman Class, University of Wisconsin. Applied Arts Course

Pass mark of school 86.4 Studies per day 4 - 5 Length of recitation period 40 min.

Number of weeks in school year 40

OK - No foreign lang

Remarks—Not Confidential

[The principal is requested here to give a general estimate of the work and character of the student. If it is desired that this statement be regarded as confidential, it should be made out on a separate sheet.]

Geo. A. Chamberlain Principal

This part of the form is to be filled out at the University.

Admitted on Certificate, from Riverside High School

to [illegible] Applied Art course.

[illegible] Registrar.

Approved by [illegible] Permit to register issued 6/27 Admitted by RWB

► Yeo's March 1923 application to attend the University of Wisconsin–Madison.

K. Godfrey J. Bailey **R. Yeo** G. Jones L. Mrkvicka O. Riegel V.Beardsley W. Wittenberg K. Butler
A. Moorhead Dorothy Burns Marguerite Widmann Agnes Zeimet Edna Walter Ruth Hewitt Doris Gormley Dorothy Strauss Mary Hussong S. Hetland
E. Giessel M. Klefeker J. Weimer Rosanna Kindschi Katherine Kennedy Florence Killilea C. Hansen W. Rorison W. Buethe

▲ Yeo in his 1925 college yearbook photograph.

Top Row—E. Keir, E. Kreimann, G. Abendroth, W. Treichel.
2nd Row—M. Rick, E. Abendroth, M. Teska, J. Trapp, F. Renner, S. Yeo, Niedercorn.
3rd Row—H. G. Holmes, W. Laut, H. Wagenknecht, H. H. Naujoks, R. R. Smith, N. Rick, C. R. Dale, **R. Yeo.**
Bottom Row—V. Scott, A. H. Reinert, E. R. Summers, E. V. Hicks, V. A. Otto, P. F. Murphy, W. H. Taylor, Wolff.

Sigma Phi Sigma

Founded at University of Pennsylvania, 1908
Number of chapters, 13
Local chapter, Mu Date established, 1922

▲ Richard Yeo in the 1926 group photograph of Sigma Phi Sigma fraternity. His elder brother Stewart is in the row above him.

▲ A Peace dollar from 1925, the year Yeo married.

He left UWM that year and secured a position in the advertising department at Mirro Aluminum Company in Manitowoc. He worked there until 1927 and, according to Brown, "tried various other jobs in Wisconsin and as far west as California." From 1929 to 1932 Dick was employed as a greeting-card distributor by the Milprint Company in Milwaukee, and for a time he and Marion lived with her aunt.

Their daughter was born on November 17, 1930. Dick embraced family life and began scouting for a better, more reliable job. In 1932 he applied for an opening at Western Printing Company in Racine. He got the position and was assigned to the firm's subsidiary, Whitman Publishing, where he started in the mail-order department (later becoming its manager) and moved up to assistant sales manager in 1934. Said Dan Brown, "Whitman wanted employees' suggestions, and this was unique at that time. Dick had many good [ideas]."

At the time, Whitman manufactured and sold stamp-collecting supplies—albums, hinges, and the like—which it marketed in five-and-ten-cent stores. In the aforementioned interview with Paul Green, Dick noted that the firm's "production of stamp items was [curtailed] by World War II. That event caused paper shortages and, in turn, the amount of paper we needed! So we dropped certain minor product lines. . . . We also had photo albums, matchbook collector cards and, of course, playing cards were very strong. . . . You might say we were very active in supplying the field of leisure time."

COLLECTING CHALLENGES

Dick was hard-wired for collecting from the start. As a child, he was heavily into stamps. His curiosity was aroused when he saw many of his grade-school classmates swapping U.S. and world postage during recess.[1] Not long after, his father instilled in him an appreciation of vintage American coins. In the course of Fred's job with Elgin's street railway, he would sort through the nickels and other coins tendered by passengers, setting aside denominations and types seldom seen in circulation.

"[My father] was not a formal collector, but he got a kick out of taking [the coins] out of a cigar box and showing them," Dick explained. "[He] gave me 2-cent pieces, 3-cent pieces, 20-cent pieces, and I can remember two rolls of 1883 nickels without 'cents.' . . . I had two brothers who showed no interest in them, so the collection came to me."[2]

By age 11 Dick was delivering the local newspaper, the *Evening Wisconsin*, published from 1868 to 1918. He vividly recalled:

> Back in those days, we newsboys didn't collect from our customers; they paid the publisher. I was entitled to sell an extra copy if I had one at the end of my route. (By the way, the price in those days was 1 cent.) The first extra I sold was paid for in the form of an Indian [Head] cent. It is dated 1894, not a rare one, and I still have it. The strange part—and it was absolutely a simple impulse—is that I took out my jackknife, found a piece of cardboard, and I cut a hole in it and stuck the coin in there. As far as I'm concerned, that was my first coin board. . . . It's still in there. I marked it, "My first cent on my route." It is 1-3/4 x 2-1/8 inches.[3]

What appealed to Dick, perhaps even then, were the stories coins could tell, the "historical aspects, with all [their] implications of adventure and romance." He trained his sights on numismatic enlightenment—"knowledge of history, particularly events commemorated on coins, and the

▲ **Quarter dollars from 1930 (the year Dick and Marion Yeo's daughter was born) and from 1932 (the year he started working at Whitman Publishing).**

◀ At first the young paperboy was more interested in collecting stamps than coins.

▲ An Indian Head "penny" from 1904, the year Yeo was born.

▼ Yeo's father would set aside odd-denomination coins from pocket change to show him.

significance of legends and symbols." These, he said in a talk he delivered in 1960, "should be a challenge to us all."[4]

His understanding and appreciation of the collector mentality would serve him well in his career, keeping him in tune with hobbyists' needs and wishes. However, in the 1930s he was acutely aware of the dearth of useful numismatic literature and resources. Early manuals, he believed, had limited appeal to "a person hopeful of finding a fortune in his change." Such books "failed to build the hobby because their promises were exaggerated and were based on finding rarities."[5] Oscar H. Dodson (president of the American Numismatic Association in the late 1950s) shared Dick's view, later commenting in the March 1969 issue of *COINage* magazine that "the old Wayte Raymond *Standard Catalogue [of United States Coins]* was difficult to use, listing coins by mint of origin and . . . in only one condition. The few books purporting to list dealers' buying prices were generally the products of individual dealers and did not reflect the whole market accurately. Even dealers themselves were very much in the dark in respect to coin values. Much of the business operated by guesswork."

▲ Dick's first collectible coin was an 1894 Indian Head cent, for which he created this rudimentary holder. It was among his most treasured possessions.

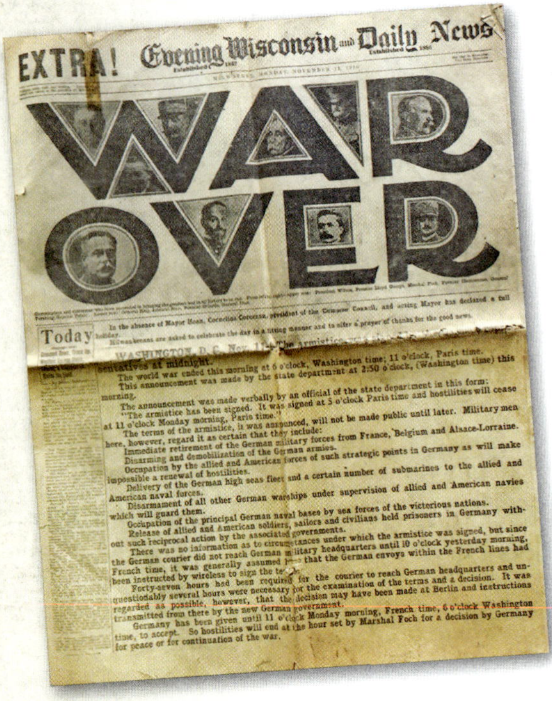
EXTRA! Evening Wisconsin and Daily News

WAR OVER

▲ The future coin collector was a paperboy for the *Evening Wisconsin* news.

Dick, like many collectors, felt that available hobby periodicals were too academic. Sophisticated numismatists, he said, were "wealthy and secretive. Some became dealers who were mostly anti–coin club. Novices were discouraged by a 'secret society' atmosphere. It was a hard door to open."

However, change was on the horizon, piloted by Dick's friend and mentor Lee F. Hewitt. "Coin collecting," Dick later wrote, "came alive in the modern sense about 1934 when [Lee introduced] his *Numismatic Scrapbook Magazine*. [His] newsy style stirred interest mainly in the exciting new series of commemorative half dollars, and in turn, proof sets.[6]

"I think he thought of himself as a conduit for people other than the elite," said Dick. "He was down to earth, the voice for the common collector who wasn't quite up there yet. He was giving them all the information he could. . . . He thought we had to come down a little closer to the level of the 'penny' collector."[7]

In the May–June 1971 issue of Whitman's *Stamp and Coin Supply Merchandiser*, Dick looked back on those early days: "The mid-1930's had a special combination of ingredients in the form of people, politics, and economics, which, when mixed together, became the numismatic cake we eat today."

Indeed, the decade proved a dynamic one for the hobby. "So it was in our fair land that economics and politics were in low gear, just the right climate for numismatic development," wrote Dick. "There was the Great Depression, and it was in full swing, truly an ill wind that unknowingly was blowing some good right into the arms of the coin collector. There were the almost idle mints—the economy needed few coins. And then there were Congress and the Administration. There were no wars, only such troubles as business downturns, W.P.A. [Works Progress Administration], and N.R.A. [National Recovery Administration]. Congress was happy to pass commemorative coin bills for everybody's morale, including its own. And the Treasury people were listening, and discovered that not only commemorative coins were being snapped up by the public, but that people were actually collecting them in sets as a series, and wonder of wonders, were eager for proof coins. So, the proof set series got started in 1936 and continued until interrupted by World War II and the coin shortage-silver boom of the sixties."[8]

◄ Commemorative half dollars were widespread collectibles in the 1930s—popular with "the common collector."

Racine, Wisconsin—Center of the Numismatic Universe

Racine is a city on the shore of Lake Michigan at the mouth of the Root River, 22 miles south of Milwaukee. Between the Civil War and the First World War the area welcomed waves of immigrants and settlers including Germans, Czechs, and Danes. (Racine has one of the largest Danish populations outside of Greenland and is famous for its Danish pastries, particularly kringle.) During the Great War and in the 1920s onward, Black and Hispanic Americans moved to the city in large numbers, as well.

Almost from its start Racine was a factory town, with mills, heavy-equipment manufactories, and machine works, and a bustling shipping center for the region. Western and Whitman Publishing were in good company in Racine: malted milk was invented there (1887), as was the garbage-disposing InSinkErator (1927), and the city was the home of industrial titans S.C. Johnson & Son, J.I. Chase, Dremel Corporation, and Arthur B. Modine.

After Whitman Publishing established itself as the leader in hobby publishing, "Racine" and "coin collecting" became linked in the minds of generations of collectors. For millions of Americans, for many decades, the beautiful and historic Wisconsin city was the center of the numismatic universe.

▶ These bronze tokens were privately issued by Racine merchants during the Civil War. They facilitated commerce when legal-tender coins were being hoarded.

▼ A $10 National Bank Note of the First National Bank of Racine, 1902.

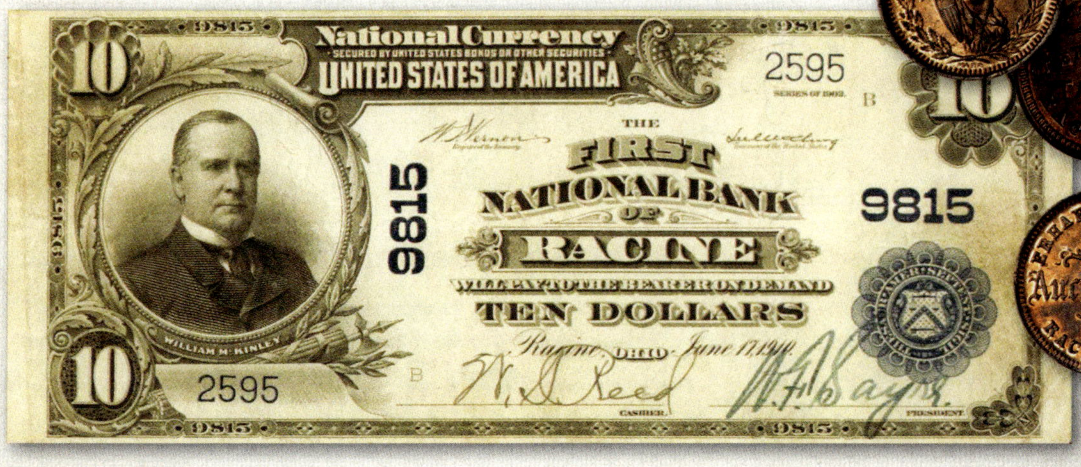

▲ A Liberty Walking half dollar from 1934, the year Whitman started printing J.K. Post's coin folders.

POST AND HIS CARDBOARD PROGENY

Given his knowledge of stamp collecting, Dick was first put in charge of Whitman's philatelic products. According to Dan Brown, he designed the firm's "United States stamp album and also the covers for various foreign stamp books."[9]

In 1934 J.K. Post of Neenah, Wisconsin, dropped in at Whitman's Racine headquarters with a proposition. Would the company be interested in manufacturing die-cut, 11 by 14–inch cardboard holders for displaying collections of low-denomination American coins? Dick recalled the meeting, not realizing at the time what a game-changer it would be for Whitman and the numismatic world.

"I think he was about 45 to 50, neatly dressed," Dick said of Post. "I'd say he had a certain amount of dignity and a pleasant demeanor. He was all businesslike. As far as our company was concerned, he was fair. He didn't demand anything."[10]

The company's quick decision to take on Post's product was not unusual. "It was a common thing for our business in those days," Dick said. "Somebody would come in with a printing job, and we'd do it. We even made the local scrip for the 1933 bank holiday. We did anything involving paper and ink you can think of doing. His was just another job."

The first board was for Lincoln cents and, as Dick reminisced later, the second was for Indian Head cents, "which were very popular in those days. They were available, and everyone had some in his home. When I was a newsboy back in the teens, half the cents I got in change were Indian cents."[11]

Post coordinated the sale of his boards for about a year, after which he agreed to turn over the distribution to Whitman on a royalty basis. Dick never saw him again. "Heck, more than 50 years have gone by, but I still wonder about him," he said in a 1986 interview. "The general feeling was that it was a novelty he and we took to market, that people would have fun with it. That's all it was. Nobody was thinking about numismatics."

► Western printed emergency scrip for the bank holiday of 1933.

The young salesman was assigned to market the company's new product. Its appeal was universal—collector satisfaction was not limited by age or educational level. The coin boards were destined to be a hit with kids and families.

That said, they were looked upon with some disdain by serious numismatists, but they were a hit with Whitman employees, who were given samples to take home and complete. Even Dick's wife, Marion, threw herself wholeheartedly into the pursuit, perhaps becoming the very first person to fill a coin board.[12] Introduced in the Chicago area, the boards "quickly spread in all directions among a Depression-ridden populace eager for any activity that might take its mind off its troubles," Dick wrote later. "This widespread fad proved to be the curtain-raiser that gave a nudge to present-day coin-collecting popularity."[13]

Dave Harper, numismatic editor for *Numismatic News*, reported in the weekly periodical's February 11, 1984, issue that the first change Whitman implemented in board design (after purchasing the rights from Post in 1939) was a color shift from black to blue. The firm produced the board in "Cellusuede," a flocked paper introduced by manufacturer Jack Sutton the year before. Harper noted that "another change was necessary when that substance was found to have a problem with fading. A switch was made to Kivar®, which [was] washable." (Later, in the 1960s, the *Red Book* was advertised as having a hard cover coated with Pyroxylin, a glossy, water- and soil-resistant nitrocellulose lacquer.[14])

Marketing the improved board was, according to Dick, "a case of growing from the roots. Our early distribution included bootblacks, gas stations, and the like. I had joined Whitman to set up a mail-order department, and this new product became quite a part of it. As dealerships became more established among retail stores, that became our focus, and we soon sought dealers in our advertising."[15]

According to Dick, the board was a primer of sorts. When a beginning collector acquired one, he had something to hold onto as he went "up the ladder."[16] The man, woman, or child on the street was drawn in by this novelty item that was, in itself, "non-numismatic in nature." Remarked Dick, "It was a convenient product offering a neat, orderly arrangement of spaces for coins from daily change, in plain view, and a challenge to form a complete series. Investment was secondary then."[17]

With increased distribution came input from collectors and dealers. "We learned that the coin board size and form was not the answer," said Dick. "It was not easy to store in a drawer. With handling, the coins popped out."[18]

Dick joined the American Numismatic Association in 1940 as Member No. 7947 and attended his first ANA convention, which was held in

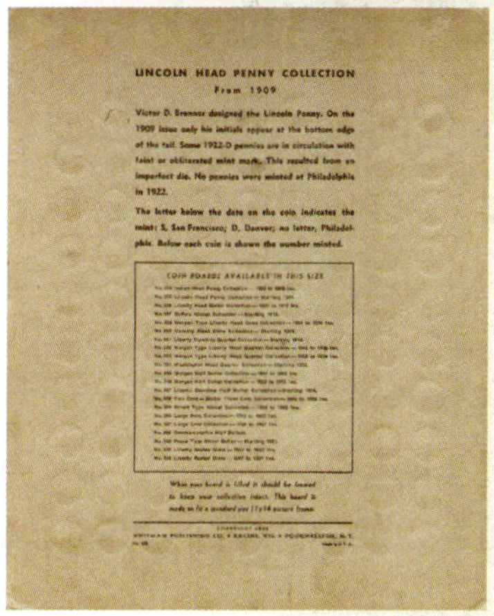

▲ Collectors were encouraged to frame their coin boards for display after completing a collection.

▲ A convention badge from the 1940 American Numismatic Association gathering in Detroit.

596 THE NUMISMATIST, August, 1940

DETROIT BECKONS TO YOU FOR THE LAST WEEK OF AUGUST.

The annual convention of the American Numismatic Association is scheduled for the last week in August. If there is any mode of conveyance for you to secure, by all means obtain it and plan to have the most thrilling, most numismatic and most enjoyable convention week you've ever had.

The Association is large. There will be all kinds of folks at the Convention, and we can guarantee that you'll find the majority of them pleasant and worth while meeting. It's strange that although they come from remote sections of the nation, they speak the same language you do; they even collect the coins you want. In a word, the most remarkable and the most enjoyable factor about a convention is being with people who have a common interest with you.

You can stake your life right now that the exhibits this year will be more spectacular than ever. American coins, foreign coins, paper money, curious moneys, and other allied numismatic material will be shown. Write the committee today for space for your exhibit. Don't plan to see what the other fellow has and leave all of your choice and prize items at home. Bring them. That's numismatics—showing the other fellow what you've been able to capture and thus sharing the real thrills. Don't hoard your treasures. Let them see the light of day at Detroit, and then they will delight you and your friends. All exhibits will be fully insured against loss of any kind.

Detroit. More importantly, that year he put his own spin on the coin board, copyrighting the folder-type album so familiar to today's collectors. The goal was to design something practical, and Dick and the Whitman team had worked on improvements throughout 1938 and 1939.[19] However, the blue color remained. "We wanted . . . something that was pleasing to the eye," explained Dick. "Another [product] had gray, and we didn't think that warm colors like red, yellow or orange were as pleasant. Jewelry or anything metallic, especially coins, seem to be harmonious with blue. We made our decisions on that basis."[20]

As Dick prepared to leave for the Detroit show, he decided to bring along a prototype of the new folder. "I remember one established rare coin dealer who looked at it and said, 'I don't know . . . that's just a novelty.' Of course, I knew that our business was with the beginning collector, and he didn't serve that segment. I showed it to many others, and those who were familiar with the boards told me we were on the right track. But there was no 100-percent acceptance at that time."[21]

"The folder taught the public that there was a systematic way to collect coins."—Clifford Mishler[22]

Convention attendance was small, perhaps 300 dealers and collectors. "It was nice, easy to move around," said Dick. "We weren't crowded. I don't even [recall] a bourse. . . . [The show] did have displays, but I can't remember anyone setting up a table to sell coins." No formal educational programs were presented, though papers were read after the banquet, and people gathered around the displays and talked about them. "I had a purpose in being there," Dick said, "so I had my eyes open and my mouth shut. If anyone was cordial to me, then I'd talk and we'd have a nice conversation. I just wasn't aggressive."[23]

In looking back, Dick believed that true collectors were fairly closeted. "You didn't know who they were. Only the elite called themselves numismatists." Whitman's market was, he determined, "the people who wanted something to do, the same people who worked picture puzzles; things you could work on, pick up and put away and then go back and work on some more. It was a novelty, not a true hobby or craft or anything of that sort."[24]

But, ultimately, the coin board, and later the coin folder, had an undeniable impact on the coin-collecting hobby. "[They] opened the door that led to a career in numismatics for thousands in all walks of life," Dick affirmed. "These people became transformed into hobbyists because of the human instinct to complete something."[25]

Whitman followed up the success of its coin folders with other products, such as removable-page albums; guide books; specialized reference books; cardboard and plastic 2 by 2–inch or Proof set holders; coin tubes, binders, boxes, and envelopes; magnifiers; and check lists. "They were sometimes crude," said Dick, "but were improved year by year and are generally taken for granted today. Without them, it is doubtful that our hobby would exist as we know it."[26]

HOBBY ROADMAPS

As Dick became better known among professional numismatists, many approached him about the need for an objective catalog of wholesale coin prices. "I told them, 'OK fellows, you help me, and I'll go to the company and see what I can do.' It was a good honest group of people who meant what they said, and they followed through with their support," he recalled.[27]

With contributors and coauthors Lee Hewitt and Charles Green, Dick began gathering data in 1941. The following year Whitman introduced the *Handbook of United States Coins*, and Dick, now known by his pen name as R.S. Yeoman, made certain that everyone who attended the banquet at the ANA's 1942 convention in Cincinnati received a copy.

"Probably 90 percent of the coin dealers at the time (just before World War II) were neophytes," Dick later explained. "They wanted to know what they should tell people who came in and couldn't afford $5 catalogs. Remember, the people were collecting 'pennies' and minor denominations, and the only catalogs for that market at the time were put out mainly by the syndicated folks, . . . [who] didn't offer a fair price compared to what they were asking when they turned around and sold the coins."[28]

Those unfair promoters were not particularly respected by the new crop of dealers in the 1940s, said Dick. "Regardless of what we thought then, a lot of the dealers were legitimate, honest people. They were saying, 'We can't give people 20 cents for a coin we're going to sell for $2.'"[29]

Whitman chose the color blue for the *Handbook* not because of the company's popular blue coin folders, but because it "had an association with the motorcar '*Blue Book*,' a familiar trade-in reference list of prices. It

▲ In the 1930s Buffalo nickels and Mercury dimes could be collected from circulation—and gathered together, date by date, in Whitman coin boards no. 357 and 359, respectively.

implied a wholesale list," said Dick. "It was the kind of thing you'd have for people who were selling something back. It seemed appropriate for that."[30] (Interestingly, coauthor Hewitt traveled with a circus band before working in the numismatic realm. His first private publishing venture was *The Circus Blue Book* in 1930, a pocket-sized reference that today is avidly sought by collectors of circus memorabilia.[31])

The *Handbook* was not an immediate hit everywhere in the numismatic community. "Many dealers, now long gone, refused to sell the *Blue Book* because the printed average values were too high for them. Some referred to it as 'the joke book.' It took some years to gain acceptance in the trade, but I feel that our *Handbook*, or any other premium catalog, is an important stabilizing influence on today's numismatic market."[32]

Frank Colletti, author of the 2009 *Guide Book of the Official Red Book of United States Coins*, writes: "The *Blue Book* was a groundbreaking publication for its day, educating consumers and forcing unscrupulous dealers (which, sadly, exist in every market) to act with honesty and accountability. It was instrumental in the process of democratizing the hobby of coin collecting."[33]

Work on the *Handbook*'s companion reference, *A Guide Book of United States Coins*, began not long after the *Blue Book* rolled off the presses,

▲ Yeo had copies of the *Blue Book* distributed to attendees of the 1942 American Numismatic Association banquet. It was the first ANA gathering he attended; this is the official convention medal he received for his participation.

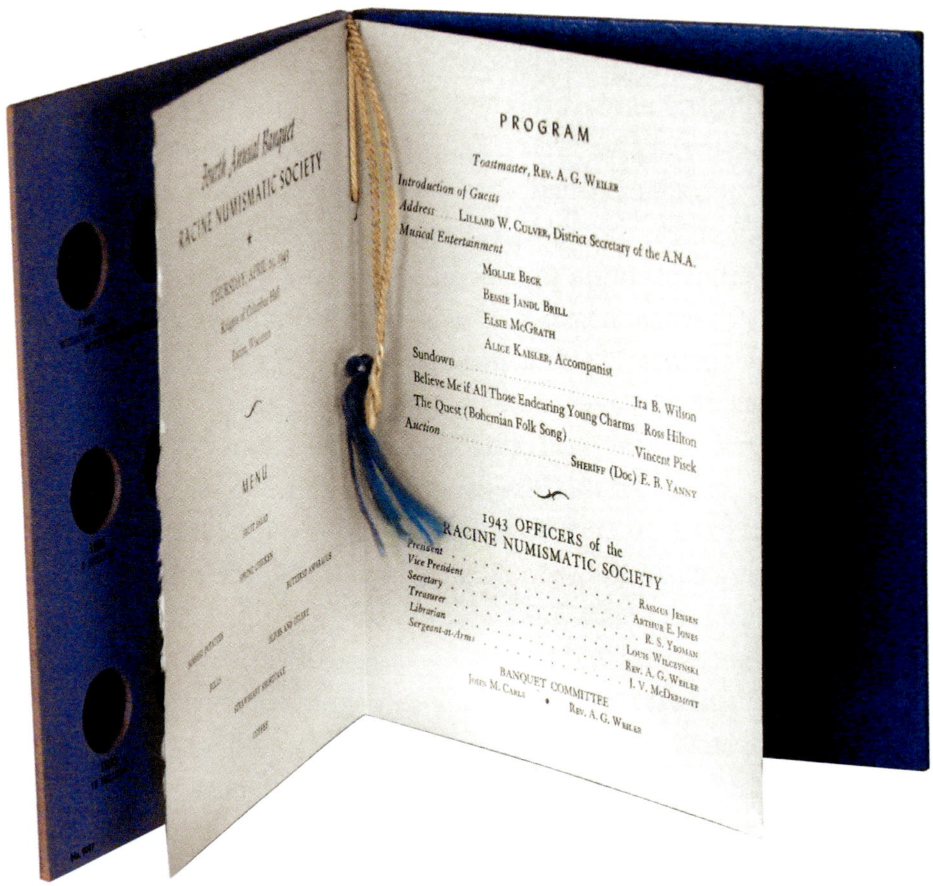

► Whitman blue coin folders were used as menu covers at the 1943 banquet of the Racine Numismatic Society. R.S. Yeoman was listed in the program as the society's secretary.

◀ Whitman editorial staff in the office library, circa 1965: (standing, from left) Lawrence Block, Edward Metzger, Ken Bressett, and Neil Shafer; (seated, from left) Dick Yeoman and office secretary Katherine Andresen.

though wartime paper shortages delayed its publication until 1946. Surprisingly, there was not a great deal of thought behind its signature red cover. Dick felt it was bright and highly visible, adding that he didn't think yellow was quite right.[34] Blue obviously was not a contender, and white would be used later for Whitman's *Current Coins of the World*.

Although sales of the *Blue Book* eclipsed its successor for several years, the *Red Book* steadily gained momentum. "There was a year or two then when we didn't sell all of them," Dick said in 1967,[35] further explaining, "we are not able to release figures on the number of copies . . . that have been sold, but we are not quite up to *Gone with the Wind* and are close behind *Peyton Place*."[36]

Readers never ceased to offer kudos or criticisms when they felt either reference was on the mark or off base. Dick valued his customers' opinions and took them back to the home office. "We had that kind of management. [Whitman was] willing to listen to my reports of [the] needs of coin-folder enthusiasts and invest many thousands of dollars in the price guides." As the face of the *Red Book* and *Blue Book*, Dick readily put his reputation on the line every day. "It's funny," he said, "as quiet a guy as I am, I was so sure of myself."[37]

"I think of the catalogs as a lubricant."
—R.S. Yeoman, 1975

Not all collectors understood the difference between the popular red and blue volumes, and Dick was asked to explain on numerous occasions. "The *Blue Book* gives wholesale prices and is smaller with less information. It is good for the beginner," he said. "But in six months a novice will be ready for the *Red Book*. It gives more grading scales and is a bigger bag of peanuts."[38]

Annual Red Book Survey Made

The Whitman Publishing Company has completed another sampling of collectors' opinions and wishes concerning the *Guide Book of United States Coins*. The results of the survey will serve as a guide for certain changes contemplated for the seventeenth edition of R. S. Yeoman's popular "Red Book."

Questionnaires were sent to thirty-five hundred subscribers, located in all parts of the country, of one of the popular numismatic publications. About one thousand replies were received, although a few did not answer all questions. Besides the answers to questions and comments requested, Whitman considers that the letters and notations received also reveal the attitudes and opinions of typical collectors. Specific questions asked and a summary of replies were as follows:

1. How often do you purchase a copy of the *Guide Book?* Replies indicated that 829 bought it every year, 111 bought it every other year, and 58 less frequently. Some bought more than one book a year.

2. Please give your opinions of the revisions and prices in the sixteenth edition. Almost everyone commented and most replies were favorable, especially to the moving of mintage figures into the listing and pricing by dates. Some constructive criticisms were offered.

3. Do you find the new grading guide helpful? Is it adequate? Of the 963 answers, only 24 replied "no" to the first part of the question. On the second part, most said it was adequate but some thought that it should be expanded to cover all grades of all series.

4. List changes that you feel would improve the usefulness of the *Guide Book.* As expected, replies gave personal opinions which were helpful but could not be tabulated easily and did not show general agreement on specific changes desired.

5. Vote on addition of the following items to the book:

	Yes	No
a. 1942-D over horizontal D nickel	228	595
b. 1955-D over S nickel	364	488
c. 1961-D over horizontal D cent	275	576
d. 1867 over small 67 Indian cent	295	524
e. 1905-O dimes with large and small mint marks	292	535
f. 1916 nickel with double obverse die	237	573
g. 1939 nickel with double obverse die	263	545
h. 1878 silver dollar with reverse of 1879 (slanting arrow feathers)	267	519
i. 1879-S silver dollar with reverse of 1878 (parallel arrow feathers)	266	519
j. 1880-CC silver dollar with reverse of 1878 (parallel arrow feathers)	269	510
k. 1900-O silver dollar with O over CC	371	427

As a result of this voting, Whitman does not plan to add any of these items to the seventeenth edition of the "Red Book."

6. List coins that you feel should be taken out of the book. There were 307 votes to remove the 1892-O micro O half dollar, against 247 votes to retain it. Others mentioned in fewer replies were the 1937-D three legged buffalo nickel, 1955 double die cent, 1942 over 41 dime, 1938-D over S nickel, and the 1945-S micro S dime.

To the seventh question, 588 (60%) indicated membership in some numismatic organization and 384 (40%) replied that they were not. Several of the smaller group indicated an intention to join a coin club or having already applied for membership.

Two specific comments seem to sum up the many received with the questionnaires returned: "The sixteenth edition was far better than the fifteenth; keep up the good work" and "The Guide Book does all that it was designed to do and more."

► In the June 1963 issue of *The Numismatist,* collector responses to a Whitman Publishing *Red Book* survey were published.

In the June–July 1964 issue of Whitman's *Coin Supply Merchandiser*, Dick recalled what a coin dealer had said to him many years before: "We collectors and dealers live in a fish bowl. It's a special buy-and-sell combination which could be called a second-hand business, where the collector knows more about wholesale and retail values than in any other product distribution. There just isn't any secret about what dealers pay for coins." In Dick's mind, a collector should not only have a book listing average prices a dealer would pay for his coins, but also one that would tell him what a dealer would ask for his coins.

To Whitman's retailers, Dick provided a little "formula" that would help them remember:

Blue = Wholesale	Red = Retail
(what a dealer pays)	(what a dealer asks)

He pressed the point with his distributors that collectors needed *both* books, which was why they were equally important on the display rack. For good measure, he offered a few more reasons for stores to carry a good supply of each: "The *Handbook* (*Blue Book*) is the smaller and lower-priced of the two and is recommended for the beginner, who, as a novice, may incidentally have a few coins to identify. The *Guide Book* (*Red Book*) is a standard price catalog of average retail prices and is larger and more costly. This book is for the more advanced and embraces a wider range of values and varieties."

And, just in case retailers failed to get the message, Dick concluded with this advice: "We print them in almost equal quantities, so be sure you show both BLUE and RED in your display at all times, or you'll be missing some important sales."

Whitman was dedicated to ensuring the fledgling *Red Book*'s reliability and accuracy, and Dick worked to build a corps of experts to review coin prices and trends. (Interestingly, he observed that the panelists' geographical location influenced their attitudes about prices and even varieties.) The selection was "as much a cross-section of dealers and experts as we can arrange it," he wrote. "[The prices provided by] some very prominent dealers are averaged with [those of] some active local dealers who may buy or sell lower grades of coins. Some panelists are liberal and interpret trends as being more rapid than others. Some price only high grades, some only low grades. A few panelists have dropped away voluntarily because we do not raise prices high or fast enough, others shy away because we go too fast. Our surveys show both opinions, but a majority accept our conservative policy of reporting," upon which he believed the future of the hobby depended.[39]

▲ The 1965 edition of the *Blue Book* listed the wholesale value of an Uncirculated 1881-CC Morgan silver dollar as $25. The 1965 *Red Book* pegged its average retail price at $50.

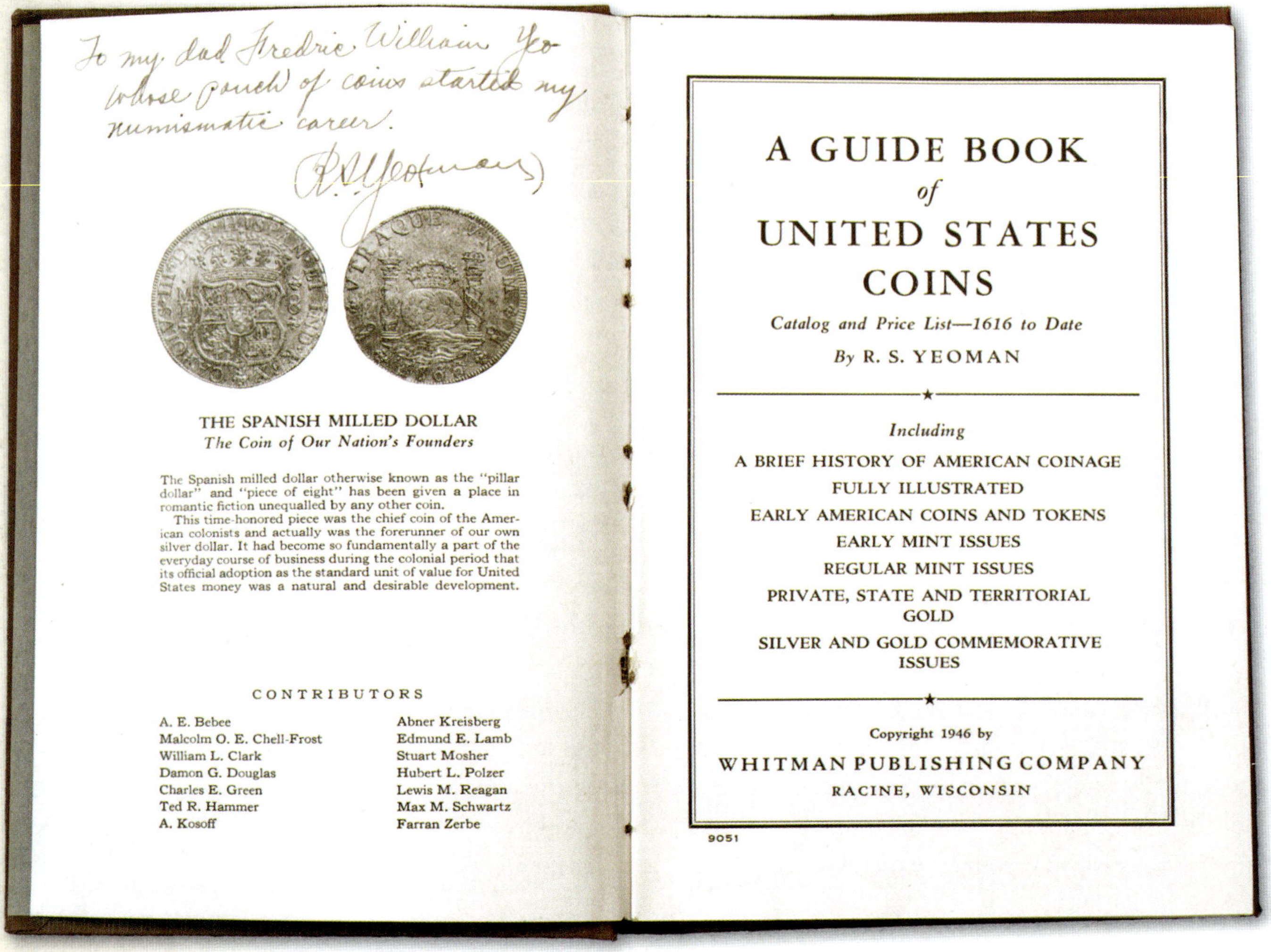

To my dad Fredric William Yeo
whose pouch of coins started my
numismatic career.
R.S. Yeo(man)

THE SPANISH MILLED DOLLAR
The Coin of Our Nation's Founders

The Spanish milled dollar otherwise known as the "pillar dollar" and "piece of eight" has been given a place in romantic fiction unequalled by any other coin.

This time-honored piece was the chief coin of the American colonists and actually was the forerunner of our own silver dollar. It had become so fundamentally a part of the everyday course of business during the colonial period that its official adoption as the standard unit of value for United States money was a natural and desirable development.

CONTRIBUTORS

A. E. Bebee
Malcolm O. E. Chell-Frost
William L. Clark
Damon G. Douglas
Charles E. Green
Ted R. Hammer
A. Kosoff
Abner Kreisberg
Edmund E. Lamb
Stuart Mosher
Hubert L. Polzer
Lewis M. Reagan
Max M. Schwartz
Farran Zerbe

A GUIDE BOOK
of
UNITED STATES
COINS

Catalog and Price List—1616 to Date

By R. S. YEOMAN

Including

A BRIEF HISTORY OF AMERICAN COINAGE
FULLY ILLUSTRATED
EARLY AMERICAN COINS AND TOKENS
EARLY MINT ISSUES
REGULAR MINT ISSUES
PRIVATE, STATE AND TERRITORIAL GOLD
SILVER AND GOLD COMMEMORATIVE ISSUES

Copyright 1946 by
WHITMAN PUBLISHING COMPANY
RACINE, WISCONSIN

9051

▲ **The Western Archives includes a first-edition copy of the *Red Book* inscribed by the author to his father, Frederic. Note it was signed *R.S. Yeo(man)*.**

As Dick later recalled, the eclectic mix of panelists occasionally fell under scrutiny:

> A Midwestern mail-order man, not too long in the commercial ranks, remarked as I paused at his bourse table that the *Guide Book* was obviously dominated by only the "Big Boys." He named a few . . . [and] I explained that he had failed to notice twenty or so other, less-prominent dealers, but he wasn't convinced. About a month later, I visited one of the large coin emporiums in New York, and was challenged by one of the partners for having nothing but a bunch of unknowns on the *Red Book* panel. So, you see, it's all a matter of whose yard you play in.[40]

In 1975 Dick further elaborated on the composition of his panel: "Publishers, such as Whitman-Western, are not supporting an arrogant, cigar-puffing gang of price-fixers; we don't have anything like the London gold market with its daily price-fixing. Nor do we have any sort of market specialists who might buy specimens to hold and stabilize the prices from day to day, such as is done in the New York and American stock markets. We collectors ought to always be ready and willing to explain to any non-collector what is right about our hobby."[41]

Year after year, the *Red Book* evolved and its popularity grew. Dick and the rest of the Whitman crew marked important milestones with appropriate fanfare.

In 1972 the essential guide celebrated its 25th anniversary. Before an audience of Florida collectors, Dick shared highlights of the "silver" edition, noting that "it's well-nigh impossible to be objective about one's own offspring. A less-involved individual could do a better job than I of reciting the merits and achievements of the catalog. He would be spared an egotism which I am bound to feel in these few uneasy moments which you have given me on this platform." Then, with great humor and modesty, he proceeded to "humanize an object which is basically only paper and ink":

> The latest edition has reached a milestone of time and numbers, for it has achieved a longevity of 25 editions, and the presses have ground out over ten million total copies. It has attained, and I hope retained, a reasonable degree of respectability and acceptance during the most exciting quarter century in the long history of numismatics. If this be egotism, make the most of it. [At the] back of the actual book, as though it were a concealed motor—a sort of quiet power source—are the many individual contributors, experts, professionals, and indeed the production personnel at Western Publishing Co., and their guiding editorial staff. They have earned the greater share of whatever commendation and endorsement the *Red Book* has accomplished. While I have great personal pride in having been identified with this popular volume, I consider my presence here as a spokesman for this dedicated group, and perhaps a symbol of the total effort and attitude of both the professional and the collector. Beyond these premises I do not intend to go. I will leave extravagant phrases to others, if they are to be expressed at all.[42]

The red cover of the 25th anniversary edition was printed in silver ink, as opposed to the standard gold. "[It] is one of only a few remaining numismatic items that can be termed 'silver' today," Dick joked. "It's getting a little expensive to give a silver wedding anniversary present in the form of coins. Many of you can recall the custom of decorating a cardboard panel with silver dollars for presentation to the celebrating couple. These coins

▲ **In 1971, when the 1972 edition of the *Red Book* was released, a collector could buy an Uncirculated 1828 half cent for $65.**

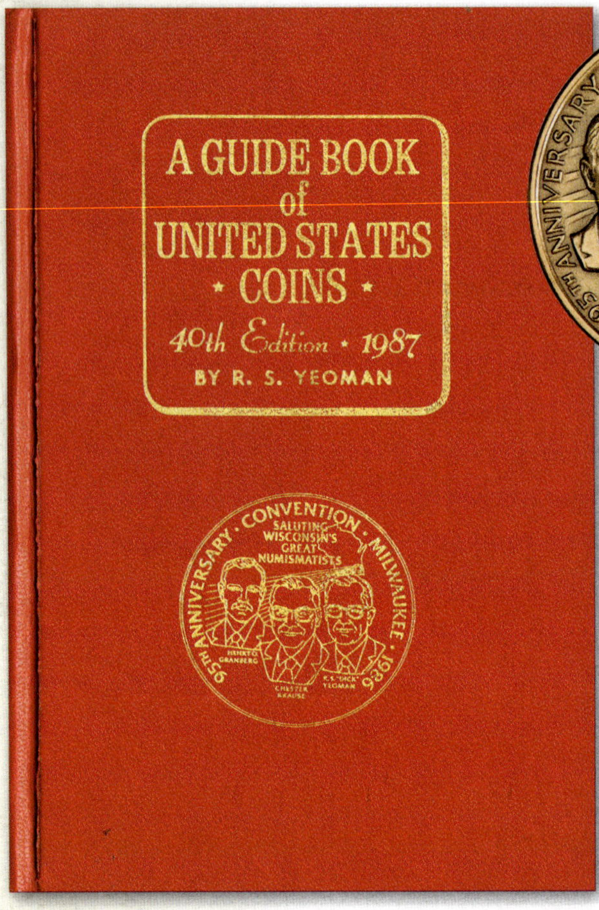

▲ A medal was issued to celebrate the ANA's 95th anniversary. Jeff Reichenberger, a member of Numismatists of Wisconsin, recalled Chester Krause's reaction to its design: "Chet handed me a medal and promptly stated, 'I don't know what the hell I was on there for. Dick Yeo should have been the only one on the medal. He did a lot more for numismatics than Granberg or I ever did.'" Krause's words reflect his own humility as well as his admiration of Yeoman.

▲ The American Numismatic Association 95th Anniversary special edition of the 1987 *Red Book*. Pictured alongside R.S. Yeoman were two more of "Wisconsin's Great Numismatists." Chester Krause (1923–2016) in 1952 had founded *Numismatic News*, the beginning of an antiques-and-collectibles publishing empire. Henry O. Granberg (1860–1946) was a member of the U.S. Assay Commission under President Woodrow Wilson, and a president of the ANA. He was instrumental in getting the Association chartered by Congress.

might come out of the local bank on a Wednesday and be redeposited at the teller's window the following Monday. Today, banks are no help at all for such anniversaries. (The coin dealer has become the only reliable source for proper gifts for such occasions.) My wife and I got safely past our silver wedding day, so we will keep our sights on our Golden Anniversary and hope we have enough friends surviving to see that we receive at least some little, old, common-date Saint-Gaudens $20 gold."[43]

The ANA held its 95th Anniversary Convention in 1986 in Milwaukee, essentially in Whitman's back yard. To mark the occasion and to pay tribute to famous Wisconsin numismatists, a collectible edition of the 1987 *Red Book* was produced, the first of its kind. The cover bore the inscription "95th Anniversary Convention Milwaukee 1986," with the names and likenesses of Henry O. Granberg (1860–1948), Chester Krause, and R.S. Yeoman above the legend "Saluting Wisconsin's Great Numismatists." An estimated 500 copies were printed and presented as souvenirs exclusively to those who attended the convention banquet.[44]

Dick never ceased to believe in the brotherhood of the numismatic community, and the role Whitman's key references played in it. "The dealer needs the collector, and the collector would be lost without the professional numismatist. They both need catalogs such as the *Blue Book* and *Red Book* to make a fair and available coin market."[45]

EXPLORING THE WORLD

In the years after World War II, Dick observed a growing interest in foreign coins as a hobby pursuit. Veterans often returned home with coinage accumulated during their overseas service, generating a natural curiosity about different cultures and currencies. Dick encouraged collectors of U.S. coins who had "reached a point of waning interest" to bring out the miscellaneous world specimens they had set aside and start a new collection. "There are literally thousands of coins of other nations obtainable at little cost—and the whole wide world to choose from."

"We are a great fraternity, a common-purpose group totaling millions. Keeping our hobby and science healthy and progressive requires a positive attitude and personal involvement. I charge each of you with the responsibility of keeping it that way." —R.S. Yeoman, circa 1971

▲ **Collectors needed handy references for identifying their non-U.S. coins.**

At the time, standard references for collectors of world coins were few and far between. Among the relevant books in a list of recommended reading, compiled by Dick in 1951, were J.W. Scott's *Silver and Gold Coins of the World* and *Copper and Nickel Coins of the World* (published in 1906, with reprints in 1913 and 1917), followed decades later by Wayte Raymond's *Coins of the World: 20th Century* (1945) and *Coins of the World: 19th Century* (1947). It became obvious that Whitman needed to produce a reference of its own, and work began in the early 1950s to organize a database, perfect a numbering system, and acquire coin images. "[When we started], the only catalog of any importance . . . was Wayte Raymond's [*Coins of the World*]," Dick stated in a 1987 interview. "[Raymond] had the American Numismatic Society take the photos for him, but he didn't own the photos. He just paid them for the prints, because they were photographing their own coins."[46]

▲ **Military members returning from overseas often brought coins back from their service. Yeoman encouraged them to jump into coin collecting.**

Books to Buy or Borrow

by Glenn Smedley (1951)

R.S. Yeoman, the well-known editor of several coin books and an associate of a firm which publishes others, gave a talk before the Chicago Coin Club on December 12, 1951, on this subject. He approached the problem of choosing books in this manner. "If my house was on fire and I had time to save just twenty-five books from my numismatic library, which twenty-five would I choose?" The list of twenty-five books which he handed out at the close of his talk has been this collector's guide ever since. To bring it up to date, a few titles have been replaced by those of later publications, and a few others have been added because I have found them to be especially helpful—including two which Mr. Yeoman edited and was too modest to include in his list.

Title	Author	Date
Early Coins of America	Sylvester Sage Crosby	1875
The State Coinages of New England	Henry C. Miller and Hillyer Ryder	1920
The United States Half Cents	Ebenezer Gilbert	1916
Early American Cents, 1793–1814	Dr. William H. Sheldon	1949
United States Copper Cents, 1814–1857	Howard R. Newcomb	1944
United States Half Dimes	D.W. Valentine	1931
United States Dimes	Abe Kosoff	1945
Type Table of U.S. Dollars, Half Dollars and Quarter Dollars	Capt. John W. Haseltine	1881
Early Quarter Dollars 1796–1838	A. W. Browning	1925
A Register of Half Dollar Die Varieties and Sub-Varieties	M.L. Beistle	1929
U.S. Pattern Trial & Experimental Pieces	Edgar H. Adams and William Woodin	1913
Fractional Money	Neil Carothers	1930
History of American Coinage	David K. Watson	1899
A History of Currency in the United States	A. Barton Hepburn	1915
U.S. Paper Money: Old Series	Dr. F.A. Limpert	1948
Private Gold Coinage of California	Edgar H. Adams	1913
California Gold Quarters, Halves & Dollars	Ed M. Lee	1932
Silver and Gold Coins of the World	J.W. Scott	1913
Copper and Nickel Coins of the World	J.W. Scott	1913
Coins of the World: 19th Century	Wayte Raymond	1947
Coins of the World: 20th Century	Wayte Raymond	1945
Historia Numorum	Barclay V. Head	1887
Roman Coins	Harold Mattingly	1928
Dictionary of Numismatic Names	Albert R. Frey	1947
Catalog of the Jenks Collection	Henry Chapman	1921

Photographs were a challenge for Whitman as well, although the ANS provided as much assistance as it could. "Common coins were the hardest ones to locate," said Dick, and the process was frustrating. "I got discouraged regularly every 30 days on that one."

Working out the bugs in the numbering system was just as vexing. "I wasn't going to sit down and just copy Wayte Raymond's numbers, . . . [but] when you're doing a numismatic project, you sometimes have to use work from other peoples' research. You can't get away from that. So even though I made my own numbering system, it was based on a reversal of his. He started out with the higher denominations from each country, and I started out with the lower denominations. Once in a while we had the same number, because we would cross in the middle."[47]

R.S. Yeoman's *Catalog of Modern World Coins* (the "Brown Book") debuted in 1957. According to the April 1957 issue of *The Numismatist*:

> This long-awaited work consists of 512 pages, has hundreds of illustrations and is priced at $4.00. The period covered is roughly the last 100 years, with coins listed chronologically and grouped by metallic content, design and denomination. Estimated values are shown for each type and denomination. Three years have been spent in compiling the book and dozens of experts have contributed their time and knowledge to make it authentic.

▲ Yeoman learned that common world coins were the hardest to find images of. It wasn't worth a dealer's time to photograph them for individual sale.

◀ Whitman capitalized on the burgeoning interest in world numismatics by releasing Yeoman's new, improved volumes of catalogs previously attempted by other authors.

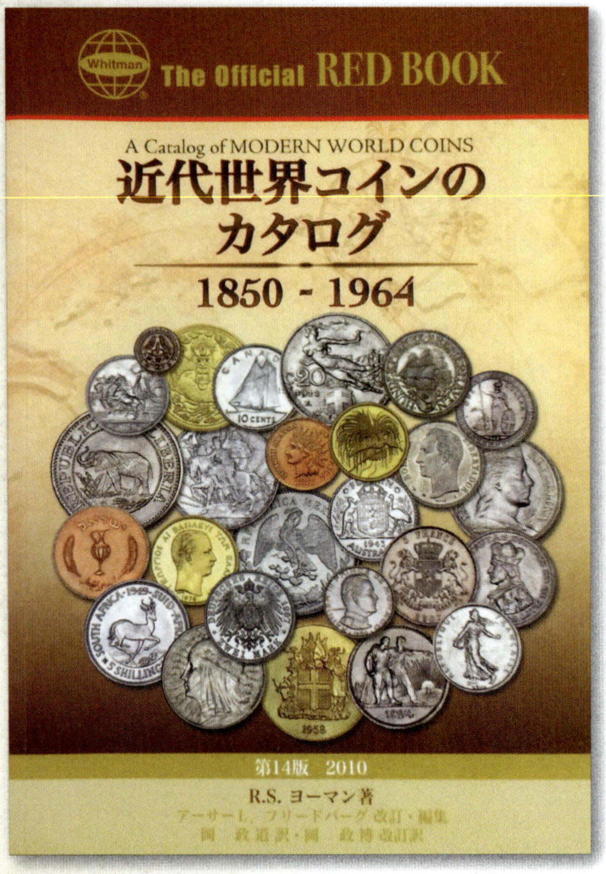

▲ The *Catalog of Modern World Coins* has even been published in Japanese-language editions.

However, the divergent numbering systems caused some confusion among experienced collectors. "They wanted to know why they should buy our book when they had been using Wayte Raymond numbers," Dick recalled. "I told them not to bother buying both, that they should just stay with Wayte Raymond. [I hoped] that the new collectors would start with my book. That proved to be true."[48]

Unfortunately, Dick's frustrations concerning the catalog did not end with its publication. In 1958 Whitman received correspondence from attorneys representing Wayte Raymond's widow, Olga, who claimed copyright infringement with regard to *A Catalog of Modern World Coins*. In a July 14, 1958, interoffice memo, Whitman's rights and royalties lawyer, Lloyd Smith, refuted the charge and emphasized that Whitman's published references to the Raymond catalog were within the bounds of fair use.

Smith suggested that Dick accompany him to New York to meet Mrs. Raymond and show that "he didn't have horns on his head." They spoke in her lawyer's office for "about an hour, and everything went well," Dick reported. The case was settled to the satisfaction of all parties.

"I worried about things like that," he later admitted. He felt strongly that publishers in the numismatic field should work together amicably. "If there is a disagreement, I think it should be kept quiet and behind the scenes. That's why I'm so pleased that presently [in the 1980s] all the elements get along with one another. That's very satisfying to me."[49]

Whitman has published more than a dozen editions of *A Catalog of Modern World Coins* and seven editions of *Current Coins of the World*, the latest volumes of which were released in 2021 and 1976, respectively. The Coin & Currency Institute (CCI), then based in Clifton, New Jersey, and operated by Arthur and Ira Friedberg (the sons of numismatist, author, cataloger, and publisher Robert Friedberg), approached Whitman Hobby Products in the early 1980s about acquiring a license to publish the two titles. Whitman agreed, and CCI introduced its revision of *Modern World Coins* in 1984 and *Current Coins of the World* in 1988.

Says Arthur Friedberg, "I always enjoyed using those two books, particularly *Modern World Coins*, which covers 1850 to 1964. This is the period where you find the greatest concentration of collecting interest for world coins. With Krause Publications' introduction of its standard catalog in the early 1970s, Whitman seemed to lose interest in the world-coin field.

However, we felt there was still a market for a reasonably priced book that gave collectors all the information they needed in a more concise and portable format. For instance, we saw no need to list individually the price for every date of a coin type when, in fact, the prices for most dates were the same. Also, we intended to market the book outside the numismatic community, and had considerable success selling it to libraries and book stores (which were abundant at the time)."[50]

▲ A Carver/Washington commemorative half dollar minted in 1953, the year Dick Yeoman became general manager of Whitman's hobby department.

MARKETING STRATEGIES

Throughout his Whitman employment, Dick was actively involved in the promotion of the company's products, even after he left the sales department to become general manager of the hobby department in 1953; then vice president and general manager of the Coin Supply Division; and a member of the board of directors in February 1963. It was not unusual for him and other Whitman staff to drop by unannounced on retail outlets to check on product displays. In 1965 Dick expressed his disappointment in a message to wholesalers (or "jobbers"):[51]

> The most discouraging experience in our travels is to go into a store with adequate display space and find that the best sellers in the Whitman line are missing. This is perhaps the greatest sales waste in the merchandising of our products.
>
> Whitman coin supplies cannot be compared to flour, wax, soap, etc. It is a specialized line of leisure-time products calling for concentrated service.
>
> Jobbers of Whitman products are selected for their knowledge of the coin market and for their merchandising experience and know-how. It is constant attention to the needs of the dealer that produces profits. These are the profits that keep your dealers satisfied with the Whitman Coin Supply Line. Profits are generated by turnover and "Maximum Turnover Comes Only from Constant InStore Service."
>
> The peddler's slogan, "You can't do business from an empty wagon," is as true today as it was a century ago. It is the responsibility of every Whitman jobber to keep Whitman Coin Supply displays filled and in stock at all times.

▶ Whitman's frameable display cards, like "American Heritage" and "Presidential American Coin Collection," were favored by beginning collectors.

Certainly Whitman wanted its dealers to make good, and it provided them a variety of tools to help ensure their success.

The bimonthly *Whitman Coin Supply Merchandiser* offered valuable information about market trends, surveys, new products, special selling features, advertising, and store displays. In addition, the company developed a variety of sales aids for retailers:

> Whitman makes available an extensive selection of advertising mats in standard one and two column widths. These can be ideally used for newspaper advertisements, dealer catalogs, periodicals and circulars (order from Whitman Coin Supply Division). Reprints of Whitman national advertisements with a space for dealer imprint may be purchased for a nominal fee. Experienced Whit-

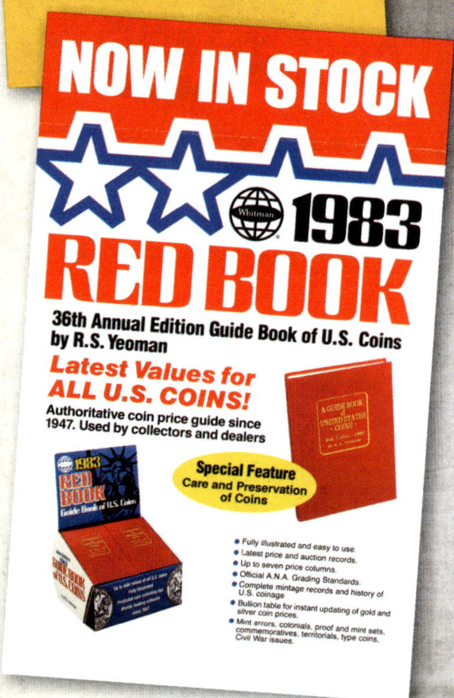

▶ A store display for an assortment of Whitman books, albums, and folders, including the 1965 *Red Book* and the latest *Catalog of Modern World Coins.*

A GUIDE BOOK OF U.S. COINS

by R.S. YEOMAN

1988 RED BOOK

41ST EDITION

A complete, easy-to-use retail guide for all U.S. Coins 1616 to present featuring:

- Latest values for ALL U.S. coins.
- Latest price and auction records.
- Detailed photographs for easy identification and grading.
- Up to seven price columns.
- Official A.N.A. Grading Standards.
- Complete mintage records and history of U.S. Coinage.
- Bullion table for instant updating of gold and silver coin prices.
- Mint errors, colonials, proof and mint sets, commemoratives, territorials, type coins, Civil War issues.

Convenient self-shipper display is easy to set up and holds 12 books for attractive presentation to customers.

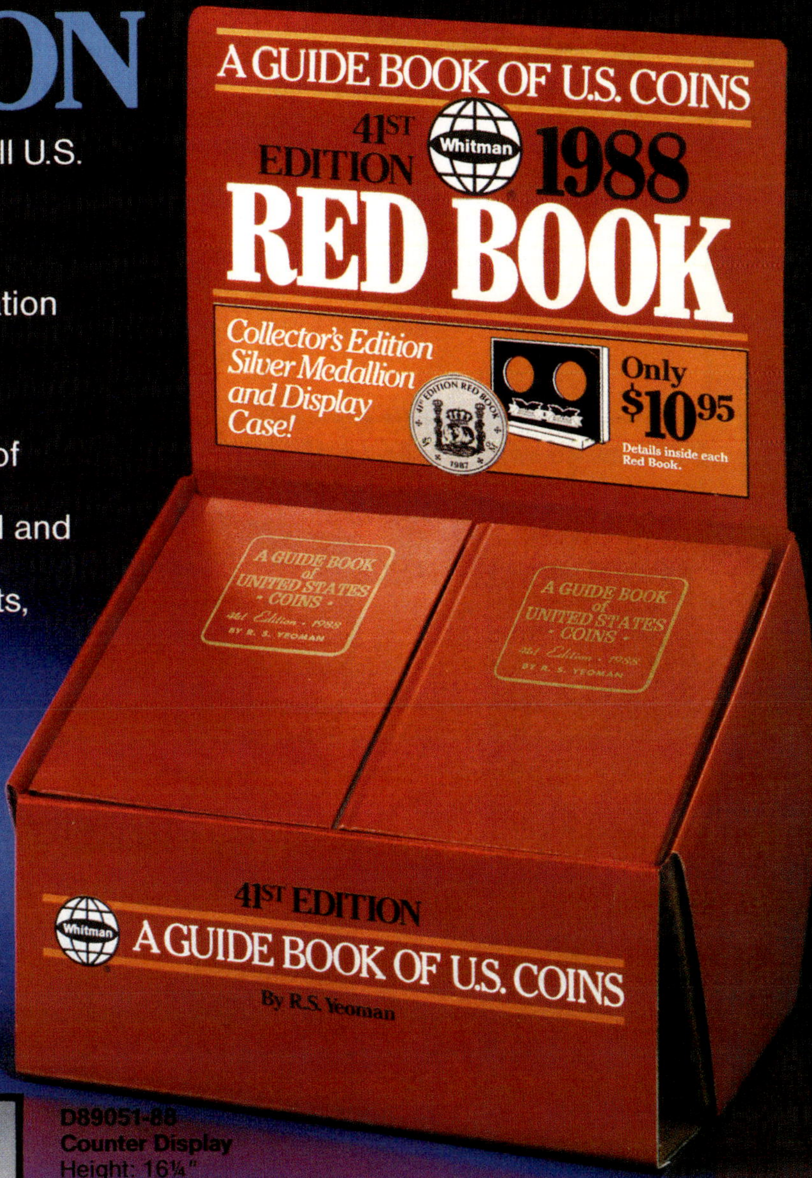

D89051-88
Counter Display
Height: 16¼"
Width: 11"
Depth: 9¼"

Special Consumer Offer

An exclusively designed and struck Red Book Collector's Edition Silver Medallion in an attractive display case. Details inside each book.

▲ **Designed to appeal to young collectors, "Current Issues" coin folders featured covers printed in different colors, depending on denomination.**

▲ **Eva Adams (seen here in a 1967 U.S. Assay Commission portrait by Frank Gasparro) was director of the United States Mint from 1961 to 1969, a time of significant changes in the hobby.**

> man jobbers assist you in ordering practical quantities and assortment, plus supplying you with window streamers and posters for attractive displays. Your jobber also offers you, free of cost, the Whitman Coin Check List. The check list is most valuable to you, creates a great amount of good will with customers, and stimulates sales. In addition, your jobber can help you select the tailor-made Eldon display racks, the efficient, up-to-date way to stock, display and sell Whitman products.[52]

Retailers were reminded of the "constant flow of new products," and indeed Whitman added more than 50 items to its line of merchandise in one year alone. "Whether it is the creation of a completely new concept of displaying and protecting a coin collection, such as the Bookshelf Coin Albums, or the [yearly edition] of the popular *Red Book* . . . there is always an enthusiastic response from your customers when you say: 'NEW from WHITMAN!'"

The year 1965 was marked by a period of retrenchment in the numismatic community, following some "hastily contrived" actions by the United States Mint that affected Whitman's bottom line and the health of the hobby. Around that time, Dick set the stage in a message ostensibly delivered to the company's sales force:[53]

> In 1964 the coin collecting market reached a peak never before enjoyed by dealers, publishers and manufacturers. A steady upward trend had been noticeable for at least two previous years, but the death of President Kennedy and the immediate issue of a half dollar with his likeness gave the hobby a great boost. Proof sets (which included the Kennedy half) and a worldwide surge of demand for anything smacking of Kennedy, by momentum alone, brought in thousands of new devotees to the ranks. Additionally silver supplies had been dwindling, and the stock of about 200,000,000 silver dollars was being withdrawn against silver certificates. Most of these coins had languished in vaults since the nineteenth century. Release of these great hoards over so short a period had a strong effect on any coin accessory [that] accommodated silver dollars. Many of these newly freed dollars changed hands rapidly during a short period.
>
> When the Treasury Department was faced with an unrelated coin shortage, [it] pointed [a] finger at coin [collectors]. Today, mint officials recognize the fact that the coin shortage was generated by a sustained high-level

business boom and inability of mints to cope with the increased demand for coins. The vanishing of [the] Kennedy [half dollars, as well as other halves] and silver dollars, from circulation is now clearly revealed as a global, free-world demand. The Kennedy souvenir market on the one hand and a belated discovery that silver had become a strategic metal in short supply on the other combined to create a crisis in coins for change in the marketplace. The coin collector, lacking a strong lobby in Washington, suffered a "Whipping Boy" image at the hands of the vending-machine and banking industries, to name only two.

For decades a letter designating the mint of origin had appeared on the coins' reverses, but in an effort to discourage hoarding, the Mint removed these marks in 1965. (They were restored and placed on obverses in 1968.) In the minds of embattled numismatists, contemporary American coinage had been stripped of its mintmarks, Proof sets, and prestige. Whitman's coin division took steps to counteract these hurtful "minus factors":

> Included are appointment of five regional field representatives, of which three are presently engaged. Standard coin reference books are nearing completion, which are expected to add impetus to our book line.[54] Sales tests are being [conducted] with a regional chain for direct service from Racine through regular Whitman salesmen. Incentives and promotional stimulants are in force. Perhaps our most hopeful program is the new line for stamp collectors to be introduced in May 1966.
>
> From the government, we already have a bright spot [with] a change to the date 1965 and are reasonably certain to get 1966 dates later this year. The new clad coins are reaching circulation but are not advertised in any coin publication, resulting from a cooperative agreement between Treasury officials and numismatic publishers. We expect proof sets late this year or early next year, and mint marks on branch-mint coins as well. A general return to normal relations between the Treasury and numismatics is expected this year.
>
> Our sales quota is tied uncertainly to such unknown factors, but our efforts nevertheless will be redoubled toward a better sales total for 1966 than for 1965.[55]

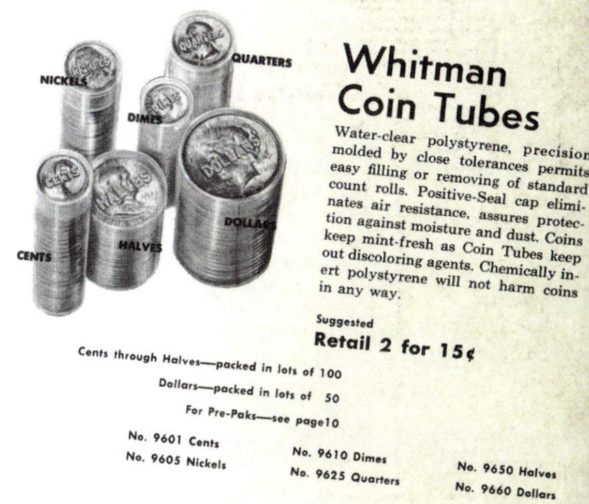

Here are 14 ways to display sell profit MORE in 1965!

Get more from your Floor Space...
Install a PROFITABLE, HIGH TURNOVER
WHITMAN COIN DEPARTMENT

Choose from 14 New custom designed Coin Department Display Units

No. 90-C Wood Floor Display — Sells approximately $450 retail
Ask your jobber or write directly to Badger Wood Products

MEMO

from R. S. Yeoman on the Importance of Good Display

For some time, Whitman has been working with experienced rack manufacturers. They have come up with some attractive and practical fixtures tailored to the Whitman Coin Supply line.

Two different companies have designed the racks shown in this brochure: Badger Wood Products and Keystone Metal Products. You will find their addresses on the back page. Write directly to them for complete information, together with prices.

Proper display of Whitman coin supplies is so important and obvious as to need no fancy persuasive word pictures. Instead we show you photos of what is available so that enterprising jobbers and dealers can procure the utmost in display effectiveness for any store location.

Sell Tested! Proven to Produce 18.1% *More Business!*

▲ Whitman gave its retailers the tools they needed to effectively market the company's products.

Dick also had a sense that some collectors, specifically the junior set, were being left behind numismatically. Since the 1940s he had served as a Boy Scout "Coin Collecting" merit badge counselor in the Racine area, an activity he found immensely rewarding. Whitman produced a "Coin Collecting Starter Set," which included an informative softcover reference, *Coins: Questions and Answers*; a pocket-size checklist and record book; two coin folders; two coin tubes; fifteen coin mounts; and a magnifier. (Similar sets subsequently were created and marketed under different names.) Whitman also marketed a kit for Boy Scouts working to complete the requirements for the "Coin Collecting" merit badge. In addition to standard supplies, the set contained a bag of 50 foreign coins and a booklet I created to guide Scouts in their quest.

▲ The Boy Scouts of America merit badge for coin collecting.

In the mid-1960s Dick thought that Whitman should do even more to encourage and involve young collectors:

> Recently I have been more than a little dismayed at the increasing difficulty these youngsters are having in locating the scarce mint marks of many dates of cents, nickels, dimes and quarters. They really leave no purse unturned to find needed coins for their folders, and to buy some of the scarce dates puts a painful strain on their weekly allowances. I observe that they have at least one coin for almost any year, but in many instances cannot locate more than one coin per year. For example, they may find a 1929 cent of the Philadelphia mint, but have no luck coming across a cent of that year struck in Denver or San Francisco . . .
>
> All of us—manufacturers, jobbers, and dealers—have a real stake in the future of coin collecting. The continuation of the hobby, as we know it, must weigh heavily on low cost and simplicity of the product, plus the very important element—minimum cost of filling in the sets of coins. If our Lincoln cents, Jefferson nickels, Roosevelt dimes and Washington quarters are giving our novices trouble in some mint mark varieties, perhaps we ought to reduce the obstacles that could easily discourage many at the start.
>
> We think we have solved the problem very nicely. In a few weeks, we plan to have four new coin folders on the market for cents, nickels, dimes and quarters which will be known as One-a-Year folders. As the name indicates, a collector need have only one coin (any mint) for a single year. Of course, after he fills his One-a-Year folders, no one could restrain him from graduating to the regular

▲ Young collectors might get frustrated trying to fill every hole in a coin folder using pocket change. Yeoman used the Wheat cents of 1929 as an example: it was easy enough to find one from Philadelphia, but more challenging to find Denver and San Francisco.

> folders and albums. All a boy or girl expects is a fighting chance to complete something, and if he stays with it and makes the grade on the first round without too much pain, he will probably be a collector for life. We are all for that, I'm sure.
>
> The One-a-Year folders will become a part of the regular 35-cent Blue Line in mid-January 1964.

U.S. ASSAY COMMISSION

One of the most meaningful moments in Dick Yeoman's life was his 1964 appointment by President Lyndon B. Johnson to the U.S. Assay Commission, which was charged with testing the quality of the nation's coinage. At the time Commission members were recommended by government officials, usually senators or congressmen; often the candidates' mayors, state representatives, or governors provided the introduction.

Recommendations were forwarded to the president, who, with input from the Mint director, chose the commission members. "That was appropriate because, after all, Eva Adams, Mary Brooks and all the rest of [the directors] had attended conventions and met a lot of people one-on-one," Dick remarked decades later. "[They] knew what they stood for, and if they were the sort of people who should be on the commission. They even had [the] FBI check on each nominee."

Dick was recommended three times before he was selected. "I've never had first-time luck in these things. I ran three times for the board of governors of the American Numismatic Association, too," he said.[56]

On February 6, 1964, Dick received a telegram from President Johnson:

> Telefax—WESTERN UNION—Telefax
> THE WHITE HOUSE WASHINGTON DC
> 1964 FEB 6 PM 2 38
> RICHARD S YEOMAN
> 1220 MOUND AVE RACINE WIS
> I SHALL SHORTLY SIGN YOUR COMMISSION APPOINTING YOU A MEMBER OF THE ANNUAL ASSAY COMMISSION.
> IT GIVES ME A GREAT DEAL OF PLEASURE TO DO THIS AND I WANT AT THE SAME TIME TO SEND YOU THIS MESSAGE TO TELL YOU HOW DELIGHTED I AM THAT YOU ARE GOING TO BE ABLE TO SERVE.
> LYNDON B. JOHNSON

President Lyndon B. Johnson in March 1964, a month after he appointed R.S. Yeoman to the U.S. Assay Commission.

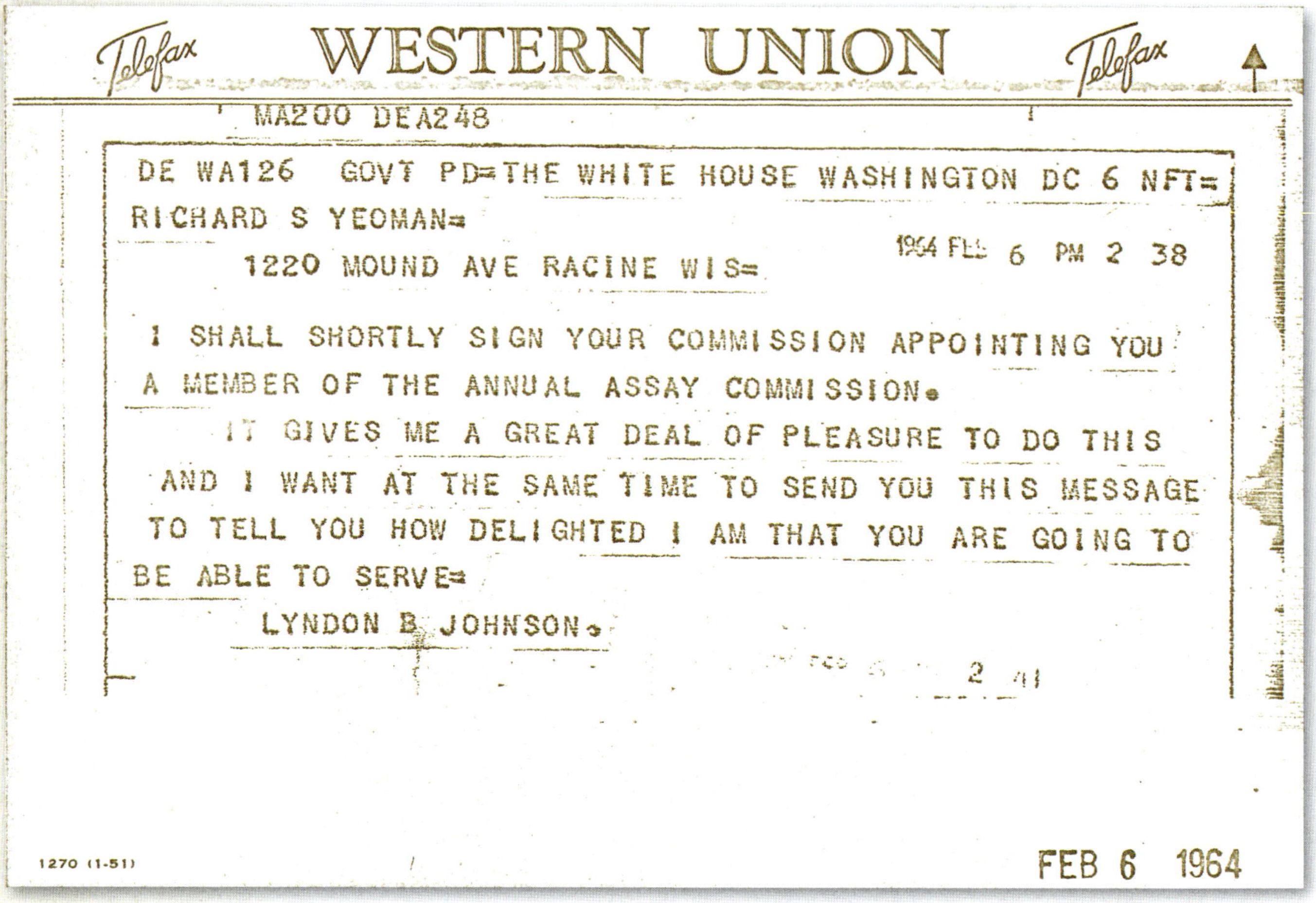
WESTERN UNION

Telefax Telefax

MA200 DEA248

DE WA126 GOVT PD=THE WHITE HOUSE WASHINGTON DC 6 NFT=

RICHARD S YEOMAN=

1220 MOUND AVE RACINE WIS= 1964 FEB 6 PM 2 38

I SHALL SHORTLY SIGN YOUR COMMISSION APPOINTING YOU A MEMBER OF THE ANNUAL ASSAY COMMISSION.

IT GIVES ME A GREAT DEAL OF PLEASURE TO DO THIS AND I WANT AT THE SAME TIME TO SEND YOU THIS MESSAGE TO TELL YOU HOW DELIGHTED I AM THAT YOU ARE GOING TO BE ABLE TO SERVE=

LYNDON B JOHNSON.

1270 (1-51) FEB 6 1964

On February 12, 1964, Dick and his 23 fellow appointees, plus three ex-officio commission members—Comptroller of the Currency James J. Saxon, U.S. Assay Office (New York) Assayer Paul J. Maguire, and Federal Judge Thomas J. Clary—met at the Philadelphia Mint at 9 a.m. in the Assay Room to assay, weigh, and count the first Kennedy half dollars. Also present were Mint Director Eva Adams, Assistant Mint Director Frederick Tate, Denver Mint Superintendent Fern Miller, Philadelphia Elected Chairman Michael Sura, and technical assistant / secretary Sidney F. Carwile.[57]

"[Eva Adams was in charge [of the meeting], and of course the first thing we had to do was elect a chairman," Dick said. "I was not in any way ready to be elected chairman, but I was."

Admittedly a little flustered, he walked to the front of the room and asked, "What do I do?" A Mint official advised Dick to call a recess so he could organize his thoughts. After a ten-minute break, Dick announced that the first priority was to appoint committee chairmen. "We went off to the side, and right away one of the members said, 'I want to be chairman of assay.' Another wanted to be chairman of counting, and someone else wanted to chair the weighing. Those were the three committees we had."

Dick assigned commission members to the committees, gave them instructions, and released them to go about their business. "As chairman, I had nothing to do," he said, so Mr. Carwile, the Mint Bureau's technical man, said, 'I'm going to take you up to the studio where the artists are,' and that's where I spent an interesting interval until the committees [came] back to report."[58]

Dick was fascinated by the process and found the count to be absolutely correct, the latter determined by a "random choice of a table-full of sealed envelopes," he said. "From every 10,000 precious-metal coins made, one was put in [an] envelope each day. The assay went well—no coin was ever below .900 fine and was above sometimes."[59]

At a banquet held that evening in the Tecumseh Room of the Bellevue-Stratford Hotel, Dick was seated next to Comptroller Saxon, who had been appointed by President John F. Kennedy. "People were coming up and asking him to sign $1 bills," he recalled. "I said to him, 'Say, I would like to have you sign one of mine.' I reached into my wallet and found that I didn't have anything smaller than a $20. So he signed my $20. I still have it."[60]

▼ **During Yeoman's service on the Assay Commission on February 12, 1964, he met with Denver Mint superintendent Fern Miller (second from left), U.S. Mint director Eva Adams, and Philadelphia Mint superintendent Michael Sura.**

▲ Yeoman's service on the U.S. Assay Commission in 1964 was recognized with the presentation of this bronze medal, illustrated at actual size.

▲ Dick's wife, Marion, was invited to serve on the 1968 U.S. Assay Commission, for which she received this medal.

When the reports were turned in, the committees' work was done. "The Mint people took the reports to Washington, and once they were digested and put in formal shape, they were sent to me, as chairman, to [review and] sign," Dick explained. He returned the documents, which became part of the Mint's annual report and were placed in the permanent archives.[61]

Following his Washington, D.C., adventure, Dick wrote to Sid Carwile:

> I consider you a sort of unsung hero in connection with my duties as chairman of the Commission. Without you, I could not have carried off the assignment nearly as well. After all, there is no opportunity for experience or even a rehearsal for the laymen members. I, therefore, am deeply indebted to you for having been at my side to keep things moving smoothly.

Mint Director Eva Adams was "delighted with the group of outstanding citizens selected by President Johnson to serve on his commission," and told Dick personally that he was "an excellent chairman." He valued his involvement and was honored to represent the hobby. The experience was "something different and exciting," he said. "It made me feel more rounded in what I knew about the Mint and more respectful of the dedication of the personnel there."[62]

In 1966 I was proud to be appointed to the Assay Commission, and Dick's wife, Marion, served two years later, likewise at Johnson's invitation. (Marion was the first Wisconsin woman to become a commissioner.) My experience on the Assay Commission was very similar to that of Dick's. I was well acquainted with all the Treasury people and, in fact, had been instrumental in promoting Dick as a worthwhile candidate. (His quiet and almost timid demeanor prevented him from being assertive about such things.) I had the honor of serving under Assay Commission Chairman R. Henry Norweb and was grateful to participate in the assaying exercise, because to me it was the most interesting part of the procedure.

THE KENNEDY HALF DOLLAR

As part of the 1964 Assay Commission proceedings, the 24 members were invited to witness the first striking of the Kennedy half dollar, which was designed by Gilroy Roberts and Frank Gasparro. "Those were the frosted proofs, the hard ones," Dick remembered. "I said to someone there, 'I can hardly keep my hands off those.'

"I liked them very much and wanted one. [Assistant Mint Director] Fred Tate [sent me one] right out of the first batch. . . . He put a little note with it that said, 'I know you wanted one of these.' Nothing can be taken out

A (Very) Brief History of the U.S. Assay Commission[63]

The U.S. Assay Commission was established on March 3, 1791, as part of the resolution that created the United States Mint. A variety of government officials served on the commission, or "Trial of the Pyx," until 1837, when President Martin Van Buren was authorized to appoint citizens to serve with the chief judge of the Eastern District of Pennsylvania, the comptroller of currency, and the assayer of the New York Assay Office. The purpose of the commission was to ensure that coiners took the utmost care in the manufacture of their products, conforming to the legal weights and fineness stipulated by the federal government. The commission reported to the president any deviation beyond the legal limits.

Thereafter, the commissioners, named by the incumbent president, met yearly at the U.S. Mint in Philadelphia on the second Wednesday of February to fulfill this responsibility. The appointment of 18 to 21 citizens to the annual Assay Commission continued until President Jimmy Carter stopped naming public members after 1976, allowing the assay to proceed for several more years with only government officials attending. March 14, 1980, was the last meeting of the Assay Commission in any form, thus ending its 188-year history.

of the Mint unless you go through the Federal Reserve. I don't think I was the only one who got one, but I'm sure Fred had to go through channels to do it. . . . I wanted to be sure the piece was preserved and protected, so after some years, I finally donated it to the American Numismatic Association."

The .900 fine silver coin—the only one of this composition to be issued in 1964—was conceived, authorized, and produced in a record 82 days. "The distribution of that half was unlike any past issue release," Dick said. "The banks all wanted to know when they would get their shipments because everyone was calling for them." He remembered talking later to Eva Adams, who said, "I just can't fill all the orders: I put them in places where they seem to be needed the most."[64] (See "The Future of the Kennedy Half Dollar" on pages 203–205 for more of Dick's personal observations about this historic coinage.)

▶ Members of the 1964 Assay Commission were invited to witness the striking of the first Kennedy half dollars. Yeoman expressed his admiration for the coin, and Assistant Mint Director Fred Tate later sent him a Proof specimen.

Old Timer Assay Commissioners Society[65]

The Old Timer Assay Commissioners Society was formed in 1964 during the American Numismatic Association's 73rd Anniversary Convention in Cleveland, Ohio, by 18 former members of the commission:

- Eva Adams
- Cab Atkins
- Elston G. Bradfield
- Vernon L. Brown
- Ernest F. Cooke
- John S. Davenport
- Oscar H. Dodson
- Polly Dodson
- Lucy Freeman
- S.W. Freeman
- John J. Gabarron
- Chester L. Krause
- Ray O. Lefman
- John H. Morris Jr.
- Matthew H. Rothert
- Margo Russell
- P.M. Williams
- Richard S. Yeoman

Dedicated to the spirit of good fellowship, the society helped former commissioners keep in touch by holding annual "meetings" at ANA conventions. The only business conducted at these informal gatherings was the election of officers, who were responsible for planning the entertainment at the following year's event: Chief Assayer (president); Chief Counter (secretary); Chief Weigher (treasurer); and Keeper of the Pyx (U.S. Mint director). Appointed officers were Chief of Medal Vault, Chief of Statistics, and Chief of Publications.

A husband-and-wife team typically volunteered as executive secretaries, coordinating the production and distribution of medals to commemorate the occasion and officially announcing OTACS guests as they arrived for the event. From 1965 through 1988 uniface medals were issued in both bronze and silver, noting the city in which the meeting was held. In 1989 25th-anniversary medals were struck in bronze, silver, and 10-karat gold to conclude the series. All bronze medals were suspended from a pin and ribbon so they might be worn during the convention. The issues were struck by Medallic Art Company, with the exception of 1977 (Art Medals, Inc.); 1978 and 1979 (Endurart, Inc.); and 1980 (The Franklin Mint).

GOVERNMENT GUIDANCE

By the 1960s Dick had become a recognized and trusted name in hobby households, and likewise was well regarded by U.S. Mint personnel and other Treasury officials. He was always happy to help the numismatic cause and seldom, if ever, expected anything in return. Perhaps that's why he never took for granted the respectful give-and-take he had with the U.S. Mint. "I had such good relations that I'm still amazed," he remarked in a June 16, 1987, interview.[66]

On July 27, 1966, he had occasion to speak before the House Banking and Currency Committee, chaired by Wright Patman (D-Texas). Dick and two others—ANA Vice President Arthur Sipe and coin dealer Abe Kosoff—supported bill H.R. 13150, which would authorize the Treasury's sale of nearly three million Carson City silver dollars at face value to the American Heart Association and American Cancer Society. The dollars would be used as incentives in a public fund drive: a contribution of $11 would entitle the donor to purchase two silver coins for $1 each; $35, five coins; and $100, ten coins. Dick delivered a brief, but impassioned message:

> I would like to speak to you gentlemen about the historical aspects of the coins which are under consideration. A true numismatist is interested in [items associated] with an event, a person, or a place, and a coin is the thing that would probably be the only representation of an event long past.
>
> . . . These are not just bags of silver that are resting in the vaults—they are real, irreplaceable mementos. They are imperishable to the historian, the same as the tetradrachms of ancient Greece, or the denarii of Rome. They represent a period that belongs to all Americans.
>
> . . . We would support any movement that would accomplish [their] fair distribution at reasonable cost. In the case of the bill before you, the funds provided by this distribution may be the means of opening the last door of research leading to the discovery of a cure of cancer, heart diseases, or stroke.[67]

"The next day," Dick recalled, "they had another session, but it was very short, and then they went into executive session. That was the last we heard of it. It developed [that] other charity groups wanted a piece of the action, and there wasn't that much to give out."

▲ Senator Robert A. Taft of Ohio (right), one of the most influential legislators of his time, toured Whitman's production plant and received a lesson in the manufacture of coin folders from employee Art Johnson.

Years later, Dick received a phone call from the Government Accountability Office, asking him for advice about how to distribute the dollars. "I told them to be sure that the price [would not] disturb the coin market. I wanted to make it very clear . . . that every dealer of any consequence in

▶ Dick Yeoman (left) and Chet Krause (right), shown here with Senator William Proxmire, testified before Congress regarding the reintroduction of mintmarks to U.S. coinage.

the country had some of those coins, that the Treasury hoard was not the only source, and that they should be careful . . . and I think they were."[68]

Meanwhile, Mint representatives played an increasingly collaborative role in the numismatic community. Eva Adams learned early in her career as U.S. Mint director (1961–1969) that hobbyists and trade organizations could help her better understand the collector mindset, so she attended conventions and did her best to be friendly to all. However, those efforts did little to combat the fallout from her decision to discontinue the use of mintmarks on coinage from 1965 to 1967, based on the erroneous assumption that collectors were contributing to the nationwide coin shortage. But, in Adams's defense, Dick said she welcomed collectors and numismatic professionals at committee hearings to voice their support of mintmark restoration.

In fact, in May 1967 in Washington, D.C., Dick and Chester Krause addressed the Senate Banking and Currency Committee, of which Senator William Proxmire (D-Wisconsin) was a member. (At the time, he also was chairman of the Subcommittee on Financial Institutions.) Said Dick, "I saw [Senator Proxmire] later in Madison, and he said they put restoring the mint marks on as an amendment to the Silver Redemption Act. . . . Nobody noticed, so [it passed] without any trouble."

▶ Yeoman was highly sought as a guest speaker.

HELLO...my name is

▲ Gerard Muhl, president of the Rochester Numismatic Association, encouraged Yeoman to attend as a celebrity guest in 1979, with Mint director Stella Hackel as guest speaker.

Throughout this period Whitman continued to expand its product line, and the U.S. Mint took notice. Of particular interest was the company's new "Perfect Lock" Proof holder. Eva Adams asked Dick if he could come to Washington and give the Mint staff a demonstration. "They liked the lock feature so much that a contract went to our special product department," he said.[69]

In May 1979 Whitman Publishing received a letter from Rochester Numismatic Association (RNA) President Gerard Muhl. The occasion was the unveiling of the Mint's new "mini dollar," to be held in conjunction with the club's "Susan B. Anthony Stamp and Coin Show" on July 2.

> Gentlemen:
>
> It has recently come to our attention that Richard Yeoman might be visiting Rochester, New York, on July 2nd. If that is indeed the case, I would like to take this opportunity to invite him to an event that the Rochester Numismatic Association will he holding that afternoon. Rochester, being the hometown of Susan B. Anthony, will be holding an official issuance ceremony for the new dollar coin. Stella Hackel, Director of the United States Mint, will be our guest speaker. She will present a major address concerning the Susan B. Anthony dollar and officially initiate public distribution of the new coin.
>
> A champagne reception will follow the ceremony, which is to be held in the [Rochester Museum and Science Center] auditorium. The event, open to the public, will begin at 3:30 p.m.
>
> I am sure the RNA members would be most pleased to meet Mr. Yeoman and share in his numismatic knowledge. Possibly we might also arrange for a "meet the author" autographing session through the Rochester Museum Shop. Please let us know if Mr. Yeoman is coming.

Norm Boughton, president of Chili Coin, Stamp & Supply, Ltd. in Rochester, followed up with a letter to Dick Thompsen of Hirschhorn, one of Western's distributors:

> Dear Dick:
>
> Following [are] the tentative plans for the Susan B. Anthony Stamp and Coin Show in Rochester, NY, on June 30, July 1 & 2, 1979.
>
> 10 a.m. Saturday, June 30: Mayor [Thomas P. Ryan Jr.] opens show; ribbon-cutting ceremony; 6 p.m. show closes

> 10 a.m. Sunday to 6 p.m.: Show is on
> 10 a.m. Monday to 6 p.m.: Show is on
>
> . . . Mrs. Hackel will arrive Monday morning, I understand. She will go to the Susan B. Anthony House to press conference there. Too small to hold any big doings. She will then go to the Chamber of Commerce for lunch and to the Rochester Museum and Science Center for an address and reception around 4 p.m.
>
> . . . Dick Yeo could be here on Thursday evening. Early Friday morning we have a local talk show I can get him on. I can also get him on another show later in the morning and an afternoon radio talk show. Saturday and Sunday, he could autograph *Red Books* at the show for 1 or 2 hours.
>
> . . . If Dick is coming and 1980 *Red Books* are going to be available, please increase my order by 3,600 pieces.

▲ Yeoman was retired from full-time corporate management by the time the Susan B. Anthony dollar debuted in 1979, but he still performed ambassadorial functions for Whitman and for the hobby community.

Dick Yeoman apparently attended the event under the umbrella of Whitman "public relations," at a cost of $425. He mentioned in a handwritten note to me that "this guy [Boughton] gave Western about $50,000 in business last year and is projecting a figure of $75,000 for '79."

Eight years later, Dick—well into his retirement by this time—turned his attention to the subject of coinage redesign. "Every once in a while, a change in the design is awfully good. It may just be a morale thing, but it seems [very] welcome to the general public, to say nothing of the collector, to see something new in his pocket change. I think it creates awareness—people start looking at their coins, instead of just counting them out."[70]

On September 8, 1987, he wrote the following letter to Senator William Proxmire, then chairman of the Committee on Banking, Housing and Urban Affairs:

> Dear Senator Proxmire:
>
> I formerly lived in Racine, Wisconsin, where I was an officer in Whitman Publishing Co., now Western Publishing Co. I am now retired and reside in Tucson, Arizona.
>
> Back in the mid-sixties, I was one who appeared at a hearing of the Banking and Currency Committee in connection with the restoration of mint marks on our coinage. American numismatists were gratified that you were instrumental in passing the legislation which restored the mint mark to our branch mint coinage.

> Briefly, I am the author of several coin catalogs, including *A Guide Book of United States Coins* and the *Handbook of United States Coins*. I was appointed by President L.B. Johnson to the 1964 Assay Commission and elected its chairman.
>
> Now, the purpose of this letter. I am joining with many coin collectors in urging our government to modernize our circulating coinage. New designs are long overdue. New patriotic symbolism in our metallic currency will command popular, progressive respect with our people, to say nothing of [the] reduction effect on our Treasury deficit.
>
> I am sure that you are familiar with the fact that most of the denominations are well past their legal limit for change. Your legislative efforts to effect design changes will be greatly appreciated by thousands of your fellow Americans and particularly hobbyists who have poured millions into the Treasury.
>
> Sincerely,
>
> R.S. Yeoman

Senator Proxmire responded cordially, thanking Dick for his support of H.R. 3314, which called for modernization of America's coin designs. "As you may be aware," he wrote, "the Secretary of the Treasury currently has the authority to change these designs at his discretion. However, I will give this bill serious consideration when it reaches the Senate."

Even into his 80s, Dick was a numismatic celebrity and an honored guest at U.S. Mint functions. On May 2, 1988, he participated in a first-strike ceremony at the Denver Mint for the Olympic silver dollar, the last such event he attended. There he hobnobbed with Treasury officials (including newly appointed Denver Mint superintendent Cynthia Grassby Baker), Olympic representatives, and fellow hobbyists. That day he was the 24th individual to strike a dollar, which bore designs by artist Patricia Lewis Verani and U.S. Mint sculptor-engraver Sherl Joseph Winter.

Two months later, Mint director Donna Pope sent Dick a letter:

> Thank you for attending the 1988 Olympic Coin First Strike Ceremony. I greatly appreciate your participation in this ceremony and the enthusiasm that you showed for

◀ Treasury Department and U.S. Mint officials heard from R.S. Yeoman as he lobbied for coinage reform and promoted the hobby. Even President Dwight Eisenhower received a letter from him. (Pictured: Eisenhower, James Baker [secretary of the Treasury in the 1980s], Senator William Proxmire, and Mint director Donna Pope.)

> this coin program. The support of individuals such as yourself help make our coin programs successful, and I am sure that the 1988 Olympic Coin Program will indeed "Help America Shine."
>
> If you are interested in purchasing the coin that you struck, it may be obtained by sending a check made out to the "U.S. Mint" for $27. . . .
>
> Again, thank you for being a part of the ceremony.

Within a week of receiving the director's correspondence, his check was in the mail.

Dick's support of the numismatic hobby was steadfast. If he knew of an individual who could advance knowledge or appreciation of the hobby, he did not hesitate to recommend him or her for a government position. In March 1953 he sent a letter to President Dwight D. Eisenhower promoting numismatist and ANA Past President Loyd B. Gettys as a candidate for director of the Mint. He received the following response (dated May 2, 1953) from Charles F. Willis Jr., special assistant to the president:

> Dear Mr. Yeoman:
>
> The President has asked me to reply to your letter of March twenty-sixth in behalf of Mr. Loyd B. Gettys, whom you recommend for appointment as Director of the Mint. He appreciates your letting him know of your high regard for Mr. Gettys and wants me to assure you that he will be given every consideration.

Though numismatically qualified, Gettys did not succeed Nellie Tayloe Ross as Mint director (1933–1953). That honor went to William H. Brett (1954–1961), who had no relevant experience.

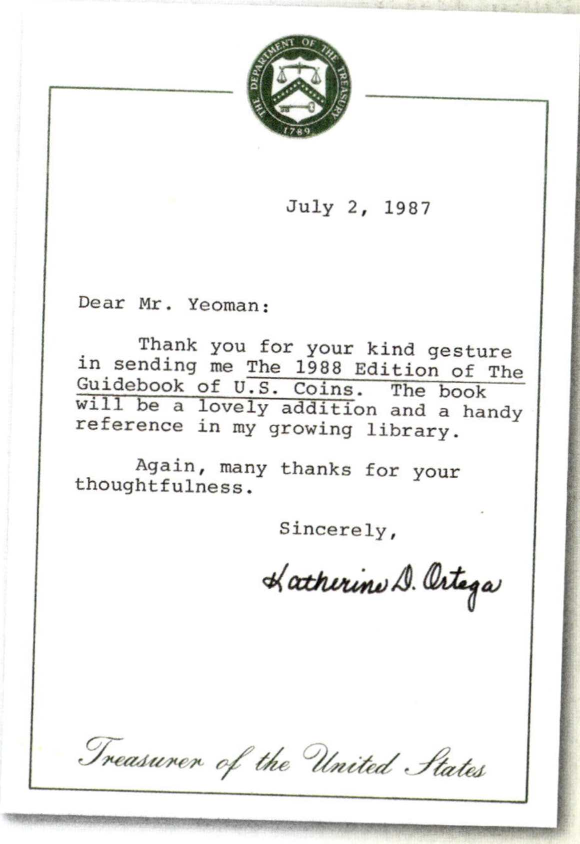

THE DEPARTMENT OF THE TREASURY 1789

July 2, 1987

Dear Mr. Yeoman:

Thank you for your kind gesture in sending me The 1988 Edition of The Guidebook of U.S. Coins. The book will be a lovely addition and a handy reference in my growing library.

Again, many thanks for your thoughtfulness.

Sincerely,

Katherine D. Ortega

Treasurer of the United States

▲ A letter of thanks from U.S. Treasurer Katherine D. Ortega.

GRASSROOTS INVOLVEMENT

In the early days of Dick's hobby participation, coin clubs were becoming popular. "The [American Numismatic Association]," he wrote, "embraced all collectors and, like an umbrella, covered the multitude. It soon showed gains in membership as novice collectors gained in knowledge and interest. In the mid-thirties, membership in the association was about 2,000. There was no Professional Numismatists Guild nor Retail Coin Dealers Association or the like. Those achievements were to come—and they did come."[71]

Dick, who had become an ANA life member (No. 84), won election to the Association's Board of Governors in 1946. He served five one-year

Dick Yeoman was a grassroots supporter of the hobby and enjoyed the camaraderie provided by numismatic meetings, conventions, and other activities.

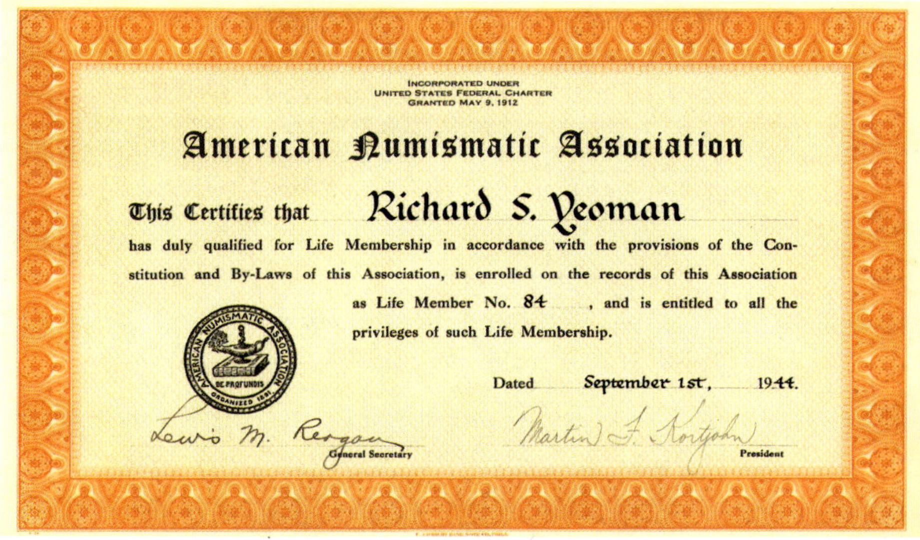

INCORPORATED UNDER
UNITED STATES FEDERAL CHARTER
GRANTED MAY 9, 1912

American Numismatic Association

This Certifies that Richard S. Yeoman
has duly qualified for Life Membership in accordance with the provisions of the Constitution and By-Laws of this Association, is enrolled on the records of this Association as Life Member No. 84, and is entitled to all the privileges of such Life Membership.

Dated September 1st, 1944.

Lewis M. Reagan, General Secretary
Martin F. Kortjohn, President

American Numismatic Association
Certificate of Award

This Certifies that Richard S. Yeoman
has been awarded the MEDAL OF MERIT *in recognition of distinguished service to the Association and to the science of numismatics.*

Date August 20, 1952.

Col. Joseph Moss, *President*
Lewis M. Reagan, *General Secretary*

◀ Yeoman became an ANA life member in 1944.

◀ In 1952 he was awarded the Association's Medal of Merit.

terms but refused all nominations for the office of president. Said ANA Past President Virgil Hancock (1975–1976) of Dick's service, "Anybody who has the wisdom *not* to run for ANA president is bound to be smart!"

Dick received the ANA's Medal of Merit in 1952; a Heath Literary Award in 1954 (for his article entitled "The 1848 Quarter Eagle with CAL.," published in *The Numismatist* in July 1953); and the Farran Zerbe Memorial Award for Distinguished Service in 1956. An accomplished exhibitor, he earned the Howland Wood Memorial Award for Best in Show in 1951, the first year the honor was presented.

In 1978 Dick was inducted into the ANA's Numismatic Hall of Fame, having been nominated by numismatist Abe Kosoff and others. ANA Executive Director Edward C. Rochette wrote in 1988 that "the present Hall [of Fame, at ANA headquarters in Colorado Springs] occupies the north

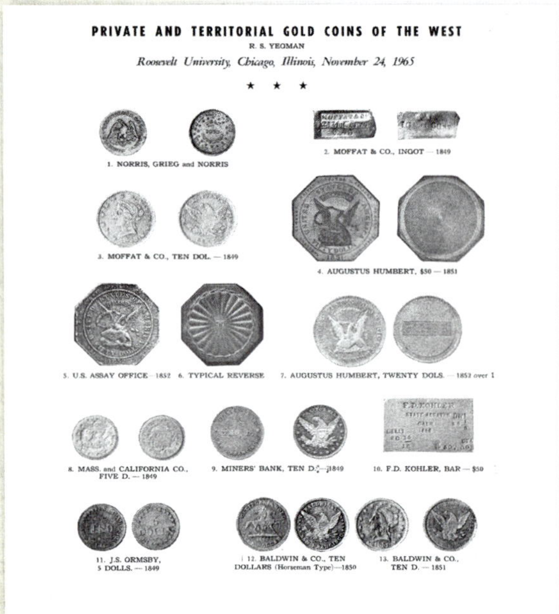

PRIVATE AND TERRITORIAL GOLD COINS OF THE WEST

R. S. YEOMAN

Roosevelt University, Chicago, Illinois, November 24, 1965

★ ★ ★

1. NORRIS, GRIEG and NORRIS

2. MOFFAT & CO., INGOT — 1849

3. MOFFAT & CO., TEN DOL. — 1849

4. AUGUSTUS HUMBERT, $50 — 1851

5. U.S. ASSAY OFFICE — 1852 6. TYPICAL REVERSE

7. AUGUSTUS HUMBERT, TWENTY DOLS. — 1853 over 1

8. MASS. and CALIFORNIA CO., FIVE D. — 1849

9. MINERS' BANK, TEN D. — 1849

10. F.D. KOHLER, BAR — $50

11. J.S. ORMSBY, 5 DOLLS. — 1849

12. BALDWIN & CO., TEN DOLLARS (Horseman Type) — 1850

13. BALDWIN & CO., TEN D. — 1851

▲ A handout Yeoman created for a November 24, 1965, presentation at Chicago's Roosevelt University about "Private and Territorial Gold Coins of the West."

▲ Dick Yeoman was a certified exhibit judge and enjoyed the opportunity to study and critique numismatic displays. At ANA events, he was qualified to judge the "Best-in-Show" category.

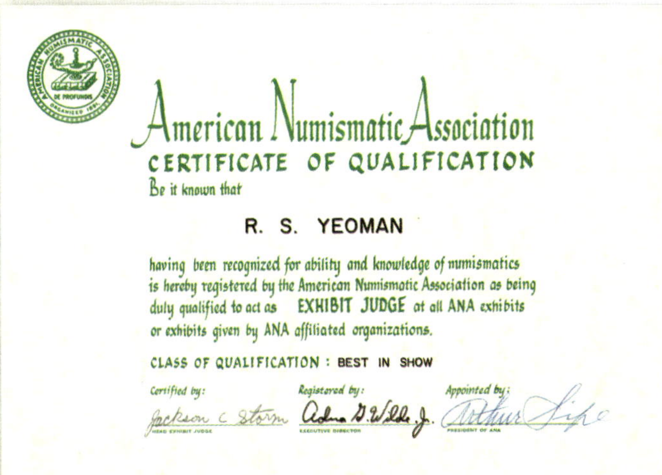

American Numismatic Association

CERTIFICATE OF QUALIFICATION

Be it known that

R. S. YEOMAN

having been recognized for ability and knowledge of numismatics is hereby registered by the American Numismatic Association as being duly qualified to act as EXHIBIT JUDGE at all ANA exhibits or exhibits given by ANA affiliated organizations.

CLASS OF QUALIFICATION : BEST IN SHOW

Certified by: Jackson C. Storm — Registered by: Adna G. Wilde, Jr. — Appointed by: Arthur Sipe

Chartered by Congress 1912

American Numismatic Association

Heath Literary Award

To: Richard S. Yeoman

in recognition of your outstanding literary contribution published in THE NUMISMATIST during the year 1953,

Third Award

Stuart Mosher, Editor — President

Elston G. Bradfield, Awards Chairman — Lewis M. Reagan, General Secretary

▲ Yeoman received a third-place ANA Heath Literary Award for his article "The 1848 Quarter Eagle with CAL.," published in the 1953 volume of *The Numismatist*.

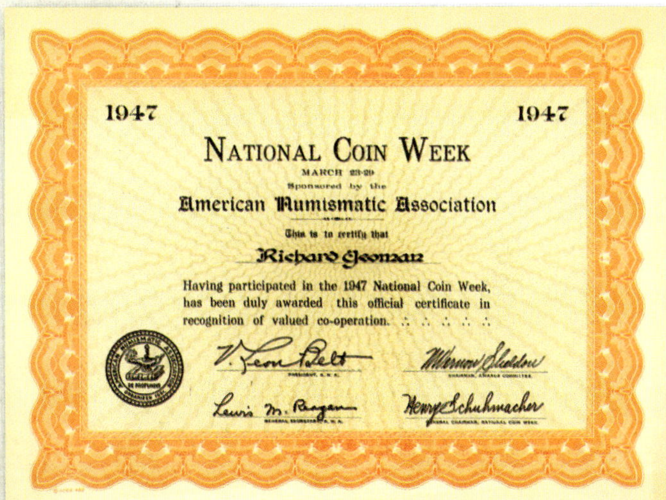

1947 1947

NATIONAL COIN WEEK

MARCH 23-29

Sponsored by the

American Numismatic Association

This is to certify that

Richard Yeoman

Having participated in the 1947 National Coin Week, has been duly awarded this official certificate in recognition of valued co-operation.

V. Leon Belt, President, A.N.A. — M. Vernon Sheldon, Chairman, Awards Committee

Lewis M. Reagan, General Secretary, A.N.A. — Henry Schuhmacher, General Chairman, National Coin Week

◀ Yeoman earned a certificate of participation for his activities during the ANA's 1947 National Coin Week.

wall of the corridor that leads from the entrance rotunda. . . . Three small alcoves are [devoted to] the honored numismatists, [and] shelf-like cases display bits of memorabilia related to [the] enshrinees. . . . Books play the more prominent role in recognizing these numismatic greats. There is an autographed copy of Richard Yeoman's *Handbook of United States Coins*, better known to us as "The *Blue Book*."[72]

Two years before Rochette's update, Dick sent a related—and uncharacteristically critical—comment to friend Glenn Smedley on April 5, 1986:

> That Hall of Fame class to which both of us have been elected has generated some thoughts. . . . What do you have in your possession that can be brought out to show friends that you are a Hall of Famer? Or, hung on a wall?
>
> At a recent ANA banquet, all the living Hall of Famers were present. We were not mentioned or recognized. I do not believe that you or I are vain persons, but we aren't here for long. . . .

▼ **Good times are always assured when old friends get together. The revelers at this 1964 ANA convention in Cleveland included (from left) Dick Yeoman, Lucy Freeman, Eva Adams, Kenneth Henderson, Elvira Clain-Stefanelli, P.M. Williams, Polly and Oscar Dodson, Vladimir Clain-Stefanelli, Paul Vincze, and Charles Hoskins.**

▲ This exotic gold ring was specially made for Yeoman by the Numismatic Literary Guild, which presented it to him at the ANA's 1971 convention in Washington, D.C.

Dick was a charter member of the Numismatic Literary Guild (NLG), which was established in 1968. At the NLG "bash" at the ANA's 1971 convention in Washington, D.C., he was presented a hand-crafted gold ring in the shape of a book, with a diamond set in the upper left corner and "Redbook" engraved diagonally in script. Inside was tucked a gold dollar. It became one of his most treasured items.

Six years later, Dick received the NLG's top honor, as reported in *Coin World*:

> The Oscar of numismatics, the "Clemy Award," went this year to Mr. Numismatics himself—Richard S. Yeoman—in Numismatic Literary Guild ceremonies during the recent Atlanta American Numismatic Association convention.
>
> The Clemy, named after its first winner, Clem Bailey, goes each year to an NLG member with numismatic writing ability, sense of humor and dedication to the hobby. Well, no one qualifies more, nor deserves the honor more than Dick Yeoman.

As national interest in coin collecting grew in the 1950s and 1960s, so did local and regional numismatic societies. Dick appreciated the social benefits, fraternal aspects, and casual nature of such groups and was an active participant. "Committee tasks are opportunities and a duty," he maintained. "Holding office should be *accepted as a responsibility*."[73] He regularly attended meetings and enjoyed new and old friendships. When he and Marion wintered in Green Valley, Arizona, he attended local stamp and coin club meetings but tried "not to be too prominent."[74]

According to his friend Dan Brown, Dick joined the Central States Numismatic Society (CSNS) in 1939 and attended its first convention, which was held in Chicago. There he met numismatists Eric Newman, B. Max Mehl, Paul and Art Kagin, Sol Kaplan, and Harry Boosel, and many other prominent collectors and dealers. He served the society as a board member, secretary, and vice president, and he was elected president in 1948.

▲ Dan Brown, a longtime friend of Yeoman's, presided over his 1977 Central States Numismatic Society celebration.

The CSNS 38th Anniversary Convention banquet, held at Milwaukee's Red Carpet Inn on May 14, 1977, was a memorable affair for Dick. Following a prime-rib dinner and presentation of awards, the event concluded with a special "R.S. Yeoman Night," over which Dan presided. (Banquet tickets were $12!) I worked for months prior to the event, organizing the guest list and inviting those who couldn't attend to write a personal message for Dick, which I placed in a scrapbook for him. I also produced a commemorative booklet for attendees featuring a brief biography of Dick, and every guest received an autographed 30th (1977) edition of the *Red Book*.

NLG SYMPOSIUM

Author-compiler, about to escape into retirement, tells all.

Confession Session

Associated with a publisher-printer which covers all phases from editorial through production to distribution
    (Like A. T. & T. or major Oil Companies)
Started in Advertising and marketing - editorial and
    numismatic career was unplanned. (Ocean - pond)
Editorial concepts:
    No perfect manuscript - deadline orbust.
    Two editors needed for each project.
    Readers enjoy being proof readers.
Various kinds of errors:
    Harmless - usually compositor's mistakes remain
        uncorrected.
    Annoying - Upside down, double-printed, blank covers.
        laminated pages, weak or smeared text. Prized.
    factual - Inaccurate data. Wrong coin values, dates.
    Serious - Any missing part. Blank pages. Missing
        and duplicated sections (misplaced signatures.
Most serious - Missing page 237 in 16th edition (1963) and
    page 239 duplicated. Some books got through before
    the plates were changed. We made good on copies reported, but strangely few complained. Private gold section.
    We kept none and none has turned up since. Such a copy of the 16th edition would be a prize mint error.

Another serious error - The very rare 1788 VERMON AUCTORI
    with reverse "C" was the object of a bizarre night
    shift incident about ten years ago. Few got into the
    market and only one complaint - John Ford.
Latest edition errors include 19o8 S VDB. Corected 2nd Prtg.

MILESSTONES

16th edition (1963) Alternate Official Title "Red Book"
    added to title page.
24th edition (1971) Special editorial study Red Books
    Never Die with new subjects in each succeeding edition.
25th edition (1972) Went past 10 million copy total and
    only cover stamped in silver.
Most unusual edition was the unique copy printed in Braille
    by another company for a 17 year old California
    collector, David Pepito.
Interesting editions are those printed in Japanese, in
    Tokyo, of the sister catalogs Modern World Coins
    and Current Coins of the World.

Yeoman's typewritten notes for the Numismatic Literary Guild Symposium at an ANA convention.

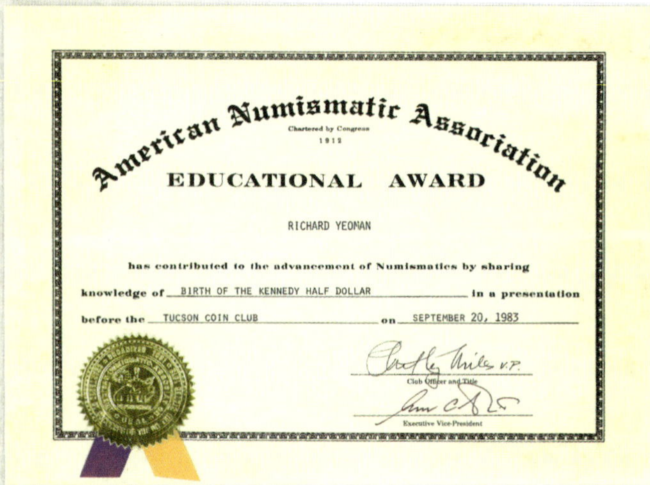

American Numismatic Association
Chartered by Congress
1912
EDUCATIONAL AWARD

RICHARD YEOMAN

has contributed to the advancement of Numismatics by sharing knowledge of BIRTH OF THE KENNEDY HALF DOLLAR in a presentation before the TUCSON COIN CLUB on SEPTEMBER 20, 1983

Club Officer and Title

Executive Vice-President

▲ On September 20, 1983, Yeoman gave a presentation on "The Birth of the Kennedy Half Dollar" to the Tucson Coin Club, as described by this ANA Educational Award.

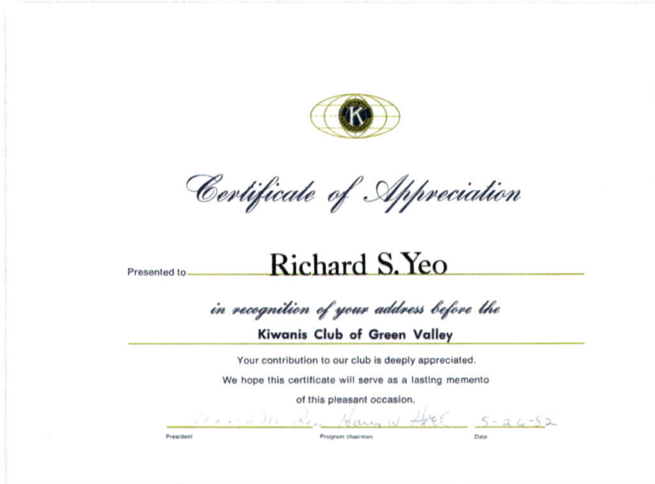

Certificate of Appreciation

Presented to Richard S. Yeo

in recognition of your address before the Kiwanis Club of Green Valley

Your contribution to our club is deeply appreciated.
We hope this certificate will serve as a lasting memento of this pleasant occasion.

President Program chairman Date

▲ This certificate was for delivering a talk to the Green Valley Kiwanis Club.

About six weeks before the tribute, I received a letter from Virgil Hancock, handwritten in bold, black marker. He wrote, in part:

> If there's one event [that] everyone who knows Dick Yeoman would not want to miss, it would be this testimonial to the one and only Richard Yeoman. And when I say "everyone who knows Dick Yeoman," that includes everyone who ever bought a *Red Book*, because Dick's name is a numismatic household word.
>
> He's the only man I know of whom everybody has spoken only good words! Of course, Dick deserves all those good words because he always has been a gentleman . . . he always finds something good to say about everybody.
>
> Please tell Dick that I'm certainly mighty sorry that I'll be out of the country when you all gather in Milwaukee, but that I wish him all the best.

On April 28, Abe Kosoff RSVP'd to my invitation:

> This is more than just a polite "sorry I cannot be with you." It is a most sincere expression of regret. Dick Yeoman and I have been long-time friends. He has been a giant in the numismatic limelight for so many years . . . he is truly a living legend! . . . . Please extend to Dick and to Marion the heartiest and warmest congratulations from Molly and Abe Kosoff.

▲ At a meeting of the newly organized Lake County Coin Club in Waukegan, Illinois, Dick Yeoman (left) spoke on the history of coinage.

I also received a handwritten letter from former U.S. Mint Director Mary Brooks, dated May 7:

> It is a distinct honor to pay tribute to the great one of our hobby! Dick Yeoman has been such a shining light to me ever since I became director of the U.S. Mint in 1969. You can't imagine how many times when I have been asked by mail, on TV or radio or in person, "What's this coin worth?"!! And with great pride and relief I say, "Oh, don't you know the numismatic Bible?" I have given [his] books to my grandchildren—and to others close to me!!
>
> Let me add to your list of tributes from near and far—"We are all better for having known you, Dick Yeoman. And may the Lord bless you with many more years of health and happiness."

CENTRAL STATES NUMISMATIC SOCIETY
1942-43 MEMBERSHIP CARD
Date Issued
Membership No. 186
This Certifies that
RICHARD S. YEOMAN
RACINE, WISCONSIN.
is a Member in Good Standing
President Secretary

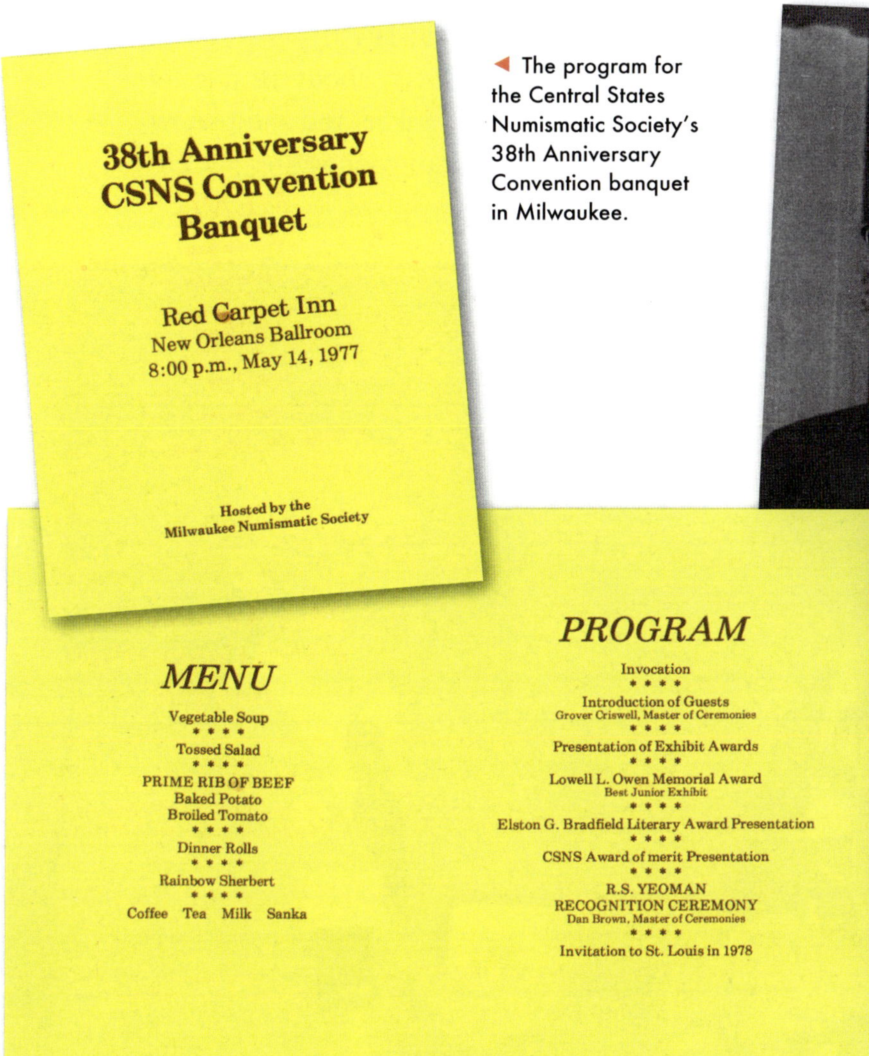
38th Anniversary CSNS Convention Banquet

Red Carpet Inn
New Orleans Ballroom
8:00 p.m., May 14, 1977

Hosted by the Milwaukee Numismatic Society

MENU

Vegetable Soup
* * * *
Tossed Salad
* * * *
PRIME RIB OF BEEF
Baked Potato
Broiled Tomato
* * * *
Dinner Rolls
* * * *
Rainbow Sherbert
* * * *
Coffee Tea Milk Sanka

PROGRAM

Invocation
* * * *
Introduction of Guests
Grover Criswell, Master of Ceremonies
* * * *
Presentation of Exhibit Awards
* * * *
Lowell L. Owen Memorial Award
Best Junior Exhibit
* * * *
Elston G. Bradfield Literary Award Presentation
* * * *
CSNS Award of merit Presentation
* * * *
R.S. YEOMAN RECOGNITION CEREMONY
Dan Brown, Master of Ceremonies
* * * *
Invitation to St. Louis in 1978

◀ The program for the Central States Numismatic Society's 38th Anniversary Convention banquet in Milwaukee.

▲ A highlight of the CSNS Convention was a special tribute to Dick Yeoman, shown here with his wife, Marion.

After the CSNS tribute, *Coin World* Feature Editor Jay Guren reported[75]:

> Disproved is the observation that "no man can be a hero in his own home town." Milwaukee is, in fact, Yeoman's birthplace, and among those who came out to honor him on this particular evening were such "non-numismatic" persons as his former college room-mate, now a successful Milwaukee attorney; and a lady who had been his secretary 18 years earlier.
>
> . . . The tall, thin man who appeared almost embarrassed by the kindnesses bestowed upon him, need not have been; Dick Yeoman was being honored that evening by the members of a numismatic world, of which he was the chief architect.

Not surprisingly, Dick wrote more than 100 personal letters of acknowledgment and thanks (with the aid of editorial assistant Jenny Tomaszek) to attendees and well-wishers. Here is a sampling:

To Dan and Thelma Brown (May 25, 1977)

> I believe there is very little left to say about the fine ceremony that you headed at Milwaukee. You and I know what a long preparation went into your Master of Ceremonies duties.

▼ In March 1988 Yeoman participated in an educational forum conducted by the California State Numismatic Association. Here CSNA President Charles Colver presents him a medal of appreciation. The symposium also featured Miguel L. Muñoz ("The Incredible Life of the 8R Mexican Peso"), Barry Jacobs ("The Frontiersman"), and John Lenker ("Odd and Unusual Money").

There are very few people who could have handled it for me, and you did a fine job.

Thelma, Marion kept those roses [you gave her] as long as they held together, and we were reminded of your thoughtfulness and generosity.

We look forward to having another visit and trip together, sometime, somewhere.

Thanks again for all your friendly gestures.

A moment with friends at the CSNA's 1970 convention in Los Angeles (from left): Herb and Rota Bergen, Alan Feinberg, Aubrey Bebee, and Dick Yeoman.

At a coin convention, Dick visits with Cory Gillilland (left) and Elvira Clain-Stefanelli, who exhibited coins from the Smithsonian Institution's National Numismatic Collection.

To Aubrey and Adeline Bebee (June 6, 1977)

Thank you so very much for the kind wishes you sent to me for the R.S. Yeoman night at the CSNS Banquet, May 14, in Milwaukee. Ken Bressett presented me with a huge scrapbook of mementos, in which your greeting was included.

I would have preferred to express my appreciation to my special friends The Bebees in person, but hope that before long I will do so at some numismatic affair.

To Mary Brooks (May 24, 1977)

I was very happy to have you among my good friends during the festivities at the Red Carpet Inn during the Central States Convention.

Your letter, which preceded your visit to Milwaukee, was also appreciated, and my family tells me they had a nice get-acquainted visit with you during the banquet.

I hope that there will soon be another opportunity to visit when we will have more time for more than a minute or two of good conversation.

To Lee F. Hewitt (May 25, 1977)

While we had very little time together, I was very pleased that you could be present during the testimonial banquet at the Central States Convention.

I have always felt disappointed that I could not be present a year ago when you were given a like recognition. You, of course, are the true founder of Central States, and no one can take that away.

To R.E. "Bob" Wallace (May 23, 1977)

Marion and I want to thank you for all your kind wishes and for coming all the way from Texas to the CSNS Banquet in Milwaukee. It is always so good to come together with such good friends, and we appreciate the fact that you were there to celebrate with us.

It was a pleasant surprise, especially, to see you at the festivities. My genuine regret is that we could find no time to really have an old-fashioned visit. It goes to say that you were one of the important people in my career. Your help was always forthcoming and meaningful.

R.S. Yeoman Club Affiliations

Life Member and Past Governor (1946-1951), American Numismatic Association
Member and Past President (1948-1950), Central States Numismatic Society
Honorary Member and Past President, Racine Numismatic Society
Member, Milwaukee Numismatic Society
Member, Chicago Coin Club
Member, San Diego Numismatic Society
Life Member, Numismatic Association of Southern California
Life Member, California State Numismatic Association
Life Member, Canadian Numismatic Association
Honorary Member, Tucson Numismatic Society
Honorary Life Member, Oklahoma City Coin Club
Co-Founder, Numismatists of Wisconsin
Member, Token and Medal Society
Member, Numismatics International
Member, California Exonumists
Member, Society of International Numismatists
Member, Sociedad Numismatica de Mexico
Fellow, American Numismatic Society
Fellow, Royal Numismatic Society
Charter Member, Numismatic Literary Guild

HOBBY HORSES

When Dick latched onto a subject that entertained—or annoyed—him, he pursued it with great vigor. His well-conceived arguments were based on decades of hands-on experience and thoughtful observation:

Speculation

Dick often was critical of numismatic "speculators," who, he said, were the "firstest with the mostest."[76] Their credo was "get in and get out before you can be hurt." However, he believed they served an important purpose: "Short issues . . . are captured immediately by alert bag dealers and speculators, [who preserve the] limited supply for posterity." (See "Coin Supply and Values," pages 203–204) That said, Dick felt they generated "inflated prices too soon—about 10 years too soon."[77]

▲ Yeoman warned would-be speculators that the 1964 Kennedy half dollar—hoarded in large quantities—had a gigantic mintage. "If you must speculate, don't follow the crowd."

The Kennedy half dollars, introduced in 1964, were snapped up by people reacting to what appeared to be scarcity. "Most [of these half dollars are] in bureau drawers," said Dick. "[They are] in circulation, but not in daily change. Some [are] hoarded by speculators, most [of whom] are not aware of [the] great mintage. . . . [The speculator believes that if] he doesn't put it away, the next fellow will."[78]

To a group of collectors at a Jacksonville, Florida, coin show in 1971, he advised:

> The climate has changed greatly in our hobby since the mid-thirties. We have seen a speculative binge go through a peak and float back to moderate levels. For many, this period has led to cynicism. One of the hardest truths to face is value decline. Coin authorities, dealers, club officers and the average collector have, since 1964, looked for positive signs of a general market upturn. After five or six years, I believe we are still looking, but are pretty well adjusted to reality.
>
> . . . No amount of persuasive editorial comment, oratory at forums such as this, or manipulating valuation books can change the facts of the marketplace, any more than pushing the needle on a barometer dial can change the weather. All the individual buyers and sellers of coins taken together create an irresistible force. As individual performers in this massive numismatic mob scene, we tend to think of ourselves as observers rather than participants, blaming the other fellow at times for what we call "the situation." The causes, the reasons, the responsibility for the situation are many-fold. Stanislaw Lee, the Polish satirist, put it very well when he wrote: "No snowflake in an avalanche ever feels responsible."[79]

In general, Dick discouraged collectors from buying great quantities of rolls or Proof sets. "The chances are that thousands of others are doing it," he said. "If you must speculate, don't follow the crowd. When there is a short issue, it is human to buy several rolls and neglect the plentiful one. Be different, quietly put away some nice uncirculated rolls of the unheralded mint (sometimes at no premium). This doesn't occur every year or in every series, but it does happen frequently enough to be important, and it usually doesn't require as much investment. Such sleepers come into their own, in time."[80]

Investment

Dick was very savvy about the world economy and the coin market, and he could speak extemporaneously on either topic. "The success of all investments in coins (based on quantity in the form of rolls and Proof sets) depend for their soundness on the ultimate, long-range demand by future collectors," he explained. "Such a market has to be a greater market, in terms of the number of collectors, than exist[s] today. The achievement of this higher level of interest rests on . . . the ability of present-day collectors, part-time dealers and professional dealers to provide a healthy climate of growth. Such growth will come only with honest and prudent attitudes and a resistance to hysterical speculation and nonnumismatic side issues."[81]

In the early 1970s Dick observed that the financial market was sensitive to world conditions: "The unpredictable potential of the European Common Market, the flight of Treasury gold stocks, and fears concerning government relationships to pricing by manufacturers are factors which have cooled off investment enthusiasm by the average citizen." He took note of a comment offered by Bradbury K. Thurlow of Winslow, Cohn & Stetson, Brokers: "We believe the current stock market is almost entirely dominated by fear of an all-powerful government that is hostile to business."

With respect to numismatics, Dick thought, "Perhaps our sphere of interest in investment can be called safe. The government is very much interested in producing great quantities of proof sets and mint sets for us.... Then, there is the other side of the coin. If investors are fearful of Wall Street investments, they might turn to coins as a haven for their investment dollars."

▼ "You and that damned *Red Book!*" Frankie Laine (who sang the theme to *Rawhide* and is seen here with Nan Grey in a scene from the television show) said to Yeoman when the coin market went south.

Indeed, Dick had firsthand knowledge of investors who set their sights on the numismatic marketplace, notably Frankie Laine, an American singer who was especially popular in the 1950s. "I visited with him [in the late sixties] after his late show at the Fremont in Las Vegas. He greeted me with, 'You and that damned *Red Book*.' Some of his buys were a little sour market-wise at the time."[82]

In a lecture he presented in June 1960, Dick offered his own philosophies of collecting and investing, and the importance of timing:

> In my thinking, I would avoid an old lament which we have all uttered: "I should have bought that coin ten years ago or even two years ago. I could have bought it for almost nothing." Values of coins are only relative, like anything else. I had my own experience in 1941 of bidding a 1936

proof set up to $17 at our Racine [Numismatic Society] Banquet Auction, and feeling like a chump for having [paid] so much. I could have had it for $1.86 in 1936.

Another mistake was committed, I thought, when I sold it, about five years ago, for the ridiculous sum of $100. In one case, I should have been earlier and in the other, later. I was off on my timing, I thought, in both instances. But, and here is an important point—I multiplied my investment sixfold. As inept as I was in buying and selling, I made a fine profit. I could have made more, but shouldn't I be consoled by the fact that I made a gain?

"The best time to buy is today—and tomorrow, and tomorrow after that."—R.S. Yeoman

Well, when *is* the best time to buy? It's somewhat as the dentist says, "The [cavity in your tooth] won't be any smaller next month. . . . One can say, *today* is the time to buy.

. . . Our population is increasing, and that means more coin collectors each year, even if the percentage for all Americans remains stationary. Our U.S. population reached 180 million in this year, about 20 percent greater than 1950. This is important because once a year is ended, our mints make no more coins of that date. Our supply of cents, nickels, dimes, etc., in any completed year, is limited and can never be increased.

. . . There is a pessimistic undercurrent concerning the rapid rise and high level which certain key coins have achieved lately. It is said that these values stifle the collector and discourage him from completing certain series. . . . Then, I say, let him turn to a less-crowded, lower-priced series and broaden his numismatic experience.

. . . When we reach those mileposts in our collecting, can we look back complacently and say, "In 1960 I had the good sense to fill in those dates when the prices were right, and kept up to date each year until the last date of the series"? Yes, [the best time to buy is] today—and tomorrow, and tomorrow after that.[83]

Supply and Demand

Dick was a student of economics and quickly saw the relevance of the laws of "supply and demand" in the numismatic industry. About the time the *Red Book* was celebrating its 25th anniversary, he remarked:

> There are collectors who might be happy Lincoln cent accumulators who believe that most collectors of anything over a hundred years old, like two-cent[s], three-cents, large cents and the like, do so just to impress their friends. There is another group which is contemptuous of the error-collector, and another which calls paper money collectors "rag pickers," and so on. Well, we who compile books and distribute them are a form of catalyst, a sort of liaison between all these groups. The whole pursuit is an act of faith. It's a good thing everyone doesn't go after the same series.[84]

He delved further into the economics of the coin hobby in a speech he delivered at a club representative breakfast hosted by the Numismatic Association of Southern California in Los Angeles on February 15, 1975:

> A great deal of attention has lately been directed toward economics. We hear a lot about a free market, supply and demand, and obscene profits. It should be no new revelation that our science and hobby has its own style of economy and reacts to consumer preferences and emotions much as the market for food, clothing, autos, or appliances. That term "obscene profits" we heard recently as a chastisement of the oil industry is not too different from a similar expression "unconscionable profit" used by former Secretary of the Treasury John Connally when he heard what the Mint Bureau was asking for the Proof silver Eisenhower dollar. The price has turned off many potential orders. The supply-demand principle and price resistance has caused a decline in the number of sales.
>
> The Bicentennial Proof sets might have had the same experience. Automation improvements have recently been announced [that] will bring the set price down from $15 to $12. The sale could be further stimulated if some way can be found to bring the price down still further. American-style economics is going to prevail, no matter what the product or the source. The reason for a high price is unimportant, for demand will always be an individual, emotional, or practical choice. If a product cannot be made cheaply enough to sell in sizeable volume, in private industry, it is discarded. It's an immutable law.
>
> So, popularity, another word for demand, or lack of popularity is a broad, basic influence on any market. This is particularly true of the numismatic market. What

"It's a good thing everyone doesn't go after the same series."—R.S. Yeoman

makes our little world exciting is the unpredictable pattern of change from one coin category to another in succeeding years. This keeps the individual collector, the dealer, and the cataloger on their toes.

. . . The common coins have the greatest spread, because the dealer contemplates holding them for months, possibly years, before disposing of them. Borrowed money to invest in such static, stored-up inventory and the uncertainty of the sale entitle the dealer to something extra for the storage period. Conversely, the scarce coins—those that move out within a few days—bring higher premium offers and narrower spread for obvious reasons. He doesn't have to borrow high-interest money to hold such pieces.

Thus, there is no standard, across-the-board discount rate for all coins. These differences naturally change with popularity—a constantly fleeting, unpredictable, changing numismatic scene.

▼ Former Treasury secretary John Connally criticized the "unconscionable profit" in the Mint's pricing for Proof Eisenhower silver dollars. Yeoman felt lower issue prices would generate stronger sales.

Errors and Die Varieties and Other Oddities

The *Red Book*'s coverage of mint errors was closely monitored by Dick and his corps of panelists. "Here the modern mass production of coins has created a controversial situation," he said. "In some ways, we must practice caution in recognizing mere poor workmanship. We can dilute the importance of varieties to a meaningless hodge-podge of variations which will repel the novice collector."[85]

Die varieties, especially those that were popular with collectors, were added to the *Red Book* from time to time.[86] The vetting process was time-consuming. "First someone would report [a variety]. At that stage, it is just a rumor," Dick explained.[87] "Then a couple of more people report[ed] finding [it]. Within about six months, as a general rule, the dealers would have a price on [it]. Then they would start to get in touch with us to ask if it was legitimate and so on."

Dick depended on his contributors for the answers, because Whitman and the *Red Book* staff were not "in the coin business." The panelists would talk it out, and, if they agreed on a variety's authenticity, they would recommend its inclusion in the next edition of the *Red Book*. They also confirmed there was a market for that variety and that there was enough to go around. "Those are things we'd do as a policy," Dick said.

▲ The 1955 doubled die—today a well-established part of the Lincoln cent series—was controversial when it was discovered.

When I became editor of the *Red Book*, I proceeded in much the same way, touching base with the experts and asking for their opinions about reported varieties. Some people on the outside lobbied for the inclusion of certain varieties, but, as Dick noted, they understood we were not a court of decision.

Perhaps the most controversial variety was the 1955 doubled-die cent. "Eastern dealers made the market for this error coin and were strongly [in favor of listing it] in the *Guide Book*," Dick remembered. "Western panelists generally were against it. Sad to say, they were not in on the ground floor, as all turned up [on] the East Coast. A survey among collectors favored including it."[88]

▲ The low-mintage 1950-D Jefferson nickel was a hot speculative item for a while, heavily promoted, with its value peaking higher than $20 in the 1960s. The *Red Book*'s pricing team had to wrestle with such market anomalies.

A similar procedure was followed for listing the 1960 large- and small-date cents. "They were easier to pinpoint because details were evident," said Dick.[89] "They were so widespread that there wasn't much of a problem there. [But] the information still had to be crystallized so we could explain which was which. I think in that case the Mint was very helpful. [It made] the information available, so it was pretty well publicized, as I recall."

The 1950-D Jefferson nickel was a questionable listing, whose value the *Red Book* listed as speculative. "The 1950-D somehow was one that never got into circulation," Dick recalled. "I think about $700 a roll was the peak. Who knew [the] next week what the price would be? That proved to be true of others, too, but the 1950-D was the shining example. I always shake my head about that coin."[90]

Coin Design

In his capacity as news editor of *Numismatic News*, Ed Reiter wrote in September 1984 that "more than anyone, R.S. Yeoman helped bring numismatics down from its ivory tower and into the everyday life of the man on the street."[91]

Reiter explained that, like many observers, Dick felt the hobby was inhibited by "the dearth of collectible coins in circulation," but what truly

▲ The nation's Bicentennial coins stirred interest among the general public. Yeoman encouraged such experimentation in coin designs.

dampened interest was not the lack of value in the nation's pocket change, but rather the lack of variety.

"What we need," Dick said, was "at least one new series of coins. Even [changing] part of a coin's design, [as] we did with the Lincoln cent in 1959, would help stimulate interest. People were tremendously interested when the Mercury dime, for instance, was replaced. We at Whitman were making folders 24 hours a day, and even then we couldn't make enough."

However, Dick cautioned that revision must be permanent. "Changing the design for just a year or two—the way we did with the three Bicentennial coins—that's not enough. That doesn't make a new series. It stirs things up a bit, but not the way we do when we have a whole new series."

Reiter noted that Dick was encouraged by the U.S. Mint's 1982 resumption of commemorative coinage but doubted that the hobby derived much benefit from the issuance of coins with hefty price tags. "What we really need to draw new collectors is not a $350 gold coin, but a part-silver coin selling for, say $5," Dick said. "The government needs to come down to the Boy Scout level—to a price where a grandfather might buy such a coin for his grandchildren. If we could get commemorative coins priced at no more than $5, we'd really stir things up."

► Yeoman recalled when the dime changed from the Winged Liberty design to a portrait of President Franklin Roosevelt. "We at Whitman were making folders 24 hours a day, and even then we couldn't make enough."

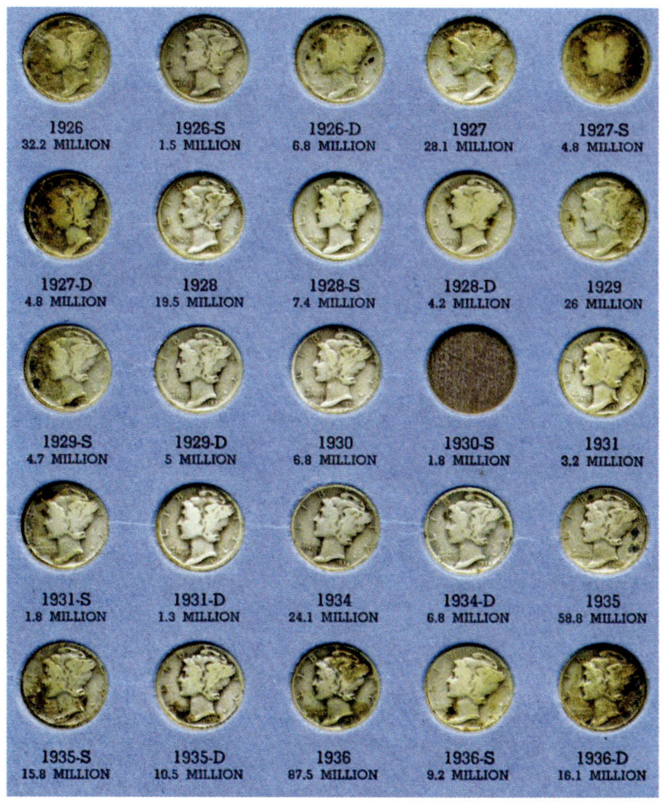

The Silent Majority

[I'd like to offer a] few words [about] the important silent majority of collectors. They may not be coin club members, subscribers to coin publications or known outside their families. They are the silent buyers of coin folders, catalogs and informational books on our hobby. They probably number in the hundreds of thousands. They pursue and collect coins from circulation and are happy with coins grading Fine. . . . Let us be sure that we do not become so elite in this group that this huge segment is ignored.[92]—R.S. Yeoman

WORD PLAY

Although generally quiet and reserved, Dick had a wonderful sense of humor. He loved a good joke and was particularly fond of quips and malapropisms. As a member of Toastmasters during his retirement years in Green Valley, Arizona, he kept a file of material for use in his presentations.

Among Dick's papers was a copy of an article titled "Using Humor in Speaking" by Charles Hampton. "It is usually expected that the speaker shall garnish his discourse with anecdotes," the author wrote, "so jokes must be dug up from some source and duly executed. . . . Make a joke file (and keep adding to it) over a period of years."

Dick obviously followed Hampton's advice—the Western Archives contain pages of notes penciled in his hand, including a fair number of malapropisms that made him chuckle. For example:

- "I call litterbugs nothing more than strewballs and scatterpillars."
- "My dentist simply drives me to extraction."
- "Ever since he retired, he's been screw loose and fancy free."

Also in his files were quotable jokes and comments he thought might provide some levity in his Toastmaster talks:

- "Your *home town* is the place where people wonder how *you've ever got as far* as you have." (Dick's emphasis)
- "Perhaps the best reason you can't take money with you is because it goes before you do."

"Coins are only lasting mementoes."
—R.S. Yeoman

- "An unknown Dublin citizen wrote or said: 'The human brain is a wonderful thing. It starts working the moment you are born, and never stops until you stand up to speak in public.'"
- "Money may be the root of all evil, but it sure grows into some beautiful shrubbery." (Dick credited this quote to his friend and fellow wordsmith Glenn Smedley.)
- "A bank vice president strolling through his domain one day saw a stranger in the tellers' cage piling $100 bills next to a small bag. The VP greeted him cheerfully, 'May I ask where you received your financial training?'

  "'Yale,' the stranger replied.

  "'I thought so,' said the VP. 'What's your name?'

  "'Yohnson.'"

"I confess to an unshakable, long-term instinct and habit—I still put the glass on many Lincoln cents that pass through my hands."—R.S. Yeoman

Dick was quite the grammarian and fondly embraced a number of pet peeves. Of considerable irritation to him was the misplacement of the word "only" in a sentence, with too many words often separating it from the intended subject. (For example, "I only have eyes for you" should be "I have eyes for only you.") Glenn Smedley had written to syndicated columnist Abigail Van Buren ("Dear Abby") on this topic, and Yeoman spotted it in his local paper. He wrote to Smedley on April 5, 1986:

> I was fascinated by your pursuit of the careless use of the term "only." For several years, I observed the placement of that elusive word in sentences used mainly by sports commentators. My surveillance was concerned by the position of "only" in the sentence. In other words, how far from its proper place it was used. . . . Those of us who write have learned, sooner or later, where the term belongs in a sentence.
>
> My latest hobby in the word-grammar game is the use of singular and plural. There is a common, almost universal, love of the word "their." It probably is an instinctive wish to avoid saying "his or hers." Anyway, I mentally reason, if the term were to be used properly, it would be followed by plural terms.

▲ Abigail Van Buren.

Murphy's Law of Perversity

▲ Ann Landers.

On November 7, 1977, syndicated newspaper columnist Ann Landers (Abigail Van Buren's twin sister) published "Murphy's Law of Perversity":

> Nothing is as easy as it looks.
>
> Everything takes longer than you expect.
>
> If anything can go wrong, it will.
>
> If there is a possibility of several things going wrong, the one that will go wrong first will be the one that will do the most damage.
>
> Left to themselves, all things go from bad to worse.
>
> If you work on a thing long enough to "improve" it, it will break.
>
> If you think everything will be O.K., you have surely overlooked something.
>
> Mother nature always sides with the hidden flaw.
>
> Mother nature is a witch. [Ann Landers told her readers that she purposely used the word *witch*, noting that "this is a family newspaper."]

Dick clipped the column from his local paper and penned his own version, which he presented at a Toastmasters meeting, complete with relevant numismatic references:

> **MURPHY'S NEW LAW**
>
> When I first heard a quote on Murphy's Law, it was simply: "IF ANYTHING CAN GO WRONG, IT WILL." . . . I propose an amendment: "If there is a vacant space, it will be filled."
>
> Now, I never met Mr. Murphy, nor learned his full name, nor from whence he came. Possibly he is of Irish extraction, which, if true, is a paradox, as the Sons of Erin have a solid tradition for cheerful optimism. We all, in one way or another, have come to know that "Nature abhors a vacuum." I contend that mankind is faced many times daily with vacant spaces, and each of us reacts consciously or unconsciously with an irresistible compulsion to put something into it.
>
> Consider the crossword puzzle, the jigsaw puzzle, or the coin board. Can we relax until the empty spaces are plugged up? Those are fun

things, of course, but our instincts are most likely to stay on the side of perversity, with which our lives are full to overflowing.

I said, "overflowing."

How about our plans when we move into a Northern-type house, with attic and basement? Doesn't the lady of the house exclaim, "How nice, lots of closets?" What happens to those beautiful spaces? Fibber Magee had one of those closets. Kitchen closets, broom closets, refrigerators—how often do they have empty spaces? We really hurt when we moved to Green Valley and [now] live without attics and basements.

I recall that when I was promoted at the office, I was thrilled to get a larger desk and my very own file. Within three months there was hardly room for the phone. Then the boss let me have another "work" table behind my chair. That turned out to be a replacement for the waste basket. And so it went.

What about our conversation and speeches? Part of our Toastmaster agenda is devoted to "stalls." We can't seem to resist those space-fillers "Uh" and "Y'know."

Have you looked for a parking space in a congested area? Usually there is none, and if you spot one in your rear-vision mirror, by the time you maneuver, some lame brain has taken it over.

They tell us to avoid tailgating on the highway. Just pull back from the car ahead an extra car length. You know what happens. Some feverish jockey in his Volks will be right in there, so you are tailgating once more.

I abhor a vacuum too, even if it is the carpet sweeper. There are many examples of space-fillers, and the space here is five minutes, but I'll bet a nickel that just as soon as I leave this space, someone will occupy it!

FANS AND FRIENDS

Over the course of his career Dick made countless friends, many of whom remained so for the rest of his life. A genuinely nice guy, he was greatly admired and respected by his peers. *Coins* magazine publisher Cliff Mishler wrote in 1977, "My reading of what the hobby is, was, and might have been at this juncture in time tells me that Dick, as R.S. Yeoman is known by his legions of hobby friends, alone was responsible for pouring the firm foundation upon which our hobby has blossomed."[93]

In the January 29, 1975, issue of *Coin World*, Abe Kosoff, a *Red Book* panelist, shared his thoughts about his longtime friend: "So much has been written about Dick that I'm sure to many readers much of this is old stuff. His interests are so varied, yet, because Dick is so quiet and unassuming, it is difficult to write about him, more so than about a flamboyant,

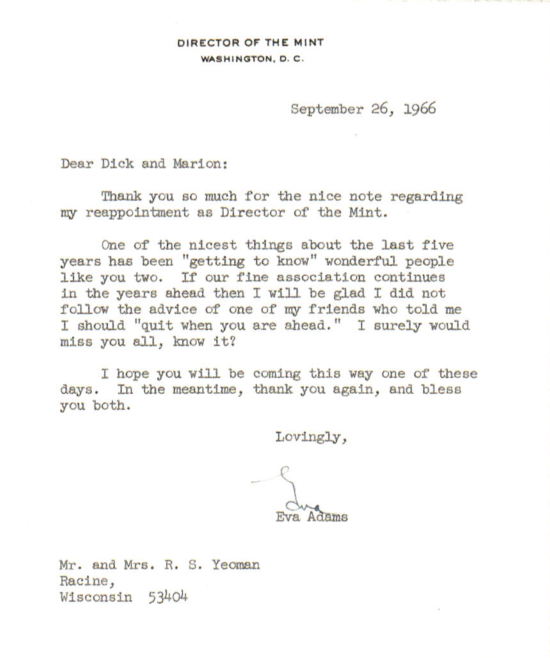

DIRECTOR OF THE MINT
WASHINGTON, D. C.

September 26, 1966

Dear Dick and Marion:

Thank you so much for the nice note regarding my reappointment as Director of the Mint.

One of the nicest things about the last five years has been "getting to know" wonderful people like you two. If our fine association continues in the years ahead then I will be glad I did not follow the advice of one of my friends who told me I should "quit when you are ahead." I surely would miss you all, know it?

I hope you will be coming this way one of these days. In the meantime, thank you again, and bless you both.

Lovingly,

Eva Adams

Mr. and Mrs. R. S. Yeoman
Racine,
Wisconsin 53404

▲ Chet Krause, Margo Russell, and Cliff Mishler. All three of these hobby legends gave credit to R.S. Yeoman for his pioneering work and influence in numismatics.

▲ A note from Eva Adams illustrates the warmth of Yeoman's many friendships.

out-going type. Funny things just didn't happen to Dick. On the other hand, his very presence as a member of a committee lends confidence and authority to it."[94]

In his presentation at a 1971 coin show in Jacksonville, Florida, Dick related:

> [T]he most rewarding part of my association with this wonderful hobby has been people. All kinds of people. I recall a few years ago discussing a rather sophisticated point of numismatics with a fellow, at the finish of which I had an ungovernable urge to ask where he lived and where he worked. When I questioned him, he quickly told me the city's name and that he worked in a school. When I asked his teaching position, he said "I am the janitor." He did not hesitate to reveal his relatively humble occupation. I am convinced that if the principal of his school were a coin collector, he would have been no better informed than my janitor friend.

Warm, casual exchanges were not unusual for Dick, who corresponded or conversed with thousands of collectors, young and old, during his nearly 50-year career. He recounted, "I remember a handwritten letter from [songwriter] Hoagy Carmichael, whose obsession was 1915-S cents, giving me the dickens for underpricing [the coin] and ending his message [with] 'and that's my story, morning glory.'"

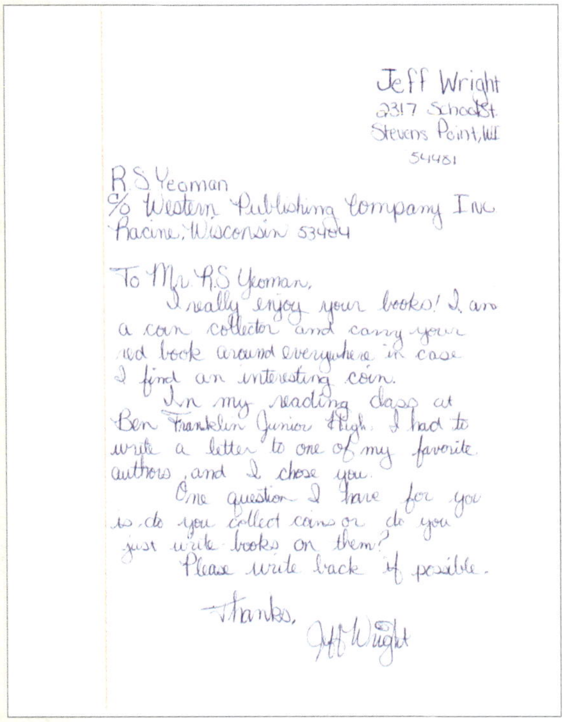

Jeff Wright
2317 School St.
Stevens Point, WI
54481

R S Yeoman
% Western Publishing Company Inc
Racine, Wisconsin 53404

To Mr R.S Yeoman,
I really enjoy your books! I am a coin collector and carry your red book around everywhere in case I find an interesting coin.
In my reading class at Ben Franklin Junior High. I had to write a letter to one of my favorite authors, and I chose you.
One question I have for you is do you collect coins or do you just write books on them?
Please write back if possible.

Thanks,
Jeff Wright

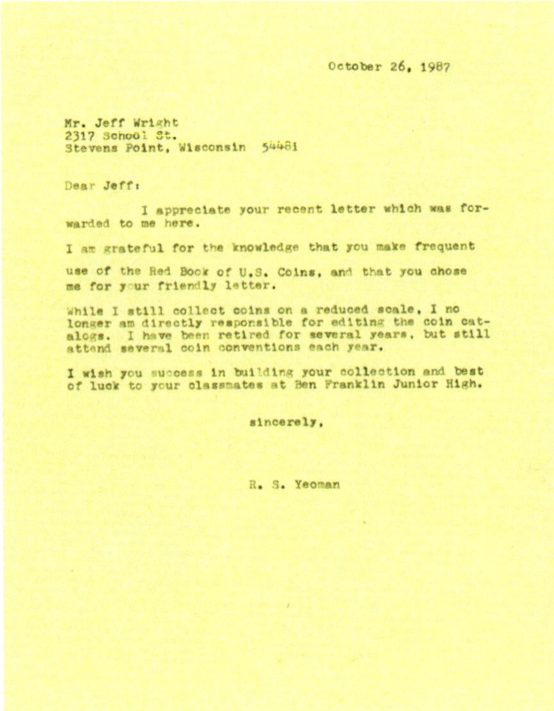

October 26, 1987

Mr. Jeff Wright
2317 School St.
Stevens Point, Wisconsin 54481

Dear Jeff:

I appreciate your recent letter which was forwarded to me here.

I am grateful for the knowledge that you make frequent use of the Red Book of U.S. Coins, and that you chose me for your friendly letter.

While I still collect coins on a reduced scale, I no longer am directly responsible for editing the coin catalogs. I have been retired for several years, but still attend several coin conventions each year.

I wish you success in building your collection and best of luck to your classmates at Ben Franklin Junior High.

Sincerely,

R. S. Yeoman

▲ Yeoman always responded to queries, especially from young collectors, such as Jeff Wright. Wright wrote to Yeoman ("one of my favorite authors") as part of a class assignment. "Do you collect coins," he asked, "or do you just write books on them?" Yeoman replied, "I still collect coins on a reduced scale" and "I wish you success in building your collection and best of luck to your classmates at Ben Franklin Junior High."

In a foreword he prepared for *Perspectives in Numismatics*, a collection of essays celebrating the Chicago Coin Club's 800th meeting on September 11, 1985, Dick talked about a few of his early acquaintances:

> In the spring of 1940, I recall meeting Eric Newman, then vice president of Central States Numismatic Society, at its convention in Burlington, Iowa. He has been a constant friend over the years. I know no researcher more thorough.
>
> . . . It seems like only a few years ago when Dave Bowers surfaced on the numismatic scene. He was an eager youth who made an early start in this fast-moving profession. He has become an authority not only in numismatics, but [also] is an expert in several classes of collectibles, a prolific writer, and a popular published author.
>
> . . . Glenn [Smedley], like Lee Hewitt and many others in the [Chicago Coin Club], was a great help to me, especially during the early *Red Book* years when he served as coordinator of the panel of contributors. He too has earned recent election to the [ANA's] Numismatic Hall of Fame.

◀ American entertainer Hoagy Carmichael had a penchant for Lincoln cents—and he let Yeoman know about it.

◄ In 1966 Dick Yeoman took Mint Director Eva Adams on a special tour of Whitman's printing operation in Racine.

In 1966 Mint Director Eva Adams toured the Western plant where *Red Books* were being bound. The occasion was memorable, as Dick related:[95]

> As we passed through our bindery, she picked up a *Red Book* just off the line, and found it to be bound upside down. "Look," she shouted above the din, "a mint error!" Later, she wrote asking for one of those *Red Book* errors, just for the fun of it. Our rejects, by that time, were either destroyed or corrected, so we took a *Guide Book* apart and rebound it upside down. I properly inscribed it as a genuine mint error and mailed it on to her.
>
> Some weeks later, a special package arrived on my desk. It was the Annual Mint Report. You guessed it. It was bound upside down . . . and [inscribed "To my good friend Dick Yeoman—with regards, even if something is up-side down! Most sincerely – Eva Adams, Director of the Mint."] It is one of my treasured mementoes, a sort of testament that in the sacred precincts of our government, lapses will occur and are recognized with good grace. It is comforting to know that a warm sense of humor can be present to season the human mix of personalities, in high and low places.

▲ Yeoman fondly remembered Q. David Bowers: "an eager youth who made an early start in this fast-moving profession."

On September 26, 1966, Adams dropped Dick and his wife a line:

> Thank you so much for the nice note regarding my reappointment as Director of the Mint. One of the nicest things about the last five years has been "getting to know" wonderful people like you two. If our fine association continues in the years ahead, then I will be glad I did not follow the advice of one of my friends who told me I should quit "when [I was] ahead." I surely would miss you all, know it?
>
> I hope you will be coming this way one of these days. In the meantime, thank you again, and bless you both.
>
> Lovingly,
> Eva

"Leave here some token of your stay."

Dick and Marion often welcomed friends—numismatic and otherwise—to their home in Racine. They made good use of a beautifully printed and embellished book they received as a wedding gift in 1925. The frontispiece read as follows:

> To the Guest in the House
>
> Write in this little book, O ye Guest, e'er ye leave this kindly roof—if only a few words and your name.—Leave here some token of your stay—some happening or pleasant thought that shall make these blank pages into a Volume of Remembrance.

Visitors seemed to pick the pre-printed quotations they liked and signed that entry, even if it meant skipping a page or two:

From Irene and Paul Smith (July 11, 1935): "Racine would never be complete without the Yeos and fried perch—but no connection."

From Adeline & Aubrey Bebee (June 21, 1952): "We will always remember the many wonderful times we have had with you grand folks."

From attendees at the Racine Numismatic Society banquet, who visited the Yeo's home before and after the event (April 19, 1952):

J. Henri Ripstra
Glenn B. Smedley
James A. Friberg
Anna Ripstra
Tillie S. Boosel
Harry X Boosel
Marcella Sheldon
Laura Grace Miller
Blanche Klein
Harold R. Klein
Margaret Palzer
Marion P. Culver
M. Vernon Sheldon—"Remember, we were the last to depart after the Breakfast. Delightful."

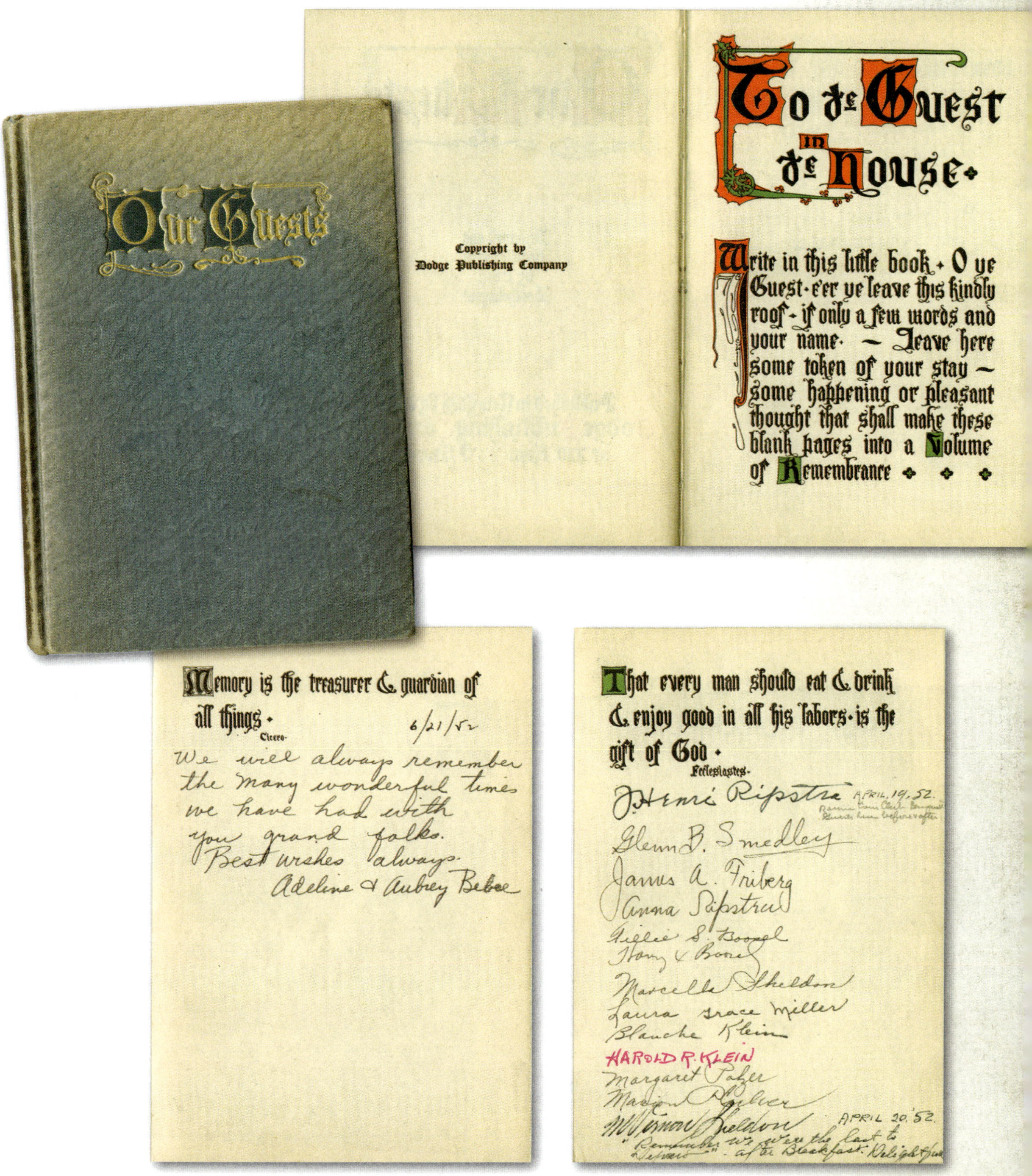

▲ Dick and Marion received this guest book as a wedding gift and frequently set it out for visiting friends. Among those signing were Adeline and Aubrey Bebee and members of the Racine Numismatic Society.

▲ Lewis Reagan, secretary of the ANA, and his wife vacationed with Marion and Dick Yeoman in 1955.

▲ Yeoman regularly attended ANA conventions, where he shared many banquet meals with friends.

▲ Dick and Marion chat with Byron Johnson.

▲ Dick with longtime friends Herb Bergen (left) and Norman Shultz (right) in 1978.

Best of friends: Aubrey and Adeline Bebee and Marion and Dick Yeoman at the 1974 ANA convention in Bal Harbour, Florida.

▲ J. Hewitt Judd.

Not surprisingly, Dick was on a first-name basis with Dr. J. Hewitt Judd, who wrote *United States Pattern, Experimental and Trial Pieces*, which Whitman first published in 1959. In April 1965 Judd and his wife were living in Omaha, Nebraska, when they received this letter from Dick commiserating on the recent burglary of their home:

> Dear Hewitt and Bunny:
>
> Word has just reached me, [a] little belatedly, that you people suffered a serious loss of your extensive coin collection. Naturally, this has shaken us up too, especially since Marion and I underwent a similar experience last Christmas Eve.[96] While our actual loss was minor, the experience was upsetting, and we want you to know that we sympathize with you and wish that we could do more than just offer words.
>
> I somehow feel that your coins are too special to be lost in the numismatic market. They ought to be easily identified, and I hope the culprits will be apprehended before very long.

Judd responded in a letter dated May 7, 1965:

> Dear Dick:
>
> Bunny and I certainly want to thank you for your nice note with regard to the Ancient Greek Coins. It was especially welcome since you had undergone a similar experience last Christmas. It gives you sort of a funny feeling to know that somebody has been in the house and made off with something you have worked at for a long time in such a short time. However, I am very grateful that we did not come home and perhaps get shot or beat up. We both are well, and I think it is much more important to be alive than to be a dead hero.
>
> I really don't know how they are going to dispose of the coins unless they have someone who buys without any questions asked. If they try to dispose of the collection through regular dealers, I am almost certain that they will be recognized. My plans for numismatics in the future, of course, are pretty uncertain at this time, but I hope to keep in touch with all my friends, as these bonds cannot be broken by any one episode like this.

(Judd mourned the loss of his ancient coins and effectively left the hobby. When thieves broke into the Yeos' home on that Christmas Eve in 1964 and made off with Marion's U.S. coin collection, she too ceased her

▲ China and Mexico both struck five-ounce silver pieces for the August 1987 ANA convention—one of the last coin shows that Yeoman would attend. "Atlanta was sort of a reunion," he wrote, recalling 47 years of such conventions.

numismatic activity, turning her attention instead to her newest hobby—collecting playing cards, of which she reportedly had many thousands.[97])

Dick kept in touch with his Elgin friends Alwin and Viola Swanson. In a letter dated September 14, 1987, he related his experiences at a recent ANA convention in Georgia:

> Atlanta was sort of a reunion. My feet came out pretty sore, but the floor duty made possible many visits with folks I have known for over 47 past years of numismatic conventions.
>
> . . . I realize that you folks are a rare couple—the only remaining contact with Elgin. Our cousin Ruth O'Connor, the last relative with whom we have communication, now lives at Holmstad in Batavia [Illinois].

He also noted that the spelling of the street on which he and Marion lived in their Arizona retirement community was one word, Carondelet (not "Caron Delet"). "The printer made the mistake on our letterhead. We made the mistake of failing to proofread."

The "No Name" Club

In 1980 Dan and Thelma Brown assembled a group of friends in a private dining room at La Maisonette restaurant in Cincinnati, where the ANA was holding its 89th Anniversary Convention. Among those in attendance were Aubrey and Adeline Bebee, Oscar and Polly Dodson, Lucy Freeman, Lester Merkin, Abe Kosoff, Ray and Betty Lefman, Matt and Janet Rothert, and Dick and Marion Yeoman. The friendly get-together became an annual affair, and the group was known affectionately as the "No Names."

Dick and Marion were regular and welcome participants, but they were unable to attend the August 4, 1988, event, again held in Cincinnati. Afterward, Dan Brown dropped them a line:

> Bebees were hosts for the No Names on Wednesday night. Bebees, Browns, Dodsons, Lefmans, Lucy attending. Missed you two. . . . Sending one bronze [OTACS medal], which I think you will want so as to keep your set complete. Cost $24. Next year will be our last year for medals, as we'll make a permanent one for the years after. [Dick wrote in margin that he replied on August 22, 1988, with a check for $24.]

▶ Dick received best-of-show exhibit honors from Numismatic Association of Southern California president Tom Fitzgerald.

▲ Dick Yeoman explained the process of hand-sewing signatures to Tom Fruit, the first professional editor of *Numismatic News*, during a tour of the bindery.

▶ In 1966, Whitman officers welcomed Mint Director Eva Adams to the Racine plant.

◀ Dick always made time to autograph the *Red Book* for collectors. (Also pictured: the simple business card he carried when he was vice president of Whitman Publishing Company.)

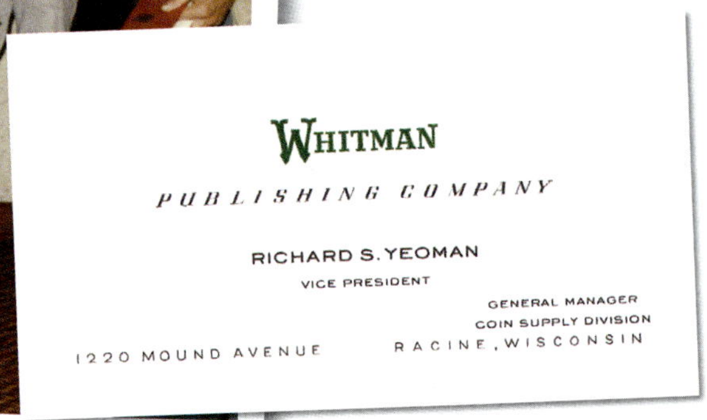

THE BEST SELLER LIST

Alice Payne Hackett's recent book, "70 Years of Best Sellers, 1895-1965", reviewed in the February 2, 1968, issue of Time Magazine, has spotlighted the success of cookbooks in the bookselling trade. Overlooked in her list of non-fiction best sellers is R. S. Yeoman's book, "A Guide Book of U. S. Coins" (Red Book), which has sold 6,758,482 copies from 1947 through 1965. Also overlooked is R. S. Yeoman's "Handbook of U. S. Coins", which has sold 4,810,304 copies from 1944 through 1965.

With these additions to the list and using 1965 as the cut-off date, the following is presented for your information.

1895 - 1965

I. TOP 15 ALL-TIME BEST SELLERS - NON-FICTION

1. The Pocket Book of Baby And Child Care (The Common Sense Book of Baby and Child Care) Dr. Benjamin Spock. 1946 ---------- 19,076,822
2. Better Homes and Gardens Cook Book. 1930 ---------- 11,325,299
3. Pocket Atlas. 1917 ---------- 11,000,000
4. Betty Crocker's Picture Cook Book. 1950 ---------- 7,000,000
5. Guide Book of U. S. Coins. 1947 ---------- 6,758,482 ✓
6. How to Win Friends and Influence People. Dale Carnegie. 1937 ---------- 6,578,314
7. 101 Famous Poems. R. J. Cook. 1916 ---------- 6,000,000
8. English-Spanish, Spanish-English Dictionary. Carlos Castillo and Otto F. Bond. 1948 ---------- 5,899,000
9. Profiles in Courage. John F. Kennedy. 1956 ---------- 5,490,651
10. Roget's Pocket Thesaurus. 1923 ---------- 5,416,857
11. Modern World Atlas. 1922 ---------- 5,000,000
12. Handbook of U. S. Coins. R. S. Yeoman. 1944 ---------- 4,810,304 ✓
13. 30 Days to a More Powerful Vocabulary. Wilfred J. Funk and Norman Lewis. 1942 ---------- 4,712,588
14. Betty Crocker's Good and Easy Cook Book. 1954 ---------- 4,500,000
15. The Pocket Cook Book. Elizabeth Woody. 1942 ---------- 4,466,200

II. TOP 11 ALL-TIME BEST SELLERS - FICTION AND NON-FICTION

1. The Pocket Book of Baby and Child Care Dr. Benjamin Spock. 1946 ---------- 19,076,822
2. Better Homes and Garden Cook Book. 1930 ---------- 11,325,299
3. Pocket Atlas. 1917 ---------- 11,000,000
4. Peyton Place. Grace Metalious. 1956 ---------- 9,919,785
5. In His Steps. Charles Monroe Sheldon. 1897 ---------- 8,065,000
6. God's Little Acre. Erskine Caldwell. 1933 ---------- 8,061,812
7. Betty Crocker's Picture Cook Book. 1950 ---------- 7,000,000
8. Gone With The Wind. Margaret Mitchell. 1937 ---------- 6,978,211
9. Guide Book of U. S. Coins. R. S. Yeoman. 1947 ---------- 6,758,482 ✓
10. How to Win Friends and Influence People Dale Carnegie. 1937 ---------- 6,578,314
11. Lady Chatterley's Lover. D. H. Lawrence. 1932 ---------- 6,326,470

Among Dick's personal files was his typed copy of "The Best Seller List" (1895–1965), in which he inserted the *Red Book* and *Blue Book* in their rightful positions.

▲ Half dollars from 1949 (the year Laura Sharon Yeo graduated high school) and from 1953 (the year she married).

ALL IN THE FAMILY

While Dick and Marion were in Milwaukee for the Central States Numismatic Society's 38th Anniversary Convention in May 1977, their Racine home was targeted again. Dick detailed the incident in a letter to his younger brother William, who lived in Glens Falls, New York: "Now I must say that we arrived home following a telephone call from Sharon [their daughter] that our house had been broken into. There was only damage; nothing was taken. We had to come up and make repairs in short order."

At the time, the Yeos were in the process of selling their house and moving to an apartment on Taylor Avenue. Dick wrote to his older brother, Stewart, that their house and grounds were "too much to keep up and a little too great a responsibility for Sharon during [our] six months' absence [in Arizona] each year." After the break-in, Dick and Marion set to work "deciding what to move and what to dispose of."

The Yeos were very close to their daughter, who lived in Racine most of her life. (Interestingly, when attending numismatic events together, the entire family went by the name Yeoman.) Sharon attended Fratt Elementary and graduated in 1949 from Washington Park High School. There, she and Eugene Z. ("Gene") Dodd met and became sweethearts; they were married on August 22, 1953, at First Congregational Church in Racine. Their daughter, Laura Jean, came along five years later.

Early in her professional life, Sharon was employed as a secretary for a dental office and insurance company. (As mentioned earlier, her maternal grandfather was a dentist.) Then, in 1983, she and Gene founded Treetop Publishing, and Sharon served as its chief financial officer. In her spare time, she was an avid reader and a fan of the arts, particularly opera. Like her mother, she enjoyed card games. (Marion was a champion bridge player.)

Dick kept in close contact with his siblings and, before his retirement, always sent them the newest editions of the *Red Book*. His niece Jane, who lived in Loudonville, New York, sent him this note on July 5, 1987, after viewing an episode of *Jeopardy!* on television:

> [Did you know] you were a question on the quiz show *Jeopardy!*? I hope you caught it! I'm not a regular watcher, and I was just thrilled when suddenly I heard them ask .... "The color of the book on U.S. coins by R.S. Yeoman."

Treetop Publishing

In 1983 Sharon and Eugene Dodd, Dick Yeoman's daughter and son-in-law, launched a new company—Treetop Publishing—out of their Racine home. The inspiration for the enterprise came from a blank book that Gene brought home from Golden Book Encyclopedia (a Whitman company), where he worked as an editorial coordinator. He gave the volume to his daughter, and she and her friends began filling the pages with stories and illustrations of their own. Gene took note of their enthusiasm, as well as the increasing popularity of bound journals for adults, and decided the blank-book business was worthy of investigation. He marketed his products as "Bare Books: Blank Books for Kids."

Wrote Marlene Salley in the September–October 1988 issue of Racine's *Journal Times*[98]:

> Someone suggested that Dodd look into the school market. In 1983 he received a call from the Stephen Bull Fine Arts School, 815 DeKoven Ave., saying that it was having an author and book fair and that the parents' group wanted to sell his books for 50 cents each. The books ordinarily [sold] for $1 each, but the parents' group planned to pay the difference in price. Dodd delivered 500 books to the school on Wednesday, then got a call on Friday requesting 500 more. The original delivery had been sold before the book fair began. In all, 1,200 of his books were sold.

However, according to Salley, Gene had little success marketing directly to school districts, so he began to attend teachers' conventions and gatherings. "He targeted conferences for reading teachers," she wrote, "because he believe[d] that reading and writing go hand in hand. Soon teachers began requesting bigger books, so he started a line called Big Bare Books, selling for $1.50 [each]."

Within a few years, Treetop Publishing's business increased fivefold, with orders received from all 50 states and Puerto Rico, every Canadian province, West Germany, Hong Kong, and Israel.

▲ Sharon Yeo's graduation from Washington Park High School in Racine, 1949.

▲ Dick and his granddaughter, Laura Jean, in 1968.

▲ Sharon and Eugene Dodd with their daughter, Laura Jean.

▲ Dick and Marion vacationed in Arizona for years.

▲ They would eventually move there in retirement, in 1977.

▲ Relaxing in the Arizona sun, 1982.

GENEROUS SPIRIT

Dick was a charitable, kind-hearted person who never hesitated to assist collectors and Whitman employees, or to donate his time, expertise, and funds to worthy causes. He was an enthusiastic supporter of the Boy and Girl Scouts of America and a benefactor of the University of Wisconsin and the United Way of Greater Tucson. He donated *Red Books* to the Tucson Numismatic Society and annually sent out more than 90 autographed copies to numismatic friends and acquaintances. He regularly presented informative and entertaining numismatic talks around the country and to local coin clubs and residents of his retirement community.

In September 1973 the American Numismatic Association was grateful to receive 1,764 world coins from Dick's personal reference collection, which he began assembling in the 1950s. The coins had been used to illustrate William D. Craig's *Coins of the World, 1750–1850*, as well as Dick's own works on more modern issues.

"My objective was to put them in the right place," he told *Numismatic News*. "It was my loyalty and interest in the ANA that dictated my action."

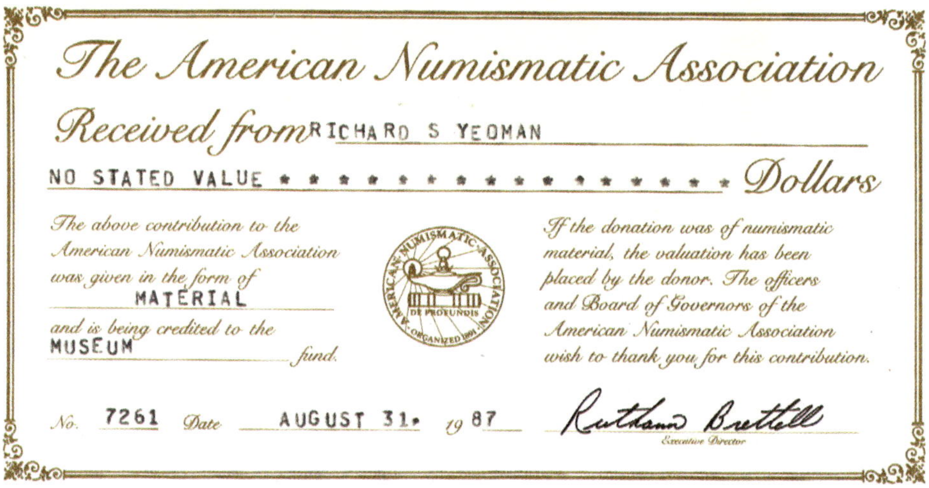

The American Numismatic Association

Received from RICHARD S YEOMAN

NO STATED VALUE * * * * * * * * * * * * * * * * Dollars

The above contribution to the American Numismatic Association was given in the form of MATERIAL and is being credited to the MUSEUM fund.

If the donation was of numismatic material, the valuation has been placed by the donor. The officers and Board of Governors of the American Numismatic Association wish to thank you for this contribution.

No. 7261 Date AUGUST 31, 19 87

Executive Director

▶ Yeoman was a staunch supporter of the ANA and donated material to its Money Museum on several occasions.

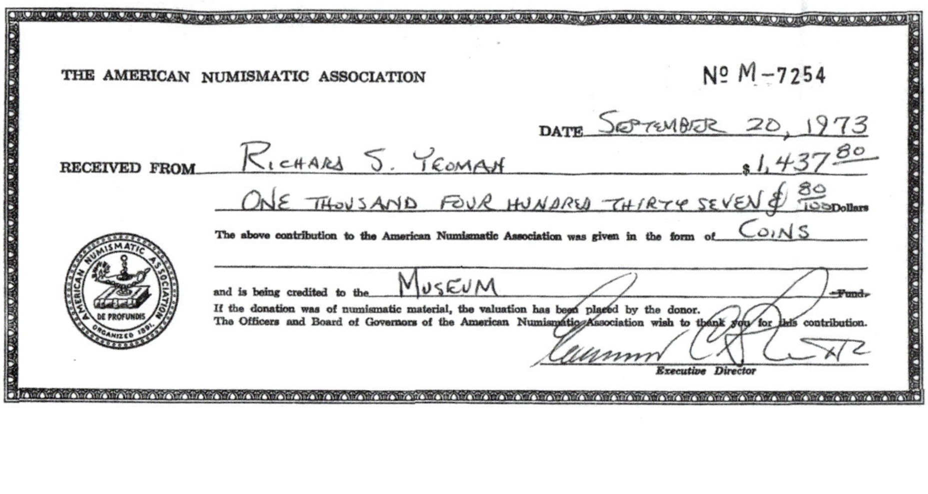

THE AMERICAN NUMISMATIC ASSOCIATION

Nº M-7254

DATE September 20, 1973

RECEIVED FROM Richard S. Yeoman $1,437 80/100

One thousand four hundred thirty seven & 80/100 Dollars

The above contribution to the American Numismatic Association was given in the form of Coins

and is being credited to the Museum Fund.

If the donation was of numismatic material, the valuation has been placed by the donor.

The Officers and Board of Governors of the American Numismatic Association wish to thank you for this contribution.

Executive Director

▶ In 1973 Dick Yeoman donated his reference collection of world coins to the American Numismatic Association. Many of the specimens were not previously represented in the ANA Museum's collection.

The ANA's plans for its museum were evolving, and Dick felt the timing of his donation was advantageous. "ANA is apt to need them more than the [American Numismatic Society], which has been around much longer." His thinking proved correct, as very few of his donated pieces were duplicated in the ANA's world collection.

Following Dick's glowing 1977 tribute in Milwaukee, *Numismatic News Weekly* published a letter to the editor from Don Bale Jr., president of Bale Publications in New Orleans:[99]

> R.S. Yeoman's numismatic talent is exceeded only by his willingness to help "small fry" like myself to get started in the numismatic publishing business.
>
> When I solicited Yeoman's editorial help on my coin book in 1963 [*Complete Guide for Profitable Coin Investing*], he immediately answered my request. I'm sure this type of cooperation partly explains why he is able to retire successfully as a numismatic literary giant, and—just as importantly—as a decent human being.

Dick helped out family and friends when he could. In the Western Archives is a February 1987 note from his son-in-law, Gene, to whom he loaned a modest amount of money to launch his publishing company. "In my first year of business, I borrowed the money and only recently remembered that I never repaid the loan. I apologize for the delay," Gene wrote, enclosing a check for the full amount.

▲ In 1973 Yeoman donated 1,764 world coins from his personal reference collection to the American Numismatic Association.

▲ Yeoman welcomed guests to visit Whitman's production facilities. In one visit, his longtime friend Dan Brown (middle) learned how coin folders were made, from Pete Foerster.

According to February 1987 correspondence from Racine businessman and friend Lesley F. Boeck and his wife, Doris, Dick apparently invested in their company, which was involved in gas stations and other real estate. "We are enjoying (what [we] think is an affluent) retirement," they wrote. "[We] often think of you folks and the others who made this possible for us [by] giving encouragement and moral support, along with your generous purchases of stock in our company when there were very few assets."

ADVENTUROUS TRAVELER

Dick's roots were firmly planted in Wisconsin and later in Arizona, where he and Marion ultimately retired. However, his work for Whitman sent him all over the United States, and he was in great demand as a numismatic speaker. It was not unusual for him to receive invitations from regional coin clubs, such as this one dated December 29, 1986, from Lorna Lebold, president of the Numismatic Association of Southern California:

> We hope that you will be able to attend the show coming in February. In fact, if you are willing, would you please be the featured speaker at the Saturday forum [February 6] at 3:00 pm. . . . Please let me know as soon as possible so we can get out some good publicity. I know that everyone would be so pleased to hear from you again. It's been too long.
>
> I forgot to mention, the topic is of your choice.

Dick responded on January 3, 1987:

> I am flattered to be asked to participate in the Saturday forum during the NASC Convention next month. I accept and will try to make my topic interesting.
>
> A few years ago, I was on a similar panel for the CSNA in Anaheim. My topic was the story of the 1848 quarter eagle with CAL. I would like to do this one again. My motive for choosing that topic is that it is California-oriented, and I believe that few folks at this event heard me on this subject.... I have, moreover, agreed to judge exhibits for [Albert and Virginia] Hall [on] Friday a.m.

At such shows, Dick and Marion often met up with numismatic friends for a few days of post-convention adventure. Aubrey Bebee waxed nostalgic in a letter dated October 12, 1988:

> [I recall] the many pleasant times we [journeyed] together. We attended a convention on the West Coast, and on our return we stopped at Las Vegas for [the ANA's] mid-winter coin convention. Our "sleeper" was coupled

▲ 1848 quarter eagle with CAL. Yeoman's example was similar to this Very Fine specimen.

> onto your train when it pulled in to Omaha. We played cards all the way to L.A. Marion, I think that you used one of your special deck of cards?
>
> Then, [there was] the time we went to the Big Island [of Hawaii]. We were stopped at the entrance by the police who inquired if we had reservations and asked our names. Then, there was a strike at the hotel, and the manager gave us a special rate with Adeline & you, Marion, making your own beds. Remember, when we left there and flew on that small plane? Dick, you didn't hesitate to sit up front with [the] pilot. Too bad we cannot travel there again and trace our footsteps.
>
> . . . As we are both semi-retired, [traveling together] is about the only way of visiting with each other—a real "come-down" in view of the close relationship that we had over the years.

▲ Card-playing was a pleasant pastime for Dick and Marion and their friends.

Decades earlier, Dick had gotten a taste of world travel. In 1966, five years after he wrote *Moneys of the Bible*, Dick and Lee Hewitt went to Israel to inspect a new mint.[100] "It was before the Six-Day War," Dick said. "The government invited editors and publishers of several publications, including representatives of Krause Publications. At that time, I was editor of the *Whitman Numismatic Journal*." The visitors' expenses were paid and they were given a great deal of freedom, but, Dick said, "some serious business . . . went on for at least two days at the beginning."[101]

The Israel Coins and Medals Corporation, established in 1958 and privatized in 2008 as The Holy Land Mint, hoped to launch an extensive series of commemorative coins. "I think they [wanted] to show us what they had and what their plans were," Dick recalled. "In fact, Lee Hewitt and I . . . went to the government center and [saw] the mint [and] the government printing office. As it happened, [the latter was] printing lottery tickets, so we had a good look at that. Being printers, we were interested in the operation. They had very modern equipment there."

Israel's goal was to maintain an office in the United States that would coordinate the distribution of its coins there. "They really wanted to get off on the right foot," said Dick. "The general idea was to [produce] commemoratives in much the same way other nations do. [It] would have coins each year for special events, religious observances and things of that nature. Over the years, [Israel has] turned out some beautiful pieces."

When asked if he remembered any specific advice he gave the mint officials, Dick said, "How to handle coins." He urged

▼ *Moneys of the Bible*, one of Whitman's popular "Black Books" published in the 1960s.

▲ Yeoman found these third- or fourth-century coins on a beach in Caesarea during his first visit to Israel.

employees to avoid fingerprints by wearing gloves. "We had to make them realize how important that was."

While exploring the area north of Haifa, he came across some young men searching for coins on a beach in Caesarea. He began looking around himself and, before long, found some imperfect third- or fourth-century specimens that had been cast aside by an ancient mint.

Dick also visited an Arab marketplace in Acre, where a local man operating a coin booth immediately recognized him and was familiar with his books. Talk about a small world!

Three years later, Dick had an opportunity to return to Israel and jumped at the chance. A study tour had been organized by Morris Bram of the Israel Numismatic Society, and Dick wanted Marion to experience the Holy Land. (She did not accompany him on his first trip.)[102] "It was more of a tourist-type thing, not going too much into numismatics," Dick explained, "but we went to some of the same places."

However, he and Marion did attend a coin club meeting in Haifa and enjoyed it very much. "There wasn't too much talk about coins," he said. "It was more a chance to get acquainted and ask how we did things in each other's country."

▲ A 1960s travel brochure for Israel.

In 1972 Dick received an unexpected telephone call from his friend Oscar Dodson.[103] He and his wife, Polly, had received a grant from the University of Illinois to go to Africa and acquire native artifacts for the school's Heritage Museum, of which Oscar was director. Knowing that the Yeos liked to travel, he suggested that they come along. Dick and Marion mulled it over for several weeks and agreed to join them. "Then we had to get our disease shots, passports and visas," Dick said. "[Oscar] had already selected the itinerary. We started out with Liberia, then Ghana, Nigeria, Kenya, and Ethiopia."

The couples did everything together, exploring places unfrequented by most tourists. "Oscar had former assignments with Foreign Service, and the State Department had alerted [the embassies in countries we visited]. They were helpful, feeling we were creating goodwill [with] what we were doing."

Naturally, Oscar and Dick were on the lookout for numismatic treasures. In Liberia they met a trader who had a bundle of 25 long iron rods known as kisi pennies. "We were [staying at] the home of a military attaché. I mentioned to [the] Marine officer's 12-year-old-daughter that I'd like to buy [the pennies] if they weren't too expensive. She said, 'You'd better let me do that. How much do you think they're worth?'" Dick replied that what he was willing to pay for them was far less than their value.

She came back with the bundle in about a half hour and said, "Give me four dollars. [The man] wanted a lot more, but he knew he wasn't going to get it."

Dick later reminisced, "You know, today I've got just one of them left. . . . I didn't want to keep the entire bundle, and gradually I gave them out here and there, which is the way I like to do things."

While in Ethiopia, the travelers found themselves in a 1,000-year-old bazaar. At one stall an older gentleman asked Dick if he was a coin collector. "He went through the curtain and came back with three Menelik 1897 *gersh* pieces in real nice condition. I told him I'd like to have them. He had no price [in mind], and I gave him the best memory I had of the catalog price and didn't miss it by much. . . . He was happy, and I still have them. I presume he thought that they were not legal anymore because they hadn't been used in years and they had changed monarchs, but that's just guessing on my part."

Years later, Oscar dropped Dick a note dated July 7, 1988: "If we plan another trip, not much is left. Should we consider the North or South Pole?" Oscar added, "About travel—I heard a fellow, who had been around the world say, 'Next time, we'll go somewhere else.'"

NOT-SO-LAZY DAYS

As Dick's 1970 retirement date approached, Whitman's executive vice president, James B. Lyle, laid out a plan of action on August 3, 1966:

> It now appears that by 1967 the marketing of the Coin and Stamp lines will be handled by the Western Publishing Trade Sales Division. Because of this rather major change, it would seem wise to put into effect by [then] some of the things which we have discussed. . . . You will be responsible particularly for editorial and public relations type of work, and this could be done in whatever fashion best [suits] you. You would maintain a desk in the office in the Coin Department and spend whatever time might be required at the desk; however, if you wish to carry on your editorial work away from the office, this would be satisfactory and you could suit yourself on this point.

After Dick's formal retirement from Whitman Publishing Company, he stayed on as the firm's ambassador, traveling to coin shows and club meetings to promote the products bearing his name. At these events, he usually signed autographs and often delivered talks on numismatic topics.

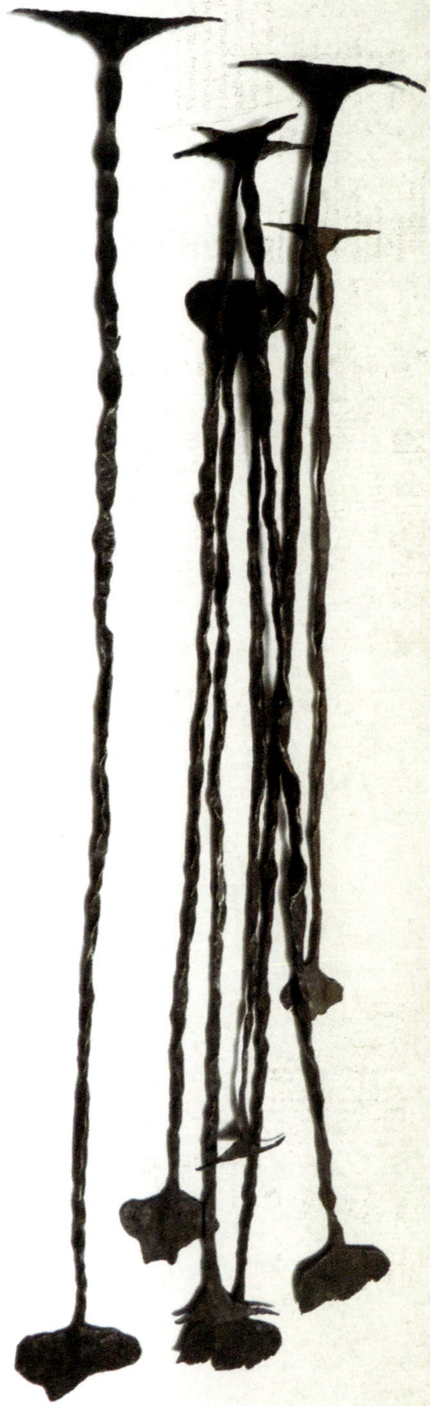

▲ During a trip to Africa, Yeoman purchased a bundle of 25 "kisi pennies" (similar to these) from a dealer in Liberia. Used as small change from about 1860 to 1900, kisi pennies typically measure 9 to 16 inches.

R.S. Yeoman: Legalities of a Bankable Name

Early in his career with Whitman Publishing, Richard S. Yeo elected to use the pseudonym "R.S. Yeoman," beginning with the release of the first edition of the *Handbook of United States Coins* (the "Blue Book") in 1942. He went on to compile and/or write *A Guide Book of United States Coins* (1946), *Moneys of the Bible* (1961), *A Catalog of Modern World Coins* (1958), and *Current Coins of the World* (1966).

In preparation for Yeo's official retirement from the company in June 1970, executive James Lyle sent him a letter dated December 29, 1969, regarding the continued use of his professional name:

> This letter sets forth the understanding between you and this Company concerning the use of your professional name, "R.S. Yeoman," in or on or in connection with, including the sale and advertising thereof, any of the books or publications which we have published and/or sold to date, or on any materials awaiting publication and/or sale which you have furnished us while in our employ or may furnish us thereafter. . . .
>
> [You agree] that you will not permit or authorize the use of your professional name . . . in connection with any similar publications, which is to say any coin catalogs or the like, to be published by anyone other than Western Publishing Company, Inc., without first obtaining our prior written consent.
>
> It is our intention that after you retire from our employ, we may engage your services for correction or revision of any of the publications listed [here]. . . . We may [also] decide at our option to correct or revise or edit any of the [listed publications] by someone other than yourself, and in that event we shall not indicate that such revisions or corrections or additional matter has been prepared or written by you but shall state that such revision or edition or additional writing is by another person.
>
> . . . We shall also have the right not to use your professional name if, at any time, we deem it advisable in our sole judgment not to continue its use, but whether we use it or not shall retain the rights to use any of the contents of the publications listed.
>
> . . . We shall not use your professional name in any way other than as stated herein without first obtaining your consent in writing.

Dick and Marion remained in Racine but wintered in Green Valley. In a letter I received from him, dated November 11, 1975, he shared a bit about his activities in Arizona:

> Out here, the weather has been dry and warm. Each day, without exception since our arrival, has been 100% sunshine. Opening the house was no problem, but getting the landscaping up-to-date has kept me busy up to now. The trimming of the greasewood, palo verde, etc. has been a catch-up job—a few months overdue.
>
> I haven't done any artwork except for a few sketches during walks in the desert. Tomorrow, I will join a small safari group from the neighborhood for a trip down around Ruby and Oro Blanco to see old mines—near the border. If I find a hoard of doubloons, you'll hear from me.
>
> The Tucson Numismatic Society has moved [its] meeting place (as all normal coin clubs are wont to do periodically), so I didn't go up last Tuesday. I was reluctant to search in strange territory after dark. Meanwhile, I'll see if I can find the spot when I'm up there in daylight sometime.

▲ By the time the nation was celebrating its Bicentennial in 1976, Dick and Marion were spending the winter months in Arizona. They were fully settled there by 1978.

By early 1977 the Yeos were solidifying their permanent relocation to Green Valley. In a letter written to Eva Adams on May 24, Dick confirmed that "our moving preparations . . . have now entered the count-down period, and we are making final decisions on bric-a-brac before the movers come into the driveway." Upon their arrival at their new home, Dick quickly stashed away his collections in a safe-deposit box.[104]

As always, Dick kept in touch with his Wisconsin friends, the Swansons. He wrote to them on November 1, 1986, sharing news of Marion's health and their life in Green Valley:

> The summer blew by fast for us. . . . Marion had been slowly recovering from cardiac arrest, which hit her in January. She was well enough to travel to Racine in August to visit with family while I attended the convention in Milwaukee for the American Numismatic Association. My publishers asked me to appear there for public relations, which in my case means autographing the catalogs [*Red Books*]. . . . We did little visiting with Racine friends—so many are gone, we found.
>
> . . . We are [as] active as we wish in our "Resort" [Villa Campana Retirement Community]. The meals are gourmet, and the entertainment is first class, with an

> occasional singing group, pianist and old-time movie video each Wednesday night. Of course, the usual bridge, bingo and exercise classes are standard.
>
> There is special room with a miniature HO gauge railway, with which I am [active]. Also, I am on the Resident Advisory Council, the conduit between the residents and management. Busy, busy!

Dick and Marion followed up with a Christmas letter to friends in December:

> Our most gratifying contemplation of the past year is Marion's steady health improvement following her cardiac arrest emergency last January.
>
> Our location at Villa Campana Retirement Center has proven to be the best move for both of us. Independence, with every health facility within reach, has done the trick.
>
> Dick made a rewarding appearance at the ANA convention in Milwaukee last August, while Marion spent several happy, quiet days with our family in Racine.
>
> Our holidays will be spent with thankful contemplation of our friendly, comfortable environment and improved health.
>
> We wish our good friends the best of everything this holiday season and during the new year.

▲ Green Valley, Arizona, is an unincorporated retirement community of several dozen homeowners' associations along the western side of the Santa Cruz River, about 20 miles south of Tucson and 40 miles north of the Mexican border. Residents enjoy beautiful views of the Santa Rita Mountains.

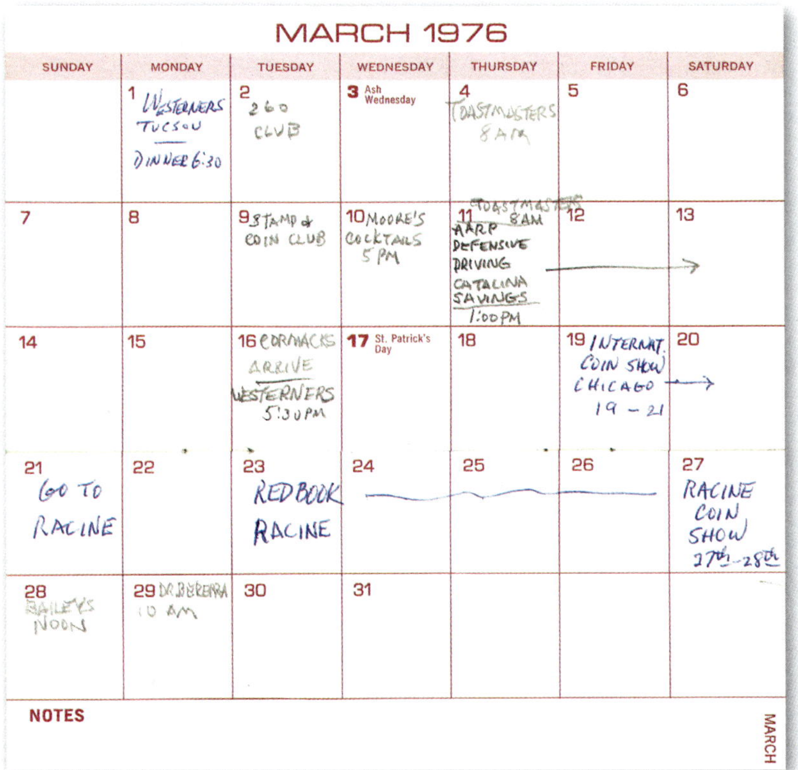

► Even in retirement, Yeoman was active in his local community and on the numismatic scene. Here are two pages from his pocket calendar for March 1976.

◀ As a gift for Ken Bressett and his wife, Yeoman sketched this view of the ghost town of Helvetia, located in the northwest corner of Arizona's Santa Rita Mountains, south of Tucson.

Dick continued to attend regular meetings of Toastmasters. During one of the speeches he delivered to the group, he examined the challenges and joys of retirement:

> Persons who have spent their productive years in business or in the professions are heard to say when they retire: "I am busier than ever."
>
> This statement is usually issued with a smile and an expression of innocent belief. And, we are entitled to a feeling of achievement that we who are retired are fully occupied with daily activities and responsibilities. Membership duties in community affairs, writing letters, getting things repaired, treating minor ailments, routine shopping, hobbies and other daily duties make up our "busier than ever" days.
>
> Now, my thought for the week starts with a question: Busier than your business or professional career, or busier than you thought you would be before you retired?

▲ Arizona governor Evan Mecham reached out to Yeoman for advice on the state's senior community.

> Speaking for myself, after seven years away from the office, I can fill every waking hour, and some days 24 hours seem hardly enough. But those busy hours are much more *my own* hours. True, there are duties we must perform for an easy conscience, but the one great difference in the doing is that the boss isn't breathing down our neck and pushing for quotas, more production, more profit, more overtime, etc.
>
> Yes, my thought for the week is as I said. I'm busier than ever, but I'm busier *my way* rather than the bosses' pressure way. To me, that's what retirement is all about.

Wrote Sandy Samples in the *Green Valley News and Sun*, "Yeo plays down all his accomplishments and seems to be content to lead a fairly quiet life in Green Valley, with his jaunts to Racine and other travels with his wife, and painting an occasional landscape." (Dick executed his works in acrylic paint, calling them "purely amateur.")

As full as Dick's days had become, when Arizona governor Evan Mecham asked him to share his knowledge and experience, he quickly made time in his schedule. On September 3, 1987, he received a letter from Richard H. Huff, the Tucson coordinator of the governor's advisory groups:

> Thank you for accepting the invitation to meet with Governor Mecham on Friday, September 11, 1987, at 2:00 p.m. in the Academy Hall at the Villa Campana Retirement Community, 6653 East Carondelet Drive.
>
> You will be joining a group whose interest and activities focus upon the Senior Community. A similar group will be formed in the Phoenix area. I am confident that your presence will make a valuable addition to this important meeting. . . .
>
> The Governor looks upon this important group as an Advisory Panel to be called upon in the future. It is his desire to establish constructive dialogue with this Panel that can be used by the Mecham administration for the benefit of all concerned.

Meanwhile, Dick did not rest on his hobby laurels. In late August 1987 he traveled by himself to the ANA's convention in Atlanta, Georgia. "Western Publishing Company thinks I shouldn't get too set in retirement's tendency to laziness," he wrote to the Swansons. Not surprisingly, Dick also was the resident numismatist at Villa Campana, giving slide presentations, offering advice, and spreading the word about coin collecting:

> Everybody seems to have keepsake coins.[105] I don't know whether I'll be able to start anybody actually collecting,

> but maybe I'll be able to enlist a few of them. . . . There are some widows here who have collections (organized and disorganized) left by their husbands, and I've helped them to dispose of the collections through dealers if they are not hobby-minded and want to do that.
>
> Of course, first I go through the collection and tell them if they have anything of value. There's one fellow who has done some traveling around the world, and he has a box full of miscellaneous foreign coins from many countries. I've been trying to get him to organize them, but he always seems to have something else he has to do.

Even in retirement, Dick received letters from collectors and, true to form, he responded to each and every one. In January 1987, a handwritten note arrived from Kean Leiker of Garden Grove, California: "I met you, sir, at the 1986 ANA show in Milwaukee, . . . you told me that it would be alright to send you books to have autographed by you. . . . If you plan to come to California again soon, please let me know and I could bring the books there. Besides, I'd like to meet you again. I think you're a neat guy."

Dick responded shortly thereafter, writing the letter in longhand rather than typing it, as was his custom with queries from the general public. As always, he was very accommodating:

> My wife and I are living in a retirement community and, frankly, mailing facilities are zero. I am able only to autograph my books at coin shows. There was a branch post office nearby a year ago, but it moved (it was in a drug store). Getting around and handling packages for mailing now are out of the picture. If you can send only one book, I can take care of it [in] a large envelope. You can decide.
>
> Our local Tucson Numismatic Society will have its show later this month, and the committee has planned a table for me. I will be available for autographing there. I have no plans for being at [the] ANA [convention] in Cincinnati this summer, but may decide later. Because our Tucson show is the same time as the [Numismatic Association of Southern California event in Los Angeles], I won't make it to California this time. Perhaps next year.
>
> Thanks for writing.
>
> R.S. Yeo

At age 84, Dick received a letter from ANA Seminar Coordinator Judy Padgett dated April 28, 1988: "As stated in my letter of December 3, the Educational Forum, where you will be the guest speaker, will be on

▲ While Dick and Marion were enjoying retirement in sunny Arizona in the early 1980s, the United States Mint resumed its commemorative coin programs, which had stopped in 1954.

Sunday evening at 6:30 p.m., June 26. We would like to know the title of your talk for publicity purposes."

The topic of Dick's presentation was "Now and Then," in which he looked back on the hobby and his involvement. He roughed out an outline in advance of his talk:

- Joined ANA in 1940 (No. 7947), almost half way to [ANA] Centennial [in] 1991. Whitman Publishing Company first subscribed to The Numismatist in 1936.
- What was numismatics like a half century ago?
  —Searching our change
  —Collecting not yet numismatics; more of a diversion
  —Emphasis on fun; no thought of speculation
- While certain conditions existed, I do not think the old days were best. At that time, there were no:
  —drip-dry clothes
  —dishwashers
  —freezers
- Back then,
  —there was the quaint notion of getting married first, and living together afterward
  —papers were read at banquets
  —a newly elected ANA president meant a new headquarters location
  —Roman Imperial coins were cheap, and bronzes exceeded demand
  —rabbits were not Volkswagens
  —coke was only a drink and for furnaces
  —pot was something we cooked in

▲ Richard S. Yeo was born in 1904, five years before the Lincoln cent. In 1986 he was in his twilight, but still active, when the United States Mint's new American Eagle bullion coins debuted.

The octogenarian's sense of humor was still very much in evidence, as was his love of the hobby and the collecting fraternity. He remained active until his final months.

WINDING DOWN

Although Marion recovered from the heart attack she suffered in January 1986, thereafter she accompanied Dick on his travels only occasionally. From personal correspondence in the Western Archives, I learned that after cataract surgery she had to wear "thick tunnel-vision glasses" because she could not tolerate contact lenses. Sometime before June 1987, Dick had "a short session with a hernia" and underwent a "repair job" on his bladder.

I also came across a handwritten outline for his participation in the California State Numismatic Association's educational symposium in Fullerton, California, on March 19, 1988. His notes were printed, rather than cursive or typewritten, and his handwriting was noticeably shaky.

Perhaps the most poignant item in his files of correspondence was a 5 by 7–inch piece of white paper, on which he jotted down his ailments, possibly in preparation for an appointment with a "Dr. Murphy." One of his complaints was that he had "no pep," difficult for a man of Dick's boundless energy and enthusiasm.

On November 9, 1988, R.S. Yeoman suffered a stroke while driving his car near his retirement community. He was dead at the scene of the resulting accident. Several days later, Marion received condolences from ANA Executive Director Robert J. Leuver:

> On behalf of President Steve Taylor, the Board of Governors and the entire membership of the ANA, I want to express our sincere sympathy to you at Dick's passing.
>
> Dick Yeo's contributions to numismatics and the hobby of coin collecting can never be adequately measured. There have been countless children and adults who have used his famous "*Red Book*" as their collecting bible and his coin boards and albums as the focus of many wonderful hours of enriching fun. Dick's activities have brought coin collecting to everyone, not just the wealthy.
>
> We all feel his loss greatly but know you do most of all. Our prayers are with you.

Dick's memorial service in Racine, attended by many friends and family members, was a celebration of his life, and I was honored and privileged to deliver the eulogy.

Ed Metzger, then-manager of the Whitman Coin Division, wrote this moving tribute, which was published in the January 1989 issue of *The Numismatist*:

> The recent death of Richard S. Yeo, who wrote under the pen name "R.S. Yeoman," leaves the numismatic hobby with a heartfelt sense of loss. Considered by many to be the father of modern-day coin collecting, Yeo's considerable contributions to the hobby have made it what it is today.
>
> Once called a "20th-century coin genius," Yeo helped to create the basic tools and framework of coin-collecting reference materials. His efforts came as a result of a keen skill in determining and fulfilling the needs of the collector.

Yeo served his hobby in a number of capacities: as author of *A Guide Book of United States Coins* ("Red Book") and the *Handbook of United States Coins* ("Blue Book"); inventor of the coin folder; speaker; exhibit judge; and noted authority on American and world coins. He took none of these roles less seriously than the others. His total commitment to the hobby was reflected in everything he did.

Among the riches Yeo gave to the coin collecting community was his constant personal goal to "do what is best for the hobby." The highest tribute coin collecting can pay to this great man would be to never lose sight of that goal.

Marion remained in Arizona after Dick's death. Wrote Dan Brown in 1977, she was a "wonderful helpmate to Dick, the mother of their child, [the] first coin-board enthusiast, [and a] listener to Dick's problems. [They took] many wonderful trips together." When Marion Junkerman Yeo passed away in 1992, her ashes, and those of her husband, were buried at West Lawn Memorial Park in Mount Pleasant, Wisconsin.

Dick and Marion's daughter, Laura Sharon Yeo Dodd, died at age 87 on September 15, 2018, at Ascension All Saints Hospital in Racine. As a long-time friend of Sharon and her husband, Gene, I attended the funeral service and afterward shared fond memories with our special group, which so often enjoyed camaraderie at monthly pot-luck supper gatherings. Sharon is survived by Gene and their daughter, Laura Jean.

LIFE AND LEGACY

R.S. Yeoman will forever be remembered as the man who introduced millions of fledgling enthusiasts to the wonderful avocation of coin collecting. His foresight, creativity, and marketing skills produced a plethora of books, albums, and related paraphernalia that made the hobby easily approachable, entertaining, and educational for three generations of collectors, students, and dealers.

Dick's mission was to make coin collecting an entertaining pursuit for everyone.

The success he achieved in this regard made him a legendary figure in the world of numismatics. He truly was a guiding force that influenced the growth and evolution of the coin hobby and related market trends. In my attempt to carry on his work, I could only tread in his shadow and try to live up to his standards. I am sure those who succeed me will continue do the same and embrace Dick's ideals. He was a man without peer and a legend in his time.

In Memory of

RICHARD S. YEO
(pseudonym: R.S. YEOMAN)
1904 - 1988

A man who will be sadly missed by the entire hobby.

Western Publishing Company, Inc.

114 THE NUMISMATIST • JANUARY 1989

▲ Western Publishing memorialized its celebrity author in the January 1989 issue of *The Numismatist*.

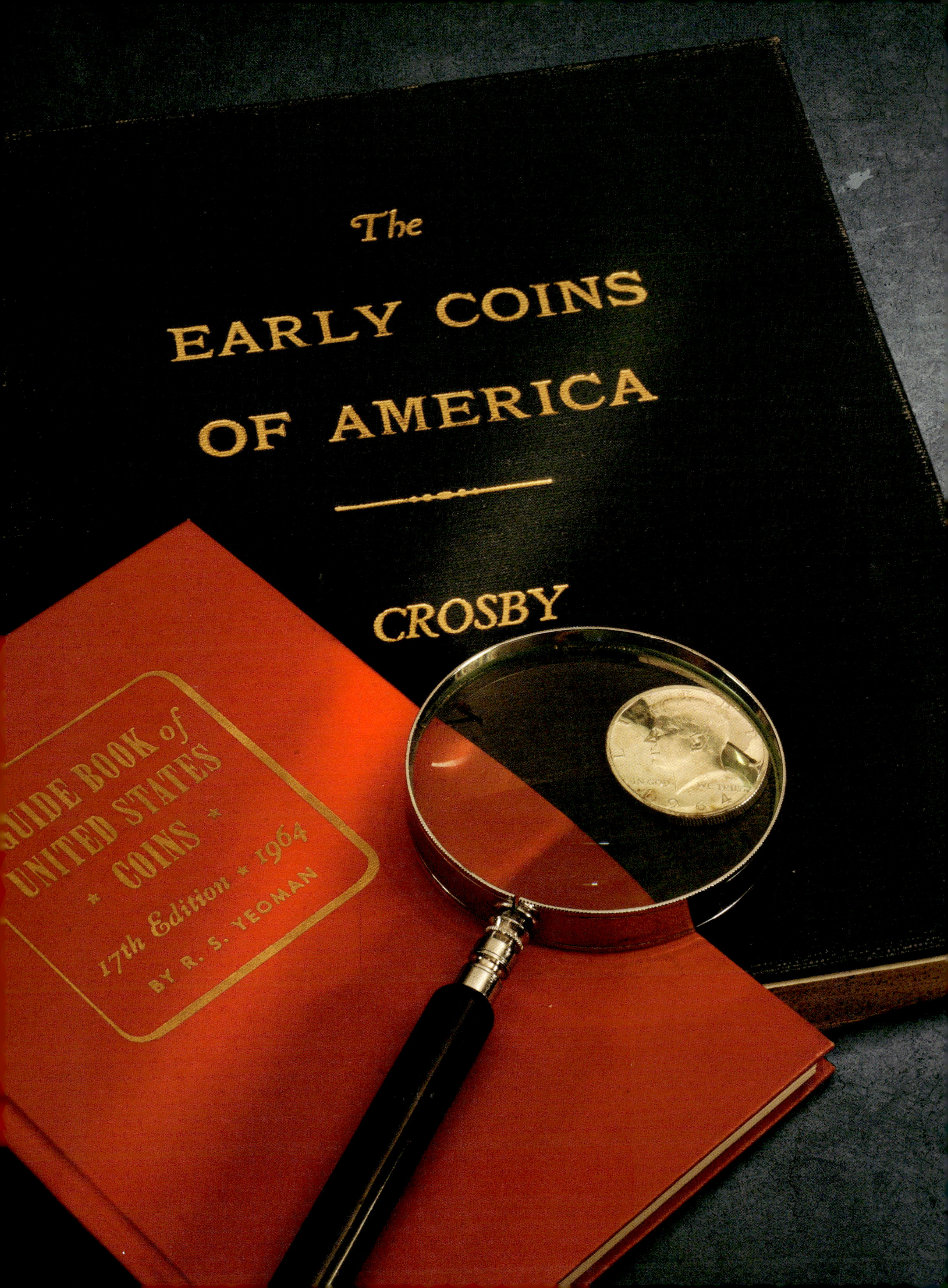
The
EARLY COINS
OF AMERICA
CROSBY
GUIDE BOOK of
UNITED STATES
COINS
17th Edition 1964
BY R. S. YEOMAN

Chapter 5

Yeoman's Wit and Wisdom

Presented here is a sampling of speeches and articles Dick Yeoman wrote during his employment at Whitman Publishing Company.

THE BENEFITS OF CONTEMPORARY LITERATURE

February 1965

I had not collected coins very long before I realized that I could not appreciate or enjoy the hobby without historical background knowledge. I don't mean a mid-twentieth-century writer's coverage of a period, say, a hundred years before either of us were born. Rather, I required, and still prefer, an account of an event that was recorded on the spot, or by one who had observed the situation, in person. In other words, I seek out the contemporary description. This, I believe, explains my lack of enthusiasm for United States commemorative coins and is the reason for my preoccupation with such specimens as the Sommer Island shilling, the 1848 quarter eagle with CAL., and others of that character.

I have no actual distaste for silver and gold United States commemorative issues. They have served a noble purpose, and the series ought to be resumed whenever the Treasury Department recovers from its difficulties and achieves a more favorable attitude toward the numismatic fraternity. These reminders of our glorious past need to be brought before the American collector and citizen at every opportunity. The best medium for these reminders, many believe, is the coinage. I simply do not receive enough challenge from this series for my historic appetite.

When I was offered an opportunity to acquire a specimen of the Sommer Island shilling back in the mid-1940s, I hesitated only long enough to mentally calculate my chances of paying for it out of a limited budget. I had read a little here and there about the piece and its fractional parts from re-edited historical accounts of the islands (now Bermuda), particularly in Sylvester Sage Crosby's *Early Coins of America*. To illustrate the point I wish to make, I could not have enjoyed ownership of this rare piece alone by judging its state of preservation, its potential investment possibilities, or its designs and legends. At the time, there was little interest in the first English-American coin to have circulated in the Western Hemisphere, and truthfully there is comparatively little enthusiasm today. Though the piece is as near to uncirculated as any known example, that is of little consequence because it is so rare. Moreover, I don't have an uglier coin in my collection. There had to be a stronger power of attraction than visual appeal or financial expectations to cause excitement in my eager brain.

"The old collectors had the same human viewpoints as we have today."

To accomplish the perspective I seek in such historical objects, I acquired, in this instance, a two-volume set of books that was a University of Glasgow reprint containing every word (with original spelling), including maps and plates personally recorded by Captain John Smith. The full title of this comprehensive work is *The General Historie of Virginia, New England & Summer Isles, together with the True Travels, Adventures and Observations and Sea Grammar by Captaine John Smith, Sometymes Governour in those Countryes and Admirall of New England.*

◀ One of Yeoman's prized possessions was this seventeenth-century Sommer Islands shilling (shown enlarged). It was part of the first series of coinage, known as Hogge Money, struck for England's colonies in the New World. The islands (now modern-day Bermuda) were named for Sir George Somers, who was shipwrecked there in 1609 as he sailed for the Virginia plantations. "Some of my forebears were Somers," said Yeoman. "I'm not a direct descendant of his, . . . just the same family. His direct descendants would be 42nd cousins of mine, I suppose." Regarding his personal specimen of the shilling, he noted, "I had to search for that one for several years. I purchased it from a dealer in Philadelphia, who got it from a stranger who said it had been picked up on the beach in Bermuda. Today, perhaps two dozen of these coins exist." In a 1985 interview published in the *Arizona Daily Star*, he explained that the coin, "worth 12.5¢ three centuries ago, is now worth about $6,000."

▲ Yeoman was captivated by the Gold Rush–era 1848 quarter eagle with CAL.—"the only known coin which commemorates itself." He spoke on this topic on numerous occasions and received an ANA Heath Literary Award for his 1953 article about the enigmatic coin. Here an example is displayed with related material at Whitman Publishing headquarters in Racine.

I have a similar relationship with my U.S. quarter eagle of 1848 with CAL. I had always been intensely devoted to California Gold Rush history. My greatest regret is that I could not afford ownership of certain pioneer specimens. Nevertheless, my search for contemporary data about the great gold discovery and all its implications has been very much a part of my numismatic career. To satisfy my thirst, many hours have been spent in libraries, including the Library of Congress and the National Archives. I have assembled a respectable bookshelf of volumes written by journalists, adventurers, early bankers, and military men who were there to witness and record the drama of the gold seekers. Most important, I have visited, as any tourist may, many of the mining towns as they are today and to visualize, as best I can, the locale where the precious gold was panned to make the coin that I possess. Others may own many specimens of this series of pioneer gold, but I have contented myself with photographs of most of them.

If I might be allowed to visit another era for a moment, I would like to mention that the few ancient coins I possess have a much greater worth to me as a result of reading *Plutarch Lives*, sets of which are obtainable in paperback editions at low cost. They cover the Greek or Roman personalities. This famous, classical writer takes one to the moments in history when our coin specimens were created and passed from hand to hand. It matters little if mythology is mixed with reality. Such were the attitudes and beliefs of the times, which to me are the important ingredients in attaining historical perspective.

We have heard many times, from more erudite researchers than I, how important a library can be to gain the fullest appreciation of a collection of coins. Such a library can open the door to any phase of numismatics, including economics, metallurgy, art, politics, and the like. I merely take this brief opportunity to suggest how this collector goes about associating his coins with history in general.

If the reader thinks that there are only a few United States coins with intriguing stories, I recommend, just for a starter, a search back through the old coin magazines. The 1909 issues of *The Numismatist* have some normal human reactions to Victor D. Brenner's new Lincoln cent. The 1913 issues have some good background comments about James Earle Fraser's radically different Indian-Bison five-cent piece. The old collectors had the same human viewpoints as we have today. Only the designs on the coins are different. The opportunities for historic study are even greater today. After all, there are more years of history to study and, happily, many more reference books to use as tools with which to dig out the facts.

THE TWENTY-FIVE YEAR RULE

Date unknown

"He has the good sense to know that they are only new material which, like wine and fruitcake, improves with age."

We had to have a generation of collecting experience to learn that an organized, orderly coin market is based on sound values and choices. At one point, some 10 years ago, we agonized through a roll-and-bag era, only to realize that this kind of material does not earn its value in so short a period. Many retreated to the sidelines and are still there, waiting for the current coins to become wanted by a new generation of collectors.

Meanwhile, the wise collector, who has learned from experience, is enjoying a market of mature numismatic material. He was the fellow who collected coins of the past, such as obsolete types of denominations, gold commemoratives, silver dollars, etc. The reason the market today is sound is that the average collector, in addition to being a more informed and instinctive numismatist, is putting emphasis on coins of past generations, and if he has coins of current or recent issue, which he should, he has the good sense to know that they are only new material which, like wine and fruitcake, improves with age and is not expected to be served as soon as made in the numismatic marketplace.

THE DATE CONCEPT IN COINAGE AND IN NUMISMATICS

1964

A presentation at a Chicago Coin Club meeting or show at the Pick Congress Hotel. Yeo mounted a complementary exhibit of vintage catalogs at the event.

In early coinage, it was important to place some indication of responsibility for the issue, such as an official's symbol and, in many instances, a numeral to indicate when the coins were struck. Usually the method of dating was simply a letter/numeral designating the year of the ruler's reign. Dating served the double purpose of furnishing a time reference and the prestige value of its relation to the king's tenure.

"Whatever the purpose for dating coins, we are quite sure that they were not placed there to accommodate the coin collector."

There is no intention to discuss early dating in more than general terms. What we are concerned with today is the beginnings and evolution of dates in modern terms, and how we, as numismatists, have come to view the system within the scope of our hobby. The recent announcement by the United States Treasury officials that the 1964 date will be continued into the 1965 calendar year, has underlined the whole subject of coin dating. I will attempt to analyze the possible effects of this recently enacted law on the coin-collecting fraternity.

Going back to the period near the end of medieval times, we encounter the earliest use of dates in terms of the Christian era. I have a well-circulated specimen—a short-cross groschen of Aachen. The date is expressed in the form of a legend that circles the border of the coin: ANNO-DOMINE MILLESIMO CCCCVI ("In the Year of Our Lord, One Thousand Four Hundred and Six"). The center of the reverse has the figure of Charlemagne holding a church in his right hand. Other early coins of this type dating include gros-tournois of Schonforst and Siehem and the short-cross and long-cross groschens of Aachen to 1424. (The specimen exhibited is the earliest I have come across.)

The Arabic or Western numerals are found in coinage of the late fifteenth century. Exhibited here are two coins of Holland. The first is dated 1484, a silver briquet issued by Maximilian during the Minority of Philip the Good. The second is a double briquet of Zeeland and Gelderland dated in the historic year 1492. A characteristic "4" is shown on both specimens. It is in the form of an X with a loop at the top. Ever since, we have had dates on coins in all Western countries in somewhat the same pattern.

Whatever the purpose for dating coins, we are quite sure that they were not placed there to accommodate the coin collector. The fact that consecutive dating is so universal has brought about an unintended challenge, at least in the United States and Canada. Coupled with the added incentive of mintmarks, a collector has a simple, understandable series to challenge his instinct to collect a complete set. This human trait is expressed similarly in completing crossword puzzles and picture puzzles. For many people, the fact that the objects are coins is secondary, but another human instinct, profit, rears itself rather soon. Fortunately, a numismatic approach—with all its facets of history, art, and engraving techniques—engages the interest of many, and we can truthfully say that the end justifies the means.

In the collecting of dates, it is necessary only that the dates and mintmarks be known and established. In other words, the collector wants to know what he is looking for. The coin board serves the collector by providing this information and in an orderly arrangement with protection for his coins. This convenient tool has been credited with the widening of interest in our hobby.

The date-and-mintmark approach is not as new as many believe. Moreover, there have been numerous instances of lapses in dates in United States coinage, as well as in foreign coin series. None, to my knowledge, have lessened the interest in collecting nor in coin values.

I was able to bring to this meeting a selection of old and valuable auction catalogs that reveal the early devotion to separate valuations of coins based on their dates and mintmarks. These may not be the oldest such printed records, but they reach back far enough in American history to impress on all of us that the peculiar character of our coin collecting is truly traditional and not a new concept or fad.

I checked through the W. Elliot Woodward catalog of 1864. United States coins are presented and offered by dates. This is early evidence that the collectors of a century ago had standardized their pattern of collecting on the date concept. It is interesting, by the way, to note the cataloger's grading terms, which were:

> Splendid
> Perfectly uncirculated
> Remarkably fine
> Very fine indeed
> Scarcely at all circulated

◄ Yeoman created slide presentations, including "The Date Concept" and "Coins Through the Ages," which he delivered at meetings of numismatic organizations and at his retirement community in Tucson. Among the issues he discussed in the former program were a 1411 shortcross groschen of Aachen; a 1492 silver double briquet of Zeeland and Gelderland; and a 1484 silver briquet of Holland, issued by Maximilian during the Minority of Philip the Good.

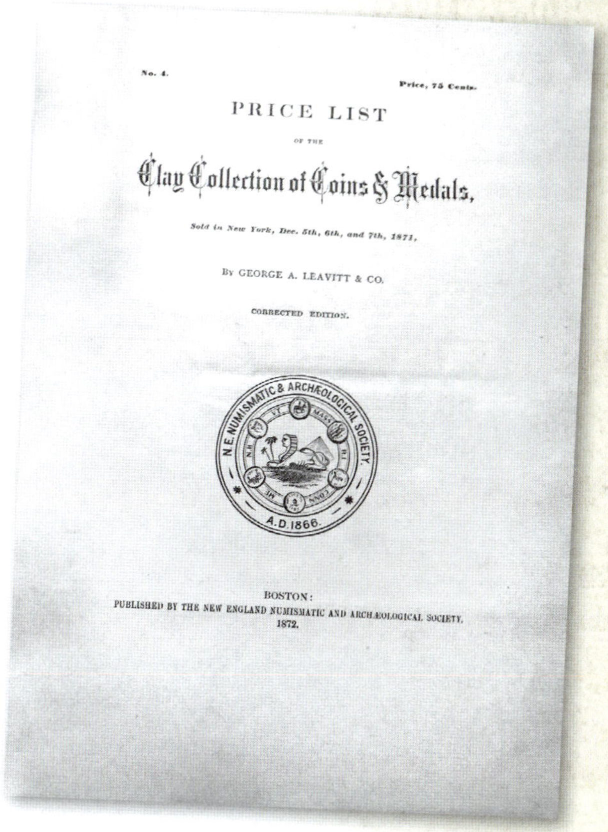

No. 4.

Price, 75 Cents.

PRICE LIST

OF THE

Clay Collection of Coins & Medals,

Sold in New York, Dec. 5th, 6th, and 7th, 1871,

By GEORGE A. LEAVITT & CO.

CORRECTED EDITION.

N.E. NUMISMATIC & ARCHÆOLOGICAL SOCIETY

A.D.1866.

BOSTON:

PUBLISHED BY THE NEW ENGLAND NUMISMATIC AND ARCHÆOLOGICAL SOCIETY,

1872.

▲ At a Chicago Coin Club gathering in 1964, Dick mounted an exhibit of "Old Catalogs." In it, he displayed a rare "price list" of Charles Clay's famous collection of coins and medals, which was sold in New York City in 1871 by George A. Leavitt & Co.

A sale listing distributed by Miner and Somerville in New York City (December 16, 1866), includes a set of U.S. cents commencing at 1800. Fifty-seven pieces sold at 1-1/2 cents each.

An old catalog carries the interesting story of the pioneer coin dealer Edward Cogan. He was an Englishman who came to America in about 1850. He set up in Camden, New Jersey, as a picture dealer. An incident in 1855 was responsible for his great interest and professional association with numismatics. Actually, a lapse in the coinage of cents was the key factor.

Cogan's friend Ryan showed him a 1791 Washington cent in his store and commented on its value. He mentioned in passing that he would pay $5 for an 1815 cent. For weeks following Ryan's visit, Cogan accumulated all the old large cents that came his way, keeping the various dates separate in pill boxes. Of course, he never found an 1815 specimen. He made occasional sales to his friends, and these transactions increased in frequency 'til he found himself in the coin business. His first public offer was called a "letter bidding" sale, which was finalized November 1, 1859.

The foregoing story points up two features that characterize present-day coin collecting methods: date series and date lapses.

Another Woodward sale catalog on display here lists the Mickley collection and is dated October 28, 1867. Part of the collection consists of United States coins by dates. The Clay Sale catalog shown here is dated December 5, 1871, and also has U.S. coins in date series offered individually.

In the Seavey Collection catalog displayed in this "Old Catalog" exhibit, the collection of Lorin G. Parmelee was offered. It is dated 1873. The cataloguer presented all coins of a year together. This would be termed "Mint Sets" today. He included varieties in some sets. Proof sets starting in 1858 were included and were complete. Seavey introduced a system of grading based on numbers:

> 1— Uncirculated
> 2— Very fine
> 3— Fine
> 4— Good
> 5— Ordinary

There is no reference to AU or extra fine.

Another item is an 1893 book by A.G. Heaton titled *A Treatise on the Coinage of the Branch Mints*. He lists, among other fascinating details, a section headed "Branch Mint Rarities." An example:

> Quarter Eagles—O 1841; D 1840, 53, 54, 55, 56, 57, and 59; C 1855; S 1858.
> Half Eagles— D 1861; S 1854, 64, 76, etc.

The most intriguing specimen here is the large aluminum token issued by the famous Farran Zerbe in 1904. He distributed these at the St. Louis World's Fair. In concentric circles he lists premium coins by date and their values. I have seldom seen so much information confined to so small a space, yet visible to the naked eye.

Let us now refer to a recent article in the No. 4, 1962, issue of the *Numismatic Review*. An article on the House of Rothschild recounts its early identity with coin dealing in Germany. The feature important to our subject is a reproduction of part of a page from a Rothschild catalog of rare coins showing thalers listed for sale individually by dates from various countries. This was published about 1775.

So, we have come to the understanding that dates/series collecting is not new, and date lapses are not to be considered a basis for panic, but in some respects have certain psychological advantages. Missing dates, now and then, introduce an element of interest. They create relief from monotony, and are subjects for tests of memory. (In the case of the 1815 cent, it's the only missing year.)

▲ Numismatist Farran Zerbe promoted his business on this unique and informative aluminum medal. Yeoman marveled at the amount of text stamped into its surface.

In more recent times, date and mintmark lapses are well known, particularly in the 1930s. Take one year, 1933, in which only cents (P and D) and halves (S) were minted in subsidiary coinage. There are frequent skipped mintmarks in all series.

In the foreign field, there are several notable examples known to most of you. In Great Britain the continuation of dates into succeeding years was a wartime expedient. The pennies struck from 1941 to and including 1943 were all dated 1940. The last silver threepence pieces were dated 1945; some of these were struck in 1946. The issue was nevertheless melted by the mint. The silver threepences dated 1944 were all minted in 1945. Shillings dated 1953 were struck in 1952, a reversal of the pattern. These were dated ahead, but the result was a lapsed date 1952, with both English and Scottish reverses.

▲ British pennies dated 1940 may have been minted as late as 1943. (In 1941, 1942, and 1943 they were produced mainly for circulation in Gibraltar and the British West Indies, using older dies.)

In Canada we have a similar date extension. The early 1948 production of cents was dated 1947, but with a maple leaf added. The new dies with IND:IMP deleted were not ready, and the old dies with 1947 were used to keep coinage flowing. There was no date lapse, for the new dies arrived late in 1948, in time to strike over 25 million cents. Nevertheless, the threat was there, and, in that respect, the situation parallels our own.

I would like to advance a thought about varieties which will probably get no farther than this occasion. It is simply this: Each new date of a coin type is a new and distinct variety. The new date 1964, for example, is unlike any other date, thus it becomes a die variety as real and different as any unintentional mint-error-style variety. I am thinking of the large- and small-date varieties of the 1960 cents.

The date variety is at least planned and (until this year) mandatory. It is deliberately contrived and with official sanction. Alas, it is so regular, expected, and obvious that it is taken completely for granted, and in a sense ignored.

The modern vehicle to coin collecting has been lubricated for the novice by the date variety system. The coin board is the very real product to further the system. I submit here and now that these people are variety collectors. Let the small change fall where it may.

CHALLENGE

1963

Commentary published in the April–May 1963 issue of the Whitman Coin Supply Merchandiser.

Did you ever consider what makes a hobby one of the most compelling of human activities? I think it is challenge. It's more than likely that there are several hours of every week that lie heavily on anyone's hands and cry out

"After the bug takes hold, the true collector doesn't wait for a rainy day."

for a change of pace. If we don't wish to submit to complete idleness and get ourselves into habits of mental laziness and the hazards of apathy, we ought to look for a personal hobby.

The challenge is strongest when nasty weather keeps us indoors. Too much reading and TV gets tiresome and leaves us in a what'll-I-do-with-myself frame of mind. Thus, we are ripe for new direction in the form of a collecting hobby. Of course, I am strongly in favor of coin collecting as a quiet, stimulating pursuit in this particular situation. Once started, naturally, the novice collector rapidly builds up a healthy enthusiasm because he becomes aware of the endless avenues of interest he can choose. In my own numismatic career, I experienced, in turn, curiosity; desire to complete set after set; the prospect of discovering a fabulous rarity; investment possibilities; historical aspects with all its implications of adventure and romance; and just plain organization of my collection and arrangements of displays for clubs and conventions.

After the bug takes hold, the true collector doesn't wait for a rainy day, he simply passes up the TV and magazines more and more and keeps accepting numismatic challenges for the rest of his life.

PROFIT OF THE MIND
1963

Commentary published in the February–March 1964 issue of the Whitman Coin Supply Merchandiser.

"Our hobby can be torn apart very thoroughly if the profit motive continues to be over-emphasized."

Whatever observation we make about the trend of coin collecting, the desire to assemble in large groups is clearly the most evident. Any week of the year, with a few obvious exceptions, there are one to ten coin shows in as many communities throughout the United States and Canada. It is a good trend, and those of us who supply the necessary accessories for arranging, protecting and pricing coins, should encourage this kind of togetherness to the utmost.

The primary objective of the convention has been and probably will continue to be the selling and buying of coins. These gatherings are basically bourses, and most dealers derive an added benefit from making contacts with new and old customers. The sale of a coin folder or *Blue Book* to a novice collector is often the start of a long-term dealer-client association.

The future of the coin show or convention, however, rests on more than the bourse, and it is encouraging to see how some local club sponsors are keeping a happy balance between the dealer's bourse, the auction, and the educational features. The show chairman is on the right track when he emphasizes exhibits and announces well in advance that handsome

A popular speaker, Yeoman appeared at forums throughout the country. Here he entertains a church group in 1950.

▲ Yeoman exhibited his extensive collection of "Milestone Coins" at the 1951 ANA Convention in Phoenix, Arizona.

▲ The Milestone Coins display earned him an award, presented by (from left) Abe Kosoff, Earl Brown, and Bob Schermerhorn.

trophies or plaques will go to the winners. He knows that newcomers to the numismatic ranks are quickly brought into the show when the local newspaper, radio, and TV announces a free exhibit of rare coins.

We have noticed that the best attendance comes to those coin shows that have a modest or free registration, accessible display room, cordial committee members to answer questions, and a place to rest when the feet start to tire. One feature in particular has been offered by only a few conventions, and that is a special educational forum. Sometimes a panel of two to four well-informed individuals can do more to further the hobby than all the coin investment plans ever devised. There ought to be more of this kind of thing.

Our hobby can be torn apart very thoroughly if the profit motive continues to be over-emphasized to the exclusion of educational features. Competitive displays, authoritative lectures, mind-stimulating forums, and displays of available numismatic literature are convention attractions that can strengthen and perpetuate the ranks of the coin collecting fraternity.

Let us have both school and marketplace, but in the right proportion. Perhaps we can plan our conventions this year with more emphasis on profit of the mind.

WHAT IS A COIN COLLECTOR?

October 1963

Speech made at a numismatic event in Kenosha, Wisconsin.

> ***"My best advice to anyone who cares to ask is to pursue coin collecting with calm intelligence."***

Is he a speculator?

He is buying rolls and Proof sets in quantity.

He ultimately becomes a dealer.

He trades surpluses with other dealers and eventually gets down to a single-coin basis. He survives if he continues to buy about as much as he sells, and makes a profit. His original stock of rolls in quantity doesn't last long. There was just too much of the same thing, and not variety enough. Suddenly everyone has 1950-D nickels.

Is he an investor?

He buys quality single coins, and some assorted rolls and Proof sets. He is selective, and works quietly and slowly. He reads about coins, studies the history of the coins combined with a check over the years of coin values. He pays little attention to sensational so-called "investment" ads and refuses to join any stampede toward a mass market in any single coin date. He may buy a few coins in Uncirculated of dates and mints being headlined, which will later be the sleepers and really scarce because they were overlooked. He knows that many times the condition is scarce even if the total minted is large. He diversifies into coins of other countries; paper money; and some medals. He is a satisfied hobbyist. He is more apt to wear a relaxed smile than a wild, vacant stare.

Is he an in-and-outer?

This type carries a check list in his pocket and inspects his change carefully. He has a few coin boards at home and knows that there are a few spaces he is going to have to fill in with "bought" coins. But he is in no hurry; the fun is in the search. He plans to leave the completed sets to his children in his will. But, he'll probably end up taking a nice profit some day and using the funds to marry off his daughter in a high-class wedding. Someday he might buy a few books other than the *Red Book*. No rush.

Is he an accumulator?

This fellow has created a well-worn path to the bank. He buys all he can carry in rolls of cents, nickels, and dimes home for the weekend. Next week, he trudges back and trades for another batch. He's being fitted early for bifocals, but his bedroom closet is loaded with partly filled plastic tubes. He religiously checks the latest offers in the coin papers and finally runs classified ads to unload the accumulations of his own. If he belongs to a coin club, he never has time to accept a committee assignment, read a coin article, or make an educational display. He has more important things to do. He is collecting coins, isn't he? He has a *Red Book* to prove it.

▲ Whitman officers and sales representatives discuss a possible youth program involving Project Head Start. Among the participants are Marsh Thomas (second from left), Dick Yeoman, and Don Hirschhorn (second from right).

Is he a bargain hunter?

This collector flies from one extreme to another. He loves to tell the boys at the meeting about his latest buy, provided he "stole" it. He has a drawer full of miscellaneous unrelated rolls, half cents, silver dollars, or foreign minor coins picked up hit and miss from anyone or anywhere. Someday he intends to straighten out the mess, but right now he wants to know if you have any duplicates of some cheap scarce dates in About Good condition. When he gets down to organizing his collection, he suddenly realizes that he completely overlooked the scarce dates, which are now 5 to 25 times higher than when he started buying, and the low-grade bargains are hardly worth the trouble. He gives up collecting because the whole business is a big fake and obviously a racket.

Is he a Mint Error Enthusiast?

One has to be careful when commenting on this specialist. He is sincere, and his interest in coin collecting has possibilities in a narrow field of research. The danger is in its magnification. He is the individual with a high-powered microscope, who is happiest when he discovers sloppy workmanship in our mint products. Our correspondence is bulging with letters from this growing fraternity. They usually start with the phrase, "I have just discovered a variety that is not in the *Red Book*." To me, a collection of mistakes is exceedingly dull, and wide of the mark of true numismatics. Genuine varieties are a part of numismatics. In short if the die is made wrong and thousands of identical coins result from it, we have a variety. But I personally make one small proviso—it must be visible to the naked eye. All else is of no consequence to the dedicated numismatist. I must state frankly that there is nothing stupid or dishonest about a mint error collector; I simply do not have any interest in this phase of coin collecting.

Is he a Numismatist?

He accumulates a modest library and adds to it from time to time. He decides on his field of interest and acquires coins in keeping with his income and interests. He lays a great deal of importance on quality. He plans his collecting pretty much on what he needs to expand his specialty. At one time, he may attend a regional convention or coin show with a list of several dozen coins and come away with some nice specimens of five or six he went after. When he reaches a point of waning interest, he switches to a new series and continues the pattern. At times, he will dispose of his earlier sets and realize a profit which will finance his new collection.

All the while, reference books are at his elbow. He will create educational exhibits, give an occasional coin talk, first at the club and later before local social, religious, and service groups. Before long, he will write articles for coin publications, and ultimately will be sought after as a coin authority. There are many satisfactions to be achieved by a numismatist, not the least of which can be pride of attainment and a certain degree of financial independence. It matters little whether the true student selects Lincoln cents or Franklin halves at the start; it's the plan of action, observation, curiosity, and patience that lead him to the goal.

"It matters little whether the true student selects Lincoln cents or Franklin halves at the start; it's the plan of action, observation, curiosity, and patience that lead him to the goal."

There are about 2,500 coin clubs in this country. All ages and all interests in coin collecting are represented. Of course, the great majority, at one time or another, is a speculator, investor, researcher, and possibly a numismatist. Only a minority, I believe, are clearly speculators. Yet this small segment of our fraternity creates the greatest commotion, runs the wildest ads, and probably will go broke soonest.

I hear statements uttered in fright that these roll-and-Proof speculators and dealers who play these fellows against each other are ruining the hobby. A lot of these wheeling and dealing fellows are temporary dealers working with other temporary dealers. With their teletypes and bold-face advertisements, they build an inflated market entirely apart from the normal, legitimate market, which will prevail after the bubble bursts. Proof that there are two distinct markets is that we see single-coin prices lower than the price on the rolls.

I repeat, the wild-eyed dealer-collectors are a small minority. They create a bad image, and the real harm is that they create the wrong picture and attitude among the new collectors. Many novices turn their backs on the hobby in disgust.

So, my best advice to anyone who cares to ask is to pursue coin collecting with calm intelligence. Look ahead to a career of pleasure, and a healthy increase in personal collecting enjoyment and a gain in value of your collection. Avoid the plunging so prevalent in quantity buying and selling. No bubble was ever blown that will not burst if expanded beyond natural limits. Ask yourself if you are a party to the bursting.

▶ Yeoman at his desk, with his "I'm busy now, come back later" look.

COIN SUPPLY AND VALUES

Date unknown

The stability of coin collecting is basically dependent on the unique situation that the supply has a maximum, known quantity:

1. No increase in quantity can legally be created after December 31 of any year, thus fixing a supply total of an issue for all time.
2. The production per year is a known and reliable figure.
3. The supply is available and reasonably well dispersed without favor.
4. Coins are a government manufacturing function, and their value is basic up to [the] point of placing in circulation. Thus, there is a built-in value unique in this "commodity," as it is at once the physical object and measuring stick by which all other commodities and services are valued. Though a coin may be a token of value intrinsically, it nevertheless is basic, and, from the collector's point of view, the face value is the minimum, or starting base, upon which a premium value is placed whenever the scarcity of supply brings it into the realm of a "collector's item."

"The supply of any date from the mint can never be more than the final total for a given year."

The supply of any date from the mint can never be more than the final total for a given year; it will never equal the published total, for losses occur, accidentally or otherwise, even during the year of issue. The chances are that not more than 90 percent remain available after five years.

Short issues that are captured immediately by alert bag dealers and speculators serve the purpose of preserving limited supply for posterity. Only the extremely small coinage years can reach a high premium under this formula, but the values have the advantage of being fair, firm, and realistic.

The handling of large lots of Uncirculated coins in years of medium or high production is a speculative adventure and should be indulged in only by the wealthy operator. Profits usually are made by trading. This is the familiar process of buying and selling over the short term, a way of financial life followed by street traders for the past half century. "Get in and get out before you can be hurt" is their credo.

SCARCITY VS. SHORTAGE

Date unknown

If the government would be more concerned with the total number of coins in circulation, there would be less cause to fear speculators as a threat to a potential coin shortage. An occasional low mintage of a date and mintmark could do no harm to the overall economy, provided other mints and production of coins in the same two- or three-year time period were adequate or greater than normal.

"One could say that 'scarcity' has a numismatic connotation quite different in meaning from 'shortage.'"

A typical merchant knows only that he has plenty of nickels in his till. He cannot be aware that a 1950-D nickel is not among the several hundred five-cent pieces he has on hand.

The collector thrives on the scarce date for numismatic conversation and a chance for a valuable find. This is not true speculation. It is more accurate to call this an occasional lucky discovery, like finding a four-leaf clover.

Thus, it would be rational to state that in a total of 10 billion cents in circulation, with a back inventory of perhaps 2 billion in Treasury vaults, a few dates and mintmarks with a mintage of two or three million would have no discernible impact on the mercantile world.

One could say that "scarcity" has a numismatic connotation quite different in meaning from "shortage," which is usually associated with "making change" in the marketplace. The shortage problem is concerned with numbers of a certain denomination, not dates on the individual coins.

THE FUTURE OF THE KENNEDY HALF DOLLARS

June 1964

Handwritten notes for a talk made at an unknown coin club meeting or convention.

I have been asked recently by many collectors and non-collectors what the investment possibilities are for the 1964 John F. Kennedy half dollar. This was a difficult question to answer during the first weeks of distribution, but as the pattern of dispersal of over 30 to 40 million of the coins became apparent by late spring, the picture becomes more clear.

At the time this is written in early June, there is barely a trickle of Kennedy halves reaching general circulation. It is evident that the great majority of them are being put away in various ways:

> 1. Collectors, a few at a time
> 2. Dealers, by the roll or bag
> 3. Speculators, same as #2
> 4. Novelty manufacturers for desk ornaments and the like, mainly for non-collectors
> 5. Banks and business houses who pass them out in holders and frames as good-will souvenirs
> 6. Non-collectors, who put them away as keepsakes or because they are different. Some believe they will be "rare" because they are likely to be "called in" (all but theirs) on account of the incomplete "E" in LIBERTY, or the mysterious "hammer and sickle" monogram "GR" of talented and dedicated Gilroy Roberts, chief sculptor-engraver of the United States Mint.

"These keepsakes will be coming out of hiding daily for the next two or three generations and will plague the marketplace."

History has a way of repeating itself. Those of us who were coin conscious way back will recall similar surges of excitement when other new issues were first distributed. Criticisms about new coins have almost always been volunteered by the public at large. Many new types in the past have been met the first day with opinions of what the coin does to the artistic sensibilities of the average citizen. It is usually a signal for pointing out design irregularities, which the critic is sure was overlooked by careless Bureau of the Mint officials, and will end up with the whole issue being called in for re-melting and a new batch re-issued in a week or two. Newspapers usually have a field day printing criticisms and opinions of a few random citizens, and after do a creditable job of garbling the whole matter as though they put real effort into bypassing the true situation and achieving unbelievable distortions, generally.

Whether or not the last half of 1964 will see more of the Kennedy coins reach avenues of trade is not easy to predict. The chances are that the souvenir market will be saturated, and the speculators probably will run out of space and turn a great many in to the banks. This would be a smart move, and I recommend it.

Over seventy years ago, another famous coin was put away—the Columbian half dollar of 1892–93. If anyone thinks that the combined citizenry of souvenir-keepers and collectors can be ignored when upward of 40 million of a single year's coin threatens the premium value, he had better ask himself a few questions.

A coin dealer of only several years' experience knows how many people present a nice Columbian half dollar every week for what they expect will be a fortune. Altogether, 2,500,000 were struck in both years, and they come to light every day in bureau drawers, grandpa's old money pouch, or in a forgotten jewelry box. They will be discovered singly for years to come, and the dealers will keep on telling hopeful non-collectors that they have drawers full of them and don't need any more.

Now, how do you think the Kennedy half dollar will fare during the next 70 years with 15 to 35 times as many specimens? It will be hard enough to dispose of the millions put away by smart hoarders within 10 years at more than compounded bank interest, without competition from the unconscious amateur who, in a mass population, discovers enough of them daily for the next three generations to drive the coin dealers batty.

. . . Well, I've given a little hint of why these coins are poor investments. Remember this when you feel the uncontrollable urge to buy rolls and bags of Kennedy half dollars. These keepsakes will be coming out of hiding daily for the next two or three generations and will plague the marketplace.

▼ Yeoman in a reflective mood, in the den of his home in Arizona.

Abbott Studio Keene N.H.
GOLD DOLLARS
LARGE CENTS
THIS IS COPY
THE MOST POPULAR WORK OF NON-FICTION OF OUR TIME
HOW TO WIN FRIENDS AND INFLUENCE PEOPLE
BY DALE CARNEGIE
POCKET BOOK EDITION COMPLETE & UNABRIDGED
1936
½ Cent
Country Holland
COIN COLLECTION
THIS TELLS YOU ALL ABOUT THE 4 FOREIGN COINS YOU RECEIVED!
AND HOW YOU CAN GET 4 MORE COINS TO COMPLETE YOUR SET IF YOU SEND IN QUICK!
Date 1936 No.
Coin ½ Anna (Pice)
Country India
Date 1893 No. 18
Coin Commerative $.50
Country America

Chapter 6

The Life and Times of Ken Bressett

THE BRESSETTS IN KEENE

It is with some trepidation that I begin writing this section of the book. Yet, it seems appropriate that much of this information needs to be included here in order to present a thorough account of how *A Guide Book of United States Coins* came to be what it is today and how so many people were involved in its origin and development throughout the years. I am proud to have played a key role in its growth and success, but I readily admit that I was only a part of the team, and a very fortunate one—a quirk of fate and opportunity put me in the right place at the right time. The story of my life, as told here, has revolved around numismatics and related matters in one way or another for as long as I can remember. In retrospect, I consider that I was somehow destined to make this my lifelong career.

Life for me began on October 5, 1928. My parents, George and Florence (Forkey) Bressett, were living in Keene, New Hampshire, at the time. Mother was born and raised in Mooers Forks, in upper New York state near the Canadian border. Father's home was in nearby Saint Albans, Vermont. Both were from large families, and both eventually moved away to seek employment in Plattsburgh, New York, where they met and married. Later they moved to Keene, where Dad's brother was working at the time as a mechanic in a local print shop. The new environment suited them well because of the family background and their knowledge of the printing business.

▲ Grandmother and Grandfather George Bressett.

▲ On the porch: Grandmother Bressett; my sister, Beverly (left); and my cousin Clair.

▲ My parents, George and Florence Bressett.

▲ Mom and Dad on their 50th wedding anniversary (1973), with many more to come.

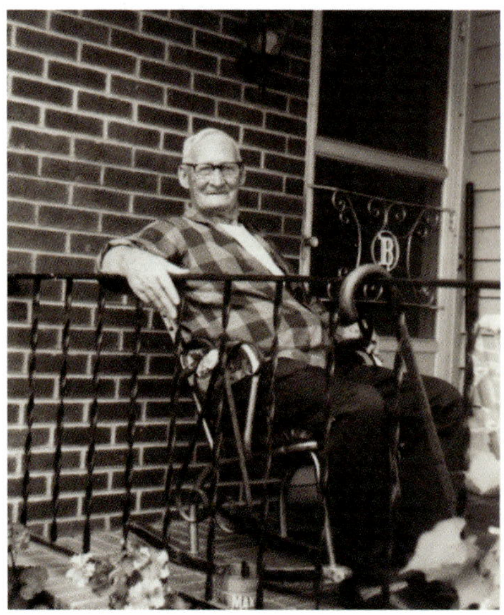

▲ Grandfather Forkey was active well into his 90s.

◄ Both my father (right) and my Uncle Victor (left) were Linotype operators at the *Sentinel*, as shown in this photo taken about the time I was born.

12 Keene Evening Sentinel — Monday, March 8, 1971

Sentinel Photo—Baker

Old Friends

George Bressett sits with linecaster, his most constant companion for 51 years before retirement.

Bressett Retiring From Paper

At 68, George E. Bressett, a man who has logged almost 50 years in the Sentinel's composing room, has decided to retire.

He's been in the business 51 years since he learned his trade at age 17. For most of that time, Bressett worked a linecaster machine which produces a single line of type, one of the many steps before the Sentinel goes to press. He retired last week as assistant composing room foreman.

A native of St. Alban's, Vt., Bressett came to Keene from Plattsburgh, N.Y. Back in 1924, the Sentinel operated out of the present G. H. Tilden Co. building.

Besides the daily evening paper, the Sentinel then published, "The New Hampshire Sentinel' which focused on county coverage.

Bressett said his retirement plans include "a few small trips." He and his wife, Florence, have two children, Kenneth, of Racine, Wisconsin and Mrs. Kenneth Devoid of Keene.

Kenneth, like his dad and granddad is in "the business." He is managing editor of the Coin Division of Whitman Publishing Co., Racine.

The senior Bressetts have four grandchildren.

◄ Dad retired from work at the *Sentinel* after more than 50 years of service.

Dad was a printer by trade and set type with a Linotype machine for the daily newspaper, the *Keene Evening Sentinel*. His father before him was one of the first ever to use the newly invented Linotype, and I have been told that he was once scorned for breaching the printer's tradition of hand-setting type one letter at a time. When I was about ten years old, I was also taught the fine art of printing, beginning with learning the "case" and setting type the old-fashioned way, with individual metal letters. In time I went through an apprenticeship, where I was a "printer's devil," a "stone man," "compositor," and eventually a Linotype operator.

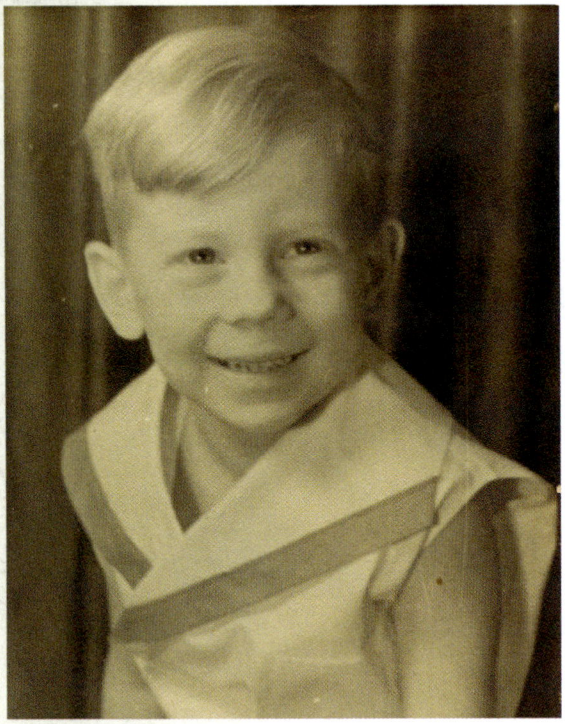

▲ I had lots of fun as a kid, even during troubled times.

My first full-time job was working at the same *Sentinel*, a commercial printing and publishing company that produces the fifth-oldest continuously published newspaper in the United States, having operated under the *Sentinel* name since its founding in March 1799. Today it still publishes the daily newspaper in Keene. Throughout my life, I have never lost my interest in printing, book layout, paper-making, and the written word. Over time I sharpened those interests with college courses in writing, graphic arts, history, and business. Fortunately, they are all skills that have been put to good use in my numismatic avocation, and they served me well when I considered expanding my career at a much larger firm, especially one that produced coin books and related products. But these things all came about much later in my life. My early memories of childhood are still very clear to me and reflect a different phase of history that was part of the story of things that influenced my career and life's journey.

Being a Depression-era baby brought with it an awareness of the hard times and belt-tightening necessities of the day. We were a family of four. My sister, Beverly, was three years older than I and often looked after me while my Mom was doing her essential household chores.

▼ My sister, Beverly, and I playing on our front porch in Keene.

▲ As a family, we always had books close at hand.

▲ Beverly and I sported trusty transportation.

I recognized just how fortunate we were that Dad had a full-time job. In fact, we even had what I think was the only telephone on our street! Of course, it was the universal two-party line, and neighbors were always welcome to use it in an emergency. That was simply the way; people helped each other in times of need. Even vagrants were treated with consideration when they wandered by and asked for food or a handout. Sometimes one would be allowed to sit on our back-porch steps and eat a sandwich or perhaps a piece of pie. When I was older, I occasionally got to talk to some and learned a little about their plight and what life was like for them on the road.

The Great Depression was a severe economic collapse that began in the United States in 1929 and lasted through most of the 1930s. By 1933 nearly half of America's banks had failed and 15 million people were unemployed. The disastrous stock-market crash of 1929 ruined thousands of investors and destroyed confidence in the nation's economy. The Depression saw rapid declines in the production and sale of goods and a sudden, severe rise in unemployment. Businesses and banks closed their doors, people lost their jobs, homes, and savings, and many had to depend on charity to survive.

▲ During the Depression I often played on the back porch, where my mother sometimes handed out food to passing drifters. I got a glimpse of what life was like for the less fortunate, who relied on charity.

▲ The Great Depression impacted everyone in 1930s America. The common refrain of the day—"Brother, can you spare a dime?"—was featured on this 20-millimeter patriotic token of the time.

President Franklin Delano Roosevelt, who was elected in 1932, created programs known as the New Deal to overcome the effects of the Great Depression. His innovative tactic expanded government aid into new areas of social and economic concerns and created social-assistance measures on a national level that changed the rapport between government and the people, many of whom came to accept and even expect federal support in their lives. Continuing on throughout the 1930s, the depression ended in the United States only when massive spending for World War II began and numerous defense jobs became available.

SOME EARLY RECOLLECTIONS

In my earliest memory, much of my playtime was spent learning about the world from my mother and sister. The first playthings I recall were improvised by my mother—putting clothes-pins in an empty milk bottle (a simple pastime then; a plastic version has recently been sold in stores as a real game), or counting pennies from the family cookie jar and sorting them by date. I have no idea if that influenced my later life, but I'd like to think it did. I was always curious and eager to learn new things. Dad encouraged me to take apart anything I could to see how it worked. An old alarm clock and pieces from a scrapped Model T Ford played a major role in my early tinkering, while he routinely tuned up his 1930 Chevrolet or listened to his Atwater Kent shortwave radio. A very special memory of those exciting days was in 1932 when my mother took me downtown with her while she voted for someone named Mr. Roosevelt. She explained to me that he was going to help make things better for all the poor people. It was my first lesson in politics.

More traditional schooling came in the usual form. I began kindergarten as the youngest in my class but adapted readily and found the situation quite agreeable, despite that it took me away from my other activities. I recall being praised for my drawing and penmanship, two talents that did not stay with me for very long. I was already reading by then, and never lost my love of that. Later I was enrolled in St. Joseph's Catholic parochial school, which provided a first-class education from 1934 through my formative years before I entered high school. Because I had started school so early, I was usually the youngest kid in my classes. That never seemed to hinder me in any way because I had been blessed with an above-average memory and sometimes even found myself disputing facts with teachers whenever I thought they said something in error. That was probably not the best way to curry favor with them, and it is a foible that has long been hard to break.

In a similar vein, I also had a vivid imagination, and when playing with others sometimes made up games with imaginary situations involving persons, places, or things—again, a flair that not everyone realized was actually a mark of creativity. Another early memory is of having my tonsils removed in 1933 at the local hospital in a group clinic, as was customary at the time. I didn't like it and resolved never to go back. It was the beginning of a lifetime effort to take proper care of myself through daily exercise, wholesome living and eating, and self-discipline. Those seem to be the main things that, together with good genes, have kept me healthy, happy, and out of hospitals for the past 92-plus years.

▲ "Stand back. . . . I just got a new bike!"

My earliest recollection of anything related to collecting coins goes back to 1934, when a neighbor gave me two strange-looking pieces. Each had a hole in the center. One was from Belgium, the other from China. I still have the one-cash coin of Chien-lung, but I don't remember what happened to the other. Over the years I went on to acquire quite a respectable collection of Asian coins and of necessity even learned to read Chinese and Japanese coinage legends.

It was only a couple of years later that I began to take a serious interest in learning more about the many different kinds of coins and paper money used throughout the world. Somehow it all seemed to fit nicely with the lessons in geography and history that I was beginning to learn in school. Those were the two subjects that I always found most interesting and stimulating. Thus I was keenly motivated when I became aware of a sales promotion that was being offered by Ovaltine in 1936. The company was presenting an opportunity to earn a set of eight different world coins just for drinking its chocolate-flavored milk supplement. It was already a favorite beverage of mine, and since it was being endorsed by Little Orphan Annie, my favorite radio personality, how could I resist? Included with the set of eight coins was a small brochure that told all about them. Interestingly, they did not show actual photographs of the coins because, like most people of that time, they believed that to be illegal. The whole package of information and coins was impressive enough to make me a lifelong collector of world coins. I still have—and treasure—those coins, along with my original homemade packaging.

▲ This coin of Chinese emperor Chien-lung (1736–1795) was the first piece in my collection, a gift from our neighbor, Mrs. Russell, around 1934.

A more serious introduction to numismatics began a little later in the 1930s, when I then became interested in learning as much as I could about our nation's coinage. In many respects it was a time that many of today's collectors envy because of the abundance of desirable currency that could be found in circulation, including gold and large-size paper money. In contrast, however, they were still the trying days of the Great Depression,

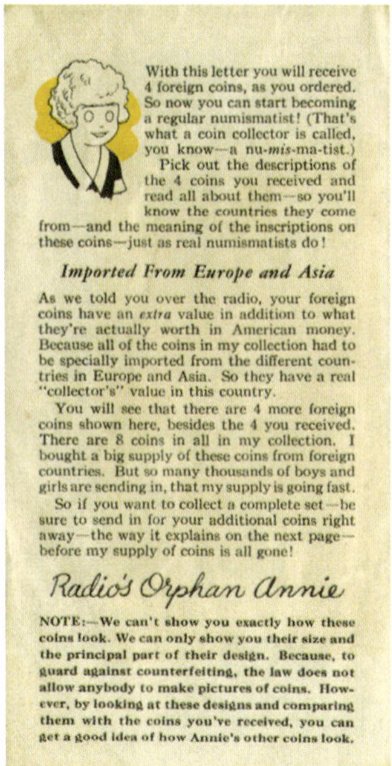

With this letter you will receive 4 foreign coins, as you ordered. So now you can start becoming a regular numismatist! (That's what a coin collector is called, you know—a nu-*mis*-ma-tist.)

Pick out the descriptions of the 4 coins you received and read all about them—so you'll know the countries they come from—and the meaning of the inscriptions on these coins—just as real numismatists do!

Imported From Europe and Asia

As we told you over the radio, your foreign coins have an *extra* value in addition to what they're actually worth in American money. Because all of the coins in my collection had to be specially imported from the different countries in Europe and Asia. So they have a real "collector's" value in this country.

You will see that there are 4 more foreign coins shown here, besides the 4 you received. There are 8 coins in all in my collection. I bought a big supply of these coins from foreign countries. But so many thousands of boys and girls are sending in, that my supply is going fast.

So if you want to collect a complete set—be sure to send in for your additional coins right away—the way it explains on the next page—before my supply of coins is all gone!

Radio's Orphan Annie

NOTE:—We can't show you exactly how these coins look. We can only show you their size and the principal part of their design. Because, to guard against counterfeiting, the law does not allow anybody to make pictures of coins. However, by looking at these designs and comparing them with the coins you've received, you can get a good idea of how Annie's other coins look.

BOYS! GIRLS! ACT NOW! GET MORE COINS TO COMPLETE YOUR COLLECTION

Hurry! Hurry! Send In Today! You Can Get Additional Coins Only While Very Limited Supply Lasts!

So many thousands of boys and girls are sending in now, that Annie's supply of coins is going fast. So if you want to get more coins—you must send in right away—because it's going to be "first come first served!" The boys and girls who send in their orders first, will get coins as long as Annie's supply lasts.

Here's All You Do!

Just fill in and send the coupon below, together with all of the thin round aluminum seal from under the lid of a can of Ovaltine. (You can order as many coins as you wish—but you must send a separate aluminum seal for each separate coin.) Mail the whole thing in to: Radio's Little Orphan Annie, 360 N. Michigan Avenue, Chicago, Illinois. Then Annie will send you your coins as fast as she can.

However, if the supply is all gone, she will substitute a different coin for the exact coin you ordered. If all of the coins are gone by the time your order is received, she will send as a substitute—one of the other premiums listed below. So mark which premium you want Annie to send you in case your order comes in too late to get any coins.

Mark Your Order Plainly

First, on the list below, draw a line straight through the names of the 4 coins you have already received. This is important—so we won't send you more of the same kind of coins by mistake. Second, mark an "X" plainly in the little square alongside each *new* coin you want us to send you. Third, send a separate aluminum seal for each coin you want. (That is, if you want one coin, send one seal—two coins, send two seals, etc.)

◀ Here is a sampling of the pieces (from India and Switzerland) I received as part of the Orphan Annie Coin Collection. I designed and produced the coin envelopes as a teenager during my printing apprenticeship.

and in reality the lowly cent or nickel was a considerable amount of money that played a very significant part in everyday life. The 25 cents that I earned by mowing lawns as a youngster had to go a long way, and paying even a dime to see a movie or purchase a comic book was a major expenditure. Setting aside even the old Shield or Liberty Head nickels that could still be found in change had to be given thoughtful consideration. One of my first completed collections, however, was a set of Buffalo nickels of every date and mint that were found in circulation. They were the beginning of my lifelong involvement as a serious collector.

Those abundant Buffalo nickels were the kind being used by everyone at that time. They were admired and appreciated by all as true American art that combined and honored both the bison and Native Americans. I remember them well and how sad I felt when I learned that a new design featuring Thomas Jefferson was going to replace them beginning in 1938. I also came to appreciate the artistry of James Earle Fraser and his other works through the kind of knowledge and familiarity one gains with numismatic study.

Aside from my interest in coins, I lived a fully normal childhood that included scrapes and broken bones and the usual games of kick-the-can, hide-and-seek, baseball, basketball, and other activities of that time.

▶ I broke my arm in only two places, but the injury kept me out of trees for most of the summer.

My summers were often spent at a relative's lakeside cabin, where I learned to swim and fish, or on one of my uncles' farms in upstate New York, where I learned about agriculture, animals, and rural life. Farming was a rough job, and thankfully I never had to do much of it, but I did learn about milking, collecting eggs, how to fill and use a kerosene lamp, and, of course, the ubiquitous outhouse, in a community that had no electricity or other conveniences. All were lessons well learned and remembered as guides to a fuller appreciation of my later life.

HOME SWEET HOME

Reminiscing about these events has made me aware of how much my hometown roots have influenced my adult thinking and demeanor. I suppose this is true of many people who have either fond or regretful memories of their birthplace. For me, I have only grown more aware of how fortunate I was to spend the first 30 years of my life in a friendly, quiet New England town tucked away in the southernmost part of New Hampshire.

"How dear to this heart are the scenes of my childhood, when fond recollection presents them to view."
—"The Old Oaken Bucket," Samuel Woodworth, 1818

The colorful town was originally called Upper Ashuelot, taking its name from the river that still runs along the southwestern border between New Hampshire and Massachusetts. It was laid out in 1734 by the province of Massachusetts, but in 1740 King George II changed the boundary line and made it part of New Hampshire. In 1753 Governor Benning Wentworth gave the town a new name, honoring Sir Benjamin Keene, a member of Parliament with a sterling reputation.

◄ The city of Keene, New Hampshire, originally was called Upper Ashuelot, after the nearby river.

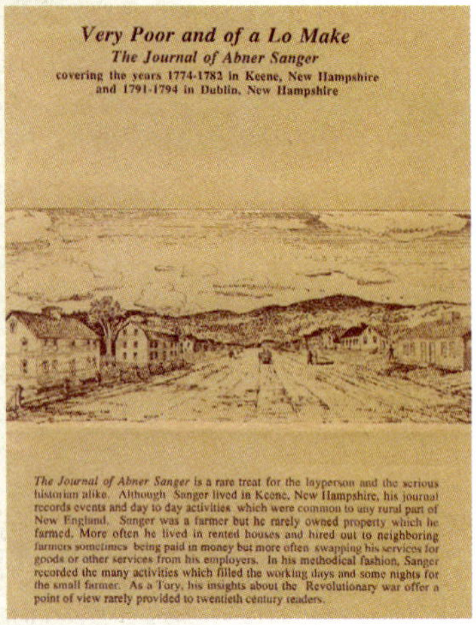

Among the area's earliest settlers were Eleazer Sanger and his descendants. The family had emigrated from England, where Eleazer was a "yeoman," or tiller of his own soil. In the emerging new environment, the family grew and thrived, leaving behind a legacy of service to their adopted land and, thanks to Abner Sanger, a journal titled *Very Poor and of a Lo Make: The Journal of Abner Sanger*, edited by Lois K. Stabler (1986).

In this book is a detailed record of what life was like in colonial America during the period from about 1773 to Sanger's death in 1822. I often refer to this book and recommend it to others because it is a factual, earthy essay on the life and times of that era. And beyond that it is part of my New England heritage, and the author was intimately involved with many of the characters we know from history and our numismatic studies. In many places, Sanger tells about the use of "coppers," credit, and various types of payment, including paper money printed in New Hampshire and Vermont, as well as many instances of counterfeits being circulated. He also presents a fresh outlook on his life as a loyal Tory coping with a changing world.

My Keene of the late 1920s was neither a bustling nor backward place to live, but rather something one might envision as being directly out of a Norman Rockwell painting. Of course, I still remember it as a friendly city of about 16,000 people, but that was nearly a century ago and it has grown and changed in many ways since then. The latest estimate shows a population of 25,000 or more, and I suspect that the racial makeup is probably about the same, with 95 percent white and a healthy amalgam of Native Americans and other races. When I lived in Keene, there were probably fewer than 2,500 families living in 6,000 homes, so just about everybody knew everyone else. And we realized how important it was to live as a community, or else face the wrath of gossip and scorn. Growing up in Keene, getting an education, and learning printing skills from an apprenticeship at the *Sentinel* has made me feel close to the very history of this country.

I shall always remember the time I heard my father tell someone that after living in Keene for the past quarter century, he was still considered a "foreigner" because his family was not born there. Both he and Mom's ancestors were from "faraway" places like Vermont and New York State and had lived there since before there even was a United States of America. Those were the sort of Yankee attitudes that prevailed in olden days and seem so strange to us today. Yet they were an indication of the fierce individualism and nationalism that prevailed in the rugged days of old. I still think myself a true Yankee and am proud of it, right down to being stubborn and obstinate, yet always ready to teach, help, and pass on to others those ideals and traditions.

◀ A 1907 postcard carries an image of Main Street in Keene, New Hampshire, during a public auction.

My love of history stems from studying the origins and ordeals of the birth of this nation. Much of the formation of our country came from the efforts and hard work of my New England ancestors, who after 1620 emerged from the Boston Bay area and sparked the ideal of freedom that built our great nation. I never cease to be proud of that heritage and constantly strive to acknowledge it with thanks and gratitude.

My interests in these things are not just idle thoughts; they are with me each time I turn on a faucet and know that I can have instant hot or cold water without going outside to a pump, or walk to the fridge for a frozen dinner, without having to rely on an old ice box that needed constant attention to replenish the ice. Things that seem so commonplace now, like electricity and all that goes with it, always refresh my memory of what once was a much harder way of life. And most of all, with each coin I study or collect, I am reminded of those who bestowed upon us these gifts, especially the nation's Founding Fathers and their contributions that have made our lives so comfortable today.

▲ New Hampshire was the first of the states to consider minting coins following the Declaration of Independence. Today even the most worn examples of the few pieces struck are very valuable.

BACKYARD ADVENTURES

One of the most memorable events of those early days was the great Category 3 hurricane of 1938 that destroyed much of Keene and the surrounding towns. We were fortunate to have only minor damage to the house and car, but we did experience a major problem with the accompanying flooding. For a period of time, we watched as the water covered the basement stairs, step by step, until it nearly reached the top floor. Fortunately, it never did. Wood, small boxes, and anything that could float drifted in and out the cellar windows. I remember vividly the cleanup efforts and

▲ After the 1938 hurricane, we surveyed the damage. That's me on the raft acting as lookout.

WIRES, POLES AND TREES ALL FALL ON LOWER MAIN STREET, KEENE

Photo by R. R. Stebbins, Keene

▲ Trees were uprooted for miles around Keene.

how we had to search the neighborhood to find property that had floated away. I sometimes helped in the search as a lookout on our improvised raft, while Father and others did the rowing. Search-and-rescue duty was a neighborhood project. Getting around to see the damage throughout the area was on everyone's mind when conditions began to return to normal.

In the middle of the storm, Dad and Uncle Vic somehow rigged up a printing press and managed to produce a small newspaper so as not to break the 138-year tradition of a daily issue of the *Sentinel*.

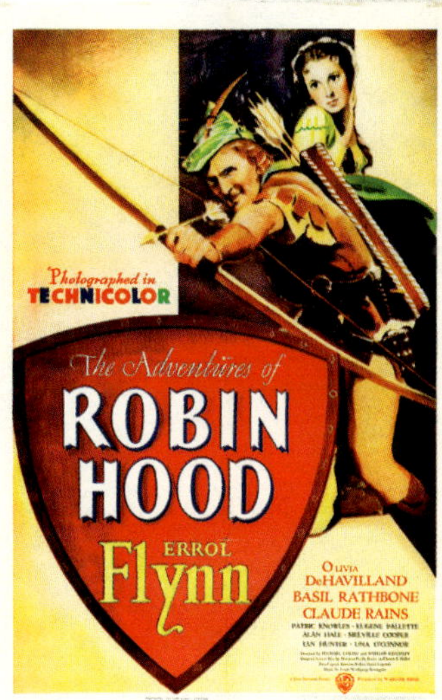

Also that year *The Adventures of Robin Hood* made its screen debut. The film left a great impression on all young boys, and our neighborhood was no exemption. Nearly half of the trees were uprooted in Keene, and they became prime places for climbing, swinging, and playing "Robin Hood" all that next summer.

GROWING AS A COLLECTOR

As my budding interest in collecting grew, I acquired many coins from friends and neighbors who knew about my hobby. I was sometimes able to trade my old comic books with other kids for the Indian Head cents or other things they had found. One major transaction was spending 60 cents for a well-worn 1892 Columbian commemorative half dollar. I could hardly wait to show it to my father, who promptly scolded me for spending so much money for something that was obviously a fake because it showed the date 1492, and they didn't even have American money back then.

▼ When I was a youngster, I recorded my coin purchases in this pocket-sized notebook.

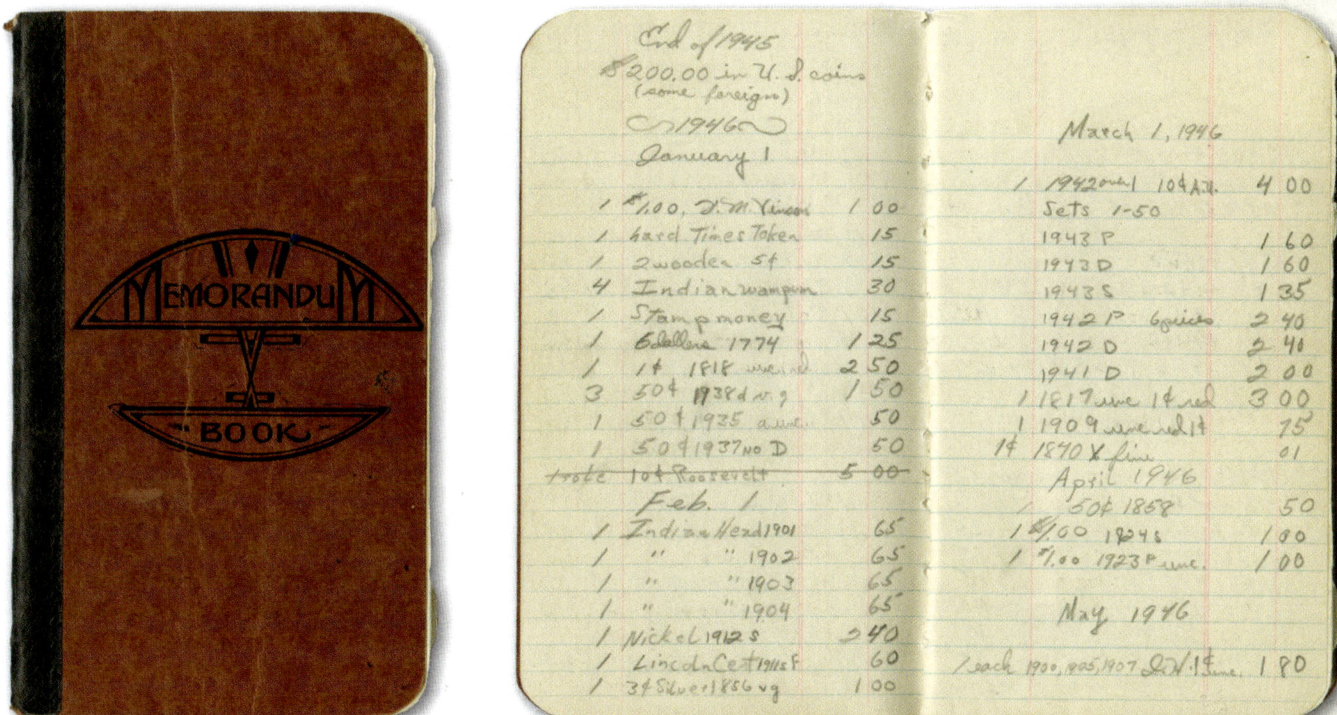

▲ This 1798 Spanish-American *half real* was given to me by Grandmother Bressett. She probably received it in change and carried it in her purse thereafter.

As usual, I couldn't resist displaying my vast knowledge of historical facts, although later I had to admit it wasn't a very good investment. The only coin that has ever been passed on to me through the family is a tiny, tattered Spanish-American 1798 silver *half real* from my Grandmother Bressett, who carried it in her purse most of her life. It still has an honored place in my collection.

A FAMILY CONNECTION

In those early days, I never knew if anyone else in my family was involved in coin collecting or connected in any way with numismatics. However, I was aware that the name "Bressett" was spelled differently by some relatives. I had seen it often with an "e" on the end, which is probably correct, and less often as "Brisset." So, I did some research. The most famous of those whom I have investigated had a very definite connection to coin production in a very tangible way. He was the one who caused me to spend years hunting down information about his existence and to locate an example of his numismatic prominence.

In the middle ages, the House of Currencies, located at the Paris Palace in France and known as the Chamber of Auditors, was responsible for controlling all minting workshops. In 1522 King François I gave Jacques Brisset the powers of a court-appointed judge concerning all matters of counterfeiting and other related royal mint matters. His principal concern seems to have been the stemming of counterfeits and devising a means of detecting them. Four very special bimetallic jetons were later made at the mint to honor him and other members of the Chamber.

▲ Nicholas Briot was an innovative French coin engraver, medalist, and mechanical engineer who immigrated to England and became chief engraver of the Royal Mint in 1633. He is credited with inventing the coining press. Briot created this bimetallic jeton honoring Jacques Brisset.

Jetons are tokens or coin-like medals, produced across Europe from the thirteenth through the seventeenth centuries. They were produced as counters for use in calculation on a counting-board similar to an abacus. They also found use as a money substitute in games, similar to modern casino or poker chips. Thousands of different jetons exist, mostly of religious and educational designs, as well as a few exceptional award pieces with portraits, crests, or coats-of-arms, like the medals given to a few special mint employees.

Only a very few jetons are bimetallic, a unique feature that shows the skills of Master Engraver Nicholas Briot. They are machine struck, beautifully engraved, and composed of both copper and brass. Four mint officials were honored by these pieces, one of whom was Jacques Brisset. His piece is dated 1616 and shows the family crest, with a hand holding two branches of holly and a flower. An example of this also now holds a cherished place in my collection.

In the very early days of my interest in coins, I realized that I needed to learn much more about the subject if I wanted to succeed in building a noteworthy collection. I sought out whatever books or literature I could locate, but little was available. I somehow found a 1932 promotional piece issued by B. Max Mehl, and later a copy of *From Barter to Banking* by Joseph Leeming. Then, in 1942, I retrieved a copy of the *Hub Coin Catalog* from scrap paper that I had collected for the war-time paper drive. Wayte Raymond's *Standard Catalogue of United States Coins* and Dick Yeoman's *Blue Book* and *Red Book* were in the works but would not be seen for another year or so. I did not become aware of *The Coin Collector's Journal*, which began publication in 1934, until a few years later. *Hobbies Magazine*, with its monthly article about coins, was my only access to current events. Just about every publication went on hiatus after 1941 and throughout the years of wartime shortages.

THANK YOU, ROBERT FROST

I probably didn't realize that I was a true New England Yankee until I reached my teenage years. Growing up within 70 miles of Walden Pond and having learned about Henry David Thoreau in school, I could hardly not become aware of the beauty of nature and life in our relatively peaceful environment, despite the harsh conditions of war and the aftermath of the Great Depression. I shall also always consider myself fortunate to have had an opportunity to become acquainted with the works of the celebrated poet Robert Frost. He considered New Hampshire his adopted home and would occasionally give a talk or recital at our local Keene High School assemblies, where he stirred my lifelong appreciation of his philosophy and inspiring poems.

It wasn't until later in life that I found and read the riveting *Journal of Abner Sanger*, which told the very real and enlightening story of colonial life in rural New Hampshire and Vermont. Sanger, like many other Yankees of that time, was someone committed to his beliefs, even though they often were a bit unorthodox. These influences, together with the reminders of New England life through the artistry of Grandma Moses and Norman Rockwell, have all shaped my life and commitment to being a dedicated Yankee, and mighty proud of it.

COMING OF AGE

World War II affected everyone, young and old alike. It was a universal topic of discussion and concern. And every abled-bodied person was willing to do their part in seeing it through. Any word of discontent brought on the omnipresent reply, "Don't you know there's a war on?" As a teenager, I was keenly aware of the situation and willing to do my part, which in the beginning was mostly helping with the scrap-metal and paper drives. Tin cans, pots, and pans had to be cleaned, flattened, and set out for pick-up. Old magazines, paper, and books likewise went off somewhere to somehow help with the war efforts. Most of all, tending the family Victory Garden was my responsibility. A plot of land was assigned to us by the city where we, along with several others, could grow vegetables for home use and canning. Anyone old enough for military service was gone from the work force, and those left at home had to carry on in every way possible.

Many essential things suddenly became scarce, not solely because they were needed for the war effort but also because of the depleted employment pool. As soon as I was old enough for an after-school job, I easily found work as a stock-boy in a local grocery store. I liked the work and felt that I was doing my part to help in the war effort. It also turned out to be an important part of my introduction to the adult world, and a major influence on my entire life.

Work in the grocery store had other perks too. Unloading the supply trucks alerted me to what would be available, and I took advantage of that by being first in line to purchase any needed household items. It was not long before the government began rationing items because they were needed for the war effort and were becoming scarce. The government established an allotment system to regulate the quantities of certain things that individuals could buy. The program was managed by the Office of Price Administration (OPA), and it issued booklets of coupons (called ration stamps) that had to be used to purchase restricted items. Shoes, meat, and certain grocery products could be purchased only by turning in the required stamps. Merchants, in turn, had to present the stamps to their suppliers to obtain replacements. Small fiber tokens could also be used as change or as payment for some items. Red tokens were used for meat and dairy products, blue tokens for other grocery items.

As I recall, gas restrictions were especially troubling. It meant that for other than essential trips, we all had to rely on bicycles or walking. Of course, in our small town walking was already a normal part of getting around. I guess that may be why I still enjoy a daily walk for exercise. Cars had to display a window sticker validating their gas quota allotment, as well as use stamps for a fill-up when it was available. Cigarettes were also in short supply and in high demand but were not rationed. The most popular brands, however, were mostly sent off to the troops, and stores were left with something called "Wings," which were probably worth about what they cost—10¢ a pack. I had no use for any of them, but while working in the grocery story I was able to see to it that some friends got preferential treatment. I never knew if that was why my history teacher, Mr. Houston, gave me such high marks, or if it was because I truly enjoyed his class.

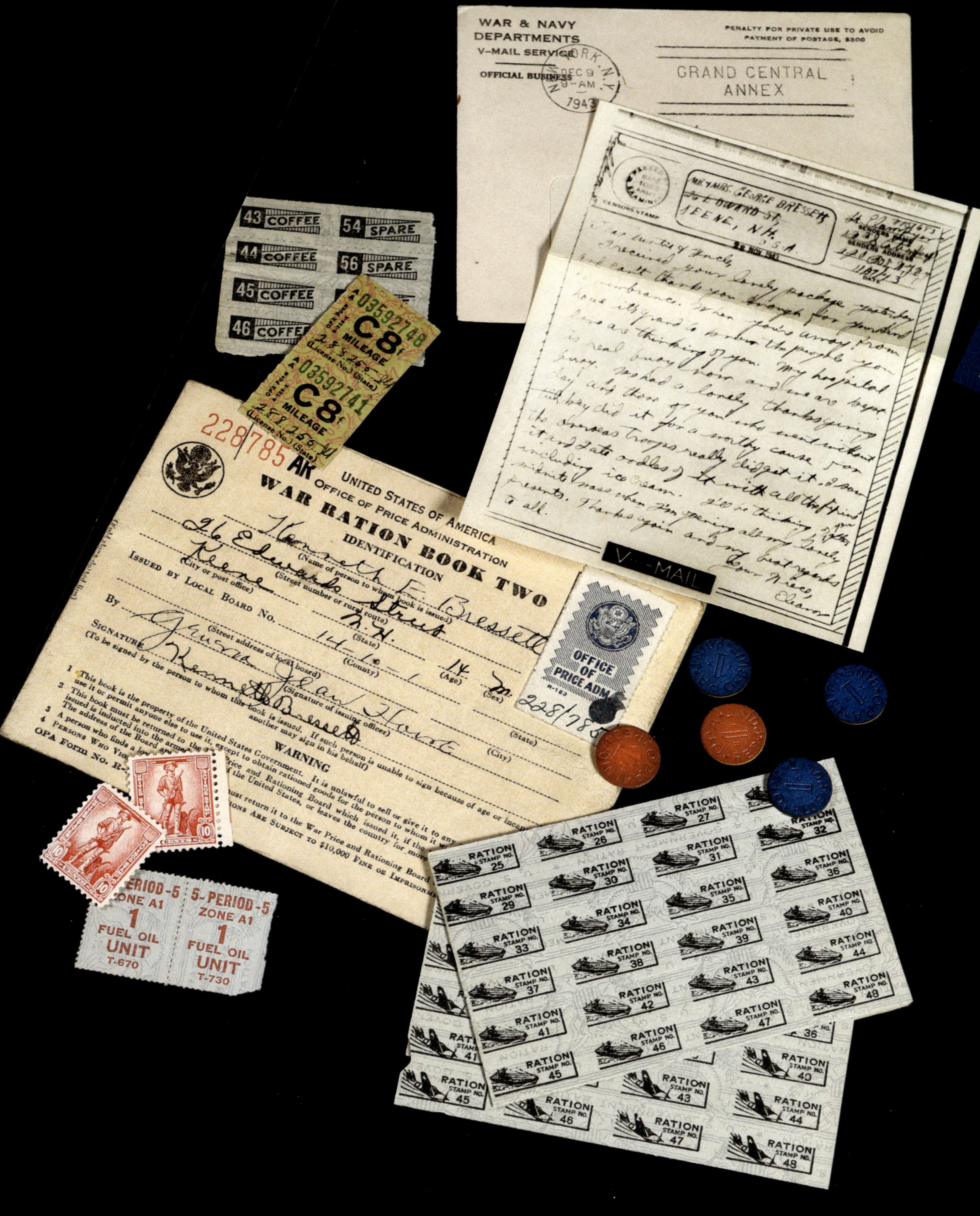

The World War II era greatly impacted my life. I vividly remember using ration books, stamps, and tokens. Shown at the top is a small-sized letter my parents received from one of my cousins by Victory Mail (popularly known as V-Mail), a process based on the British "Airgraph."

▲ Wartime brought changes to our nation's circulating coins: silver "war nickels" and zinc-coated steel cents.

Throughout those belt-tightening times I was aware of a paper shortage, but not to the extent of knowing much of anything about it, like why or how it affected the *Red* and *Blue Books*. I have subsequently learned that the lumber industry suffered from a manpower shortage caused by the draft and those who left to seek higher-paying jobs in the defense industry. Publishers had their supplies cut or limited as to quality and variety of what was available. In most cases, their allotments did not allow for new items to be printed, which meant that while the *Blue Book* could be continued, plans for the *Red Book* had to be put on hold. There was also a problem with getting specific shades of colors for the covers, which accounts for the variations seen on many of the early editions of those books. Much of Western's wartime work focused on Bibles and maps.

One of the innovative remedies the military made to alleviate the paper shortage was the use of what was called "V-mail," or Victory Mail.

Correspondence was heavy back and forth between home and the military. To save paper and speed things up, the Post Office accepted letters written on special forms that were available in local stores. Letters were censored and microfilmed for transportation to processing centers, where they were printed out and distributed to the recipients. The delivered letter was only about half the size of the original, but readable and always a welcome message from a loved one.

I was enrolled in Keene High School in 1942 and spent the next four years there. It was a time of meeting new friends, growing up, and getting on with life. It was also a time of coping with the war and all the problems that went with that. Involvement in the fray was not unexpected. We all knew about the troubles brewing in Europe since 1938. One of my dearest friends since 1934 was a German schoolmate, Hubert Spicher, who taught me basic vocabulary and some of the history of his country. I was saddened when for political reasons the language was dropped as a high-school elective, then doubly disappointed when French was also excluded for reasons unknown. We never spoke French at home, even though Dad and many of the neighbors did. I had to learn some of that out of necessity and because of my church's bilingual sermons. As an alternative, in school I quickly picked up Spanish, only to find that too was eventually dropped as an option. Fortunately, today Google Translate fills in as a substitute for my failure as a polyglot.

High-school days were pretty much alike for everyone back then. Boys and girls formed groups of friends that socialized, played sports, studied, and mostly all got along well together. I remember clearly that there was little or no class distinction or bigotry in our little city. There was only one African American family, and everyone knew them as friends. Their daughter was one of the most popular girls in our school.

My very best neighborhood friend, Bob Reinelt, was a year older than me, and we remained close for the rest of his life. Bob's great ambition was to become a commercial artist, which he did with great success. It was he who taught me to "follow your heart, do your best, and you will succeed in whatever career you choose, even if it is something as untraditional as being an artist or a numismatist." He also taught me the technique and value of doing research and preserving files of information as a resource for illustrations and data that could someday be useful. All such things became marvelous resource tools in an era before the Internet.

▼ My longtime high-school friend Bob Reinelt.

As mentioned, I was a stock-boy at one of our local grocery stores. The store manager, Eugene Gallagher, was a business-savvy, hard-working, tolerant tutor, who taught me well in every respect. I quickly became a cashier and later supervisor of the dairy department. I learned that Bertha, one of the checker girls—the really cute one—was very fond of cheese. Like any sensible teenager, I took advantage of that and made sure that she could always have some samples whenever she passed by. One day she rewarded me with a most unexpected surprise.

While vacationing in Boston in 1947, she found a copy of a brand-new publication called *A Guide Book of United States Coins*, and, knowing that I was interested in coin collecting, she bought it for me as a gift. I was thrilled and amazed at the amount of information instantly available in such a wonderful book. It opened a whole new world of knowledge for me. I used that book until it was worn thin and chock-full of notations, clippings, pictures, and comments. I even had to rebind it eventually, using an unprinted blue covering. I still have it on my bookshelf to remind me of those early days.

Three years later, that same Bertha "Bert" Britton became my wife and soulmate for the next 61 years. Throughout that long and happy marriage, we had three children: Philip in 1951, Richard in 1954, and Mary in 1955. (A third son, Mark, died at birth.) Only Philip inherited the numismatics gene, and he has excelled in the field as a dealer, storeowner, and consulting helper, working on the *Red Book* and *Blue Book* every year for the past four decades. All our children were born in New Hampshire and, like their parents, are true Yankees. Growing up in Wisconsin was no hardship or hindrance for them, except for inheriting our New England twang.

▶ Bert and I shared a casual four-year friendship prior to our marriage in 1950.

Bert and me on our wedding day, October 7, 1950.

Bert was never seriously involved in coin collecting, but she did accompany me whenever possible to numerous shows and on trips, where she loved to socialize with other "coin widows," work at registration tables, or do whatever she could to be a help. I was always amazed at the vast number of people she knew and remembered. One of her favorites was Dave Bowers, and she took several of his ANA Summer Seminar classes to learn about coins and because she had so much fun. Over the years she was recognized with the ANA's prestigious Farran Zerbe Memorial Award for Distinguished Service, named a Numismatic Ambassador by *Numismatic News*, given an ANA Presidential Award, and received several other citations and honors.

▲ Our son Philip, who looked a lot like his father at that age.

Working in the grocery store also held another advantage for me. As a cashier, I was able to see all sorts of coins and paper money passing through the tills. And at the end of each day, I was allowed to select whatever I wanted and replace it with my own money. By then, I had instructed all of the checkers in what to look for and to set aside for my inspection. It was a bonanza that lasted from about 1943 to 1947, when I attended Dresser Business School in preparation for an advancement to a full-time store manager. Soon I had to decide between continuing that line of work or taking up the printing trade, enrolling in college, or joining the armed service. Each had its own merits. At that time I didn't even think about the possibilities of a numismatic career, marriage, or a family. As it turned out, I accepted an offer from the *Sentinel* to become a journeyman printer. It meant putting off college for a while and joining the National Guard instead of enlisting in the U.S. Navy.

▼ Philip would ride his rocking horse for hours on end.

My stint with the New Hampshire National Guard turned out to be an ideal choice. It meant that I would be able to fulfill my service requirements and at the same time continue my training as a printer. I was assigned to Company I, 195th Regiment, New Hampshire National Guard in 1948, and after basic training I was soon made company clerk and promoted to the rank of corporal. My enlistment lasted four years and still brings back fond memories of a stimulating experience.

▶ Philip (left), Richard, and Mary Elizabeth Bressett.

▲ Members of Company "I," 195th Regiment, New Hampshire National Guard. That's me, Corporal Bressett, at center, in 1950.

DEEPER INVOLVEMENT IN NUMISMATICS

1947 was also the year that I joined the American Numismatic Association as a junior member. A candidate had to be at least 18 years old and have two sponsors. There were less than a hundred or so junior members back then. I recently researched a listing of those who were identified as junior members in 1948 and found only four notable names. Norman Stack and Walter Breen, both of whom are now deceased, preceded me in joining. Harvey Stack and I joined at nearly the same time, but my number, J-14350, was lower than his, J-14872. As such, I presently hold the record for being the longest continually active member of the association. Harvey and I first met in the early 1950s and have remained close friends ever since. We share many fond memories of times spent working together on projects like the *ANA Official Grading Standards* book and other efforts to improve the hobby. The first ANA convention that I attended was in Boston, Massachusetts, in 1948, and I have attended nearly all of them since then.

While working at the *Sentinel*, I honed my writing skills and had time to experiment with printing some numismatic items for myself or others. One thing was a pocket-size listing of prices paid for U.S., Canadian, and some world coins. I chuckle to see gold coins priced at about double face value, or a decent 1877 Indian Head cent for about $5. This was when I added several interesting coins to my collection at remarkably low prices; for instance, a 1792 half disme from B. Max Mehl for $100 and a decadrachm of Syracuse for the same price from another dealer. It was around that time that I also began writing a small newsletter, and later the beginnings of its journal, for the New England Numismatic Association (NENA). Occasionally I would write a few short articles or news pieces for *The Numismatist*.

I also began investigating the possibility of taking close-up pictures of coins with an old 35mm camera. Microphotography was something quite new back then, and fancy cameras were scarce and expensive. Many of the pictures of coins in books, ads, and auction catalogs were of such poor quality that they were hardly recognizable. Those printed by the collotype method were the best, but screen-dot printing was cheaper and mostly in vogue. Color pictures were virtually unheard of. The scarcity of such pictures was exemplified by an incident where B. Max Mehl reused a black-and-white "stock picture" of the Stickney 1804 dollar as an illustration for the Cohen specimen he was auctioning in the 1921 Manning sale.

► I received this badge for attending the ANA's 1948 convention in Boston. The unusual piece was struck by Whitehead & Hoag Company of Newark, New Jersey.

My reason for dabbling in photography was to be able to record as many different varieties of coins as possible. Because I was not able to afford the more expensive pieces, I thought that a good photograph would suit me just as well. Through research I learned that supplemental lenses on a normal camera would produce fairly decent close-up pictures. Some dentists were using a special technique and equipment that worked well, and I found ways to duplicate that using homemade stands, lights, and other gadgets. When I got that system working quite nicely, I figured out ways to miniaturize the equipment and make it portable so I could take it to conventions and museums, where I could photograph large numbers of coins for my growing reference collection.

Part of getting the best-quality prints was finding someone who would print to my specifications. When I was told that I was "too fussy about size and sharpness," I built my own darkroom at home, bought all the necessary equipment, and learned how to roll my own film, develop, and print to my satisfaction. I was then prepared to begin shooting decent coin pictures in earnest and sought out collections wherever I could find them. One of the first was at the Massachusetts Historical Society in Boston. I

"The gods do not subtract from man's allotted span, the hours spent in fishing [or, in my case, numismatics]."
—Babylonian Proverb

▼ Good photographs were a must for Whitman publications, so I contrived my own setups for shooting coins—one for black and white (left) and one for color (right).

knew it had an 1804 dollar and several rare colonial pieces, so I was pleased when I was given permission to shoot whatever I wanted. It was a grand experience that I will never forget. I trembled as I was handed an 1804 dollar. I had studied them and knew exactly what I was looking at, but it was the first one that I actually held in my hands.

A second fortunate opportunity came in the early 1950s, when I got to photograph selected pieces from the collection of U.S. coins formed by Louis Eliasberg Sr. His famed collection contained examples of practically every date and mint of every issue, all beautifully preserved and displayed in special plastic holders. I was told that I could photograph whatever I wanted but that it would be nearly impossible to get decent pictures with any ordinary camera. As it happened, mine worked just fine. I also used a copy of my handy *Red Book* to keep a record of each of the various specimens in the collection to verify that each existed and was there.

Then, in 1957, I was able to photograph nearly all the large cents in the collection of William H. Sheldon. I wanted to learn more about them because I was attempting to collect the early dates and varieties, and I hoped to learn more about grading them. I shot roll after roll of the collection in

Speech! Speech!

Sometime during 1948, while still in Keene, I was asked to be a banquet speaker for a local fraternal organization. At that time, I was organizing my collection of coins of the Bible for an exhibit and felt ready enough to try my hand at public speaking using that theme. It wasn't until I got to the meeting that I learned the special event of the evening was their annual oyster stew festival. Being a New Englander, I was naturally fond of just about everything from the ocean or anything near that. Clams, snails, mussels, or even calamari were all fair game, but I had never tried oysters. I wondered how they would mix with the butterflies already in my tummy. Fortunately, I enjoyed the chowder and accompanying oyster crackers, but declined the omnipresent rounds of beer. The talk went well, with many compliments on my memory and knowledge of Biblical names, places, and events. Receiving the $20 stipend topped the evening and made my day.

black and white, then a set of color slides of the various types in several different grades of condition, as determined by Sheldon himself. Many of the variety pictures were used in the 1958 edition of *Penny Whimsy*, in which I was given credit for the photography. The work was done at my house and Dorothy Paschal, Sheldon's assistant and co-author, brought the collection to me to shoot and study. My son Philip, who was beginning to take an interest in coins, unfortunately was confined to his room with a case of measles, and he missed out on the excitement.

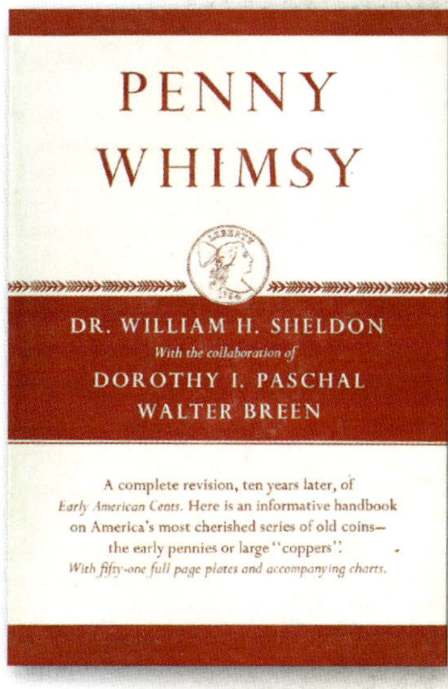

I have continued accumulating photographs of all sorts of coins ever since and was particularly active in doing so from 1948 to 1970. During that period I shot coins at the Bennington Historical Museum in Vermont while researching material for my treatise on the subject of early Vermont coinage. Photographing items in the Detroit National Bank Money Collection was another learning experience, as was shooting Civil War and patriotic tokens for George Fuld while he was writing his seminal works on the subject. Stock photos that I took for use in the *Red Book* and other Whitman publications were always my number-one priority and kept the shutter snapping for many years. Even today I continue to add to my resource of color illustrations of nearly every variety of all U.S. coins, and I use them frequently. It is something that I would encourage every serious numismatist to try now that it is so easy and convenient to do with an iPhone and cloud storage. Q. David Bowers commented on my early use of photography in his historical account of numismatic happenings of the 1960s:

> News was carried about a prominent numismatist who recently had a change in employment: Kenneth E. Bressett, well known for his research in early American coins, has joined the staff of the coin supply division of the Whitman Publishing Company, Racine, Wisconsin. As an assistant to Richard S. Yeoman, division manager, he will specialize in numismatic editorial and research work.
>
> Mr. Bressett was the first to develop a portable camera for photographing coins and has used it picturing rare coins in collections of Eastern museums. During the last three years, with the use of his camera, he has discovered 12 American colonial coins previously unknown or unrecorded by collectors. His performance has been matched by only one other modern researcher.

▶ Vermont coppers, among my favorite early American coins.

THE 1950S

It was during the 1950s that my life changed probably in more ways than I can remember. As I mentioned before, I began the decade still working as an assistant manager of the grocery store and fresh out of business school, when the opportunity came up for me to think seriously about accepting a position in the printing trade. All things considered, I chose to become a printer and honed that skill at the *Sentinel* from 1948 to 1959, when I switched over to working for the much larger Western Printing Company and jumped at the opportunity to become an editorial assistant to the famous R.S. Yeoman. Again, it was an opportunity that simply could not be refused.

Throughout that important time of my life, I was constantly advancing my interest in collecting all kinds of coins and learning as much as possible about them. Paper money was of only secondary interest because it was not considered part of the numismatic culture, and many collectors were leery of the legality of "gold backed" notes or the possibility of older pieces being demonetized. There was also the belief that paper currency could not be photographed, and thus there was a paucity of books and information about older notes. Whenever I got large-size notes, I would spend them as tips or jokes to watch the curious reaction. Imagine who's laughing now!

In 1950 I felt confident enough about my knowledge of numismatics to form a local coin club, the Cheshire County Numismatic Society, in Keene.

It was the first ever in the state as far as I know, and it lasted for many years after I moved on. Retired general M.S. Newton of Vermont was a member—not only a wonderful friend and mentor, but he also allowed me to photograph his nearly complete collection of all U.S. coins, from

▼ Dick Yeoman and I joined the Canadian Numismatic Association in 1950 and applied together for life membership in December 1960. Today I am the association's longest-active member.

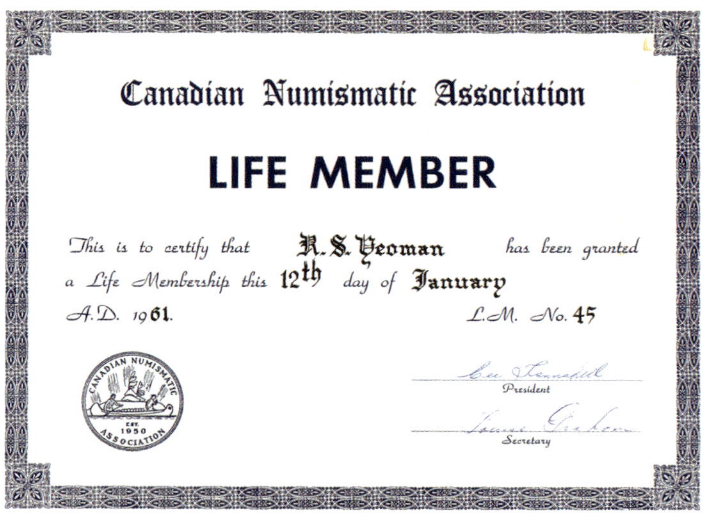

Canadian Numismatic Association

LIFE MEMBER

This is to certify that R.S. Yeoman has been granted a Life Membership this 12th day of January A.D. 1961. L.M. No. 45

President

Secretary

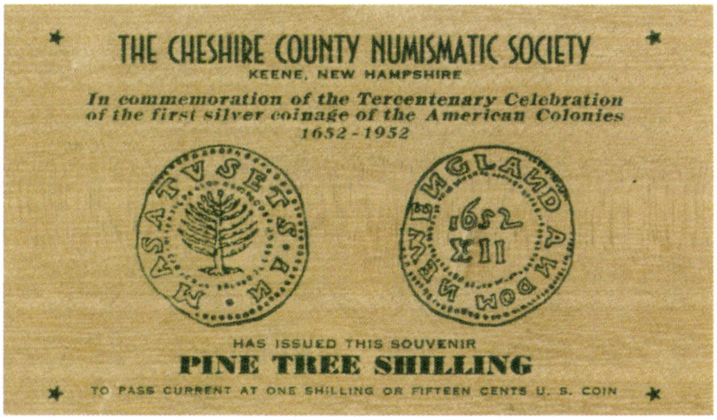

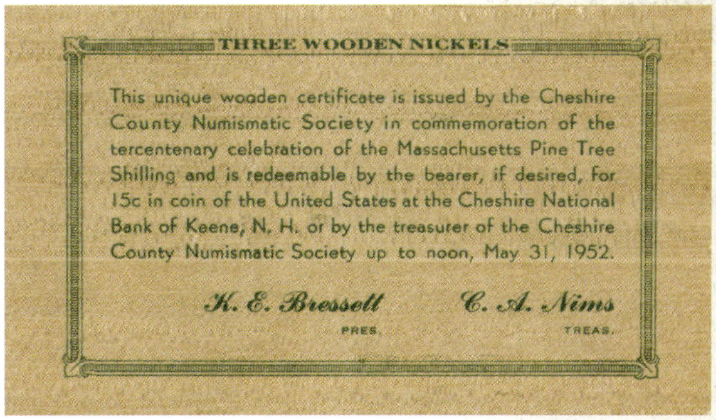

▲ Charles Nims and I made these "wooden pine tree shillings" as a fundraising gimmick for the Cheshire County Numismatic Society.

half cents to gold, and to use the type coins as illustrations for the *Red Book*. Later, after his death, I was allowed to acquire his magnificent collection of Chinese silver dollars that he obtained while serving in that country. Adding those pieces to my already growing collection of Chinese minor denominations added to its significance. Sadly, many of the finer pieces were later lost through a burglary or disposed of at public auction.

Among the early members was Charles Nims, who became a lifelong friend and helped in many ways to make the club a success. In 1952 Nims and I boldly made and issued "wooden pine tree shillings" as a fundraising gimmick. I designed the piece, set the type, and printed the "flats," as they were called back then. They were made of a thin sheet of wood supplied by a specialty company. The entire venture was paid for by Howard Macintosh, proprietor of the Tatham Stamp and Coin Company of Springfield, Massachusetts. One of the items he was selling at the time was a set of wooden nickels from various states, and because there were none from New Hampshire, he agreed to back the venture and purchase most of them for his store. To add to the novelty of the pieces, instead of calling them wooden nickels, we denominated them "three wooden nickels," which was more in line with the value of a shilling.

Howard was a friend to many at that time, and our relationship was very special for me because he appreciated my basic knowledge of ancient coins. He allowed me to work at home sorting and classifying his supply of common Roman bronzes and packaging them for his inventory. It was another enjoyable and educational "moonlighting" job that lasted a couple of years during the early 1950s.

Another famous member of the Keene club at that time was Sam Jillette, a part-time dealer from Greenfield, Massachusetts. We had children about the same age and thus became family friends. When his son was born, they had expected another girl and intended to name her Penny, so the son was named Penn. He was near my Philip's age, and they often played together until Penn moved away and enrolled in the Ringling Bros. and Barnum &

Bailey Clown College in Florida. Later he became world famous for his magic and entertainment act, popularly known as Penn & Teller.

I was also active in many regional clubs throughout the 1950s and joined the Canadian Numismatic Association in 1950, making me its longest active member today. I became a member of the American Numismatic Society in 1954 and must have joined the New England Numismatic Association somewhat earlier (in 1948, I think), and participated in shows and activities with all of them. One of my most noteworthy conventions was the 1952 New York ANA annual show. It was there that a group of youngsters with a common interest in numismatics met in person pretty much for the first time and formed a lasting bond. Included were Q. David Bowers, Dick Johnson, Walter Breen, Grover Criswell, George Fuld, and myself.

By 1957 we established a more formal group of young, interested researchers and banded together to form what we called the Rittenhouse Society, after the first director of the Philadelphia Mint. Membership was by invitation and available only to those under the age of 30. Unfortunately, that excluded Eric P. Newman, but that oversight was soon corrected. In October 1959 our annual meeting was held at the ANA show in Atlantic City with Dave Bowers, Walter Breen, and Grover Criswell in attendance. Dick Johnson, George Fuld, and Ken Rendell were not able to be there. Our first "official" breakfast meeting was in Boston in 1960 and has been held ever since as an official event at each ANA anniversary convention. Current membership consists of 50-plus authors, researchers, and students representing all aspects of numismatics.

Of course, the most important event of all was on October 7, 1950, when Bert and I were married. Our honeymoon trip was a tour throughout New England, from New Hampshire to Philadelphia. Yes, there was a bit of numismatics involved with that. While in Philly, I visited dealer Catherine Bullowa and purchased a spectacular Egyptian tetradrachm for a whopping $25. That practice became a standard ploy whenever we traveled and gave me an excuse to visit many shops, museums, and other numismatic venues around the country, as long as my companion came with me.

The frequent traveling, however, came to a halt in 1952 when caring for our first son, Philip, took precedent. Later Richard, and then Mary, added further restrictions for Bert and kept me from spending too much time away from home. Most of my trips from around 1955 on were to Boston to sell coins to dealers there. My prime buyers were Maurice Gould and Frank Washburn. Their requirement for bulk lots of Indian Head cents, two-cent coins, Civil War tokens, and other common items was at least 100 of each. Prices ranged from 3¢ to 10¢ each for most of them. Philip

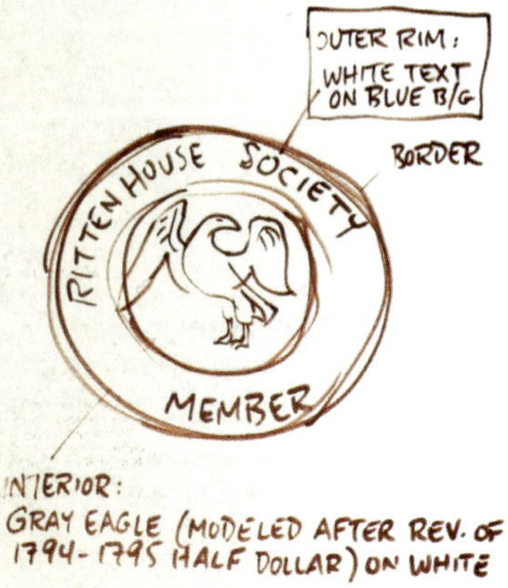

▲ I was a co-founder of the Rittenhouse Society in 1957. This membership pin was distributed in August 2017 at the Society's 60th-anniversary breakfast, held at the ANA convention in Denver. Whitman Publishing sponsors the annual breakfast meeting; publisher Dennis Tucker sketched the basic design for the membership pin, and it was executed by Thinh Bui of the company's Art Department.

often accompanied me on those trips and enjoyed the experience, while Bert liked the relief, and I made a bit of extra spending money.

I can't remember exactly when I first met Dick Yeoman. It must have been somewhere around 1955, possibly earlier at one of the regional conventions or at the ANA's 1952 New York show. Even the major ANA conventions were much smaller back then, and everybody knew each other because there was always time to sit and talk. Dealers would often chat with interested collectors, rather than rushing around the floor making deals or trying to buy and sell whatever they could. Some of my most enjoyable visits were talking with Dave Bowers, Richard Picker, John Ford, Grover Criswell, and Dick Yeoman. Picker was an extraordinary dealer. He always had time to talk at length about colonial coins, especially the Vermont coppers that were some of his favorites. He was noted for never commenting on the grade of his coins, but would say "my grade is $400," or whatever his valuation of the piece might be. Ford, while often irascible, was always informative and especially entertaining as a dinner companion. A fussy eater, he sometimes brought his own food to the hotel and instructed the chef how to prepare it.

▲ Dick Johnson, a renowned authority on medallic art, proposed making special medals honoring members of the Rittenhouse Society. Unfortunately, only two were ever produced. The first recognized Eric P. Newman, and the second (shown) was dedicated to me.

A MEMORABLE MEETING

At some point, probably around 1955, I asked Dick Yeoman about some of the things in the *Red Book* that seemed to be missing, unknown, or misleading. He was intrigued and asked me to write to him with specific information. That I did, and he was very appreciative. The next year he asked if I would offer more suggestions and recommendations and said that he would pay me for my work as a freelance consultant. Naturally, I was delighted, and in the course of doing this I asked my wife what she thought I should charge for my work. With her usual wisdom, she said that if I asked too much, he would never ask me again; or if too little, he might not respect the work. She suggested $50. I held out for $100, although she said I would never get it. Being a savvy businessman, Dick not only paid the $100 but asked if I would consider doing the same in the future for both the *Red* and *Blue Books*. In 1958 he invited me to visit him in Racine to discuss the possibility of moving there to work full time as an editorial assistant.

His offer was an opportunity that I could not resist, and in 1959 Bert and I made arrangements to sell the house, packed up the family, and headed off to Wisconsin for a new chapter in our lives. It was the beginning of a career that I have followed forever since, and one that I have never regretted. Working with and learning from the talented Dick Yeoman was a once-in-a-lifetime experience. Dick was a man of superior intellect, business acumen, moral convictions, and concern for the welfare of others. His

◀ The Village of Racine was incorporated in 1841. Located where the Root River empties into Lake Michigan, it began as the settlement of "Port Gilbert," founded in 1834.

keen sense of humor and good nature made him a friend to all. On my arrival for work, I was even more impressed by the quality and scope of the Western Publishing operation.

The executive offices at Western were elaborate. Its origin as a privately owned company gave the officers an opportunity to design the building complex as they pleased. I was particularly delighted with the indoor parking facility that had an attendant who saw that cars were properly cleaned, gassed, and cared for in every way. In the building there was a nurse's office, cafeteria, travel facilitator, and even a barber shop. A short walk from the offices were the factories and the composing room where type was set for the books, and farther on was the actual printing facility and giant presses. One of the unique facilities was the plate-making department, where duplicate printing plates were made by the electrotype process and huge photographic plates were shot with a camera the size of a small room in which the operator actually worked with the film.

▲ The Johnson Wax Administration and Research Center in Racine was designed by famed architect Frank Lloyd Wright in 1936. Then, as now, it was a major employer in the area.

One of the more interesting departments was the Production Room, where a staff of professionals managed the printing of all ongoing jobs throughout the corporation. These were tracked on a huge blackboard showing the daily progress of each project, from initial planning through composition, design layout, typesetting, ordering paper and components, press time, and everything else, right up to when the final product was shipped. If a single part of the process was not done on schedule, the entire process was reassigned to a different time slot, which sometimes meant a delay of weeks or months. It was working under those constraints that taught me the value and importance of meeting deadlines. It was a necessary value that I have never overlooked, and to this day I am proud of having never negligently missed an assigned deadline.

Professional graphic-arts skills, and everything one would ever need to know about printing and publishing, were taught in night courses at the Western offices and in conjunction with the University of Wisconsin for degree credits. Many of the employees availed themselves of the opportunity, as did I for a long time.

◀ Always on the lookout for imperfections, R.S. Yeoman often visited the Whitman production department.

When I began work at Western, my first assignment was to organize and prepare for publication the 1962 edition of Jim Charlton's *Standard Catalogue of Canadian Coins*. It was thrilling to see my name listed on the credits page as "R.S. Yeoman and Kenneth E. Bressett, editorial assistants." Perhaps equally thrilling was having my own office and desk, with a secretarial pool and a neat numismatic reference library close at hand to assist with my research and writing work. It was a dream come true. My family was soon nicely settled into the community, with Philip, Richard, and Mary in school and Bert and I beginning to mingle with new friends and neighbors. It was easy to get to know and like Racine because of its pleasant weather and colorful waterfront location.

Some of our earliest acquaintances were neighbors, coworkers, and members of the local coin club, who have remained close friends ever since. Among the most unforgettable were Bill Spencer and Fred Dickfoss and his delightful and lovely wife, Hazel. I soon found and joined a small group of neighborhood card players who met every Friday night for beer and a friendly game of penny poker. All went well with that until our wives got wise to the fact that they were missing out somehow by having to stay home and fix the sandwiches and snacks. So, they ganged up on us and insisted we take them out for dinner once a week for compensation. That

▶ Orientation classes, as well as courses for college credit, were offered to Western employees. R.S. Yeoman (back row, right) signed up in 1959 to learn about some new equipment.

was the happy beginning of what became a traditional "Friday Fish Fry" dinner that lasted for many years.

Part of that gang was Dick's son-in-law, Eugene Dodd, and his daughter, Sharon, who is now deceased. Another couple, John and Jean Hawes, became our closest family friends. They were married about the same time as Bert and me. Then, in 2012, Jean and I lost our spouses within weeks of each other. Since then, the two of us have continued to stay closely in touch and enhance our unique bond through correspondence, visits, and vacation trips.

▼ Sharon Yeo Dodd and her husband, Eugene, were part of our "Friday Fish Fry" gang.

▶ "Miller Time"—relaxing at a picnic with my potluck poker group, around 1965. Left to right: Jim Minert, John Hawes, and me. In Wisconsin we all paid tribute to "The Beer That Made Milwaukee Famous."

BEGINNING WORK AT WESTERN

During those very early days of working at Western, I spent much of my time organizing, editing, and writing for all of their coin products. I also took on the task of revising and updating the entire line of coin albums. The most enjoyable part of these activities was having the time and opportunity to use the office library for research. The core library originally belonged to Dr. J. Hewitt Judd. I was allowed to supplement it with additional references and whatever else was needed for daily work.

"Buy the book before the coin." **— *Aaron Feldman***

Throughout the years I have always tried to accumulate or read whatever books I could find locally or in nearby libraries. Regrettably, there were very few, but I was able to acquire some through the help of George Fuld, Eric Newman, and a few other bibliophiles. Frank Katen and Aaron Feldman were good sources, and I believed in "Buy the Book *Instead* of the Coin," rather than Aaron's usual advice. By the time I made numismatics my lifelong avocation, I had acquired a personal, wide-ranging library of basic information about the hobby.

A Library of Old Friends

As my library grew and my interests expanded, I was eventually able to acquire references on a great many subjects. Many are treasured autographed copies from fellow authors, others are "working" copies that are stuffed with clippings, notations, corrections, and additional information. All are now old friends and can be easily located by their place on the shelf, their size, color, or binding. Some are actually organized by country, subject, or theme! Nearly 1,000 books devoted to U.S. material are closest at hand in my office, and they cover everything from the 1652 coins of Massachusetts to articles about the use of ramen noodles as currency in some of today's prisons. The rest of the world, from 700 B.C. to the present, is covered in the main library room that holds in excess of 3,000 volumes. Today much of this information is instantly available through Google or the Internet. Yet nothing can surpass the pleasure of holding an actual book in my hand and doing research the good old-fashioned way.

▶ Planning sessions with Yeoman and Production Manager Pete Foerster (center) were frequent and productive. The Carl Wuermer painting on the wall was Dick's favorite and later hung in his home.

▶ Distributor Don Hirschhorn (left) often weighed in at sales meetings with Whitman staff.

At Western, after finishing my first editing assignment for expanding and updating the Charlton *Standard Catalogue of Canadian Coins*, I immediately got started planning a few monographs that I felt would be important references connected with the formation of the two or three new states that were under consideration for being added to the Union. The first of these, published in 1960, was *Alaska's Coinage Through the Years*, written in cooperation with Maurice M. Gould. It was a small, black-covered essay on the subject that became the first attempt at listing all of the many

Dick and I frequently visited the plant to inspect production.

tokens and money substitutes used in Alaska before statehood. It later continued in book form for several additional, enlarged editions with the added assistance of collectors Kaye and Nancy Dethridge.

In succeeding years the Whitman inventory of "black books" was expanded to include such diverse titles as *Hawaiian Coins, Tokens and Paper Money; The Colonial Coinage of the U.S. Virgin Islands; United States Territorial Coinage for the Philippine Islands; The Money of Puerto Rico; Moneys of the Bible; Confederate States Paper Money; A Guide Book of United States Fractional Currency; A Guide to Civil War Store Card Tokens; Foreign Coins Struck at United States Mints;* and *Money Tells the Story*. All of these were written by carefully selected authors under my supervision and sometimes with my help. It was the beginning of a grand experience of collaborating with specialists of all stripes and talents, and a new wave of publishing for Whitman that had heretofore concentrated on only the basic U.S. classic *Red Book* and *Blue Book*, along with Dick's *Modern World Coins* catalogs.

In addition to working on book publishing, I also took on the responsibilities of keeping the coin albums and other products updated and adding a few entirely new items to the line, like plastic tubes, magnifying glasses, and other related supplies. Dick's philosophy was "you can't do business from an empty cart, or sell only the most popular sizes of shoes," and he encouraged the development of new products.

The demands of expansion and accelerated sales called for adding to the staff in order to keep up with production. An experienced sales force,

► "Yes, we make *Red Books* here!" Western Publishing president Terry Daniels (left), Dick Thompsen (center), and Dick Yeoman inspect a shipment about to be sent to a customer.

◀ Final inspection of *Red Books* prior to shipping.

production coordinator, and others were already in place when I began work at the Racine office, and of course the corporate printing facilities took care of all the detailed business of producing high-quality products. So, my duties mostly centered on working in tandem with Dick and his experienced crew to bring new items to the line and to see that things were factually accurate and in tune with current market demands.

NEW RESPONSIBILITIES

In 1962 I was named coordinating editor of the *Red Book* and continued to serve in that capacity for all of the other publications, under Dick's supervision and with his help. Little by little, the staff began to expand with needed assistance in the editorial department and other functions of the growing business. The coin market was active in general, and especially all related holders and supplies were in high demand throughout the country. I remember calling it the "Soaring Sixties" and thought it would never end. No one suspected that by the close of the decade much of the novel interest in coin collecting would begin to fade.

The May 1962 issue of *The Numismatist* included a report of my activities at the Empire State Numismatic Association convention, at which I was the featured speaker:

> The combined "Coin is King" show of Triple Cities Coin Club and 24th semiannual convention of Empire State Numismatic Association was a grand success—a conservative statement indeed. Upward of 700 who attended included 55 bourse dealers and exhibitors who filled 160 cases with fine numismatic material. Over 150 persons filled the Colonial Room for the banquet and to hear guest speaker Kenneth E. Bressett, Numismatic Editor of Whitman Publishing Company.

Bressett's after dinner talk dealt with "The Fantastic 1804 Silver Dollar," which is the title of a book that is about ready for release. He gave us facts based on the most modern methods of examining coins, and reached the conclusion that all known 1804 silver dollars were struck considerably after that date. Master of ceremonies John J. Pittman conducted a lively question-and-answer period which elicited the comment that such programs are a help to the hobby and the finest thing being done for it.

Among the outstanding numismatists in attendance were Dr. and Mrs. V. Clain-Stefanelli, curators of the Division of Numismatics, Smithsonian Institution. Together with Ken Bressett, they served as exhibit judges.

As a merchandising aid for our growing cadre of wholesale customers, Dick proposed that we publish a marketing piece that could be mailed to our list of supply dealers. Organizing and preparing the publication of course fell to me, and from 1960 to 1973 I wrote a quarterly, four-page mailer featuring our publishing activities, notices of new products in the works, tips about promotional items, and notes about current market activities. Retailers who stocked Whitman coin products received the newsletter, which kept them informed of the latest news about the *Red Book*, the *Blue Book*, and other Whitman coin titles. It was published as the *Whitman Coin Supply Merchandiser* from 1960 to 1966, then resumed in 1969 as the *Stamp and Coin Supply Merchandiser*, reflecting the company's acquisition of a stamp division over the interim. By 1971 the philatelic line had been cancelled, and the newsletter was discontinued. The next year it was revived as the *Coin Supply Merchandiser*, and it ran under that name through the end of 1973. In its various incarnations, the *Merchandiser* holds a wealth of inside information on the evolution of the *Red Book* and has now been preserved in the Newman Numismatic Portal (nnp.wustl.edu).

Dick's daily work on his products ended when he retired in 1970, and I became the de facto editor of all Whitman publications in 1971. The announcement of my new title was delayed to retain the prominence and respect for the Yeoman name. From 1974 to the 2018 edition my name appeared on the title page of the *Red Book* as editor, and as editor emeritus thereafter.

▼ In 1969 Whitman created a nine-volume Braille edition of the *Red Book* for Davyd Pepito, a blind 17-year-old coin collector from California.

▶ One of my favorite aspects of the numismatic hobby is sharing knowledge with others. I found that joining local, regional, national, and specialty clubs is a great way to do this. Cartoonist Bill King recognized my involvement in 1972 by creating the fun profile shown here.

HE BECAME INTERESTED IN COINS WHILE WORKING PART-TIME IN A GROCERY STORE IN HIS HOMETOWN OF KEENE, N.H.
SMILE
KENNETH E. "Ken" BRESSETT
IS NOW MANAGER OF WHITMAN COIN PRODUCTS AND COORDINATING EDITOR OF THE RED BOOK.
HE IS ALSO RESPONSIBLE FOR THE BLUE AND BROWN BOOKS PLUS OTHER COIN PRODUCTS.
BILL KING
KENNETH E. BRESSETT
AMERICAN NUMISMATIC ASSOCIATION
DE PROFUNDIS
ORGANIZED 1891
NO. 14350
HELSINKI FINLAND 1994
FOR MERIT OF SERVICE
FORUM SPEAKER
Kenneth Bressett
COLORADO SPRINGS NUMISMATIC SOCIETY
AWARD OF THE MONTH
96TH ANNIVERSARY CONVENTION
PITTSBURGH AUGUST 9 - 13, 1989
SPEAKER
800th MEETING BANQUET
SEPTEMBER 14, 1985
PITTSBURGH AUGUST 9 - 13, 1989
1891 CLUB
RITTENHOUSE SOCIETY MEMBER
MDC XVIII HELSINKI FINLAND
KENNETH BRESSETT U.S.A.
Hawaii State Numismatic Association Convention
OFFICIAL
Member
HONORING KENNETH BRESSETT
EDITOR EMERITUS
"Mr. Red Book"

▲ Eric P. Newman.

THE MYSTERIOUS 1804 DOLLAR

The early days of the 1960s had brought other opportunities and duties for me, along with the chance to work with some of the most talented authors and researchers of that time. Most important of all was Eric Newman, who became my most ardent friend and mentor. We had known each other from earlier encounters, but at this point we decided to begin working together in earnest on solving the origin of the rare 1804 dollars that had mystified the numismatic world for generations. Both of us had previously studied the conundrum, along with Walter Breen and a few others, and now we had a chance to collaborate, with the likely possibility of having the results published in book form.

Eric was a good friend and teacher but, being somewhat older than me, was always treated with great deference. Even so, he had a keen sense of humor and had to be watched. His favorite joke was, when hosting guests for dinner, suggesting they look at the hallmark on the silverware. While that is perhaps not a socially polite thing to do, for a numismatist it held a very special meaning when they discovered they were actually using items made, and marked, by the renowned Ephraim Brasher, maker of the famous Brasher doubloons! At other times, he might casually prompt a visitor to look at an old document on the wall, which astonishingly was a 1776 Solomon Southwick broadside copy of the Declaration of Independence, which was made for the original states and was one of only seven still in existence. In 2015 this historic document was gifted to Washington University in St. Louis.

Eric would occasionally limp. I once asked why, and he replied, "I'm just practicing for the time that I may need to." Inspired by the master, I have sometimes used a version about my "old football injury," which happened when I was at home watching a game on TV, got up to get another beer, and twisted my ankle.

The mysterious 1804 dollars had intrigued and baffled investigators for eons because information about their origin was clouded by deception and lies from Mint officials and others involved in their coinage. When I first attempted to learn why and how these coins were made, and what made them so valuable, I was stymied by the lack of reliable information or even a basic understanding of their nature. The first piece of useful information I found appeared in R.S. Yeoman's 1942 first edition of the *Handbook of United States Coins*. The listings for 1804 dollars were described as Type 1 and Type 2, stating that this was "the first time this fact has been mentioned." Subsequent research has revealed that was not the first time and that a great deal of information and speculation had been around ever since the coins were first made, but finding such references was extremely difficult in those days without the help of today's instantaneous research tools.

Continued on page 251.

A typical day at the Whitman office.

Selecting appropriate pictures for the *Red Book* was a never-ending task.

I always enjoyed Chet Krause's visits to the Racine office. Here we are looking at covers for Whitman coin folders.

Coin World
THE WEEKLY NEWSPAPER OF THE ENTIRE NUMISMATIC FIELD
SIDNEY NEWS BUILDING
SIDNEY, OHIO

A Birthday Gift for YOU!

It's COIN WORLD's tenth birthday. . .

We want to wish you, OUR READER, many, many happy returns!

We are ever so pleased to give YOU a gift on OUR birthday!

Enclosed is a specially-marked COLLECTOR EDITION of the 1970 "A Guide Book of United States Coins," the famous Red Book by R. S. Yeoman.

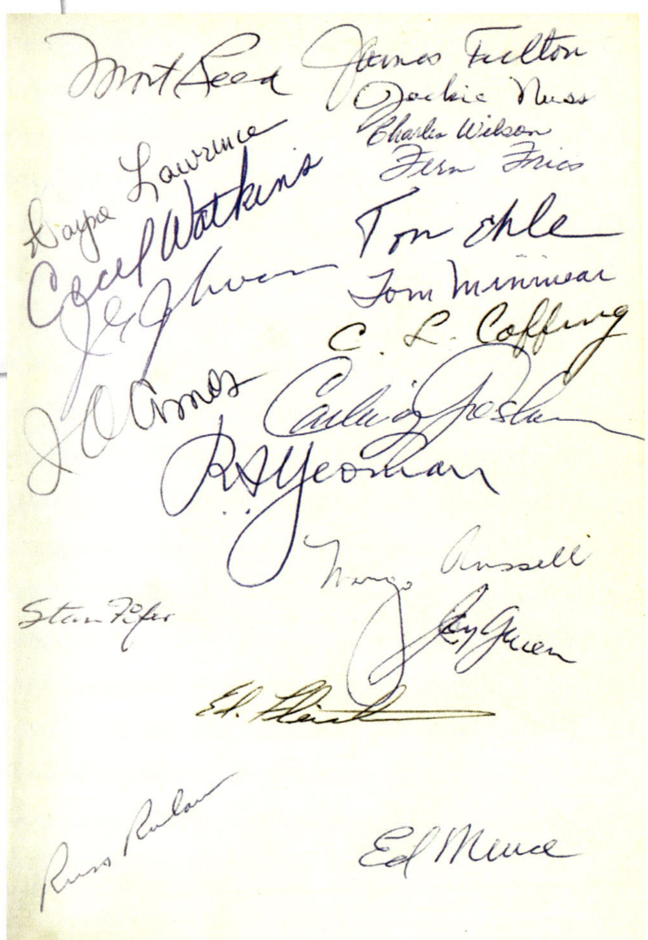

► To celebrate the 10th anniversary of *Coin World*, Whitman authorized a special *Red Book* with an overprinted front cover. Approximately 3,000 were made to be given away. The autographs seen here are from a copy of this authorized edition.

Ed Metzger and I were interviewed by Charles Beaudoin (center), managing editor of *La Tribune*, a Canadian publication printed in Quebec.

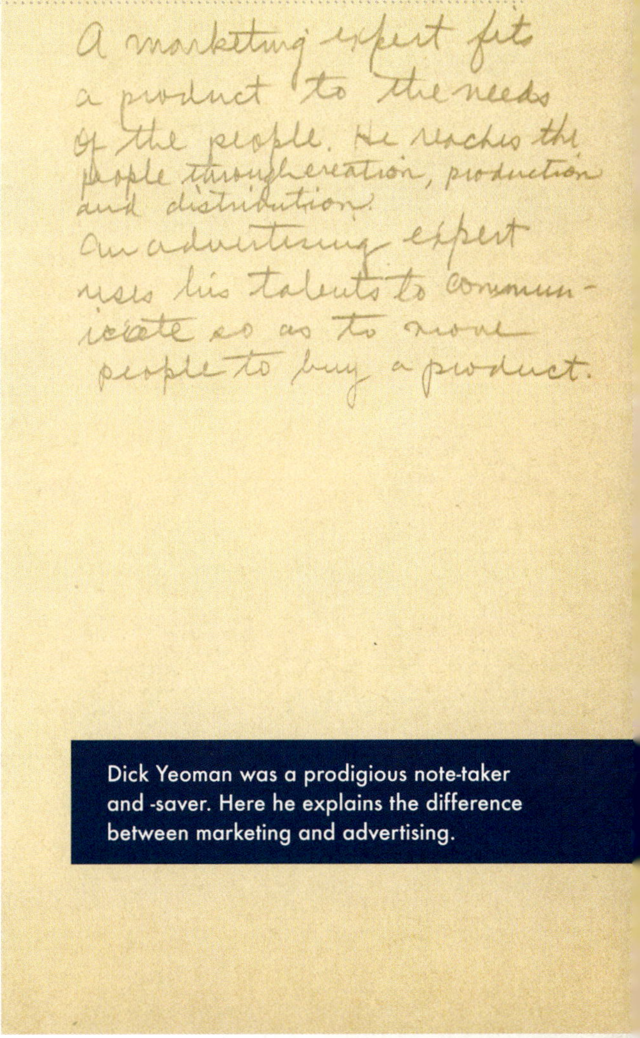

A marketing expert fits a product to the needs of the people. He reaches the people through creation, production and distribution.
An advertising expert uses his talents to communicate so as to move people to buy a product.

Dick Yeoman was a prodigious note-taker and -saver. Here he explains the difference between marketing and advertising.

Production Manager Pete Foerster reviewed the manufacture of coin folders on a daily basis. It was estimated that the quantity of coin folders produced outnumbered some of the coins they were intended to display.

A special silver bar was created by the Whitman staff and presented to Yeoman to celebrate the silver anniversary of his famous *Red Book*.

Here I watch as a Whitman worker boxes up books on the loading dock for nationwide distribution.

At the time of writing and publishing the book on 1804 dollars, it never occurred to us that we might someday, by an unimaginable quirk of fate, become a party to actually adding to the mystery. Yet, that happened just as work on the book was essentially finished and it was ready to go to press. (In the Winter 2020 issue of *The Asylum*, the quarterly journal of the Numismatic Bibliomania Society, a new team of researchers—Leonard Augsburger and Joel Orosz—chronicled the events leading to what could be called an aborted edition of a book that should never have been printed.)

In early July 1962 our work on the 1804 dollar book was finished and in the final stages of being ready for press-time scheduling. Around the middle of the month we received word that there would be a slight delay because of a difficulty in obtaining the right kind of Kivar®, the material used for making the covers. This, however, should not have delayed printing, and with a sense of relief I went forward with my plans to attend the annual summer convention of the American Numismatic Association, which was scheduled for the following month in Detroit, Michigan.

▲ The King of Siam presentation specimen.

What ensued next was a publisher's nightmare. Near the end of July, I learned that a prominent London coin dealer, David Spink, and an American, James Risk, had discovered some new information about the dollars and would be presenting a talk on the subject at the ANA convention. Naturally, I was eager to hear their talk because I knew and respected both of them. I planned on attending the ANA show and rejoiced in having finished the book on schedule. I had a few press sheets bound to take with me for "show and tell." Now I would have a chance to find out what others had learned about the origin of these coins. The title of their talk was "New Facts About an Old American Coin."

The gist of their presentation was the discovery of a new specimen of the dollar, which they traced to the King of Siam. As such, it proved our theory about when and why the coins were made in 1834, and this proof needed to be added to our book to make it complete. Immediately after the lecture, I ran out of the room directly to a pay telephone to call the factory and actually yell, "Stop the press!" There was much new information to be added to the story. The Western production team was understanding and granted us another month or so to finish the project. The work was completed in record time, and the revised books were shipped on October 1, 1962.

When the dust had settled, a press foreman asked me what I wanted to do with the sheets that had been printed prior to stopping the press run. I arranged to have a few copies of the unpublished books bound for archives and friends. As I recall, a total of about 40 to 42 copies were made, and the rest of the sheets were destroyed. A number of them were sent to

▲ The Sultan of Muscat presentation specimen of the 1804 silver dollar, for many years owned by the Childs family.

Newman for his use. Most of the others were later distributed as gifts to those who were involved with the original research. A few, but certainly not all of them, were autographed by Newman and myself. Others were either left unsigned or individually inscribed to recipients by either of us. I have been told that autographed copies are considered great rarities and have sold at auction for over $1,000!

The so-called "1st edition" copies of *The Fantastic 1804 Dollar* are not identified on the cover or inside to distinguish them from the published version. They are, however, readily distinguishable by the changes in Chapter IX, which was re-titled "The Origin of 1804 Originals," and many other additions. As near as I can recall, there were some changes to at least 60 pages.

I've probably told this part of the 1804 dollar story too often, but it's one of my favorites. When I was doing research on the location of all the known specimens, I became friends with F. Newell Childs, the owner of the best preserved and perhaps most valuable specimen. I was living in Wisconsin then, and he nearby just outside of Chicago. Newell was custodian of the dollar, along with an equally fabulous collection of other rare United States material. I made it a point to visit with him every time I was in the area, and we often went to lunch in town or just "played" with his coins at home. Much of the collection was stored unprotected in old-time trays. Some of the early Proof gold coins were still wrapped in the original tissue coverings as received from the mint.

I made it a point to correct his storage problems whenever possible and repackaged most of the pieces in safer containers. Newell also relied on me as a consultant to keep him apprised of market conditions and as his agent to purchase additional items that were missing from the nearly complete run of date and mint pieces. Most of the coins were stored in a special safe in his bank, where we sometimes worked. However, one day while we were looking at some of the pieces he had at home, he suggested we go to his club in town for lunch. I cautioned him to put the coins in a safe place. With our work finished, we had a nice meal and I headed back home. A few days later, I got a furious call from him, shouting, "Where's my '04 dollar?!!" Struggling for a reply to defend myself, I came up with a likely probability: "We were working in the dining room; have you looked on top of the china cabinet where you sometimes hide things?" My hunch was right, and the piece was quickly returned to the bank.

Newell had recommended that his father, Charles Frederick Childs, buy the coin to add to the family collection when it was being offered by Ruth and C.E. Green for $5,000. From 1945 to 1952 the senior Childs held the 1804 dollar. In 1952 it was given, with the balance of the Childs coin collection, to Charles Frederick Childs II, age eight, whose father, F. Newell

Childs, acted as custodian from 1952 to 1999. The family sold the collection on August 30, 1999, at the Walter H. Childs Collection auction by Bowers and Merena, Inc., where the coin sold for $4,140,000, a world-record auction price for any coin at the time.

MY SERVICE ON THE U.S. ASSAY COMMISSION

As exhilarating as work was on the 1804 dollar book, my most memorable event of that era was being selected by President Lyndon Johnson to serve on the United States Annual Assay Commission, which was an agency of the United States government from 1792 to 1980. Its function was to supervise the annual testing of the gold, silver, and (in its final years) base-metal coins produced by the United States Mint to ensure that they met specifications. Although some members were designated by statute, for the most part the commission, which was freshly appointed each year, consisted of prominent Americans, including numismatists. Appointment to the Assay Commission was eagerly sought after, in part because commissioners received a commemorative medal. These medals, different each year, are extremely rare, with the exception of the 1977 issue, which was sold to the general public.

▼ During my service on the 1966 U.S. Assay Commission, I worked with Opal Morris and Mint Assayer Dr. Paul Maguire to select packets of coins to be examined.

▶ Mint Director Eva Adams counseled me and fellow commissioner Philip L. Budd about our duties as commissioners.

Each year the president of the United States appointed unpaid members, who would gather in Philadelphia to ensure the weight and fineness of silver and gold coins issued the previous year were made to specifications. The commission met in 1971 but for the first time had no gold or silver to test, with the end of silver coinage.

My involvement with the Assay Commission actually started when I endeavored to help Dick secure an appointment. I began the quest by contacting influential friends and people I knew in the Treasury and Mint departments to gain their support. It was relatively easy because Dick's prominence and reputation were already well known to most.

Inevitably, my name and standing in the numismatic community became familiar to the same influential people, and in 1966 the mantle was passed to me. My odyssey began in the last days of January, when I received a call from Mint Director Eva Adams informing me that I had been appointed by President Lyndon B. Johnson to serve on the 1966 Assay Commission. The meeting convened on February 9 and, as mentioned previously, I was appointed by Chairman R. Henry Norweb to the Assaying Committee.

As the day unfolded, we watched as the Mint workmen sorted, cut, and melted the designated coins to ensure they were of the correct weight and fineness. As expected, all were within the proper tolerance. The Assaying Committee was fortunate to be the only one to ever assay silver and clad coins, because both were minted during 1965. When we concluded our

Opal Morris and I watched carefully as selected coins were elongated and prepared for assay by Mint worker William Badger.

▲ I received this bronze medal for my service on the 1966 U.S. Assay Commission.

duties, our group of 22 commissioners received specially minted medals and certificates for our participation. Afterward, we were treated to a spectacular tour of the Philadelphia Mint and dinner at a local restaurant. It was a day I shall never forget.

It was during those heady times that I had the privilege of meeting and working with many prominent Mint and Treasury officials. Among my favorites were Gilroy Roberts, the designer and engraver of the Kennedy half dollar in 1964, and Frank Gasparro, who designed the Eisenhower dollar in 1971. Both were very approachable and interesting because of their hands-on connection with many of the country's most famous coin designs. Gasparro was a particular favorite because he had also designed and engraved the obverse of the Assay Commission medal awarded to me in 1966. Both had at one time held the position of chief engraver of the United States Mint. Gasparro, in addition to producing many Mint medals, designed and engraved the obverse and reverse of both the Eisenhower dollar and the Susan B. Anthony dollar; the Lincoln Memorial reverse of the cent; and the reverse of the Kennedy half dollar.

▲ After my service, I regularly attended annual meetings of the Old Timer Assay Commissioners Society, held in conjunction with ANA's anniversary conventions. The group issued this badge for its 1985 gathering in Baltimore.

▲ Coin designer Gilroy Roberts and I frequently corresponded. As a token of our friendship, he gave me one of the first Kennedy half dollars, which he had encased in plastic.

FRANK GASPARRO
216 WESTWOOD PARK DRIVE
HAVERTOWN, PENNSYLVANIA 19083

January 16, 1971

Mr. Kenneth E. Bressett
Manager, Whitman Coin Supply
Division
Western Publishing Co., Inc.
1220 Mound Ave.
Racine, Wis. 53404

Dear Ken:

Since you are a distinguished authority on coins I am very glad to have your comments on the Eisenhower Dollar. Thank you for writing and for the fine compliments you have given this work.

As to the eagle, I have always been fascinated by this beautiful bird and as a young art student I spent many hours sketching the eagles in their aerie at the Philadelphia Zoo. I had great pleasure in designing this one.

As to the Eisenhower portrait, after a great deal of study and experimentation I decided on a profile because it seemed to lend itself best to my interpretation of him both as to appearance and character and as I wished him to be remembered by posterity. Of course, I kept in mind that my portrait would be used on a coin and not a medal and I treated it differently.

You can probably appreciate the effort I put into my designs and I hope this coin will be accepted as graciously by others as you have accepted it.

Thank you again for your comments and interest in my work.

Sincerely,

Frank

Frank Gasparro

▲ Mint engraver Frank Gasparro and I were longtime friends and correspondents who enjoyed discussing the ins and outs of coin design. *Overset:* A bust of Dwight Eisenhower sculpted by Gasparro; a portrait sketch he made in 1945; and his designs for the Eisenhower dollar coin.

BACK TO WORK AGAIN

Western's coin department had more than enough work not only for the dedicated staff but also for experienced numismatic assistants. Dick suggested a young member of the Racine Numismatic Society whom he had known for some time, and Lincoln W. ("Bill") Higgie III was hired to help in numerous ways. He was a skillful writer and especially knowledgeable about ancient coins. To complete his studies, he eventually moved on to finish his education and travel throughout Europe, then to become a prominent dealer in coins and artwork. He often recounted stories of his many trips to the ancient lands around Turkey and the Mediterranean in a fashion not unlike the voyages of Sinbad and Marco Polo. As a frequent visitor to the bazaars, he knew where and how to bargain successfully and to avoid the many fake coins that were sold to tourists. Genuine silver pieces-of-eight and other world coins were often there in quantity and priced only slightly above their bullion value.

It was Bill who first introduced me to medieval Turkoman and Armenian coinage and encouraged me to form a representative collection . . . odd as that may seem for a specialist in United States coinage. I began by reading Jacques de Morgan's *The History of the Armenian People* and quickly realized that here was an entire chapter of history that was new to me. It is still one of my favorite books because it is a perfect blend of history and numismatics. It also gave me an even greater awareness of my many Armenian friends who were a significant part of the population around Chicago, Racine, and Milwaukee, where I was living at that time.

Remembrances of My Early Days in Racine

by *Lincoln W. Higgie III*

My interest in coin collecting began around 1950 when my father brought me to meetings of the Racine Numismatic Society. A typical meeting included collectors, dealers, and hobby leaders like Yeoman, who often displayed interesting world coins, and J.V. McDermott, who would invariably bring his famous 1913 Liberty Head nickel.

One evening Yeoman introduced the club to a new member of his staff, a numismatic author, editor, and printer named Ken Bressett, who quickly became involved with club activities. An exciting speaker, he frequently entertained us with coin narratives and related stories, displaying his quick wit and extensive knowledge.

▲ Dick gave Marion a necklace from which was suspended a counterstamped Spanish piece-of-eight, much like the specimen shown enlarged here. In this photo she wears the controversial neck piece at the Numismatic Association of Southern California's 1978 convention in Los Angeles.

Bressett had grown up as a printer in Keene, New Hampshire. At an early age he had fallen in love with numismatics. Add to this the gift of an expressive writing style as sharp as Yeoman's. He understood how to work with collectors and dealers, as well as typesetters, pressmen, and binders, to deliver a quality product. To this list of qualifications, add a lovely wife who often assisted collectors and dealers at shows where Whitman was represented.

In January 1961 Yeoman asked me to work for him as an editorial assistant. He assigned me to editing and writing some of the books then in progress, and to a desk directly behind Bressett. They helped me to learn the ropes of writing, publishing, and printing. Both wrote in a clear, concise style, which I quickly learned to appreciate. I owe an immense debt of gratitude to those two men for their patience and help at an important time in my life.

One unforgettable event for me was when Dick gave his wife, Marion, a piece of jewelry containing a Spanish piece-of-eight that was counter-stamped with the head of King George. It is a well-known collector item referred to as "The head of a fool on the neck of an ass." Bressett noticed her wearing the item and recited the saying, something she neither understood nor appreciated. At that point, I stepped in to explain the situation and left us all laughing.

For many decades, Bressett has maintained the integrity of Yeoman's *Guide Book* and has expanded its scope with changing times. Thanks to both these scholars, it remains the most trusted and widely read collector reference book ever written. Its formula for coin-book text and layout is the accepted standard of excellence not only for Whitman books but also for the outstanding works of Yeoman's old friend Chet Krause. So, I thank Dick Yeo and Ken Bressett for the many good things they did for me personally and for illuminating the lives of so many other people who love numismatics.

Bill Higgie's departure meant that we had to find a suitable replacement. My immediate choice was Neil Shafer, a writer whom I had come to know from his brilliant articles on Philippine coinage that were published in Lee Hewitt's *Numismatic Scrapbook Magazine*. It was one of the most fortunate decisions of my life. Not only did he accept the editorial position, but he proved to meet all of my most hopeful expectations, and it was the beginning of a life-long friendship that extended well beyond our mutual interest in numismatics. Throughout the 20 years that Neil worked at Western Publishing, we jointly or independently wrote more books, articles, and promotional pieces than I can recall. Our lunchtime chess games became legendary, and we both constantly increased our numismatic knowledge and skills by sharing research, data, and information. Our success in solving the mystery of the background and use of Allied military currency, as described in the November 1968 issue of the *Whitman Numismatic Journal*, will forever be the seminal work on the subject.

▼ Neil Shafer, right, as a representative from the coin department, makes a final check before the presses start to roll—a necessary step in production.

▲ Neil and I often visited the typesetting room and offered suggestions for layouts. Here we are with typesetter Wil Winters in 1962.

Even with Neil's additional help, one of the major tasks that he and I faced was trying to keep up with the ever-mounting workload. I accepted the challenge when Dick wanted to publish the aforementioned *Coin Supply Merchandiser*, but when he came up with the idea of a monthly magazine, Neil had to be included, and he loudly complained that it just couldn't be done. Somehow I eventually convinced him that it really was a good idea, and with Dick's assistance and a few more extra helpers we could manage to pull it off. We did, but only with the support of numerous friends and authors, plus the eventual addition of two other very skillful writers, Holland Wallace and Lawrence Block. The magazine was launched in 1964 and ran monthly for a full five years. In an effort to make our miniscule staff seem larger, each of us wrote articles for the magazine under our own names and a variety of pseudonyms. I used my wife's maiden name in some cases, and, as I recall, Neil and later Lawrence Block occasionally used their spouses' names too.

Working with Ken Bressett at Whitman Publishing

by Neil Shafer

The following is a memory-laden description of the time in August of 1962 when I first joined Whitman's editorial staff in Racine, Wisconsin.

Toward the end of 1961 I was offered a position in the editorial department of Whitman Publishing Company, then operating out of Racine, Wisconsin. At that time I was in the midst of my first semester at Georgetown University in Washington, D.C., studying law. My regular job consisted of teaching fourth- through sixth-graders instrumental music in the public schools of Montgomery County, Maryland, just north of Washington.

I was able to finish that semester at law school and also complete the school year with the music classes, so it was not until August of 1962 that I finally arrived at the office in Racine. I was quite surprised to find everyone busily scrambling from office to office with various papers; no one had much time to introduce me around or help me get settled. One could easily tell that something big was happening.

It was the exact time that Ken was his busiest, trying to change some text in a book he had just completed with Eric Newman—*The Fantastic 1804 Dollar*. Proofs of the full text had been run, covers were being made ready, and the book was 99 percent ready to go. Then the ANA's annual summer convention took place, and a figurative bombshell went off there. Spink of London made an unbelievable surprise report that an 1804-dated U.S. silver dollar was a member of an otherwise 1834-dated presentation set of Proof coins in a special holder that was given to the Imam of Muscat!

The book, as it was before this incredible announcement, had included a chapter called "The Diplomatic Gift Delusion," in which it categorically stated that such a piece did not exist. You can just imagine what this revelation did to the plans for imminent release of the book. I believe the best way I could have helped was to stay out of the way and let those doing work on the updating finish what they were engaged in. Perhaps they asked me to assist with text or other editorial work—I don't recall exactly. I hope I actually helped in some way.

Shafer and I have always been more like brothers than just good friends. Our favorite game was buying, selling, locating, and trading coins with each other in what we called a "baksheesh" exchange. The only rule was that both of us had to end up being happy with the transaction, and whomever really needed the piece most should get it. A baksheesh "credit" often made up for any disagreement over the value. Come to think of it, I probably still owe him a couple of them.

Neil was a master joker, and I could rarely top his clever puns, no matter how hard I tried. He can best describe one of my most diabolical pranks. It happened during a visit to our home for dinner:

> One time at his home, fairly soon after I came to Racine, Ken indicated to me that his wife, Bert, had received a certain Philippine 10-centavo silver coin in change, and that was dated 1910-S. It was pretty worn but looked genuine enough. My first book published by Whitman covered U.S.-Philippine coinage, and in that book I said there was only a suspected coinage of 5 to 10 pieces of the 1910-S 10 centavos. I considered that coin to be the rarest issue in the whole book. No one could provide an example anywhere, but at the time I thought there was possibly some piece someplace . . . but how was it possible that such an item could be found right here in Racine and in this way?
>
> Being young and gullible—I don't remember if I actually believed them, but knowing that stranger things have happened—the first thing I had to do was examine the piece for myself under magnification. I then asked Ken for a glass, and in a few minutes he brought me one of those dime-store, 3-power jobs … with the most apologetic kinds of excuses as to why he just could not produce a better magnifier. I remember trying all sorts of positions with that useless glass in the vain hope of being able to see if was truly a 1910-S issue. Of course, it was an altered 1919-S and in a low-enough grade that the 9 could more easily be altered to a zero, and Ken did quite a nice job of altering it too, I must say.

The *Whitman Numismatic Journal* began publication in January 1964 under my direction as managing editor. Articles were solicited from interested authors. Early that year, two were received from Lawrence Block. The first was "Raymond Chandler and the Brasher Doubloon," which was published in the July issue. The second appeared in the August issue and featured a profile of Archduchess Maria Theresa of Austria.

▲ **Philippine 10-centavo coins are known to have been minted in San Francisco in 1909 and 1911 (among other years). Finding one from 1910 would be a major numismatic event!**

▲ Larry Block and Neil Shafer shared office space when they worked on the *Whitman Numismatic Journal*.

Considering the quality and aptness of his work, Block was soon invited to join the Whitman staff as an associate editor, and he accepted the position in October 1964, continuing in that capacity until February 1966. Much of his work consisted of writing for the magazine and creating promotional material, advertising, and newsletters. He also participated in reviewing and selecting the articles and books submitted to Whitman for publication. In 1966 he edited and assisted in the publication of *Swiss Shooting Talers and Medals* by Delbert Ray Krause.

From then on, Block's byline was frequently Horace Bull, although other names were used occasionally. His then-wife's name, L.A. Kallett, appeared in a June 1965 article; the book reviews he wrote for the "Light from Many Lamps" column in the magazine were signed "L.B." (Using initials was customary for the rest of the staff, who occasionally wrote similar reviews.) That section of the magazine was my favorite, and I wrote most of it by reviewing the latest numismatic books and related materials. It was a marvelous learning experience for all of us. Block resigned as associate editor of the magazine in February 1966 to pursue a career in freelance writing. (Best known for his fictional crime stories, he was named a Grand Master by the Mystery Writers of America in 1994.) He was replaced by Holland Wallace, who joined the staff in April. The backlog of articles by Horace Bull continued to be published in *WNJ* for several months after his departure, with the last in September of that year.

The Whitman Numismatic Journal

by Lawrence Block

From my point of view, the *Whitman Numismatic Journal* came along at just the right time. In early 1964, I was living with a wife and two young daughters in a Buffalo, New York, suburb. I'd been making a living for several years as a freelance writer, and some months previously I'd had a falling out with my agent; consequently, the publishers who'd furnished the greater portion of my income were no longer accessible to me. I was a college dropout with an essentially empty résumé and, aside from writing, the only job I had much chance of getting was bagging groceries at the supermarket. So, I soldiered on and set about seeking and finding new markets for my work.

By then I'd been a very ardent coin collector for several years, and I accordingly tried writing for some of the numismatic publications. "Raymond Chandler and the Brasher Doubloon" was my first piece for the *Whitman Numismatic Journal*, and I'm not even sure I was familiar with the magazine when I submitted it. It was graciously accepted by Ken Bressett, as was a second effort. And sometime in the spring, Ken got in touch to say that he was going to be in Buffalo and suggested we meet for dinner. I thought this might lead to more assignments. It never occurred to me that the man would offer me a job, or that I would take it.

Continued on next page.

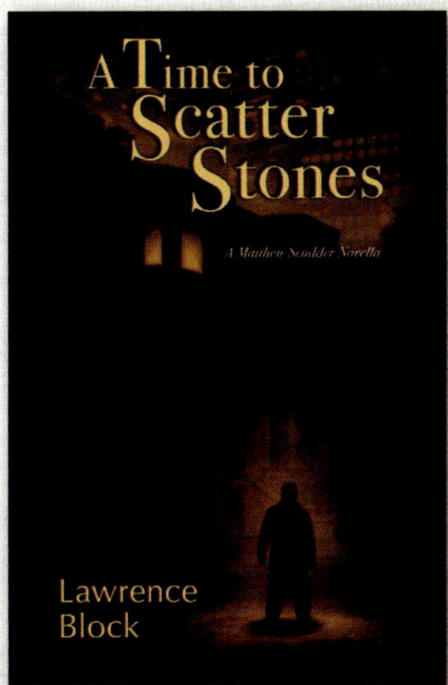

▲ Lawrence Block (left) and Harlan Coben at the Waldorf Astoria Book Brunch, September 28, 2008; and one of Block's recent Matthew Scudder mysteries (*A Time to Scatter Stones*, 2019).

But, see, it was perfect timing. Within a couple of months we'd sold our house and moved to Racine, where I entirely reversed the habits of a lifetime (well, not a very long lifetime) and went to work for Western Printing as an associate editor in Whitman's Coin Supply division. I got up every morning, put on a shirt and tie, and went to the office. I wrote articles for the magazine, edited articles submitted by other writers, laid out each month's issue—and increasingly found myself involved in product development and advertising and sales promotion.

Over the next year and a half, I thrived. I'd always assumed I'd be a failure in any sort of corporate environment, and that wasn't the case at all. I enjoyed the company of my fellow workers, and I found the work very much of interest. And I also realized that, while I could in fact make a go of this, it would never really be what I wanted to do with my life. I wanted to be back in New York, and I wanted to make my living writing fiction. I accordingly left Whitman and Racine early in 1966, but I've never regretted one moment of the time I spent there.

Adding Holland Wallace to the staff in 1966 was another fortunate event. His many talents were exactly what was needed to continue and expand the number and variety of books that were then under consideration or in progress. His specialty was world coins, especially those of Central America. He went right to work updating and adding to *A Catalog of Modern World Coins* and the first issue of *Current Coins of the World*. By the second edition he was named assistant editor, along with Neil Shafer. As staff writers, we always accepted that the name Yeoman was kept as author on all publications. They were his creations, and he deserved the credit. Even though we sometimes joked about all of us doing "yeoman work," we were always proud to work for him, with him, and under his guiding genius.

▼ **Holland Wallace joined the *Whitman Numismatic Journal* staff in 1966.**

During his ten years at Whitman, Holland authored, contributed to, or edited many articles and books including two editions of *A Guide Book of Mexican Coins, 1822 to Date* and *Coins of the World, 1750–1850*, as well as working on various books authored by Dick Yeoman. Several of his articles were also published in the *Whitman Numismatic Journal* and other periodicals. Wallace continued to contribute to the expansion and success of the organization until his retirement in 1976. Regrettably, the numismatic world lost a good friend when he died in 2018.

The rest of this decade was equally busy for me and all of the Western employees. With the expanded staff, I was able to dedicate more time to increasing the product line and promoting existing projects. Much of this required traveling to conventions, participating in forums, or giving talks. From 1973 to 1976 I volunteered to be the director of an entertaining group of fun-loving authors called the Numismatic Literary Guild, an organization that continues to thrive and has become an expected part of the entertainment at annual ANA World's Fair of Money conventions.

GRADING STANDARDS

I became increasingly concerned about the problems of grading standards when the numerous definitions and names being used to describe the condition or state of preservation of coins were getting beyond control or comprehension. Dick and I, like so many others, were strong advocates of establishing industry rules and standards, and, whenever possible, we were particularly vocal about the cause in our talks and writings. Influential dealers like Abe Kosoff and Harvey Stack were especially forceful in presenting their opinions and recommendations. Here is an account of the times as remembered by Harvey Stack:

> In the spring of 1973, the American Numismatic Association invited a group of over 50 professionals, including myself, to its Colorado Springs headquarters to address the variance that existed among collectors and dealers when grading coins, and to try to unify the system so that all coins could be graded using the same methodology.
>
> Within the hobby were many debates about Mint State coins, and prooflike pieces. The standards were different for each denomination and mint; technology differed, as did planchet preparation, planchet stock quality, and striking. Addressing the need for a more unified system was the intent of the ANA conference.
>
> While there were many different people with many different ideas, members of the conference agreed that it might be worthwhile to consider adopting the Sheldon System. It was almost a quarter of a century old and had been used for coppers (large cents), as discussed and explained in William Sheldon's book. It was thought that combining adjectival letter grading with numerical grading could make the system clearer.

"Somebody said that it couldn't be done, But he with a chuckle replied, That 'maybe it couldn't,' but he would be one, Who wouldn't say no till he'd tried."
—Edgar Guest

▼ Jim Ruddy and I often shared thoughts about grading standards and our respective books on the subject.

▲ Harvey Stack.

Dick Yeoman, the original editor of *A Guide Book of United States Coins*, and Ken Bressett, who assisted him, re-did the grades as [they] would be listed in the forthcoming issue of the *Guide Book*, and showed us a copy. It had one flaw [that] I noticed. Adopting the new names for grades that included letters and numbers worked fine for grades where the letters were the same as the previously used adjectival grading. For example, AU-50 was easily understood, as "About Uncirculated" had been used as a grade in the past. The new system used MS or Mint State for Uncirculated coins. But many coins had previously been called Brilliant Uncirculated (BU).

I was concerned that Mint State grades might be questioned by those who were used to the old adjectives. So, I suggested to Ken, "Why not for the first few years list values using both sets of adjectival lettering and also the numerical grades?" It would surely get readers familiar, more quickly than just having just an "MS" abbreviation with the new numerical grade in the *Guide Book*. It took me about two weeks of talking with Ken on the phone to convince him that this was important and would be helpful.

. . . Eventually the numerical part of the grade came to be used more often, as collectors became accustomed to seeing both in print and more commonly used. Within a short time after this conference was held, the ANA established an authentication and grading service that, for a fee, would examine and photograph each coin, attach the photo to a certificate, and return it to the sender. However, as the coin was not in any way physically attached to the certificate, there was no way to definitively guarantee that the certificate was for a specific coin.

It was more than a decade after the ANA grading conference, in the mid-1980s, that PCGS [Professional Coin Grading Service] and NGC [Numismatic Guaranty Corporation] came into existence. They provided a service that graded coins and also put them in a sealed plastic holder so that switching was nearly impossible.

There were other ways that the coin market was changing. By 1972 the ANA had launched the American Numismatic Association Certification Service (ANACS)

> to combat the counterfeit and altered coins that continued to enter the market.
>
> The ANA continued to work on its grading guidelines. Finally, they were ready, and *The Official ANA Grading Standards for United States Coins* was published in 1977. In time, ANACS would use these standards to assess the coins that were sent in and assign them grades, beginning the move toward third-party coin grading that would eventually cause a sea change in numismatics.

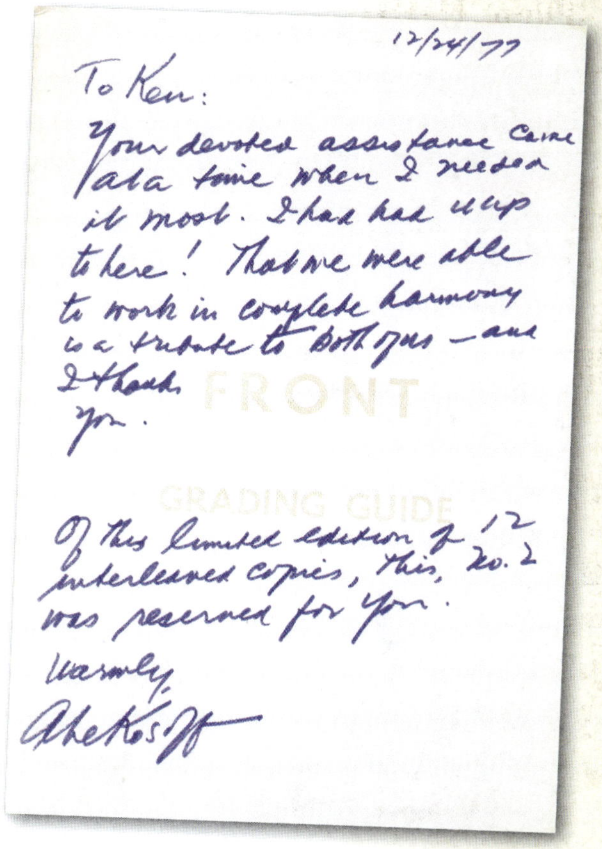

12/24/77

To Ken:

Your devoted assistance came at a time when I needed it most. I had had it up to here! That we were able to work in complete harmony is a tribute to both of us — and I thank you.

Of this limited edition of 12 interleaved copies, this, no. 2 was reserved for you.

Warmly

Abe Kosoff

▲ Friend and consultant Abe Kosoff inscribed an interleaved copy (number 2 of 12) of *Official ANA Grading Standards for United States Coins* on December 24, 1977, with the following message: "Your devoted assistance came at a time when I needed it most. . . . That we [are] able to work in complete harmony is a tribute to both of us—and I thank you."

My efforts to bring stability to the grading problem extended in many directions. When the ANA approved the concept of publishing an officially authorized book, I determined to get the printing contract for Whitman. With that in hand, I had to enlist a group of experienced collectors and dealers and consolidate their opinions about an "ideal" description of each grade for every United States coin. I then had to write those descriptions in acceptable and understandable words that everyone could agree upon. Most of that was done with the indispensable aid of Kosoff's criticizing and Stack's nagging, which I learned to both tolerate and appreciate.

What Abe never knew was that when these were made, the jolly jokers at Whitman also made one copy without his name on the title page as co-editor along with mine. They then brought it to me for a final press check before printing. Of course, I nearly had a heart attack before they admitted to their dirty deed.

Once the text was agreed upon, the next burden was finding coins or pictures to illustrate each grade. I had already tackled that problem before, when Whitman got the contract to print *A Guide to the Grading of United States Coins* by Martin Brown and John Dunn. In their fourth edition, which we printed in 1964, I was asked to make line drawings for each grade. With no talent for illustration, I solicited the help of Arthur Mueller, a professional artist, and assisted him in making detailed renderings of each coin type. I then made several copies of every image and, using white correction fluid, removed each portion of the coin in succession, according to the amount and location of wear.

When I did the same thing for the *Grading Standards* book, I used the newly established "official" standards, which were slightly different than those of Brown and Dunn. And I made one significant change that has probably been ignored or overlooked by just about everyone. In the process of making the doctored drawings and new word descriptions, I had

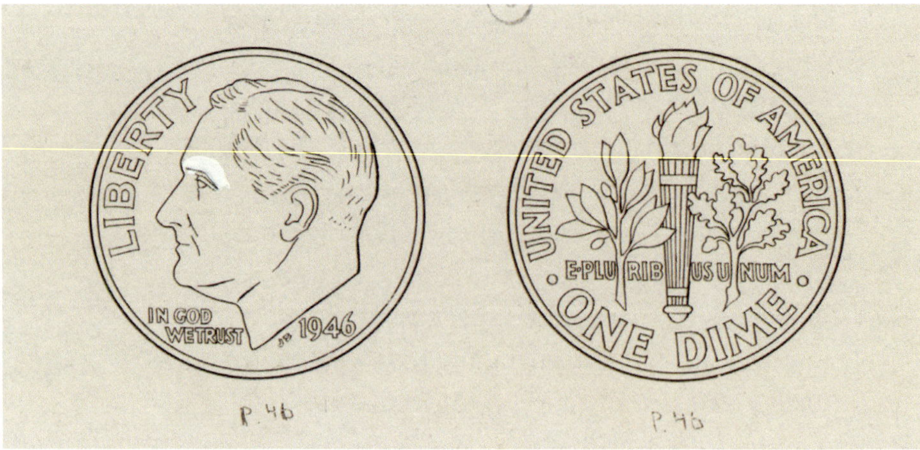

▶ Altering hundreds of line-drawings with white correction fluid was a tedious job.

my work reviewed by a quality-control committee at Whitman. These were non-numismatic people who independently offered their assessments of the grading process. Through experimentation, I learned that those people who knew nothing about grading consistently did better in learning to grade when the descriptions were listed from Uncirculated down to Poor, rather than from Poor up to Uncirculated, as was the custom in all other publications. Thus, a new tradition was established that is still used throughout the industry. In a way, it was similar to Dick's original arrangement used in the *Red Book*, which listed coins from the lowest denomination to the highest.

The ANA standards, published in 1977 in hopes of bringing stability to the market, were widely accepted by collectors and dealers alike, although it was only the beginning of an ongoing process. The following year also stands out in my mind as the time I received the ANA Medal of Merit, which was one of the first in a string of honors that are still greatly appreciated and esteemed. This one, I have always assumed, was because of my dedicated work on the *Grading Standards* book. In a similar vein, in 2009 I was named an honorary Doctor of Numismatics for my lectures at the ANA Summer Seminars.

ANA SUMMER SEMINARS

Beginning in 1974, and continuing each year thereafter, I have participated as an instructor at the American Numismatic Association's annual Summer Seminar. This event has often been called the most important and esteemed educational event in the hobby. It is a two-week program conducted at the campus of Colorado College, adjacent to ANA headquarters in Colorado Springs, with an annual attendance of several hundred students and scores of volunteer instructors. When the Seminar was introduced in 1968, it was only a week long. In 2001 it was expanded to two weeks. Some of the classes were also held at off-site locations in California,

Vermont, Wisconsin, and other places. Jeff Garrett—past president of the ANA, a dedicated fan of the seminars, and a young student in the first class I taught there—frequently remarks: "There is no better numismatic education for new collectors, prospective dealers, and professionals seeking to sharpen their skills."

▲ With my co-instructors (Dennis Tucker, Robert W. Hoge, and Beth Deisher) and students at the 2013 ANA Summer Seminar. Our "Legends of Numismatics" class was billed as "an exciting journey through the world of numismatic writing, publishing, and research."

Each year the ANA provides experienced instructors to teach during the two-week-long Summer Seminar sessions. Over the years, favored instructors have become staples at these events and are treated as celebrities by the students. Many of them—Bob Campbell, J.P. Martin, Bill Fivaz, Ricardo de Léon Tallavas, John Kraljevich, and Fred Schwan, to name but a few—have been teaching for decades. The ANA is always grateful to the individuals and companies who donate their time and talent to this amazing program. The Summer Seminar could not happen without them. Similarly, over half of those in attendance are repeat students, many of whom are able to attend because of full scholarships made available by the ANA, local coin clubs, and other numismatic organizations and businesses.

◄ Discussing ancient and medieval coins with ANA Summer Seminar co-instructor Robert W. Hoge, July 2013.

▲ Talking shop at the 2018 ANA Summer Seminar graduation banquet with ANA immediate past president Jeff Garrett and then-current president Gary Adkins.

For several years, around 1985 to 1988, I served as educational director at the ANA and was in charge of the seminar, so it has always held fond memories for me. Attending the seminar is a stellar opportunity to visit ANA headquarters, the Edward C. Rochette Money Museum, and the Dwight N. Manley Numismatic Library. The library is the largest numismatic lending library in the world and is a treat to visit in person. The museum features the Harry W. Bass Jr. collection of gold coins, which is among the finest in the world. Life on the Colorado College campus, and the interaction of students with each other after classes and over meals in the famous cafeteria, all add to the experience.

Most seminar classes last four days and are designed to provide full numismatic immersion. The grading classes are the most popular and usually sell out well in advance. They are quite challenging but enable students to learn the art of coin grading in a short amount of time. Several students have told me that the hands-on experience of learning to grade is invaluable because they have a chance to examine coins they may never see in any other way. The instructors work closely with every student, making sure they are ready for the next skill level before moving on.

The counterfeit-detection classes are also favored. This subject has become even more relevant in recent years, and students have the opportunity to examine the ANA's large reference collection. One of the best ways to learn about counterfeits is to examine genuine and fake coins side by side. This, with expert instruction, gives students the best possible education on the subject.

As I write this, the COVID-19 epidemic has temporarily halted traditional classes, and in their place are the new ANA eLearning Academy programs that may well become the wave of the future.

2013 Summer Seminar Catalog
Session II–Legends in Numismatics

Learn from the best and rub elbows with some of the world's most renowned numismatists. Let Hall-of-Famer Ken Bressett, Robert Hoge, Dennis Tucker, and Beth Deisher take you on an exciting journey through the world of numismatic writing, publishing, and research while engaging students in discussions about the many ways that people can—and do—collect. Topics include:

Cross-pollinating Numismatics with Mainstream America—Learn how to effectively reach general audiences through your presentations, writing, and publishing.

So You Want to Publish—Learn how to determine the best audience for your writing and research and get tips from the pros on how to approach and work with editors and publishers of daily, weekly, and monthly commercial numismatic publications as well as book publishers.

The *Red Book*—Learn all about the history of the hobby's bible: *A Guide Book of United States Coins*, as well as the behind-the-scenes workings of publishing the #1 best-selling price guide in the hobby.

The Ways People Collect—So many ways to collect; so little time. We'll take a look at a variety of ways in which people can build interesting collections.

Roundtable—An open forum for questions and answers with the Legends Team and students.

Instructors:

Kenneth E. Bressett—Longtime editor of the *Red Book*, he is a former ANA President, a member of the Numismatic Hall of Fame, and a Farran Zerbe Award winner.

Robert Wilson Hoge—Curator of North American Coins and Currency at the American Numismatic Society, he is the former curator of the ANA Money Museum.

Dennis Tucker—In 2004 he became the youngest publisher in Whitman Publishing history and has since published more than 100 numismatic books including the Bowers Series.

Beth Deisher—Recently retiring after 27 years as editor of *Coin World*, Beth also was the founding editor of *Coin Values*, *Paper Money Values*, and *WorldWide Coins*.

ADDITIONAL ACTIVITIES

Yes, I kept busy during the 1960s and 1970s, but I also made sure to maintain a healthy social and family life. With the children in school, Bert became involved in volunteer work as a hospital "candy-striper" and was engaged with her ceramic classes, while I was occupied with my coin interests. We needed to find some time just for ourselves, so we sat down and resolved to find something that we could enjoy together. The decision to make it square dancing was unanimous. We joined a local dance group, learned all we needed to know, and spent the next 15 years enjoying one of the most entertaining activities of our lives. Along the way, our dance group participated in exhibitions at state fairs and special events, and we traveled to Nashville and other places to perform. With our colorful costumes and all we were quite a spectacle, and it all took place totally outside my world of numismatics.

During that time, we made numerous family motor trips from our adopted home in Wisconsin back to Keene to visit with old friends and relatives. Sometimes we would extend the trip by circling north through Canada and returning at Niagara Falls. On one such trip, in 1969, we were fortunate to see the falls actually shut down for repairs and dry enough to walk upon. Another memorable family trip was to the 1967 World's Fair (known as Expo 67), held in Montreal, Quebec.

The 1970s were also special for us in that it was the time we became better acquainted with Marilyn and Bill Fivaz. I don't remember exactly when I first met Bill, but surely it was sometime before 1976 because I remember him showing up for one of my coin-grading classes at the ANA Summer Seminar. My reaction was, "What are you doing here? You should be doing the teaching"—which he did to help with the class. He continued to teach nearly every year thereafter, sharing his incredible knowledge as a teacher, student, and researcher, as well as one of the country's leading numismatic authors. His ever-popular *Cherrypickers' Guide to Rare Die Varieties*, coauthored with J.T. Stanton, is legendary. Bill is also a prime contributor to the *Red Book* and one of the decision-making panelists for adding new varieties to that book. As an experienced photographer, Bill has generously contributed numerous close-up pictures to Whitman books as a teaching aid.

▼ Seems like Bert and I were always laughing about something behind the scenes.

But I'm getting ahead of the story. Bill, Marilyn, Bert, and I became instant friends and were companions at so many coin events that we decided to try vacationing together. Someone suggested

Hawaii, and we all agreed. From that point on, we made it an annual event to rent a condo and spend a couple weeks there, as well as to enjoy some occasional cruise-ship trips and other visits. Lifelong friendships abound in numismatics, but I am sure ours is one of the best.

▲ Bill Fivaz and me in 2020, speaking at an ANA grading seminar in Atlanta.

In retrospect, the years from around 1965 to 1975 were some of the busiest ever for me. It was a time that involved me in many hobby-related activities, such as writing, speaking, and promoting the numerous Whitman products and ideals. My early interest in the coinage of Vermont was well known to Eric Newman, and when he selected authors to participate in the American Numismatic Society's 1976 *Studies on Money in Early America*, I was asked to submit an article on that subject. The resulting thesis turned out to be a seminal work and die study of the Vermont coinage from 1785 to 1788, and since then "Bressett" identification numbers have been universally used to designate the varieties of those coins. Needless to say, I still get a thrill when I see coins listed that way in auction catalogs or other citations.

Another event that stands out in my memory was my participation in a course held in 1965–1966 at Roosevelt University in Chicago. The program was conceived and fostered by well-known coin dealer Arthur Kagin, whose objective was to make "Numismatics" an accredited college course. Fifty or more prominent numismatists were involved as consultants and teachers. Arthur was persuasive and got numerous people to support it in one way or another.

▲ This variety of 1786 Vermont copper coin is identified as "Bressett 5-E."

The program, overseen by Roosevelt University's Division of Continuing Education, was titled "Numismatics: The Story of Civilization." The first semester ran from September 29 to December 16, 1965; the second semester was February 16 to May 18, 1966. I participated in the first semester and was joined by fellow instructors Grover Criswell, Bernard Feinberg, George Fonda, George Fuld, Leland Howard, J. Hewitt Judd, Charles Ricard, Gilroy Roberts, Matt Rothert, Margo Russell, Joseph Segel, and Leonard Stark. Second-semester teachers were Eva Adams, Amon Carter, John Davenport, Admiral Oscar Dodson, Nathan Eglit, Arthur Kagin, Paul Kagin, Eric Newman, John Jay Pittman, Hans Schulman, Nate Shapero, Don Taxay, and Dick Yeoman.

I do not remember why the program was not continued beyond that, but I cherish the special silver medal that was given to me for my participation, and I have many fond memories of all the prominent numismatists I got to know through association and by working with them.

► As a participant in Roosevelt University's Numismatic Education Program in 1965–1966, I received this attractive, engraved silver medal.

The 1960s saw great changes in collector habits. From 1945 to 1950 and beyond, interest in collecting had blossomed and prices rose sharply as dealer advertising and large auctions helped fuel broader public attention. 1963 was clearly the year of the investor. The unwarranted hype, however, brought about a crash in 1966; the resultant slump lasted until about 1970. In the following decade there was considerable collector and speculator participation that extended from about 1973 to 1977.

Subsequently, just about every facet of the popular collectibles market saw changes. Stamps, baseball cards, dolls, Jim Beam bottles, semi-precious stones, and others were affected. In an effort to enhance the line of Whitman products, I began to explore the possibilities for introducing specialty holders and related items that would be of interest to stamp and card collectors. To get a feel for the potential market demands, I did field research

► A typical Whitman sales booth at a coin convention.

by going to some of the specialty conventions or meetings. To keep my mission undisclosed, I did everything under the pseudonym Bert Britton, my wife's maiden name. My research into button collecting revealed that several well-known coin dealers were also involved in that hobby. I further learned that collectors were very individualistic in ways of storing and displaying their buttons. Holders and other things were of no special interest to them. There were very few books on the subject, and not many full-time professional dealers.

In an effort to build new awareness of the hobby, I wrote an article for one of the button-collector magazines giving my views on things that might be helpful in expanding public interest. It was so well received that I was asked to deliver a talk on the subject at an upcoming national convention. That I did, and "Bert Britton" was even introduced as some sort of an expert on the subject. It was a valiant effort, but to no avail, and nothing more ever came of the experiment.

▲ To encourage collecting and make the hobby fun for all, Whitman created and promoted "Coin Collecting Starter Kits" under a variety of names.

In an attempt to sum up the problems that were influencing the market, I gave a talk for the Numismatic Literary Guild in 1978. In doing so, I discussed the concerns expressed by collectors in 1878 as mirrored a century

▼ Whitman staff produced this prototype of a Disney-themed coin-collecting kit featuring Scrooge McDuck. The boxed set, perhaps intended to be sold at Disneyland's Story Book Shop, was never released.

The Call of Numismatics

by Phil Bressett

My first memories of coins began about 1955, at the age of four or five. As the oldest of three children, I was the lucky one that got to go on numismatic adventures with Dad, while my younger brother and sister stayed home with Mom. We lived in southern New Hampshire; Boston was our closest "big city" and a very exciting place to visit. Those trips would always include a visit to Maury Gould and Frank Washburn at the Copley Coin Company. Mr. Gould was very nice and would show me many interesting coins. So, by the age of about five, I was hooked for life!

In 1959 Dick Yeoman asked Dad to move to Racine, Wisconsin, and work at Whitman, so the family packed up and off we went to a new adventure! When I was in the fourth grade at school, I met a fellow coin collector. The new Memorial reverse had just been added to the Lincoln cent, and so the hunt was on for us to find the better-date old Wheat cents. Many weekends were spent looking through bags of cents. We could not wait for the next edition of the *Red Book* to see all the new higher values. Dad would not let even me know in advance what those prices would be!

In the early sixties Neil Shafer began working at Whitman. Silver Certificates had been recently replaced by Federal Reserve Notes, and collectors' new interest in paper money caught my attention. One of Neil's first projects was writing *A Guide Book of Modern United States Currency*. His influence started me on a lifelong interest in paper money of all kinds, both American and foreign.

In 1976—after school, the Navy, and a two-year motorcycle trip around the country—I rented some counter space in a pharmacy owned by a family friend and opened my first "coin store." In no time I had outgrown the space and moved into my own store. Soon gold and silver began to move up in value and business was booming. Even Dad began to recognize that I had become a professional dealer. In 1978 I was invited to join my first *Red Book* pricing session for the 1979 edition. Others in this group were Dad, Neil Shafer, Dick Thompsen, and Don Kagin.

As the years went by, this group would change and different experts would sit in on these meetings, depending on what was hot in the market at that time. These special pricing finalizers who helped over the years included Don Kagin, James A. Simek, William (Bill) Spencer, Gary Adkins, Leonard R. Saunders, and Robert Rhue. Many other specialists often lent their expertise for a day or two. I feel very lucky to have been a part of *Red Book* history for over 40 years. I thank all who helped make this possible and who made *A Guide Book of United States Coins* the great reference that it is.

later. Interestingly, the very same problems can be seen in the market today, some 40 years beyond that.

It seems there have always been four major complaints:

1) Overpriced and overgraded material.
2) Ever-increasing prices, from 15¢ to $1.50 in 1878, and similar upsurges in 1978. (Today's increases are in the thousands.)
3) Government-issued "collector coins" at higher-than-ever prices for patterns and Proofs (similar to today's special finishes, mintmarks, and packaging).
4) Counterfeits that included electrotypes and copies of American colonial coins struck by Thomas Wyatt and John Bolen in the mid-1800s (reminiscent of the current plague of outright fraudulent Chinese fakery).

CAREER MOVES IN THE 1980S

During the 1970s the number of walk-in coin shops throughout the country was growing rapidly, mostly due to a rise in bullion prices, and the demand for related collector products was obvious. Keeping up with innovative new items and sales incentives was a constant challenge for the Whitman staff. We did our best to cope with the situation, but clearly bold changes were inevitable. My assessment was that it might be to my advantage to become a coin dealer, rather than a teacher and enabler. With that thought in mind, and with some encouragement from Don Kagin, I accepted a position of vice president in the firm of A.M. "Art" Kagin in Des

▼ While employed at Kagin's, I had the pleasure of working with talented numismatist Ingrid Smith, who later moved to Canada to run her own business and coin shows.

▲ The 1981 ANA convention in Hawaii brought many families and friends together. From left: Bert Bressett; Al and Dorothy Baber; me; Bill and Marilyn Fivaz; and Joyce and Lee Kuntz.

▶ The motley crew of the ANA Certification Service under the direction of "Captain Ken" in 1983.

▼ Mid-1980s portrait.

Moines, Iowa. And so in 1981 we packed up our belongings again and headed off to a new adventure.

Life in Iowa was somewhat different from that in Wisconsin, but pleasant in many ways. I worked hard to adapt to the new challenges of being a member of the dealer community. It was indeed exhilarating to be involved with so many extraordinary rare coins, not to mention the auctions, travel, and buying and selling on a major scale. Soon, however, the company decided to open an office in California, and I was asked to relocate there along with Don and some of the staff. While weighing the feasibility of such a move, I was informed by ANA Executive Director Edward C. Rochette that the association was looking for someone to head its new coin authentication department.

It seemed like an ideal opportunity for someone with my background. I had known Ed and his wife, Faye, since 1958. Ed and I were members of the same coin club in Worcester, Massachusetts, and were confident

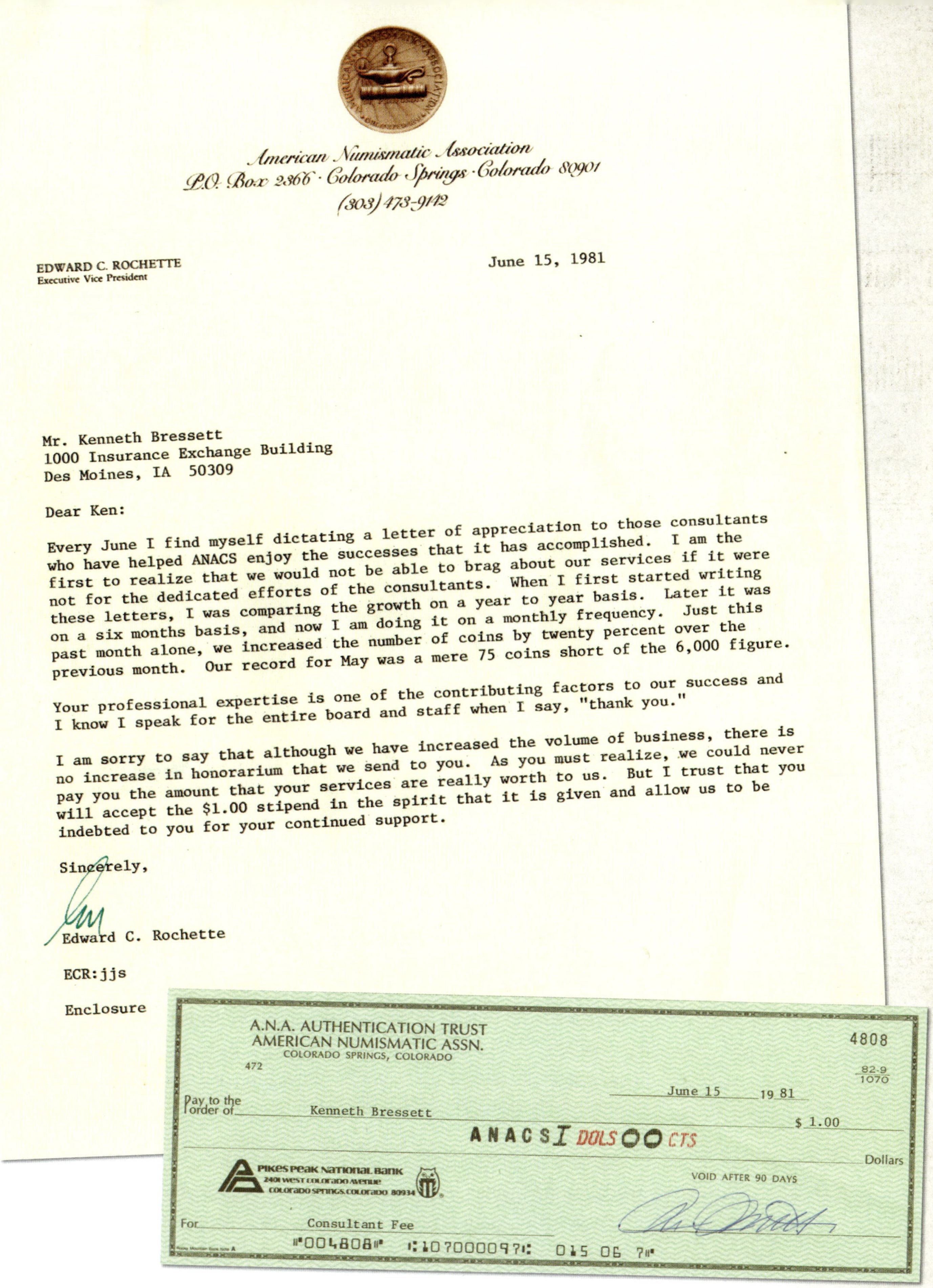

American Numismatic Association
P.O. Box 2366 · Colorado Springs · Colorado 80901
(303) 473-9142

EDWARD C. ROCHETTE
Executive Vice President

June 15, 1981

Mr. Kenneth Bressett
1000 Insurance Exchange Building
Des Moines, IA 50309

Dear Ken:

Every June I find myself dictating a letter of appreciation to those consultants who have helped ANACS enjoy the successes that it has accomplished. I am the first to realize that we would not be able to brag about our services if it were not for the dedicated efforts of the consultants. When I first started writing these letters, I was comparing the growth on a year to year basis. Later it was on a six months basis, and now I am doing it on a monthly frequency. Just this past month alone, we increased the number of coins by twenty percent over the previous month. Our record for May was a mere 75 coins short of the 6,000 figure.

Your professional expertise is one of the contributing factors to our success and I know I speak for the entire board and staff when I say, "thank you."

I am sorry to say that although we have increased the volume of business, there is no increase in honorarium that we send to you. As you must realize, we could never pay you the amount that your services are really worth to us. But I trust that you will accept the $1.00 stipend in the spirit that it is given and allow us to be indebted to you for your continued support.

Sincerely,

Edward C. Rochette

ECR:jjs

Enclosure

A.N.A. AUTHENTICATION TRUST
AMERICAN NUMISMATIC ASSN.
COLORADO SPRINGS, COLORADO
472

4808

82-9
1070

June 15 19 81

Pay to the order of Kenneth Bressett $ 1.00

ANACS I DOLS 00 CTS Dollars

PIKES PEAK NATIONAL BANK
2401 WEST COLORADO AVENUE
COLORADO SPRINGS, COLORADO 80934

VOID AFTER 90 DAYS

For Consultant Fee

⑈004808⑈ ⑆107000097⑆ 015 06 7⑈

▲ As a consultant to the ANA Certification Service, I received a letter of thanks from ANA Executive Director Ed Rochette and "payment" in the amount of $1.

▲ Edward C. Rochette.

that we could work well together as members of the ANA team. So, without much hesitation, Bert and I packed up again and headed off to another new adventure, which lasted from 1982 to 1988.

Meanwhile, back at the Whitman offices, work continued to function pretty much as usual under the guidance of Richard Thompsen and most of the original staff. I was retained as a freelance consultant and continued to assist with many aspects of the business, as well as editing and pricing the *Red* and *Blue Books*. Holland Wallace had already left in 1976. Neil Shafer left in 1981 to pursue his avocation as a consultant, dealer, and author in the field of paper money. Times were changing throughout the hobby.

In 1979, after the ANA adopted and published its official grading standards, we began grading coins using those guidelines. One of my tasks was to hire and train a staff for this work. Many of them have since moved on to become some of the most famous names in the industry, while others are dealers, researchers, and authors.

In 1990 the ANA Board of Governors sold ANACS to Amos Press, publishers of *Coin World*, who later sold ANACS to Anderson Press in 2005. In December 2007 it was acquired by Driving Force, LLC, of Colorado.

ADVENTURES WITH DEEP SEA TREASURES

Being a numismatic authenticator wasn't just another ordinary job. In fact, it could get rather exciting, as was the case when I was asked to verify a quantity of coins reportedly found on a long-lost treasure ship that sank off the coast of Florida more than 300 years earlier. Credit for the discovery goes to Mel Fisher, who has been called the world's greatest treasure hunter because he followed his dream of discovering what is now recognized to be the most valuable sunken treasure ever recovered. His mantra, "Today's the day!" carried him through numerous trials and heartbreaking losses until on July 20, 1985, he discovered the fabled galleon *Nuestra Señora de Atocha* that sank during a hurricane in September 1622, off the coast of Key West, Florida. The ship was laden with over 40 tons of silver, gold, emeralds, and other valuable items. Included were some 100,000 Spanish silver coins of various denominations and more than 1,000 silver bars.

Today's the day!"
—Mel Fisher

Fisher formed a company called Treasure Salvors, Inc., which used a sand-clearing wash deflector device to unearth metal objects at the bottom of the sea. After perilous searching, they discovered the ship in the Marquesas Keys and continued work there beginning in 1971. In 1973 three silver bars were found, and in 1975 nine brass cannons were recovered. Subsequently, a flood of precious treasure was salvaged.

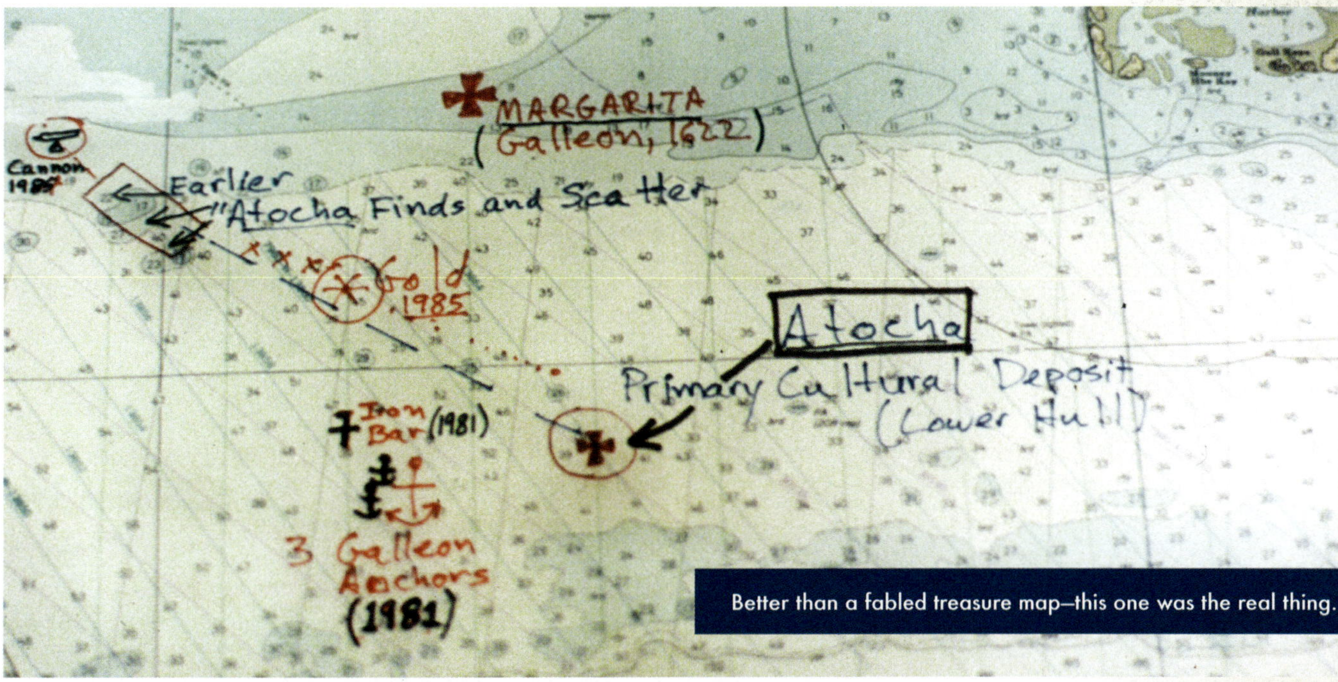

Better than a fabled treasure map—this one was the real thing.

▲ This vessel, one of several used to recover the *Atocha* treasure, was old but seaworthy.

◀ ANA Museum Curator Robert W. Hoge observes the process used to conserve some of the coins.

▲ I found several silver bars near the sunken ship, but of course had to leave them there.

▲ I grew attached to this gold chain salvaged from the wreck but was not allowed to keep it as a souvenir of my dive.

▲ Recovered from the ocean floor were enough pieces-of-eight to please a band of swashbucklers.

▲ Treasure Salvors maintained its headquarters and an exhibit area in an old Navy base building, just a block from Key West Harbor.

Prior to the discoveries, Fisher had sold stock in his company to investors, some of whom were anxiously awaiting verification of the find. To allay any question of the validity of the treasure, an ANA authentication team was invited to dive with the Fisher crew to inspect the coins and examine the wreck.

In September 1985, as director of ANA educational programs, I was selected to be one of the examiners, along with ANA museum curator Robert W. Hoge and N. Neil Harris, editor of *The Numismatist*. We began by taking lessons to become PADI-certified scuba divers. Susan Mobley, an archeology student at the University of Colorado who had assisted in the ANA museum in the past, accompanied the group at her own expense, as did videographer David Lisot and some of our wives. Our journey to Florida early in 1986 was uneventful but filled with anticipation and excitement about what we were about to experience with professional divers and chests full of pieces-of-eight, gold chains, emeralds, silver bars, and the like.

As landlubbers, we were nervous about our first dive, but with the reassurance and guidance of our divemaster everything went smoothly as we explored the areas where much of the treasure had been found. The second day's dive was more thrilling when we saw some of the actual artifacts that were being recovered and were permitted to hold and examine pieces to our heart's content. Later in the week, we got to see the entire operation where coins were being conserved, cataloged, and recorded.

▲ Bolivian 4-reales silver coins of King Philip III from the shipwrecked *Atocha*.

A CHANGING MILIEU

The balance of the 1980s brought about other changes and new opportunities for me. I continued to work independently as editor of the *Red Book* and various Whitman products, but I also contributed to several other publications. One favorite was writing an article for every issue of a now mostly forgotten ANA magazine called *First Strike*, which was published quarterly from 1987 to 1989 and sent to all ANA junior members and coin clubs. It was basically aimed at young and beginning collectors but included quality articles by a number of well-known writers. In keeping with the magazine's title, each of my articles dealt with a distinct numismatic event. At about this same time, in recognition of some of my activities, I was named a Numismatic Ambassador by *Numismatic News*, a Krause Publications weekly.

Numismatic Ambassadorship

by *Dennis Tucker*

Ken Bressett was named a Numismatic Ambassador in 1986. I was very happy to join him in those ranks in 2018. About 400 ambassadors total have been named since 1974, when Krause Publications and *Numismatic News* bestowed the first such recognition. Florida United Numismatists took over the administration of the awards with the 2015 nomination and election cycle. I remember first reading about the Numismatic Ambassador awards when I was a young collector back in the 1980s. To me, the recognition is a heartwarming honor, but it's also a call to further action. A Numismatic Ambassador is a person who energetically represents and promotes the hobby, both inside and outside our community. We do it because we love numismatics. We've been recognized for the work we do—and now we have a job to keep doing!

▲ 1987 FIDEM medal.

Much of my time at the ANA during 1985 was spent working on programs, books, and other things in preparation for the coming centennial celebration of the association, to be held in Chicago in 1991. I was also working with Mort Reed editing and doing the layout for *Coinology*, a book that was underwritten by the ANA. I also served as a professional witness, or *amicus curiae* ("friend of the court"), for the district attorney in a Post Office case involving fraudulent advertising. I still chuckle about the defendant protesting, "Of course Bressett can grade coins better than I do; he uses a magnifying glass!"

Over the next couple of years I handled other complaints and collaborated with the FBI and the Treasury Department. Somehow, I found time to work on the ANA's "Book of the Month" project, educational videos, and interviews. I helped coordinate the 50th Anniversary Congress and Exposition of the Fédération Internationale de la Médaille d'Art (FIDEM), which the ANA hosted September 11–15, 1987, the first time the event was held in the United States. (FIDEM is an international organization of medalists, mints, and museums founded in Paris in 1937 to encourage artistic experimentation and innovation in medal design.) Separately, and on my own, I also helped update the Boy Scouts' *Coin Collecting* manual that I had originally written in 1975.

▲ *First Strike* was published quarterly by the ANA from 1987 to 1989. I was happy to contribute to this magazine for beginning collectors.

▲ Here I am with Teresa de Francisci, wife of coin designer Anthony de Francisci and the model for his 1921 Peace dollar (see below).

Internal strife at ANA headquarters in 1988 was causing several employees to seek better working conditions elsewhere, and I agreed that moving on was easier than disagreeing with management. I felt sure that a career as a freelance consultant and writer would be far more to my liking. Thus, in 1988 I resigned from the ANA staff and made the move to independence that I have never regretted.

▲ Anthony de Francisci's Peace dollar design as submitted to the U.S. Commission of Fine Arts in December 1921.

1988 was also the year that my dear friend and mentor, Dick Yeoman, died in a motor-vehicle accident. My sorrow was softened only slightly by the honor of being asked to deliver the eulogy at his funeral.

From 1989 to 1990 I worked from my home in Colorado Springs for Premier Coin Investments of Minneapolis, along with coin dealer Gary Adkins, mostly writing promotional sales material, helping at coin shows, and doing public-relations work. Later, around 1997 to 2005, I continued working with Adkins at his firm Numismatic Services, Inc., and then with John Taitt when he bought the business in 2005.

Leaving the ANA's employ in 1988 did not diminish my ardor for trying to improve conditions within the organization, or for wanting to better relations between dealers and collectors. From May 1986 through December 2002 I wrote a monthly column in *The Numismatist* called "Consumer Alert." It was basically an exposé of dealers and promoters using hype or outright deceptive advertising gimmicks. Inevitably, I stepped on the toes

▲ My meetings with U.S. Treasurer Mary Ellen Withrow were always a special treat.

of some who were involved in advertising beyond the acceptable bounds of "puffery." Readership surveys during that period showed that my column rated either number one or number two each month, usually competing only with those of Q. David Bowers. Then, without explanation, my columns were dropped and never again requested, leaving me to wonder why they were no longer wanted. Undeterred, I continued to use other avenues to keep unabashed advertising to a minimum.

Recognizing the importance of the rapidly growing electronic age, I was determined to keep up with changing modes and the importance of online communications. Here is what I said in an interview with Alan Herbert that was published in the March 7, 1995, issue of *Numismatic News*. Although I didn't predict everything exactly right, it did provide a glimpse of today's trending:

> "I'm doing everything I can to keep up with the trend. I think it's very important," [Bressett said]. Then, in a somewhat surprising comment, he revealed some of his thoughts about online collectors: "It may very well develop that the on-line computers will replace coin clubs in the future. I could visualize that. The role of the clubs

◀ In 1993 I was elected vice president of the ANA Board of Governors. Serving the two-year term were (back row, from left) Ken Hallenbeck, me, President David Ganz, and Anthony Swiatek; and (front row, from left) David Lisot, Helen Carmody, John Pittman, Florence Schook, and Nancy Wilson.

◀ The American Numismatic Association Board of Governors during my 1995–1997 term as president: (standing, from left) J.T. Stanton, Kay Edgerton Lenker, Helen Carmody, and Scott Travers; (seated, from left) John Wilson, Will Rossman, me, Anthony Swiatek, and Gary Lewis.

and coin conventions and shows is changing. I don't think it will ever go back to what it was." He cited his own youth as an example. "When I was a boy, I could walk to the coin club meeting. Today, for a youth in a big city, it's neither safe nor practical. Today's collector can sit at a computer terminal and have a lot of fun. I'm going to do as much as I can to be on. One problem is that the majority of collectors are in their 50s, and that's not the computer generation.

▲ ANA Librarian and National Coin Week Chair Nancy Green (left), Executive Director Ruthann Brettell, and I draw a name from a hat to determine the recipient of a Summer Seminar scholarship.

▲ Cutting the ceremonial ribbon to open the ANA's 1996 show in Denver (from left): U.S. Mint Director Philip Diehl, ANA Convention Chairman Tom Hallenbeck, U.S. Treasurer Mary Ellen Withrow, and me.

▲ Another show, another grand opening—this time at the ANA's 1997 convention in New York City.

▲ It was a pleasure to present the ANA Presidential Award to former *Coin World* editor Margo Russell in 1997.

In an effort to help with what I felt would be for the betterment of the ANA, I decided to run for the Board of Governors after I left employment there in 1988. In 1989 I was elected to the board and later became vice president in 1993. From 1995 to 1997 I proudly served as president, subsequently relinquishing my option of returning to the board for another term.

I felt it was time to move along and get on with my work as a self-employed consultant and writer. There were other obligations that needed my attention about that same time. From 1993 to 1996 my aging mother was ill and in elder care. Shortly after losing her, my beloved wife suffered from a blood clot and complications that eventually resulted in her death in 2012, ending our 61-year journey together through life.

ROUNDING OUT THE CENTURY

Yes, the entire decade that ended the twentieth century was laden with electrifying activities for me, but the most stimulating was being appointed by the director of the Mint in 1996 to serve on the Citizens Commemorative Coin Advisory Committee (CCCAC). Established by Congress under Public Law 108-15, the Committee advised the secretary of the Treasury on the themes and designs of all U.S. coins and medals and represented the interests of American citizens and collectors. My term lasted until 2003, when the commission was reformed as the Citizens Coinage Advisory Committee (CCAC) to advise the secretary of the Treasury on mintage levels, themes, and memorial design proposals related to circulating coinage, bullion issues, and medals.

The original committee on which I served had the honor of selecting the earliest designs for the newly instituted 50 State Quarters™ program. Previously, I had testified before Congress about the benefits of adopting such a program and was party to seeing it through to fruition. Serving with me on the committee were: Elsie Sterling Howard (chairman), Charles Atherton, Reed Hawn, Jules Reiver, Thomas V. Shockley III, and Elvira Clain-Stefanelli. For my part in working on this and many other Mint activities, in 1996 I received a citation from Treasury Secretary Robert Ruben for assistance in coinage matters. Working with a numismatic authority like Reed Hawn was a special treat and learning experience. His collections of super-high-grade and rare items like the 1804 dollar and 1913 nickel have never been forgotten, nor have his sage guidance and observations on how things work in the mysterious world of Washington politics.

◀ I participated in selecting designs to recommend for the 50 State Quarters Program with CCCAC chair Elsie Sterling Howard.

▲ In 1999 Bert received the Numismatic Ambassador award from *Numismatic News* publisher Clifford Mishler.

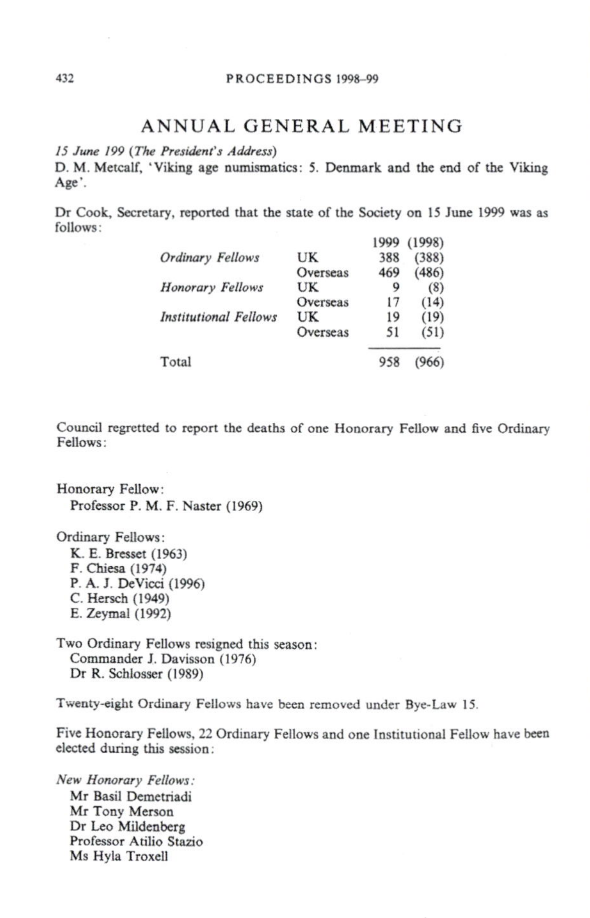

432 PROCEEDINGS 1998–99

ANNUAL GENERAL MEETING

15 June 199 (The President's Address)
D. M. Metcalf, 'Viking age numismatics: 5. Denmark and the end of the Viking Age'.

Dr Cook, Secretary, reported that the state of the Society on 15 June 1999 was as follows:

		1999	(1998)
Ordinary Fellows	UK	388	(388)
	Overseas	469	(486)
Honorary Fellows	UK	9	(8)
	Overseas	17	(14)
Institutional Fellows	UK	19	(19)
	Overseas	51	(51)
Total		958	(966)

Council regretted to report the deaths of one Honorary Fellow and five Ordinary Fellows:

Honorary Fellow:
Professor P. M. F. Naster (1969)

Ordinary Fellows:
K. E. Bresset (1963)
F. Chiesa (1974)
P. A. J. DeVicci (1996)
C. Hersch (1949)
E. Zeymal (1992)

Two Ordinary Fellows resigned this season:
Commander J. Davisson (1976)
Dr R. Schlosser (1989)

Twenty-eight Ordinary Fellows have been removed under Bye-Law 15.

Five Honorary Fellows, 22 Ordinary Fellows and one Institutional Fellow have been elected during this session:

New Honorary Fellows:
Mr Basil Demetriadi
Mr Tony Merson
Dr Leo Mildenberg
Professor Atilio Stazio
Ms Hyla Troxell

▲ The Royal Numismatic Society's 1999 report of my death was greatly exaggerated.

While being involved with these activities, I had plenty of opportunities to meet and speak with Mint and Treasury officials. Philip Diehl, the director of the Mint at that time, was very interested in the possibility of building a new museum in Washington, D.C., where the public would be able to view the National Numismatic Collection (then housed in the Museum of American History at the Smithsonian Institution). He hoped it could be a part of the Mint's recently constructed headquarters and administrative building. In an interview in the January 4, 2000, issue of *Numismatic News*, Diehl remarked:

> I very much want to see a new home for American numismatics. What I'm really talking about is a visitor's center and/or museum here in Washington, D.C., that pays tribute to the American coin collector and to numismatics. There has been a lot of talk about the National Numismatic Collection and the fact that there hasn't been a great deal invested in it over the last several years. We have been talking to the Smithsonian about the possi-

bility of entering into an agreement that would allow the Mint to take a more active role in that collection.

The new Mint headquarters building was designed to have a visitor's center on the ground floor. It would be an interesting turn of events to see part of the collection come full circle and return to the Mint, where it was started (albeit in Philadelphia, not Washington). Having driven past the building this spring while it was under construction, I can attest to the fact that it is a substantial structure, located at the edge of Washington's Chinatown, with plenty of restaurants nearby.

▲ At the invitation of U.S. Mint Director Philip Diehl, I worked with HOK / Studio E of St. Louis, Missouri, to design an area in the Mint's administration building that would highlight the National Numismatic Collection. I was also asked to choose appropriate coins and artifacts for exhibition and to write the accompanying descriptions. The Western Archives contain the plans for the ill-fated project.

The National Numismatic Collection had its beginnings in 1792, when Chief Coiner Adam Eckfeldt began saving samples of coins minted each year. In 1838 it became known officially as The Mint Collection. In 1923 the coins were transferred to the Smithsonian Institution, and for many years the Mint sent examples of each year's coinage. In 2002 a decision was made to remodel a portion of the museum to make way for a new exhibit dedicated to the "Star Spangled Banner," providing an opportunity to move the coin exhibit.

As strategizing progressed, HOK / Studio E of St. Louis, Missouri, was selected to design a new display area in the Mint's administration building, and I was asked to write the discourse and choose appropriate coins and artifacts for exhibition. My instructions were to go to the Smithsonian and select whatever items necessary for a comprehensive and instructive exhibit. This I did with great enthusiasm, and all went well until internal disputes erupted over who actually had rights to the material. In the end, the project was aborted and my work was largely discarded and forgotten. The collection now is featured in the Smithsonian's permanent Gallery of Numismatics in an exhibit titled "The Value of Money," which debuted in 2015. Much of the success of the display is due to the support and efforts of individual collectors and donations made by NGC, Lee and Saundra Minshull, Bill Gale, Jeff Garrett, Lilly Foundation, Charles and Joel Anderson, and many others.

▲ I was inducted into the ANA's Numismatic Hall of Fame in 1996 and have worn this lapel pin with pride.

LOCAL ACTIVITIES

Meanwhile, in Colorado Springs an increasing number of dedicated numismatists began getting together to share common interests and research projects. Larry Johnson, a local collector and specialist in Hard Times tokens, suggested we all gather occasionally for dinner and conversation. I agreed, and we proposed the idea to several of our friends. After a slow beginning in 1996, we decided to form a supper club with monthly meetings but no officers, dues, or special agendas. The idea caught on and, although necessarily limited to only 20 members, it is one of the most successful, interesting, and enjoyable coin clubs in existence. Although now severely curtailed because of pandemic restrictions, it has survived through monthly online get-togethers.

That year I was also inducted into the Numismatic Hall of Fame. The stated purpose of that honor is to perpetuate and enshrine the names of the most important numismatists of all time. The American Numismatic Association established the Hall of Fame in August 1964, with a public gallery at its headquarters in Colorado Springs, Colorado. (The honor was the brainchild of Jack W. Ogilvie, a Hollywood film writer and editor who served as ANA historian from 1950 to 1970.)

A constitution and bylaws were drafted that year, and the first inductees were named in 1969. The next group was enshrined in 1970, with subsequent honorees inducted every two years thereafter. As might be expected, R.S. Yeoman was one of the early living members, being inducted in 1978. As trustee of the Numismatic Hall of Fame, the ANA ensures that the intent and purpose of the shrine is preserved without bias or prejudice. Prior

► Bert and I enjoying the beach during a mid-1990s Caribbean cruise.

to each induction year, nominations are accepted from the membership. After review by a five-member Hall of Fame council, the names and qualifications of the nominees are passed on to an elector panel. Members of the council, the ANA Board of Governors, and ANA-appointed officers and staff are ineligible to serve as electors.

The physical Hall of Fame is currently in the plaza outside ANA headquarters and features photographs and brief biographies of the honorees. Prior to 2012, Numismatic Hall of Fame nominations were sought every two years. Beginning that year, Hall of Fame nominations became an annual tradition, with historic numismatists honored in odd-numbered years and modern collectors inducted in even-number years.

Other changes were on the horizon in 1997. Western Publishing was absorbed into Golden Books Publishing Company, and I was invited to continue as a consultant and editor of the *Red Book*. Golden sold the adult books division to St. Martin's Press in 1999, and I was retained as editor, author, and manager of the Coin Products Division (as I was at Western Publishing Company from 1980 to February 1997). I continued work on the *Red Book* for St. Martin's Press from March 1999 to 2002.

LET THERE BE PEACE

In 1994 I initiated a project to promote world peace through messages on national coinage. I named the concept "Peace 2000" and was pleased when the ANA pledged its support through its "Future of the Hobby" Committee, which I co-chaired with Reed Hawn. Here is an early draft of a press release that explained the program in some detail:

> **Worldwide Circulating Peace Coins**
> **Proposed for the Year 2000**
>
> A unique concept of circulating commemorative coins with designs promoting global peace is being considered by several mints for implementation in the year 2000. The proposal for spreading a message of peace around the world was developed by a group known as the Future of the Hobby Committee. Representatives of all aspects of the hobby serve on the committee, which was developed and

▶ The Peace 2000 movement was launched at the American Numismatic Association's convention in Detroit in July 1994 and enthusiastically received. Artist Virginia Janssen sculpted two beautiful medals celebrating the concept.

▶ A limited number of "concept coins" were created and minted by Ron Landis of the Gallery Mint.

supported by the American Numismatic Association. The Peace Coin Program is being spearheaded and managed by ANA Vice President Kenneth E. Bressett.

The year 2000 will be a time of special importance to collectors, Bressett said. This is a date we have all waited to see on our coins. It is a time when people everywhere will stop to take a careful look at their money and its message. This program is designed to encourage and support all nations in the issuance of circulating coins that embody peace, freedom and human rights. It is a massive undertaking but one that will spread a most vital message around the world.

Mints have not been asked to follow any specific guidelines but are urged to utilize a circulating coin from their nation, imprinting it with the word "Peace" or "Peace 2000." Countries are being encouraged to conduct design contests to involve the public in producing special designs that follow a theme of peace. The denomination should be that which is the most common in circulation, Bressett said. A portion of each nation's seignorage, the difference between the cost of production and the face value of each coin, is requested to be used to foster peace efforts throughout the world. It is anticipated that other special coins, beyond the circulating issues, will be produced by many countries to add to the interest in collecting these coins in sets and series.

"I see this global project creating a renewed interest in numismatics and expanding the market for all numismatic products," Bressett said. "We will be serving the collector and the marketplace by interesting a new generation of people in noticing and collecting circulating coins."

According to Bressett, "The movement started by the Future of the Hobby Committee may soon develop into a 'groundswell movement' supported by collectors everywhere. It is a window of opportunity to return numismatics to a hobby that can be enjoyed by everyone through coins in circulation." Bressett recently returned from the World Mint Directors' Conference in Helsinki, Finland, where he experienced a warm reception and acceptance to his proposal of the international program.

"World mints are looking for themes that will be popular, and the 'Peace 2000' program seems to fit the bill,"

> Bressett reported. "It was enthusiastically received by all of the officials contacted at the conference, and could very well prove to be the catalyst for bringing thousands of new members into the hobby." Bressett said that he has spoken with representatives of the United States Mint and submitted the proposal to the Mint's Citizens' Advisory Committee on Commemorative Coinage, which has solicited themes for U.S. commemorative coins.
>
> The Peace 2000 program was developed by the Future of the Hobby Committee after a series of meetings at major coin conventions. ANA President David L. Ganz serves as counselor to the committee, which is co-chaired by Bressett and collector Reed Hawn of Austin, Texas. ANA Governor David Lisot serves as committee secretary, and Governor Anthony Swiatek is a member.
>
> Other committee members include Ann Marie Aldrich, publisher of *Coin World*; Q. David Bowers, principal of Bowers & Merena Galleries; Ms. Michael Burke and Carmen Cook, both of the U.S. Mint; collector Brian Cornwall of Canada; David Hall, principal of the Professional Coin Grading Service; FAO coin promoter Raymond Lloyd of London; Edward Metzger of Whitman Coin Products; James Miller, publisher of *COINage*; Clifford Mishler, president of Krause Publications; dealer Harvey Stack; numismatic researcher Robert Turfboer; Murray Church, consultant; [and] ANA Executive Director Robert Leuver and Educational Services Director James Taylor.

Future committee meetings, as well as special efforts to promote the Peace 2000 program around the world, were being planned. The movement was launched at the American Numismatic Association's convention in Detroit in July 1994 with considerable enthusiasm and acceptance. Unfortunately, nothing much ensued beyond the initial response. A scant half-dozen countries took the initiative seriously or adopted thematic designs. Most felt the complicated task of changing coinage design requirements was too daunting. Lack of support from the U.S. government was a major disappointment and cause of diminishing interest from other nations. With deep regret, the incentive was essentially discontinued after 1997, and I turned my attention to other activities.

▲ Peace coins by Israel, Mexico, and Great Britain.

Gallery Mint Concept Dollars and Other Peace Incentive Medals

In 1997 Arkansas-based Gallery Mint struck some concept dollars to give the media an idea of what the proposed Peace 2000 small gold-colored dollar would look and feel like. This was well before the U.S. Mint's first Sacagawea dollar coins were issued. The "One Concept" medals had a traditional Liberty Head motif on the obverse and an eagle with spread wings on the reverse. The Gallery Mint struck 110 of these and 50 or 60 were distributed to the media, world mints, and others at the 1997 ANA convention in New York City.

Subsequently, other versions of a Peace concept design were made using the same reverse, and similar obverse designs but dated 2000. One has the familiar image of the Statue of Liberty.

◀ 2000-dated prototypes made by the Gallery Mint.

▶ An experimental Ron Landis test piece; only 12 were struck, in April 1998.

◀ Two test pieces were made in 1998 overstruck on Susan B. Anthony dollars.

In addition to the Gallery Mint pieces, nickel and silver medals were made by Clifford Mishler to promote the Peace program.

Still other medals, made of brass, were produced in quantity to distribute at conventions and other gatherings. Some of these had a loop attached for wearing or other uses.

Quantities of elongated pieces were made by Raymond W. Dillard for collectors and for publicity.

A limited number of international mints cooperated by issuing coins with special peace-related designs. I think those of Israel and Mexico are the most attractive.

◀ Brass Peace medals.

▲ Privately made "Search for Peace" medals.

▲ Related medals by Clifford Mishler.

▼ An elongated Peace token by Raymond Dillard.

▶ A "Peace" dollar (silver fantasy piece) made by the Gallery Mint.

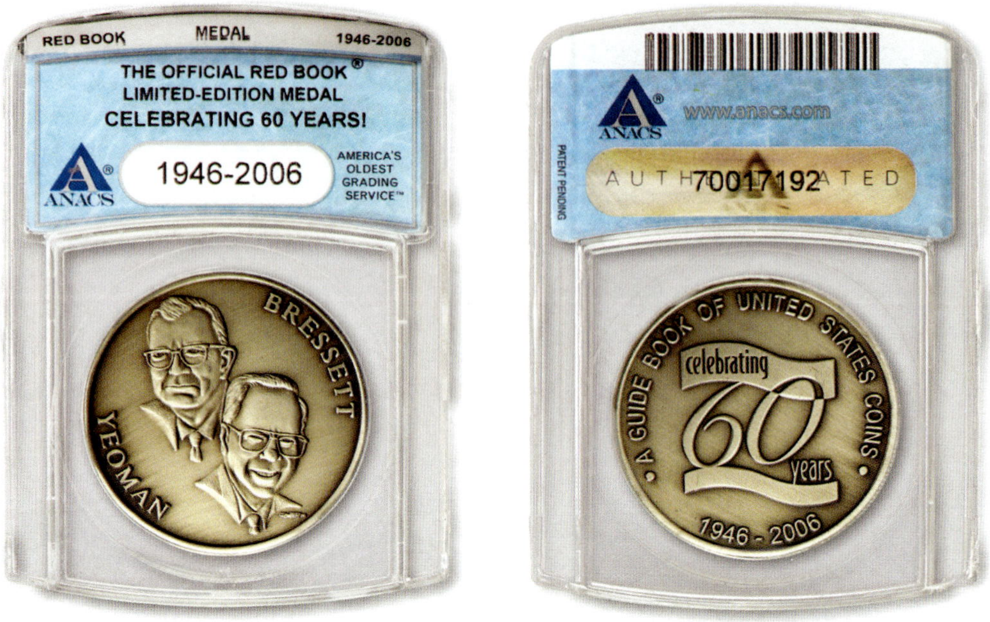

▶ In 2006 Whitman Publishing issued a limited-edition medal to commemorate the 60th anniversary of the *Red Book*.

REWARDS AND AWARDS

These heady days were also overlaid with additional work and some special honors. I served as editor and consultant for St. Martin's Press's coin products program from 1999 until 2002. The company's ownership then passed to Anderson Press and the modern-day Whitman Publishing Company was reborn.

In recent years I have been fortunate to receive a number of honors, for which I am most grateful. The American Numismatic Association presented me the Glenn Smedley Memorial Award in 1997; the Farran Zerbe Memorial Award for Distinguished Service in 1998; and the Lifetime Achievement Award in 2001. Three years later I was named Numismatist of the Year, and in 2017 I received the Adna G. Wilde Jr. Award for Excellence.

In 2016 I was presented the American Numismatic Society's Distinguished Service Award, and in 2018 I earned the Burnett Anderson Memorial Award for Excellence in Numismatic Writing, a joint recognition of the ANA, the American Numismatic Society, and the Numismatic Literary Guild. From the NLG I had received its highest recognition, the Clemy, in 1983.

In a rather extraordinary honor, in 2010 my publisher established the Kenneth E. Bressett Young Numismatist Literary Award (for researchers and writers aged 18 to 22), which is sponsored annually by the American Numismatic Association and Whitman Publishing.

Receiving so many of these very special and kind accolades sometimes seems to me undeserved and almost embarrassing, but each and every one is treasured with pride and fond memories. They constantly remind me how important it is to continue working for the good of the hobby, and to pass on to others whatever information, advice, and counsel I can.

With each of these awards comes the realization that they have been bestowed by my friends, who mean even more to me than the tributes they convey. They are the inspiration that continues to keep me deeply involved in numismatic activities, thankfully in a healthy, happy, and productive way.

▲ **In 2016 I was presented the American Numismatic Society's Distinguished Service Award.**

MILLIONS FOR THE TREASURY, NOT ONE CENT FOR COLLECTORS

Starting sometime around 1998, I became involved in yet another program intended to call attention to collecting coins and to their usefulness as an educational tool. In 1992 Canada had issued a 12-piece set of their quarters with designs commemorating their provinces and territories. The program was hugely popular and could work equally well with United States coins, so many of us were interested in promoting the concept. Freed from my commitment to the "Peace 2000" project, I turned my attention to what eventually would be called the 50 State Quarters Program.

The new plan originated in December 1993 with the CCCAC, under Secretary of the Treasury Lloyd Bentsen and Director of the Mint Philip Diehl. One CCCAC member, David Ganz, suggested the 50 Statehood quarters program, and the council moved to gain support through the House Banking Committee, led by Representative Michael Castle (R-Delaware). A leading force in promoting the effort was *Coin World* editor Margo Russell. Joining her were several leading numismatic figures of the day, including Reed Hawn and myself.

The 50 State Quarters Program was authorized by Public Law 105-124 and signed by President William Jefferson Clinton near the end of 1997, under legislation introduced by Congressman Castle. Launched in 1999, the program was a ten-year initiative that honored each of the nation's states in the order they ratified the Constitution or were admitted into the Union.

The reverse designs for each quarter were created through consultation with the governor of each state, then reviewed by the governor, the Commission of Fine Arts, and the CCCAC (and, later, the Citizens Coinage Advisory Committee). Final approval for each design would be at the discretion of the secretary of the

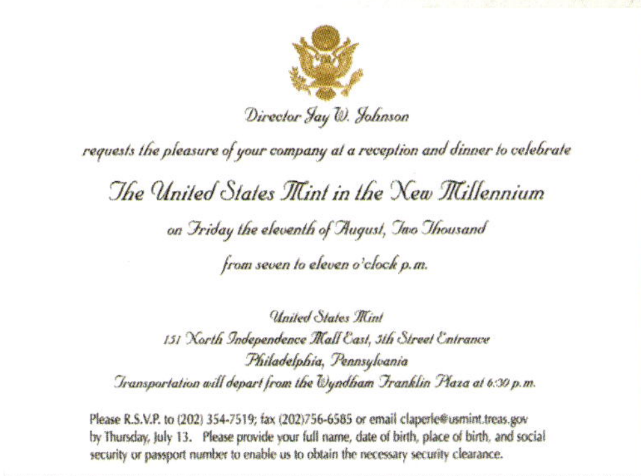

Director Jay W. Johnson

requests the pleasure of your company at a reception and dinner to celebrate

The United States Mint in the New Millennium

on Friday the eleventh of August, Two Thousand

from seven to eleven o'clock p.m.

United States Mint
151 North Independence Mall East, 5th Street Entrance
Philadelphia, Pennsylvania
Transportation will depart from the Wyndham Franklin Plaza at 6:30 p.m.

Please R.S.V.P. to (202) 354-7519; fax (202)756-6585 or email claperle@usmint.treas.gov by Thursday, July 13. Please provide your full name, date of birth, place of birth, and social security or passport number to enable us to obtain the necessary security clearance.

Lawrence Summers
Deputy Secretary of the Treasury
and Philip N. Diehl
Director of the United States Mint
request your presence
to dedicate and tour the new

United States Mint Denver Die Shop

on Monday, the thirteenth of May
at ten o'clock a.m.
luncheon to be held at twelve o'clock p.m.

R.S.V.P. by April 29
Tel: (202) 874-6400
Fax: (202) 874-6343

320 West Colfax Avenue
Denver, Colorado 80204

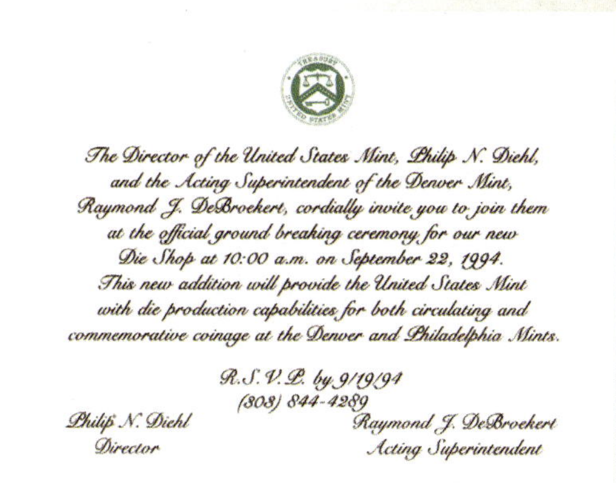

The Director of the United States Mint, Philip N. Diehl,
and the Acting Superintendent of the Denver Mint,
Raymond J. DeBroekert, cordially invite you to join them
at the official ground breaking ceremony for our new
Die Shop at 10:00 a.m. on September 22, 1994.
This new addition will provide the United States Mint
with die production capabilities for both circulating and
commemorative coinage at the Denver and Philadelphia Mints.

R.S.V.P. by 9/19/94
(303) 844-4289

Philip N. Diehl
Director

Raymond J. DeBroekert
Acting Superintendent

▶ **Over the years I've been fortunate to be invited to a variety of special events hosted by the United States Mint.**

Treasury. As a member of the CCCAC, I was honored and excited to help select the designs. In the years that have passed since then, the seigniorage from this coinage has been estimated to have produced more than $6 billion of proceeds to the Treasury. Little of this financial benefit, however, has ever gone to the numismatic community that initiated the program.

A REWARDING FAMILY LIFE

True to my New England upbringing, the most significant part of my life has revolved around my family. On October 7, 1950, Bert and I were married, and we enjoyed a full and happy union for over 61 years before the culmination of her illness brought it to an end in 2012.

It sometimes seems like much of our time together was spent packing and moving from one place to another, traveling, making friends, coping with changes, and adapting to new situations. All were very normal things, fraught with challenges both rewarding and disappointing. The most gratifying parts of our marriage were the births of our children. As a family, we lived for a time in New Hampshire, Wisconsin, Iowa, and Colorado, but we have never forgotten our Yankee roots.

▼ I often used ancient artifacts from my personal collection when giving my children history lessons.

Our first son, Philip, was born November 18, 1951. After a rather normal childhood and upbringing, he left home as a teenager to join the U.S. Navy and see the world. There he grew to manhood, studied, and learned many new skills. Upon returning home, he soon left on a motorcycle trip that lasted a couple of years. When he came back to Wisconsin, he pursued his original desire of working in the numismatic field. In 1977 he began with a small office in Racine and later opened a full-service walk-in store specializing in coins, stamps, and baseball cards. Throughout that time, and continuing to the present, he has been closely involved with the editing and pricing operations of the *Red Book* and has been a helper to me in many related projects.

▲ Philip in full Navy dress for the first time.

Richard was born March 11, 1954. He too left home at an early age to find his place in the world. With little or no special interest in numismatics, his major leaning was in the field of medicine and therapy. He received advanced training when he became a brother with the Cistercian monks of northern Wisconsin. Richard later worked as an anesthesia technician at Meriter Hospital in Madison, Wisconsin. Along the way, he also served in the U.S. Navy and as a computer specialist for an insurance company. Unfortunately, he was frequently incapacitated with various illnesses, migraine headaches, arthritis, and heart trouble that led to his untimely death at 66 in 2020. Richard spent most of his life living and working in Madison.

Our daughter, Mary Bressett Sauder—born June 27, 1955, and the youngest member of the family—was, of course, her father's pride and joy. Over the years, she showed some interest in numismatics, but probably

◄ Our children (from left): Philip, Mary, and Richard.

▲ Hawaii was one of our favorite vacation spots.

more to please her "Pops" than to become truly involved in collecting. This is not to say she does not have the collector instinct, for she enjoys her accumulation of countless giraffes of every color, size, shape, and stripe. Mary lives a full life at her home in Massachusetts and faithfully telephones me every evening to check on my welfare. She also is the only member of the family to have presented me with a grandchild, Robert, born in 1983 and now living in South Carolina. He is the father of my only great-grandchild—his daughter, Maisie.

▲ Bert and me in 1998, not long before our receipt of the ANA's Farran Zerbe Memorial Award for Distinguished Service.

▲ Marilyn Fivaz (left) and Bert, sharing a laugh during one of our Hawaii vacations.

▲ Constant companions for more than 61 years.

A Tribute to Bert Bressett

by D. Wayne ("Dick") Johnson

Bert was at Ken's side for 61 years, often as a hostess at numismatic events where Ken had some major function. Numismatists knew her, and she knew numismatists. On February 12, 2012, Bert Bressett died after coping with COPD for years. Funeral services were held in Colorado Springs, with a Catholic Mass for the Dead at Saint Paul's Catholic Church in Colorado Springs. Interment was in Keene, with a memorial service on June 8.

Coincidentally, my daughter, Sandra Johnson Carazza, chose to attend Antioch College in Keene, New Hampshire, for her doctorate in psychology. She had been living in Keene for four years attending classes. How fortunate, I thought, that I could go to Bert Bressett's memorial service and also visit my daughter.

The gravesite service was attended by a large number of family and friends. The only numismatic personalities there—aside from Ken—were Bill Fivaz and his wife, Marilyn, along with my wife, Shirley, and myself. The Fivazs and the Bressetts had traveled together to Hawaii many times. When the priest asked for remembrances of Bert, Bill recounted their Hawaiian trips and his fond memories of her.

My most recent recollection of Bert was at the banquet following the 70th FIDEM Congress and Exhibition in Colorado Springs in 2007. While the guests went out on the veranda to overlook the night lights of Colorado Springs from the mountainside restaurant, I noticed Bert at her table. I went over and had a 45-minute conversation with her about Ken and their travels, family activities, and mutual friends. This will remain my fond memory of Bert Bressett.

CONSIDERING RETIREMENT, AGAIN

I have intended to retire several times. It seems like the thing to do, but actually complying is not easy, especially when doing what you like best is so rewarding. The beginning of a new century made it seem more inviting this time, and I realized that it was now going to be up to a new generation to meet the challenges of the future. The perennial glitches of grading, deceptive counterfeits, coins touting "first day of whatever," special finishes, or contrived rarity were problems that were just not going

► Autographing *Red Books* was always a pleasure.

away. And they seem a bit too much for a traditionalist to continue battling, like Don Quixote tilting at windmills.

Fortunately, there is a new, invigorated cadre of involved collectors and professional numismatists who have taken up the challenge and are doing a splendid job of ushering us into the new world of hobby activity. Recently, I have been following the progress made by the staff of the American Numismatic Association under the direction of its multi-talented executive director, Kim Kiick, and can say without hesitation that she will go down in history as one who has seen the future and paved the way for a new generation to embrace it.

The dedicated ANA staff is already hosting a multitude of outreach programs designed to make involvement in the hobby easily approachable and inviting to targeted age groups. Staffers like Rod Gillis, Brianna Victor, and others are on the forefront of innovation. And to everyone's delight, teenagers like Abby Zechman, Garrett Ziss, Kellen Hoard, and Kenny Sammut seem destined to be the hobby leaders of tomorrow.

▲ Executive Director Kim Kiick leads a talented and productive staff at the ANA.

Already in place are Facebook, Instagram, Twitter, LinkedIn, and specialty blogs and pages. These, together with several ongoing virtual educational programs, and the ANA eLearning Academy, are currently being conducted through online meeting services.

On a grand scale, the Newman Numismatic Portal and Wayne Homren's electronic *E-Sylum* publication have altered the way collectors think, participate, and enjoy their avocation. For serious researchers, these events and venues and the advent of instantaneous information and communications have already changed the world.

I am equally confident in the future of my longtime publishing family. Throughout my association with the staff of Western Publishing Company, and more recently Whitman Publishing, I have always been mindful of the contributions and helpful support of a cadre of secretarial and editorial assistants. No author alone composes a successful book. I have already mentioned Jeff Garrett and other numismatic contributors. In recent years another helper in particular has guided me through the trials of editing and producing much of my work, and I gratefully acknowledge and thank Whitman senior editor Diana Plattner for her patience, understanding, and help in so many ways to make the publishing process both tranquil and enjoyable.

Like most authors, I am always hesitant to reveal what I am working on at any given moment. Some feel it is bad luck, confidential information, or just plain meddlesome. I simply don't like to break my immediate preoccupation. Sometimes I offer a bogus reply. For anyone wanting to know my current plans for the future, I am herewith happy to share. My goal now is to continue writing and to enjoy numismatic research and coaching. Perhaps I might even add additional information and concepts to the hobby, as it expands to include a yet-to-be seen variety of items that are unimaginable today. Will coins even circulate in the future? Will colored or novelty designs come and go? Will individuals still be able to own anything other than current coins in circulation in their own country? Frankly, I have every confidence that things will right themselves in time, and I am both curious and anxious to see the outcome. What a wonderful opportunity this is to be part of an emerging chapter in numismatic history.

"My goal now is to continue writing and to enjoy numismatic research and coaching."

At the moment, we are all living through tumultuous times brought on by COVID-19, economic troubles, and other concerns that seem insurmountable. Eventually, they will lessen, and we will awaken to a new and radically altered way of interacting with others. Those who accept the changes will be the beneficiaries of a more cooperative and peaceful way of life.

At my age, I have no hesitancy in admitting that I have a brief siesta nearly every day. In fact, I have done this most of my life whenever possible. Even ten minutes is enough to recharge my batteries and get me going again. I recommend it to everyone. Perhaps that will change when or if I ever retire. Perhaps it won't matter then, because I fully intend to live beyond 100 before slowing down, and then only if I have completed all the unfinished work revealed as I researched this present treatise. Numismatics is a lifetime commitment for many of us who enjoy the challenge of discovering new avenues of learning, teaching, and sharing with others. I have frequently said, "Art and history have been reflected throughout the ages by coinage. We are but custodians of these historical relics, and must appreciate and care for them while they are in our possession."

And here are a few other things you might be interested in knowing about what I enjoy and find inspirational:

Ken Bressett's Favorite Things

Music: "Canon in D," by Johann Pachelbel; "Che gelida manina" from *La Bohème*, by Giacomo Puccini; the Beatles.

Foods: Grain cereals; yogurt; ice cream; filet mignon.

Movies: *The Grapes of Wrath*; *The Maltese Falcon*.

Coin: 1652 Massachusetts Pine Tree shilling.

Coin books: *Coins of the World*, by R.A.G. Carson; *Greek Coins*, by C.M. Kraay and Max Hirmer.

Non-numismatic books: *How to Win Friends and Influence People*, by Dale Carnegie; *All Creatures Great and Small*, by James Herriot.

▲ The 1652 Massachusetts Pine Tree shilling.

PAST, PRESENT, FUTURE

"The old order changes, yielding place to new, and God fulfils Himself in many ways, lest one good custom should corrupt the world."—"Morte d'Arthur" by Alfred, Lord Tennyson

Looking back on my life as a professional numismatist has been a delightful stroll down memory lane. Yes, I have had a few disappointments, but the many adventures, honors, and friends encountered along the way have more than made up for any setbacks, and I have always enjoyed each of the numerous new and exciting experiences.

I began working for the rejuvenated Whitman Publishing on September 9, 2003, and was named editor emeritus of the *Red Book* in 2018. To commemorate my retirement and the appointment of Jeff Garrett as the new-generation senior editor, a reception was held at the Whitman Baltimore Convention in October 2018. Among the many trappings for the event, the entrance to the convention was specially decorated. For me, this seemed like the doorway to a new phase in my life.

Recently I had the good fortune to have access to the "Western Archives" with many of the notes, papers, mementos, and files that Dick Yeoman accumulated throughout his career. Studying them is what has inspired me to write this tribute to him and the scores of others who have made the *Red Book* what it is today. It also called to mind some of the things that I also am proud to say I contributed to its content. With these thoughts, I began research on this *Red Book* project soon after my official retirement. It has been a pleasure sharing these recollections with the multitude of readers, helpers, and contributors to this very special book as we celebrate its 75th anniversary.

▲ The entrance of the Whitman Baltimore Winter Expo in October 2018 commemorated my transition from *Red Book* senior editor to editor emeritus.

Books written, coauthored, or edited by Ken Bressett

Handbook of United States Coins (the Blue Book).

A Guide Book of United States Coins (the Red Book).

Alaska's Coinage Through the Years, with Maurice Gould (1960). A 2nd edition (1965) included Kaye and Nancy Dethridge as co-authors.

Hawaiian Coins, Tokens, and Paper Money, with Maurice Gould (1960), revised in 1961.

The Fantastic 1804 Dollar, with Eric Newman (1962). A "Tribute Edition" was published in 2009, with expanded information.

A Guide Book of English Coins (1962). Eight more editions were published (through 1982).

Let's Collect Coins! An Introduction to a Fascinating Hobby, with Price Guide of Valuable Coins (1966). The 9th edition was published in 1990.

Buying and Selling United States Coins (1970). The 12th edition was published in 1982.

"Coin Collecting," Boy Scout Merit Badge pamphlet (1975 to 1985).

Official ANA Grading Standards for United States Coins (1977). Updated and revised several times since.

Basics of Coin Grading for U.S. Coins (1982).

United States Coin Price Trends, with Q. David Bowers (1990).

Collectible American Coins (1991).

Collecting U.S. Coins: A Guide for Beginners (1992). Published in association with the American Numismatic Association.

A Guide Book of United States Currency (1993–). The 8th edition was published in 2019.

Handbook of Ancient Greek and Roman Coins (editor), based on the text by Zander H. Klawans (1994).

Coin Collecting: A Beginner's Guide to the World of Coins (1999). The 2nd edition was published in 2003 and went through several printings.

Official Whitman Statehood Quarters Collector's Handbook (2000).

Money of the Bible (2005). The 3rd edition was published in 2013.

Milestone Coins: A Pageant of the World's Most Significant and Popular Money (2007).

The Fantastic 1804 Dollar, Tribute Edition (2009). An expanded edition released on the 50th anniversary of the start of the original book's research collaboration.

Mega Red (2015 to date). The expanded *Deluxe Edition* of the *Red Book.*

Whitman Guide to Coin Collecting: An Introduction to the World of Coins (2017). This is a revised, updated, and enlarged "Golden Edition" of *Coin Collecting* (1999).

A Penny Saved: R.S. Yeoman and His Remarkable Red Book (2021).

Always happy to autograph books for hobbyists! Here, I sign a copy of *Mega Red* for *Numismatist* news editor (now editor in chief) Caleb Noel, at the August 2017 ANA show in Denver.

Looking Ahead

As the concluding parts of this book are being written, the world is slowly emerging from the disastrous effects of the COVID-19 pandemic. Nearly everyone has been negatively affected in one way or another, and some of the people and events described herein have been lost or changed forever. On a personal note, the year began for me with significant losses from a burglary, followed by the death of my sister Beverly. Soon after that my youngest son, Richard, passed away after a long illness. Over the following months many other relatives and friends have died from the virus or other causes.

Now, after being vaccinated myself, and determined to successfully meet life's challenges, I look forward to a brighter new day with enthusiasm.

Personal tragedies invoke hardships and chaos for everyone, and must be met with patience, faith, and the courage to accept changes and move forward. Fortunately, in time the numismatic fraternity will continue to function normally, albeit with some modifications to conventions, meetings, conferences, new books, and revised coin valuations.

In a way we are all fortunate to have been part of this transition, and witnesses to changes we never envisioned. As coin collectors are apt to say, "The change will do us good."

▶ In addition to the *Red Book*, I have written, edited, or contributed to a variety of publications, including the *Whitman Numismatic Journal*, *The Fantastic 1804 Dollar*, *Milestone Coins*, *A Guide Book of English Coins*, and *Money of the Bible* . . . with more to come!

THE FANTASTIC 1804 DOLLAR
By ERIC P. NEWMAN and KENNETH E. BRESSETT
MONEY OF THE BIBLE
Milestone Coins
Whitman Numismatic Journal
JANUARY 1964 VOL 1 No 1
FEATURE ARTICLES:
★ Foreign Coins Struck at U. S. Mints
★ New Listings for World Coin Catalog
★ Latest Coin Value Guide Line
★ Coin Chronicle of the Roman Republic
HAWAIIAN COINS, TOKENS AND PAPER MONEY
BY MAURICE M. GOULD
Whitman
EIGHTH EDITION
a guide book of English coins
By KEN BRESSETT
NINETEENTH AND TWENTIETH CENTURIES
12th Edition
Official Guide to BUYING $ SELLING U.S. COINS
$1.95
by Ken Bressett

Appendix A

COLLECTING AND GRADING THE *RED BOOK*

For many years, since the days when R.S. Yeoman was at the helm, coin collectors have been interested in assembling sets of *Red Books*. The demand for older editions has created a healthy buy-and-sell market. Some collectors who acquire these old volumes maintain reference libraries of all kinds of coin publications. To them, having one of each edition is essential, because that is the way old books are collected. Others are speculators who believe that the value of old editions will go up as interest and demand increases. Many people who save *Red Books* do so to keep a consistent record of coin values and price trends going back further than any other source.

Old *Red Books* are also a handy way to take the pulse of the hobby community. They show how grading has changed over the years, what new coins have been discovered and added to the listings, and which areas are growing in popularity. Studying old *Red Books* can be educational as well as nostalgic.

THE FIRST EDITION: DIFFERENCES BETWEEN THE FIRST AND SECOND PRINTINGS

The first edition of the *Guide Book of United States Coins*, cover-dated 1947, was released in two print runs. Before sending the book back to press for its second printing, author R.S. Yeoman took the opportunity to order several corrections. The most famous edit—the one that collectors most often use to quickly tell whether their first edition is from the first or second printing—is on page 135. There, a paragraph discussing the Morgan dollar states:

> 270,232,722 silver dollars were melted under the Pittman Act of April, 1918. 259 121,554 for export to India, and 11,111,168 for domestic subsidiary coins, which probably accounts for the scarcity of this date.

In the second printing, the text *for the scarcity of this date* was clarified to *for the scarcity of 1903 O*. (For some reason, Yeoman didn't order the correction of a typographical error in the same sentence: a missing comma in *259,121,554*.)

Longtime *Red Book* collector and historian Frank J. Colletti, author of the *Guide Book of the Official Red Book of United States Coins*, has made a page-by-page study of the two printings of the 1947 *Red Book*. Colletti has compiled several other significant corrections and additions made in the second printing. These modifications have never been publicized before; they are described in this appendix for the first time.

- **Page 29 (Connecticut coppers).** In the second printing, the photographs for the obverses of the "1787 Cent, Mailed Bust Facing Left" and "1787 Cent, CONNECT Variety" were properly switched.
- **Page 41 (Higley or Granby coppers).** In the second printing, the caption for the third set of photographs was clarified with better typography and punctuation. The text *(1737) UNDATED OBVERSE SIMILAR TO ABOVE REVERSE "I CUT MY WAY THROUGH"* was edited to *(1737) Undated, Obverse Similar to Above. Reverse "I CUT MY WAY THROUGH"*
- **Page 51 (Washington medals).** In the second printing, the chart for the second Washington medal was corrected from *1783 UNITED STATES* to *1783 UNITY STATES*.
- **Page 81 (Indian Head cents).** In the chart, the first entry's listing of *1865 (L on ribbon, rare)* was corrected to *1864 (L on ribbon, rare)*.
- **Page 90 (silver three-cent pieces).** In the third row of the first chart, the date 1851 was corrected to 1852.
- **Page 117 (Capped Bust half dollars).** In the second printing, the text *All of her years (except 1916-17) mint-mark is on Rev.* was corrected to *All other years (except 1916-17) mint-mark is on Rev.*
- **Page 145 (half eagles).** In the second printing, the price of the 1795, Small Eagle, was lowered from $100 in Fine to $75. The price of the 1796 Over 95, Small Eagle, was increased from $75 in Fine to $100.
- **Page 183 (commemorative coins).** In the second printing, mintages and values were added for the 1946 Booker T. Washington half dollar, and the D and S mint coins were also added:

1946	Booker T. Washington	1,000,000	$1.00
1946D	Same type D mint	250,000	1.50
1946S	Same type S mint	500,000	1.00

In addition, Colletti notes that there are a number of typographical errors in the first printing that were *not* corrected in the second printing—for example, on pages 189 and 190, the name of Georgia jeweler and gunsmith Templeton Reid is misspelled in the headlines (but not in the narrative text) as Templeton *Ried*. (That correction would finally be made in the third edition.)

In some years a very limited number of *Red Books* were made for use by price contributors. Those were interleaved with blank pages. No more than 50 copies were ever made for any one year. Perhaps fewer than 20 were made in the first few years. Three of these of the first edition, and one of the second edition, are currently known. Their value is now in the four figures. Those made in the 1960s sell for about $300 to $500 today.

Error books are popular with collectors. The most common error is double-stamped printing on the cover. The second most frequently seen is an upside-down cover. Probably the best known of the error books is the 1963-dated 16th edition with a missing page. In those error books, page 239 is duplicated, and page 237 is missing. The mistake was corrected on most of the printing.

In Whitman's modern era, *Red Book* contributor copies have been distributed annually. These have a special illustrated autograph page bound in the front, bearing the contributor's name and the signature of the current senior editor. These contributor copies are rare, with about 120 issued each year from Whitman Publishing headquarters. In recent years they have been accompanied by an "Official Red Book Contributor" lapel pin.

GRADING *RED BOOKS*

Red Book collectors have adopted grading terms similar to those used for coins. Agreed-upon terms make it easier to understand the condition of a book being discussed or perhaps offered for sale sight-unseen. While there are no official regulations, the descriptions offered here are commonly used by most experienced collectors and dealers.

- **New**—Pristine condition. The book has never been opened, and the pages are tightly compressed. Slight blemishes may be present on the cover or spine due to the printing process.
- **Very Fine / Near Mint**—May appear new at first glance. The binding is tight, but not necessarily compact. The pages look and sound crisp when being separated from each other for the first time. There may be evidence of slight use, but the book has no evidence of marks or stains.
- **Fine**—Still attractive, with little obvious wear. The entire book is clean and unblemished. A few minor problems may be evident under close inspection. Pages are bright, and the cover not noticeably worn. Pencil markings, folds, and creases are minimal and unobtrusive.
- **Very Good**—Obviously worn from repeated use. May have notations and marks that are not blatantly noticeable. The owner's name or stamp on the flysheet will probably affect its desirability but may be tolerated on early editions that are rarely seen without some sort of imperfection.
- **Good and Fair**—Well worn, ragged, and/or tattered.

Early editions of the *Red Book* are rarely if ever found in anything approaching New condition. Exceptionally well-preserved older editions command a substantial premium and are in great demand. Nice used copies that are still clean and in good shape, but slightly worn from use, are also desirable.

Serious collectors rarely desire books in Good or Fair condition. Exceptions are sometimes made in the case of especially rare editions. Books in readable condition are often used for reference purposes, or as duplicates to avoid handling more valuable copies.

RED BOOK VALUES AND CHECK LIST

Values given here are for unsigned books. Those signed by R.S. Yeoman are worth substantially more. Books autographed by Kenneth Bressett, Jeff Garrett, and/or Q. David Bowers are more readily available. They may also command premiums.

Classic Hardcover Binding

Year/Edition	Issue Price	VG	F	VF	New
❑ 1947 (1st ed.), 1st Printing	$1.50	$225	$425	$675	$1,350 **(a)**
❑ 1947 (1st ed.), 2nd Printing	1.50	175	350	600	1,100 **(a)**
❑ 1948 (2nd ed.)	1.50	60	125	210	475 **(a)**
❑ 1949 (3rd ed.)	$1.50	$60	$100	$210	$500 **(a)**
❑ 1951/52 (4th ed.)	1.50	50	90	175	350 **(a)**
❑ 1952/53 (5th ed.)	1.50	85	150	375	975 **(a)**
❑ 1953/54 (6th ed.)	1.75	30	50	65	85
❑ 1954/55 (7th ed.)	1.75	30	45	60	85
❑ 1955 (8th ed.)	1.75	30	35	55	75
❑ 1956 (9th ed.)	1.75	20	35	45	70
❑ 1957 (10th ed.)	1.75	10	15	35	45
❑ 1958 (11th ed.)	1.75		8	12	20
❑ 1959 (12th ed.)	1.75		8	10	20
❑ 1960 (13th ed.)	1.75		7	9	20
❑ 1961 (14th ed.)	1.75		4	6	20
❑ 1962 (15th ed.)	1.75		4	6	15
❑ 1963 (16th ed.)	1.75		4	6	15
❑ 1964 (17th ed.)	1.75		3	4	10
❑ 1965 (18th ed.)	1.75		3	4	10
❑ 1966 (19th ed.)	1.75		3	4	10
❑ 1967 (20th ed.)	1.75		2	3	8
❑ 1968 (21st ed.)	2.00		2	3	8
❑ 1969 (22nd ed.)	2.00		2	3	8
❑ 1970 (23rd ed.)	2.50		2	3	8
❑ 1971 (24th ed.)	2.50		2	3	7
❑ 1972 (25th ed.)	2.50		2	3	7
❑ 1973 (26th ed.)	2.50		2	3	7
❑ 1974 (27th ed.)	2.50		2	3	7
❑ 1975 (28th ed.)	3.00			3	6
❑ 1976 (29th ed.)	3.95			3	6

a. Values are for books in Near Mint condition, as truly New copies are effectively nonexistent.

Year/Edition	Issue Price	VF	New
❑ 1977 (30th ed.)	$3.95	$3	$6
❑ 1978 (31st ed.)	3.95	3	6
❑ 1979 (32nd ed.)	3.95	3	6
❑ 1980 (33rd ed.)	3.95	3	6
❑ 1981 (34th ed.)	4.95	2	5
❑ 1982 (35th ed.)	4.95	2	5
❑ 1983 (36th ed.)	5.95	2	5
❑ 1984 (37th ed.)	5.95	2	5
❑ 1985 (38th ed.)	5.95	2	5
❑ 1986 (39th ed.)	5.95	2	5
❑ 1987 (40th ed.)	6.95	2	5
❑ 1988 (41st ed.)	6.95	2	5
❑ 1989 (42nd ed.)	6.95	2	5
❑ 1990 (43rd ed.)	7.95	2	5
❑ 1991 (44th ed.)	8.95	2	5
❑ 1992 (45th ed.)	8.95	2	5
❑ 1993 (46th ed.)	9.95		5
❑ 1994 (47th ed.)	9.95		3
❑ 1995 (48th ed.)	10.95		3
❑ 1996 (49th ed.)	10.95		3
❑ 1997 (50th ed.)	11.95		3
❑ 1998 (51st ed.)	11.95		2
❑ 1999 (52nd ed.)	11.95		2
❑ 2000 (53rd ed.)	12.95		2
❑ 2001 (54th ed.)	13.95		2
❑ 2002 (55th ed.)	14.95		2
❑ 2003 (56th ed.)	15.95		2
❑ 2004 (57th ed.)	15.95		2
❑ 2005 (58th ed.)	15.95		2
❑ 2006 (59th ed.)	16.95		2
❑ 2007 (60th ed.)	16.95		2
❑ 2008 (61st ed.)	16.95		2
❑ 2009 (62nd ed.)	16.95		2
❑ 2010 (63rd ed.)	16.95		2
❑ 2011 (64th ed.)	16.95		2
❑ 2012 (65th ed.)	16.95		2
❑ 2013 (66th ed.)	16.95		2

Year/Edition	Issue Price	VF	New
❑ 2014 (67th ed.)	$16.95		$2
❑ 2015 (68th ed.)	16.95		2
❑ 2016 (69th ed.)	16.95		2
❑ 2017 (70th ed.)	16.95		2
❑ 2018 (71st ed.) **(b)**	16.95		2
❑ 2019 (72nd ed.) **(c)**	17.95		2
❑ 2020 (73rd ed.)	17.95		2
❑ 2021 (74th ed.)	17.95		2
❑ 2022 (75th ed.) **(d)**	17.95		

a. Values are for books in Near Mint condition, as truly New copies are effectively nonexistent. **b.** Features a gold-foil portrait of first Mint director David Rittenhouse. **c.** Features a gold-foil portrait of Editor Emeritus Kenneth Bressett. **d.** Features a silver-foil emblem for the 75th anniversary of the *Red Book.*

• ***Softcovers (1993–2007).*** The first softcover (trade paperback) *Red Book* was the 1993 (46th) edition. The softcover binding was offered (alongside other formats) in the 1993, 1994, 1995, and 1996 editions; again in the 1998 edition; and from 2003 through 2007. All are fairly common and easily collectible today. Values in New condition range from $2 up to $4 for the earlier editions.

• ***Spiralbound Softcovers (1997 to Date).*** The first spiralbound softcover *Red Book* was the 1997 (50th) edition. The format was next available in the 1999 edition, and it has been an annually offered format since then. Today the spiralbound softcovers all are easily collectible. The 1997 edition is worth $4 in New condition, and later editions are valued around $2.

• ***Spiralbound Hardcovers (2008 to Date).*** The first spiralbound hardcover *Red Book* was the 2008 (61st) edition. The format has been available (alongside other formats) every edition since. All spiralbound hardcovers are readily available to collectors, and are valued from $2 to $4.

• ***Journal Edition (2009).*** The large-sized *Journal Edition*, featuring a three-ring binder, color-coded tabbed dividers, and removable pages, was issued only for the 2009 (62nd) edition. Today it is valued at $5 in VF and $30 in New condition.

• ***Large Print Editions (2010 to Date).*** An oversized format has been offered annually since the 2010 (63rd) edition. All editions are readily available to collectors and are valued at $5 in New condition.

• ***Essential Edition (2013–2017).*** The magazine-sized softcover *Essential Edition* was published annually from 2013 to 2017. Aimed at mainstream readers, it featured large print and focused on the most popular federal coins. Copies are rarely seen on the secondary market; valued around $10.

Leather Limited Editions (2005 to Date)

Year/Edition	Print Run	Issue Price	New
❑ 2005 (58th ed.)	3,000	$69.95	$70
❑ 2006 (59th ed.)	3,000	69.95	70
❑ 2007 (60th ed.)	3,000	69.95	70
❑ 2007 1947 Tribute Edition	500	49.95	100
❑ 2008 (61st ed.)	3,000	69.95	70
❑ 2008 (61st ed.), Numismatic Literary Guild **(a)**	135*		650
❑ 2008 (61st ed.), American Numismatic Society **(b)**	250*		400
❑ 2009 (62nd ed.)	3,000	69.95	75
❑ 2010 (63rd ed.)	1,500	69.95	75
❑ 2011 (64th ed.)	1,500	69.95	75
❑ 2012 (65th ed.)	1,000	69.95	75
❑ 2013 (66th ed.)	1,000	69.95	75
❑ 2014 (67th ed.)	1,000	69.95	75
❑ 2015 (68th ed.)	500	99.95	100
❑ 2016 (69th ed.)	500	99.95	100
❑ 2017 (70th ed.)	500	99.95	100
❑ 2018 (71st ed.)	500	99.95	100
❑ 2019 (72nd ed.)	500	99.95	100

* Included in total print-run quantity. **a.** One hundred thirty-five imprinted copies of the 2008 leather Limited Edition were created. Of these, 125 were distributed to members of the NLG at its 2007 literary awards ceremony; the remaining 10 were distributed from Whitman Publishing headquarters in Atlanta. **b.** Two hundred fifty copies of the 2008 leather Limited Edition were issued with a special bookplate honoring the 150th anniversary of the ANS. They were distributed to attendees of the January 2008 celebratory banquet in New York.

Special Editions

Year/Edition	Print Run	Issue Price	VF	New
❑ 1987 (40th ed.), American Numismatic Association 95th Anniversary	*500*		$600	$750
❑ 1992 (45th ed.), American Numismatic Association 100th Anniversary	*600*		120	225
❑ 1997 (50th ed.), *Red Book* 50th Anniversary	1,200	$24.95	50	90
❑ 2002 (55th ed.), American Numismatic Association "Target 2001"	500	100.00	25	40
❑ 2002 (55th ed.), SS Central America		35.00	20	35
❑ 2005 (58th ed.), FUN (Florida United Numismatists) 50th Anniversary	*1,100*		50	90
❑ 2007 (60th ed.), American Numismatic Association 115th Anniversary	500		50	90
❑ 2007 (60th ed.), Michigan State Numismatic Society 50th Anniversary	*500*		50	90
❑ 2007 (1st ed.), 1947 Tribute Edition		17.95	5	20
❑ 2008 (61st ed.), ANA Milwaukee World's Fair of Money	*1,080*		25	50
❑ 2008 (61st ed.), Stack's Rare Coins			5	15
❑ 2010 (63rd ed.), Philadelphia Expo **(a)**		24.95	20	40
❑ 2011 (64th ed.), Boston Numismatic Society		85.00	45	90
❑ 2012 (65th ed.), American Numismatic Association	800	100.00	30	60
❑ 2013 (66th ed.), American Numismatic Society **(b)**	250		100	250
❑ 2015 (68th ed.), Central States Numismatic Society	500	15.00	25	60
❑ 2016 (69th ed.), American Numismatic Association 125th Anniversary		100.00	40	75
❑ 2018 (71st ed.) NGC 30th Anniversary			60	100
❑ 2020 (73rd ed.) Chicago Coin Club 100th Anniversary	250			75
❑ 2021 (74th ed.) Philippine Collectors Forum / 100th Anniversary of the Manila Mint **(c)**	250	25.00		90

a. Two thousand and nine copies of a special 2010 hardcover edition were made for distribution to dealers at the premiere Whitman Coin and Collectibles Philadelphia Expo (September 2009). Extra copies were sold at $50 apiece with proceeds benefiting the National Federation for the Blind. **b.** Two hundred fifty copies of the 2013 hardcover were issued with a special bookplate honoring ANS Trustees' Award recipient (and *Red Book* contributor) Roger Siboni. **c.** Two hundred fifty copies were printed, but some were destroyed in shipping, resulting in total distribution of 212 books.

Appendix B

COLLECTING THE *BLUE BOOK*

The 1942 first-edition *Handbook of United States Coins* was unique in many ways in its shape and content. The cover consisted of a cardboard case, covered with blue Kivar®, with rounded corners and pages. The color had been selected for its availability during wartime shortages, although perhaps also because of its similarity to the blue cover and rounded corners of Charles Green's 1936 *Mint Record and Type Table*. Whatever the reason its color was chosen, the guide was soon popularly known as the *Blue Book*. A copy of the first edition with author R.S. Yeoman's signature, still preserved in wartime gift-wrap paper, is in the Western Archives.

There were two press-run printings of the first edition. Yeoman made notations on two books that he preserved, indicating first and second printings. Until recently, it was thought that the two print runs were identical in every respect. However, Ken Bressett made an important discovery while reviewing the Western Archives in December 2020. He relates it here:

> While examining the treasure trove of heretofore unknown material in Yeoman's personal possessions, I was astounded to discover two very carefully preserved copies of the 1942 first-edition *Blue Book*. On careful examination I found they had been saved for a special reason well beyond the fact that they were likely some of the first books off the press. True to Yeoman's famous style, he purposely intended to preserve them as documents of the evolution of the *Blue Book* during its first year of production.
>
> The inside front sheets of these books are inscribed and autographed as *First Printing Jan 1942* and *Second Printing April 1942*. That alone would have been important information, but it was also a hint that I should carefully examine the content of each. The effort was well rewarded—it revealed that many changes had been made in the second printing, resulting in a very distinctive second variety of the first edition. The differences are even more astounding than the very similar well-known situation with the two varieties of first editions of the *Red Book*.
>
> Most notable of the changes in the second-printing *Blue Book* are the mintage figures that were brought up to date to reflect revised 1942 Mint reports. In the first printing, mintages shown for current issues are for only the first nine months of 1941, and do not include Proof figures. In each case, the second printing also includes a lengthy "Reminder" stating that coins are priced in ordinary condition, and may bring more money when Uncirculated. On page 61 a typographical error was corrected (referring the reader to page 13, not page 12). And page 121 was updated to include the 1942 Proof sets.

This information has never been published before. Collectors are encouraged to study their first editions of the *Blue Book* and report their varieties to Whitman Publishing. This will allow an understanding of the rarity and availability of each variety to emerge.

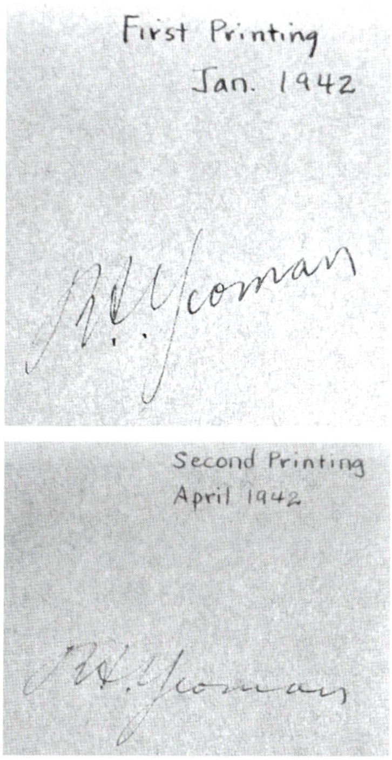

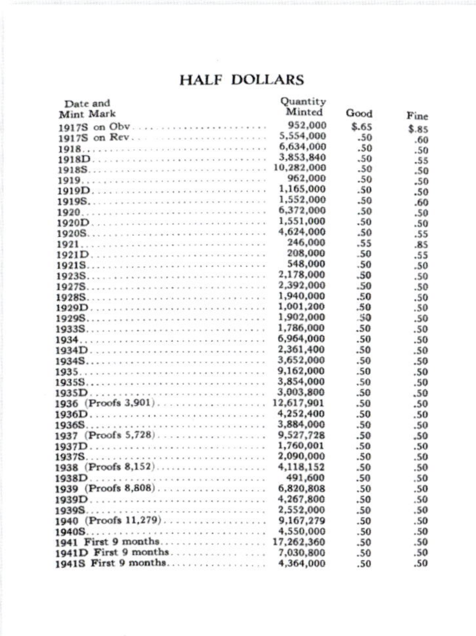

HALF DOLLARS

Date and Mint Mark	Quantity Minted	Good	Fine
1917S on Obv	952,000	$.65	$.85
1917S on Rev	5,554,000	.50	.60
1918	6,634,000	.50	.50
1918D	3,853,840	.50	.55
1918S	10,282,000	.50	.50
1919	962,000	.50	.50
1919D	1,165,000	.50	.50
1919S	1,552,000	.50	.60
1920	6,372,000	.50	.50
1920D	1,551,000	.50	.50
1920S	4,624,000	.50	.55
1921	246,000	.55	.85
1921D	208,000	.50	.55
1921S	548,000	.50	.50
1923S	2,178,000	.50	.50
1927S	2,392,000	.50	.50
1928S	1,940,000	.50	.50
1929D	1,001,200	.50	.50
1929S	1,902,000	.50	.50
1933S	1,786,000	.50	.50
1934	6,964,000	.50	.50
1934D	2,361,400	.50	.50
1934S	3,652,000	.50	.50
1935	9,162,000	.50	.50
1935S	3,854,000	.50	.50
1935D	3,003,800	.50	.50
1936 (Proofs 3,901)	12,617,901	.50	.50
1936D	4,252,400	.50	.50
1936S	3,884,000	.50	.50
1937 (Proofs 5,728)	9,527,728	.50	.50
1937D	1,760,001	.50	.50
1937S	2,090,000	.50	.50
1938 (Proofs 8,152)	4,118,152	.50	.50
1938D	491,600	.50	.50
1939 (Proofs 8,808)	6,820,808	.50	.50
1939D	4,267,800	.50	.50
1939S	2,552,000	.50	.50
1940 (Proofs 11,279)	9,167,279	.50	.50
1940S	4,550,000	.50	.50
1941 First 9 months	17,262,360	.50	.50
1941D First 9 months	7,030,800	.50	.50
1941S First 9 months	4,364,000	.50	.50

▲ First printing of the *Blue Book*, first edition, page 70.

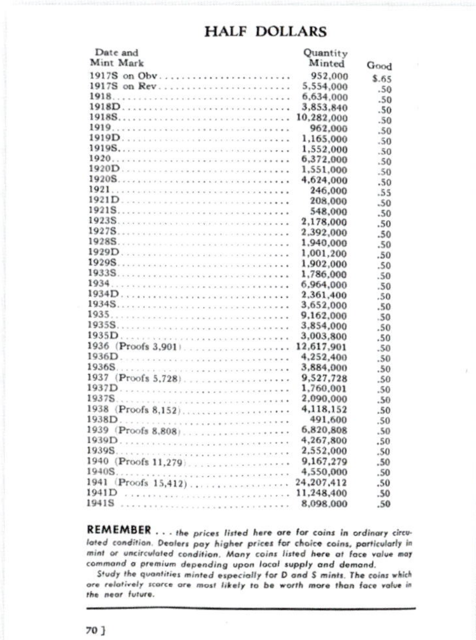

HALF DOLLARS

Date and Mint Mark	Quantity Minted	Good
1917S on Obv	952,000	$.65
1917S on Rev	5,554,000	.50
1918	6,634,000	.50
1918D	3,853,840	.50
1918S	10,282,000	.50
1919	962,000	.50
1919D	1,165,000	.50
1919S	1,552,000	.50
1920	6,372,000	.50
1920D	1,551,000	.50
1920S	4,624,000	.50
1921	246,000	.55
1921D	208,000	.50
1921S	548,000	.50
1923S	2,178,000	.50
1927S	2,392,000	.50
1928S	1,940,000	.50
1929D	1,001,200	.50
1929S	1,902,000	.50
1933S	1,786,000	.50
1934	6,964,000	.50
1934D	2,361,400	.50
1934S	3,652,000	.50
1935	9,162,000	.50
1935S	3,854,000	.50
1935D	3,003,800	.50
1936 (Proofs 3,901)	12,617,901	.50
1936D	4,252,400	.50
1936S	3,884,000	.50
1937 (Proofs 5,728)	9,527,728	.50
1937D	1,760,001	.50
1937S	2,090,000	.50
1938 (Proofs 8,152)	4,118,152	.50
1938D	491,600	.50
1939 (Proofs 8,808)	6,820,808	.50
1939D	4,267,800	.50
1939S	2,552,000	.50
1940 (Proofs 11,279)	9,167,279	.50
1940S	4,550,000	.50
1941 (Proofs 15,412)	24,207,412	.50
1941D	11,248,400	.50
1941S	8,098,000	.50

REMEMBER . . . *the prices listed here are for coins in ordinary circulated condition. Dealers pay higher prices for choice coins, particularly in mint or uncirculated condition. Many coins listed here at face value may command a premium depending upon local supply and demand.*

Study the quantities minted especially for D and S mints. The coins which are relatively scarce are most likely to be worth more than face value in the near future.

70]

▲ Second printing of the *Blue Book*, first edition, page 70.

VARIETIES AND FORMATS OF THE *BLUE BOOK*

The early years of the *Blue Book* yielded a treasure trove of varieties as Whitman experimented with different styles and materials for the covers. Other changes over the years provide hobbyists the opportunity to build a substantial and visually interesting collection.

Whitman released the 2nd edition later in the same year as the first edition. It, too, had a copyright date of 1942, but this time the cover date was 1943. The corners on the cover were squared off. The 2nd edition had a great number of improvements, such as many new photos. Another major change was in the price listings. The valuations of many key-date coins increased by 50 to 100 percent.

Approximately 10,000 copies of each yearly edition of the *Blue Book* were printed during the following decade.

Collectors should be aware that the dating system for the *Blue Book* was not always consistent. Although the second edition initiated the convention of dating the volume one year ahead of the copyright date, a change took place after publication skipped 1944, and the 5th and 6th editions (published in 1945 and 1946, respectively) bore no identifying date. The delay between the 8th and 9th editions (published in 1949 and 1951, respectively) adds to the confusion. The valuation chart in this appendix clarifies the relationship between edition number, stated date, and copyright date for the early *Blue Books*.

The 3rd edition of the *Blue Book*, published in 1943 with a cover date of 1944, offers several interesting varieties. Books for this year were issued with covers in many different shades of blue.

The 4th edition was published in 1945, two years after the 3rd edition. Perhaps because of the hiatus, it had no title-page date. The 5th edition would reset the series' dating conventions, with a title-page date of 1947 and a copyright date of 1946. From this point on, the Blue Book would match the Red Book in bearing a title-page date (and, starting with the 20th edition, a cover date) one year ahead of publication

The 4th-edition *Blue Book*, like the 3rd, was also made with several different cover styles, reflecting the wartime shortages of cover materials. The most common has a normal blue cover. However, some other varieties are more popular among collectors because they are fairly unusual. For reasons we can only speculate, some 4th-edition *Blue Books* have a cover that was recycled from the 3rd edition and over-stamped "Fourth Edition." These *Blue Books* (along with the similar over-stamped 9th-edition issues) might be the only "overdate" books in American numismatic publishing! It is possible that this was a means of using up extra covers from the previous year's edition, or perhaps the older covers were used to correct a printing error. The gilt wears off these covers more readily than on others, and this reuse of the covers may be the cause. In addition to the use of various shades of blue, some covers have a noticeably different texture. Another variant of the 4th edition is particularly unusual in that it features a *black* cover. This and a variety of the 9th edition were the only editions of the *Blue Book* whose covers were a color other than blue. The black *Blue Books* are very scarce, particularly in Very Fine condition.

The 9th edition was released in 1951 with a title-page date of 1952. As they had for the 4th edition, the publishers utilized the previous year's leftover covers. They were overprinted with the words "Ninth Edition." This variation is very scarce and one of the most difficult *Blue Books* to obtain in nice condition. As a result, even copies of poor quality are very collectible. Any available copies usually sell immediately to knowledgeable collectors.

One version of the 12th edition was produced with a regular cover, but another version was released with a much darker blue cover with a pebbled texture. This experimental cover was an improvement over the regular surface in that it did not absorb stains as readily, and its shiny finish was easier to clean. There were, however, other problems because it was brittle and chipped easily.

In the Western Archives are specimens of the 6th-edition *Blue Book* with a blue cover, without gold stamping; an 8th-edition Blue Book with a red cover, without gold stamping; and a 1955 *Red Book* with a blue cover, without gold stamping.

There is a noteworthy error in the 19th edition: the listing of contributors is incorrectly labeled with the notation "Contributors to the Eighteenth Edition."

The first *Blue Book* had a plain (unprinted) spine, which was maintained until the 21st (1964) edition. The title was printed on the spine starting with the 22nd (1965) edition.

Note that the spine of the 45th edition (1988 cover date) has a typographical error: it reads *Handbook of United Stated Coins* (instead of *United States Coins*). The error was caught during production; most copies had already been printed and shipped, so printing was allowed to continue without a correction. In this case, a *correctly* spelled title on the spine would be an error!

From the 40th edition (1983 cover date, published in 1982) to the 60th edition (2003 cover date), *Blue Books* were released only in softcover format. Starting with the 61st edition, published in 2003, Whitman reintroduced the hardcover format, while also continuing production of the softcover. Both hardcover and softcover formats have been produced since.

The 58th, 59th, and 60th editions (cover dates of 2001, 2002, and 2003) were made in a slightly oversized format of 5-1/2 by 8-1/4 inches.

Errors of the *Blue Book* exist, but in smaller numbers than for the *Red Book*. Editing copies (interleaved editions or marked-up standard editions) are also known.

THE MARKET FOR THE *BLUE BOOK*

Collectors seek old editions of the *Blue Book* for many of the same reasons they collect the *Red Book*. They offer many attractions, such as information on changes in the coin market, news in numismatic research, and insight into the growth and development of coin collecting.

Copies of the first edition are desirable but not particularly rare, other than those signed by R.S. Yeoman. However, this appendix's newly published information about two different first-edition varieties (first printing and second printing) may change the market, if one variety proves rarer than the other. Currently, average-condition examples are priced around $100; near-new copies, with full gilt on the cover, are available for between $150 and $200.

In general, copies of the *Blue Book* are available at a modest price, and editions after the 12th are likely to cost the collector only a few dollars, even in Very Fine or better condition.

Valuation Guide for Select Past Editions of the Blue Book

Edition	Date*		VF	New
	Title-Page	Copyright		
1st	1942	1942	$100	$225
2nd	1943	1942	35	55
3rd	1944	1943	30	50
4th	None	1945	30	45
5th	None	1946	20	45
6th	1948	1947	15	30
7th	1949	1948	12	25
8th	1950	1949	10	20
9th	1952	1951	5	10
10th	1953	1952	5	10
11th	1954	1953	3	7
12th	1955	1954	3	7

* During its early years of production, the *Blue Book*'s date presentation was not standardized. Full information is given here to aid in precise identification of early editions.

BLUE BOOK–RELATED COLLECTIBLES

A significant collectible item related to the *Blue Book* is the *Handbook of United States Type Coins*, a 32-page booklet first published in 1943. This short guide, produced by Yeoman with the assistance of A.S. Porter Jr., was inserted as a part of the Whitman coin folder for type coins. It contained no coin values (wholesale or otherwise) but provided descriptions and black-and-white photographs of regular-issue U.S. coins and varieties, from half cents through dollars, along with capsule histories of their production. The original 1943 pamphlet featured a self-cover and was slightly smaller than the 1948 version (shown here), which is roughly the size of the *Blue Book*, at 5-3/4 by 7-1/2 inches. The 1948 printing was only slightly changed: it was given a blue cover and featured updated content that included the newly issued Roosevelt dime and Franklin half dollar. These booklets were no longer included in the type-coin folder but were sold separately because of popular interest in the subject. Two versions are known and can be distinguished by the advertisement on the inside back cover. The earlier version gives a price of 75¢ for the *Hand Book* [*sic*] and $1.50 for the *Guide Book*; the later printing, from circa 1961, shows prices of $1 and $1.75, respectively.

As noted in chapter 3, Whitman issued one-ounce, .999 fine silver medals for both the *Red Book* and the *Blue Book* from 1986 through 1997. These are pictured and discussed in detail in the *Guide Book of the Official Red Book of United States Coins* (Colletti). Several are illustrated here.

Notes

1. O.H. Dodson, "The World's Number One Coin Collector: Richard S. Yeoman, A Legend in His Own Time." *The Numismatist* (January 1970).
2. R.S. Yeoman, interview by Paul Green. *Numismatic News* (December 16, 1986).
3. R.S. Yeoman, interview by Paul Green. *Numismatic News* (December 16, 1986).
4. "What's Ahead for the U.S. Coin Collector," a talk presented by R.S. Yeoman in June 1960 and later adapted for a lecture in 1962.
5. "The Importance of Collecting Aids in the Growth of the Hobby," a talk presented by R.S. Yeoman to the Numismatists of Wisconsin (June 29, 1969).
6. R.S. Yeoman, foreword to *Perspectives in Numismatics*, a collection of 19 manuscripts celebrating the Chicago Coin Club's 800th meeting on September 11, 1985.
7. R.S. Yeoman, interview by Paul Green. *Numismatic News* (August 18, 1987).
8. R.S. Yeoman, "A Quarter Century of *Red Book* Progress." *Stamp & Coin Supply Merchandiser* (May–June 1971).
9. Speech delivered by Master of Ceremonies Dan Brown at the Central State Numismatic Society's tribute to R.S. Yeoman in Milwaukee on May 14, 1977.
10. R.S. Yeoman, interview by Paul Green. *Numismatic News* (December 30, 1986).
11. R.S. Yeoman, interview by Paul Green. *Numismatic News* (December 30, 1986).
12. Speech delivered by Master of Ceremonies Dan Brown at the Central State Numismatic Society's tribute to R.S. Yeoman in Milwaukee on May 14, 1977.
13. R.S. Yeoman, foreword to *Perspectives in Numismatics*, a collection of 19 manuscripts celebrating the Chicago Coin Club's 800th meeting on September 11, 1985.
14. As advertised in a 16-page promotional brochure titled "Whitman Proudly Presents the World's Most Complete Line of Numismatic Books and Accessories" (circa 1963).
15. "The Importance of Collecting Aids in the Growth of the Hobby," a talk presented by R.S. Yeoman to the Numismatists of Wisconsin (June 29, 1969).
16. Dave Harper, "Introduction of coin board made hobby popular." *Numismatic News* (February 11, 1984).
17. "The Importance of Collecting Aids in the Growth of the Hobby," a talk presented by R.S. Yeoman to the Numismatists of Wisconsin (June 29, 1969).
18. R.S. Yeoman, interview by Paul Green. *Numismatic News* (August 30, 1988).
19. R.S. Yeoman, interview by Paul Green. *Numismatic News* (August 30, 1988).
20. R.S. Yeoman, interview by Paul Green. *Numismatic News* (February 10, 1987).
21. R.S. Yeoman, interview by Paul Green. *Numismatic News* (September 6, 1988).
22. Clifford Mishler, "MEMO: from the publisher." *Coins* magazine (August 1977).
23. R.S. Yeoman, interview by Paul Green. *Numismatic News* (September 6, 1988).
24. R.S. Yeoman, interview by Paul Green. *Numismatic News* (February 10, 1987)
25. "The Importance of Collecting Aids in the Growth of the Hobby," a talk presented by R.S. Yeoman to the Numismatists of Wisconsin (June 29, 1969).
26. "The Importance of Collecting Aids in the Growth of the Hobby," a talk presented by R.S. Yeoman to the Numismatists of Wisconsin (June 29, 1969).
27. R.S. Yeoman, interview by Paul Green. *Numismatic News* (January 27, 1987).
28. R.S. Yeoman, interview by Paul Green. *Numismatic News* (January 27, 1987).
29. R.S. Yeoman, interview by Paul Green. *Numismatic News* (January 27, 1987).
30. R.S. Yeoman, interview by Paul Green. *Numismatic News* (January 27, 1987).
31. Lee Hewitt obituary, *Coin World* (April 29, 1987).
32. A speech presented by Yeoman to 145 people attending the Numismatic Association of Southern California club representative breakfast in Los Angeles (February 15, 1975).
33. Frank J. Colletti, *A Guide Book of the Official Red Book of United States Coins* (2009).
34. R.S. Yeoman, interview by Paul Green. *Numismatic News* (March 24, 1987).
35. R.S. Yeoman, interview by Paul Green. *Numismatic News* (March 24, 1987).
36. Marie Slivka, "*Red Book* Took a Yeoman Effort to Write," *The Plain Dealer* (September 17, 1967). Yeoman was in Cleveland for *The Plain Dealer*'s Midwest Fall Book Festival, "his first such event." However, he told interviewer Slivka that he was not "an author in search of a publisher."
37. R.S. Yeoman, interview by Paul Green. *Numismatic News* (August 30, 1988).
38. Marie Slivka, "*Red Book* Took a Yeoman Effort to Write," *The Plain Dealer* (September 17, 1967).
39. "Prices and Values of United States Coins," handwritten notes by R.S. Yeoman (circa mid-1960s, perhaps about the time the *Whitman Numismatic Journal* was introduced).
40. "25 Colorful *Red Book* Years," a talk presented by R.S. Yeoman at a 1971 convention in Jacksonville, Florida.
41. A speech presented by Yeoman to 145 people attending the Numismatic Association of Southern California club representative breakfast in Los Angeles (February 15, 1975).
42. "25 Colorful *Red Book* Years," a talk presented by R.S. Yeoman at a 1971 convention in Jacksonville, Florida.
43. "25 Colorful *Red Book* Years," a talk presented by R.S. Yeoman at a 1971 convention in Jacksonville, Florida.
44. Frank J. Colletti, *A Guide Book of the Official Red Book of United States Coins* (2009).
45. A speech presented by Yeoman to 145 people attending the Numismatic Association of Southern California club representative breakfast in Los Angeles (February 15, 1975).
46. R.S. Yeoman, interview by Paul Green. *Numismatic News* (March 10, 1987).
47. R.S. Yeoman, interview by Paul Green. *Numismatic News* (March 10, 1987).
48. R.S. Yeoman, interview by Paul Green. *Numismatic News* (March 10, 1987).
49. R.S. Yeoman, interview by Paul Green. *Numismatic News* (March 10, 1987).
50. Personal communication.
51. "Too Many Empty 'Wagons': Important Message from R.S. Yeoman," printed in a flier for distributors.
52. "What Whitman Does for Its Dealers," featured on the back of a 16-page promotional brochure titled "Whitman Proudly Presents the World's Most Complete Line of Numismatic Books and Accessories" (circa 1963).
53. R.S. Yeoman, "The Relationship of Coin Division Sales to Economic and U.S. Mint Policies." Letter or program thought to have been presented to Whitman's sales force, bearing the date January 18, 1968, and the notation "Written for H.M. Benstead."
54. These books included *Swiss Shooting Talers and Medals* by Delbert Ray Krause; *A Guide Book of Philippine Paper Money* by Neil

Shafer; and *Standard Grading Guide to Canadian Decimal Coins* by James Charlton and Robert Willey.

55. R.S. Yeoman, "The Relationship of Coin Division Sales to Economic and U.S. Mint Policies."
56. R.S. Yeoman, interview by Paul Green. *Numismatic News* (June 2, 1987).
57. "Birth of the Kennedy Half Dollar," handwritten notes for talk made by R.S. Yeoman at a coin convention held at the Princess Kaiulani Hotel in 1983.
58. R.S. Yeoman, interview by Paul Green. *Numismatic News* (June 2, 1987).
59. R.S. Yeoman, interview by Paul Green. *Numismatic News* (June 2, 1987).
60. R.S. Yeoman, interview by Paul Green. *Numismatic News* (June 2, 1987).
61. R.S. Yeoman, interview by Paul Green. *Numismatic News* (June 2, 1987).
62. R.S. Yeoman, interview by Paul Green. *Numismatic News* (June 2, 1987).
63. "OTACS: Old Timer Assay Commissioners Society," 1993 souvenir program, with history provided by Lester Davis as part of his exhibit of OTACS medals at the ANA's Early Spring Convention in Colorado Springs (March 1012, 1993).
64. "Numismatic Memories: 1952–87," dated August 1987 (origin/publication unknown).
65. "OTACS: Old Timer Assay Commissioners Society," 1993 souvenir program, with history provided by Lester Davis as part of his exhibit of OTACS medals at the ANA's Early Spring Convention in Colorado Springs (March 10–12, 1993).
66. R.S. Yeoman, interview by Paul Green. *Numismatic News* (June 16, 1987).
67. "Sale of Standard Silver Dollars Held by the Treasury, Hearings Before the Committee on Banking and Currency, House of Representatives, Eighty-Ninth Congress, Second Session, on H.R. 13150 (and Related Bills), a Bill Authorizing the Sale of Standard Silver Dollars Held by the Treasury." (July 26–28, 1966.)
68. R.S. Yeoman, interview by Paul Green. *Numismatic News* (June 16, 1987).
69. R.S. Yeoman, interview by Paul Green. *Numismatic News* (August 25, 1987).
70. R.S. Yeoman, interview by Paul Green. *Numismatic News* (October 4, 1988).
71. R.S. Yeoman, "A Quarter Century of Red Book Progress." *Stamp & Coin Supply Merchandiser* (May–June 1971).
72. Edward C. Rochette, *Numismatic News* (April 19, 1988). Today Numismatic Hall of Famers are commemorated on engraved stone plaques displayed in an outdoor gallery to the right of the entrance of the American Numismatic Association's Colorado Springs headquarters.
73. From "The [Compleat] Numismatist," handwritten notes by R.S. Yeoman, likely for a talk at a club meeting or convention (date unknown).
74. R.S. Yeoman, Sandy Samples. *Green Valley News and Sun* (November 4, 1981).
75. Publication date unknown.
76. From Yeoman's handwritten notes on stationery from the Admiral Semmes Hotel & Motor Hotel, Mobile, Alabama (date unknown).
77. From Yeoman's handwritten notes on stationery from the Admiral Semmes Hotel & Motor Hotel, Mobile, Alabama (date unknown).
78. Interview with R.S. Yeoman, broadcast NBC "Monitor" radio program (circa 1967). According to an article in *The Milwaukee Journal* (Sunday edition, April 2, 1967), he was a guest on "Monitor" three times.
79. "25 Colorful *Red Book* Years," a talk presented by R.S. Yeoman at a Jacksonville, Florida, convention (c. 1971).
80. "What's Ahead for the U.S. Coin Collector," a talk presented by R.S. Yeoman in June 1960 and later adapted for a lecture in 1962.
81. Brief, handwritten note, likely jotted down prior to the aforementioned Jacksonville talk (circa 1971).
82. "25 Colorful *Red Book* Years," a talk presented by R.S. Yeoman at a Jacksonville, Florida, convention (circa 1971).
83. "What's Ahead for the U.S. Coin Collector," a talk presented by R.S. Yeoman in June 1960 and later adapted for a lecture in 1962.
84. "25 Colorful *Red Book* Years," a talk presented by R.S. Yeoman at a Jacksonville, Florida, convention (circa 1971).
85. From "The [Compleat] Numismatist," handwritten notes by R.S. Yeoman, likely for a talk at a club meeting or convention (date unknown).
86. "25 Colorful *Red Book* Years," a talk presented by R.S. Yeoman at a Jacksonville, Florida, convention (circa 1971).
87. R.S. Yeoman, interview by Paul Green. *Numismatic News* (June 30, 1987).
88. "25 Colorful *Red Book* Years," a talk presented by R.S. Yeoman at a 1971 convention in Jacksonville, Florida.
89. R.S. Yeoman, interview by Paul Green. *Numismatic News* (June 30, 1987).
90. R.S. Yeoman, interview by Paul Green. *Numismatic News* (June 30, 1987).
91. Ed Reiter, "*Red Book* author at 80 looks back." *Numismatic News* (September 15, 1984).
92. From "Now and Then," a talk delivered by Yeoman at the ANA's 1988 Summer Seminar in Colorado Springs.
93. Clifford Mishler, "MEMO: from the publisher." *Coins* magazine (August 1977).
94. Abe Kosoff. *Coin World* (January 29, 1975).
95. 25 Colorful *Red Book* Years," a talk presented by R.S. Yeoman at a Jacksonville, Florida, convention (circa 1971).
96. Dick and Marion would suffer three burglaries and break-ins during their life together.
97. Speech delivered by Master of Ceremonies Dan Brown at the Central State Numismatic Society's tribute to R.S. Yeoman in Milwaukee on May 14, 1977.
98. Marlene Salley, "Racine Book Seller Turns Over New Leaf." *The Journal Times* (September–October 1988).
99. "Yeoman Fan." *Numismatic News* (June 18, 1977).
100. Ray Panzarella. *The Arizona Daily Star* (January 17, 1985).
101. R.S. Yeoman, interview by Paul Green. *Numismatic News* (February 2, 1988).
102. R.S. Yeoman, interview by Paul Green. *Numismatic News* (March 15, 1988).
103. R.S. Yeoman, interview by Paul Green. *Numismatic News* (December 8, 1987).
104. Sandy Samples. *Green Valley News and Sun* (November 4, 1981).
105. R.S. Yeoman, interview by Paul Green. *Numismatic News* (November 24, 1987).

About the Author

Kenneth Bressett has been involved in the numismatic hobby since the 1940s. He has written many articles and is author or editor of more than a dozen related books. He is a past governor, vice president, and president of the American Numismatic Association, and a highly accomplished teacher and researcher. He has served for many years as the editor, senior editor, and now editor emeritus of *A Guide Book of United States Coins*—at more than 25 million copies, one of the best-selling nonfiction titles in American publishing. As a former consultant to the U.S. Mint, he was instrumental in helping to implement the 50 State Quarters Program and in selecting many of the coins' reverse designs. Ken is a founder of the Rittenhouse Society, a past appointee to the Annual Assay Commission, a recipient of the Numismatic Literary Guild's Clemy Award, and an inductee in the Numismatic Hall of Fame (at ANA Headquarters in Colorado Springs).

Barbara Gregory served as research and editorial assistant to Ken Bressett for *A Penny Saved*. Barbara earned her degree in English and American literature from Alfred University (New York), and began post-college work as a medical illustrator and typesetter / layout artist in Rochester and Syracuse. Her editorial career started with a staff position with *Aeronautics Digest*, United States Air Force Academy, Colorado Springs. She then jumped into life in numismatics with *The Numismatist*, serving as editorial assistant, assistant editor, associate editor, and production editor, before taking the reins as editor-in-chief in 1988. *The Numismatist* is the American Numismatic Association's award-winning national educational publication for collectors of coins, medals, tokens, and paper money.

Credits and Acknowledgements

Author Kenneth Bressett would like to recognize the following individuals, many of whom knew, admired, and/or worked with R.S. Yeoman during his more than 50 years in the numismatic hobby: Lawrence Block, Q. David Bowers, Phil Bressett, Frank J. Colletti, Arthur Friedberg, Jeff Garrett, Rod Gillis, Lincoln W. Higgie III, Robert B. Kelley, Kimberly S. Kiick, D. Wayne Johnson, Ed Metzger, Douglas Mudd, Joel J. Orosz, Neil Shafer, and John Wilson.

Eugene Dodd and Sharon Dodd supplied much family information. William Spencer and Fred Dickfoss related stories of their early association with Yeoman at Racine Coin Club meetings. Jean Hawes contributed information about the Yeoman family. Harvey Stack and Holland Wallace supplied memories and their connections with Yeoman and the *Red Book*.

The publisher would like to thank: the American Numismatic Association (Caleb Noel, editor, *The Numismatist*, and Robert Kelley, museum specialist and photography director) for assisting with photography and image research. Q. David Bowers for help in many ways, including sharing recollections of the *Red Book* and R.S. Yeoman, and other memories. Frank J. Colletti for sharing insight and information on collecting the *Red Book*. Charles Daughtrey for contributing a dual portrait of R.S. Yeoman and Kenneth Bressett. Amanda DeWees for her research work on the *Guide Book of the Official Red Book of United States Coins*. Jeff Garrett for writing the foreword and contributing photographs. Barbara Gregory for her yeoman work on the text manuscript, editorial organization, and image-coordinating. David W. Lange for helping to preserve the history of the hobby's coin boards and folders, and for sharing information and photographs. The Library of Congress for historical images. Joel J. Orosz for reviewing portions of the manuscript and sharing feedback, and for contributing an essay. The Racine Yacht Club (Past Commodore Gregg Henning; Office Manager Kimberly A. Shortess; and Editor Paul Tobias) for sharing historical information and photographs. The Rochester Numismatic Association (President Scott Annechino, and Past President Gerald Muhl) for sharing an image and information. Bob Shippee for reviewing the galleys. Stack's Bowers Galleries for allowing access to their numismatic image archives. Steve Wheeler for writing the biography of Otto Wadewitz in *RYC Roots* magazine.

Thanks also to Lawrence Block, Phil Bressett, Rod Gillis, Lincoln Higgie, D. Wayne Johnson, Ed Metzger, Neil Shafer, Harvey Stack, Doug Winter, and John Wilson, for sharing recollections; and to Charles Davis, David Fanning, and George F. Kolbe for pricing the *Red Book* in the appendix.

Thanks to every Whitman employee who has worked on the *Red Book*, in hundreds of important capacities, for 75 years. Thanks to every volunteer contributor who has shared knowledge of pricing, die varieties, and other content since the book debuted in 1946. And thanks to every collector who has shared ideas, spotted mistakes, and voiced opinions over the decades.

Thanks to the United States Mint (staff and officers too numerous to list individually), for producing the coins studied in the *Red Book*, and for providing information and assistance in many ways.

Whitman Publishing associates who have worked on the *Red Book* during its Anderson Press renaissance include: Ray Berg, Edwin Bevens, Jeff Bolte, Henri Bui, Thinh Bui, Dawn Burbank, Eleanor Burden, Mary Burleson, Jeri Burke, Jeff Campbell, Bob Cashatt, Chris Chapel, Robert Clark, Jennifer Corbett, David Crenshaw, Sydney Cromwell, Amanda DeWees, Joel Edler, Susan Goggins, Brandon C. Hall, Janet Hatfield, Adam Helewski, Matt Heller, Will Hollis, Dan Holmes, Michelle Hudson, Jan Humphreys, Matt Jeffirs, Montana Kitterman, Lori Kraft, Tammy Lawrence, Bob Lemke, Tatia Lockridge, Teresa Lyle, Christopher Marsden, John McCurdy, John McDowell, Tom Mulvaney, Amanda Piarino, Stephen Pirtle, Diana Plattner, Emily Sewell, Peyton Smith, Rachel Street, Caitlyn Trautwein, Dennis Tucker, Sydnei Wheat, Brad White, Jen Williams, Brandon Woods, and Keith Zaner.

Image Credits

Unless otherwise noted below, images are from the Western Publishing Archives and Whitman Publishing Archives. Family photos in chapter 6 are taken from Ken Bressett's personal photo archives.

Images are credited by page number. Where multiple illustrations are found on a given page, they are credited by location, starting with number 1 at upper left and reading left to right, top to bottom.

Preface: Pg xi.1, American Numismatic Association / Robert B. Kelley. Pg xii.1, *Coin World* / Steve Roach.

Chapter 1: Pg xviii, American Numismatic Association / Robert B. Kelley. Pg 4.1–2, Racine Yacht Club. Pg 10.1–2, Shutterstock / Silver Spiral Arts. Pg 10.3, Shutterstock / a98ntfp. Pg 10.4, Shutterstock / Gregory James Van Raalte.

Chapter 2: Pg 12, American Numismatic Association / Robert B. Kelley. Pg 14.1, Shutterstock / Mark Kostich. Pg 14.2–3, Shutterstock / Yaroslaff. Pg 14.4–5, Shutterstock / Daniel D. Malone. Pg 14.6, Shutterstock / Mark Kostich. Pg 17.1, Library of Congress. Pg 17.2–3, Stack's Bowers Galleries. Pg 25.1–2, Carl Schrieber.

Chapter 3: Pg 30, American Numismatic Association / Robert B. Kelley. Pg 32.1–3, Library of Congress. Pg 33, Library of Congress. Pg 34, Library of Congress. Pg 40, Central States Numismatic Society. Pg 55.1–2, David W. Lange. Pg 62.1–2, Library of Congress. Pg 65.1, Library of Congress.

Chapter 4: Pg 84, American Numismatic Association / Robert B. Kelley. Pg 87.1–4, Stack's Bowers Galleries. Pg 88.1, Library of Congress. Pg 88.2–4, Stack's Bowers Galleries. Pg 89.3, Stack's Bowers Galleries. Pg 90.1–2, Stack's Bowers Galleries. Pg 91.3–4, Stack's Bowers Galleries. Pg 92.1–4, Stack's Bowers Galleries. Pg 93.1–4, H.E. Harris & Company. Pg 93.5–6, Stack's Bowers Galleries. Pg 93.9–14, Stack's Bowers Galleries. Pg 94.2–7, Stack's Bowers Galleries. Pg 95.1–5, Stack's Bowers Galleries. Pg 96.1–2, Stack's Bowers Galleries. Pg 98.1, Stack's Bowers Galleries. Pg 99.1–6, Stack's Bowers Galleries. Pg 100.1, Heritage Auctions. Pg 102, American Numismatic Association. Pg 103.1–2, Stack's Bowers Galleries. Pg 105.1–2, Stack's Bowers Galleries. Pg 107.1–5, Stack's Bowers Galleries. Pg 111.1–2, Stack's Bowers Galleries. Pg 111.3, David W. Lange. Pg 114.1–2, David W. Lange. Pg 114.3, Stack's Bowers Galleries. Pg 118.1–4, Stack' Bowers Galleries. Pg 119, White House Press Office. Pg 124.1–6, Heritage Auctions. Pg 128, Rochester Numismatic Association. Pg 129, Stack's Bowers Galleries. Pg 130.1, Library of Congress. Pg 130.2, U.S. State Department. Pg 130.4, *Coin World*. Pg 132, American Numismatic Association / Robert B. Kelley. Pg 143.1, Royal Numismatic Society. Pg 143.2, Token and Medal Society. Pg 144, Shutterstock / Bart Sherkow. Pg 147.1–4, Stack's Bowers Galleries. Pg 148.1, National Archives and Research Administration. Pg 148.2–3, Stack's Bowers Galleries. Pg 149.1–3, Stack's Bowers Galleries. Pg 150.1–5, Stack's Bowers Galleries. Pg 153, Library of Congress. Pg 155.1, *Numismatic News*. Pg 162.1, Newman Numismatic Portal. Pg 162.2–3, Stack's Bowers Galleries. Pg 166.1–2, Stack's Bowers Galleries. Pg 171.1–4, American Numismatic Association Museum. Pg 173.1, Shutterstock / Be Good. Pg 177.1–2, Stack's Bowers Galleries. Pg 178.1–2, Wikimedia / Ken Bosma. Pg 178.3, Wikimedia / James Brooks. Pg 181.1–3, Stack's Bowers Galleries. Pg 182.1–4, Stack's Bowers Galleries.

Chapter 5: Pg 186, American Numismatic Association / Robert B. Kelley.

Chapter 6: Pg 206, American Numismatic Association / Robert B. Kelley. Pg 221.2–3, Stack's Bowers Galleries. Pg 222.1–2, National Archives and Research Administration. Pg 222.3, Library of Congress. Pg 223, American Numismatic Association / Robert B. Kelley. Pg 224.1–4, Stack's Bowers Galleries. Pg 231.2–4, Stack's Bowers Galleries. Pg 245, American Numismatic Association / Robert B. Kelley. Pg 246, Newman Numismatic Portal. Pg 252.1–2, Stack's Bowers Galleries. Pg 257.2–3, Q. David Bowers. Pg 257.4–5, Stack's Bowers Galleries. Pg 263.1–4, Stack's Bowers Galleries. Pg 265.1, Wikimedia / Annulla. Pg 265.2, Subterranean Press. Pg 268, Stack's Bowers Galleries. Pg 272.1, American Numismatic Association / Robert B. Kelley. Pg 272.2, Dennis Tucker. Pg 277.1–2, David W. Lange. Pg 281.3, National Archives and Research Administration. Pg 282, American Numismatic Association Archives. Pg 285.1–4, Stack's Bowers Galleries. Pg 297.1, APMEX. Pg 297.2, NGC. Pg 306.2, American Numismatic Association / Robert B. Kelley. Pg 313, American Numismatic Association / Robert B. Kelley.

Index

"A penny saved is a penny got."
—Benjamin Franklin